About the

Hannah Rose Woods is a writer and ⸻
from the University of Cambridge, ⸻
history, and in 2016 captained her ⸻
most nostalgic of television progran⸻
has written on history, politics and ⸻
Guardian, *History Today*, *Art UK* and *Elle* magazine, and has
appeared as a contributor on *Dan Snow's History Hit* podcast,
Tortoise Media ThinkIns, *BBC Radio 5 Live* and *Radio 4's Front
Row*, the *Today* programme, *The World at One* and *The World
Tonight* to discuss topics including nostalgia, public history, Victorian
culture, gender equality and universities.

Praise for *Rule, Nostalgia*

'Fascinating and timely, *Rule, Nostalgia* is an eye-opening history
of Britain's enduring fixation with its own past'
Jeremy Paxman, bestselling author of *The English* and *Black Gold:
The History of How Coal Made Britain*

'Well-argued, timely and hugely entertaining. A great
piece of popular history'
Jonathan Coe, bestselling author of *Middle England*

'Our national story is so much stranger than we think: this book
brilliantly insists that we look at it afresh'
James Hawes, bestselling author of *The Shortest History of England*

'*Rule, Nostalgia* announces Woods as one of the most
interesting new historians of her generation'
Dan Jones, *Sunday Times*

'Hannah Rose Woods explores how illusory and contested
golden ages have haunted Britain since medieval times . . .
[An] intelligent and eminently readable book'
Richard Evans, *New Statesman* (Book of the Day)

'A sharp new history of longing for the good old days'
Tristram Hunt, *Financial Times*

'A timely book . . . persuading the reader [that] a feeling full of
sweetness and sadness is also a dark and dangerous force'
The Times

'Woods is a sharp, iconoclastic writer . . . A great book'
John Harris, *Guardian Politics Weekly UK*

'Eye-opening and thoughtful . . . Woods has
a bright future ahead of her'
The Telegraph

'A must read for anyone wanting to understand where the
roots of our sense of a nation originated'
Janina Ramirez, bestselling author of *Femina*

'A great, scholarly history, and so searingly relevant. Hannah
Rose Woods is clever, witty and perceptive. They don't make
'em like they used to; now they make 'em better'
Dan Snow, author of *On This Day in History*

'An utterly eye-opening and enthralling debut, clearly laying out our
uniquely British obsession with nostalgia. Required reading for anyone
who wants to use the term "culture war". I absolutely loved it'
Fern Riddell, author of *Death in Ten Minutes: The forgotten life of
radical suffragette Kitty Marion*

'A smart, entertaining and meticulously researched backwards look
(quite literally) at Britain's history of looking over its shoulder.
Deconstructs the lure of the fictitious "good old days" and how they
have been weaponised throughout history. Excellent'
Otto English, author of *Fake History*

'Outstanding. A thrilling, elegant and highly original
interrogation of how we use our pasts'
Musa Okwonga, author of *One of Them: An Eton
College Memoir*

'Nostalgia was once considered a terminal condition.
Hannah Rose Woods suggests that the culture needs to book
itself in for a check-up. Provocative and well-argued, *Rule,
Nostalgia* offers the diagnosis that might lead us to a cure'
Matthew Sweet, author of *Inventing the Victorians*

'A triumphal backwards tour through the history of
Britain's relationship with its own past. This funny, sad,
wise and brilliantly informative book is a crash course in the
many pasts that have made our presents'
Peter Mitchell, author of *Imperial Nostalgia:
How the British Conquered Themselves*

RULE, NOSTALGIA

A Backwards History of Britain

Hannah Rose Woods

WH
ALLEN

1

WH Allen an imprint of Ebury Publishing,
20 Vauxhall Bridge Road,
London SW1V 2SA

WH Allen is part of the Penguin Random House group of companies
whose addresses can be found at global.penguinrandomhouse.com

Lines from 'MCMXIV' from *The Whitsun Weddings* by Philip Larkin
reprinted by permission of Faber and Faber Ltd.

Lines from '1916 seen from 1921' from *Selected Poems* by Edmund
Blunden (Carcanet Press) reproduced by permission of David Higham Associates.

Lines from 'The English Spirit' by Siegfried Sassoon reproduced by
permission of the Estate of George Sassoon.

Lines from 'East Coker' from *Four Quartets* by T.S. Eliot
reprinted by permission of Faber and Faber Ltd.

The authors and publisher gratefully acknowledge the permission granted
to reproduce the copyright material in this book. Every effort has been
made to trace copyright holders and to obtain their permission.
The publisher apologises for any errors or omissions and, if notified
of any corrections, will make suitable acknowledgment in
future reprints or editions of this book.

First published by WH Allen in 2022
This edition published by WH Allen in 2023

www.penguin.co.uk

A CIP catalogue record for this book is available from the British Library

ISBN 9780753558744

Printed and bound in Great Britain by Clays Ltd, Elcograf S.p.A.

The authorised representative in the EEA is Penguin Random House Ireland,
Morrison Chambers, 32 Nassau Street, Dublin D02 YH68

Penguin Random House is committed to a sustainable future
for our business, our readers and our planet. This book is made
from Forest Stewardship Council® certified paper.

Contents

Introduction

Nostalgia Tells it Like it Wasn't

It can seem as if Britain is a nation obsessed with its history, yearning for the stability and certainty of a vanished golden age. Or, as James Bond has it in the 2012 juggernaut *Skyfall*, 'we're going back to the past ... where we have the advantage.' At a time of change and uncertainty, amid fierce political disputes both over Britain's past and its future, it has never been more important to interrogate the ways in which we remember the past.

I began writing this book in the final weeks of Britain's exit from the European Union, when imperial nostalgia was being blamed for Britain's inability to recognise that it was unprepared to face the challenges of the future. A few months later, I was legally confined to my home as a pandemic ripped its way around the globe, which newspapers and politicians told me I could make sense of by imagining it was the Second World War. And then the statue of Edward Colston was tipped into Bristol harbour, and historians were cast as unlikely enemies of the state, as Prime Minister Boris Johnson suggested that telling the truth about slavery and empire was a 'cringing embarrassment about our history', and cabinet ministers accused historians and heritage workers of waging a shamefully unpatriotic campaign to 'do Britain down.'[1] Writing a history book that has something new to say about the past used to be a normal thing to do. Now, according to the government and a swathe of the national media, it is apparently a sinister attempt to 'rewrite history' and discredit Britain in the present, and we would do better to realign ourselves with the official narrative that Britain's past is a seamless roll call of glittering triumphs and inspirations; stirring pride; and other less glorious episodes that we don't need to think about because it was 'just how things were' at the time. Not only this, but they tell us we can only find our way as a nation again if we 'rediscover . . . the dynamism of the bearded Victorians', or summon up the 'buccaneering', 'swashbuckling' spirit of Elizabethan explorers and nineteenth-century free-traders.[2] And I want to find out what on earth is going on.

Nostalgia, however, has a long history of its own. For more than 500 years, British politicians, poets, novelists and social commentators have mourned the loss of older national identities, and called for a revival of simpler, better ways of life – from Margaret Thatcher's call for a return to 'Victorian values' in the 1980s, to William Blake's protest against the 'dark Satanic mills' of the Industrial Revolution that were fast transforming England's green and pleasant land, or sixteenth-century observers looking back to a 'Merry England' before the upheavals of the Reformation.

Beginning with an exploration of nostalgia in the twenty-first century, I delve further back in time to uncover the nostalgias of the past, from the 'history wars' in the present day to the English Reformation of the sixteenth century. While conservatives today yearn for the supposed 'Blitz spirit' of wartime Britain, those who had lived through two world wars often yearned for the lost innocence of rural life, reimagining the Edwardian era as a long summer garden party free from anxiety and upheaval. The Edwardians, in turn, looked back longingly to a golden era of Victorian optimism – a time before imperial competition, urbanisation and technological change were transforming their world at a seemingly ever-accelerating rate – or else retreated into nostalgic visions of endless childhood through tales such as *Peter Pan*. And while the Victorians themselves have often been viewed as the apogee of national self-certainty, many, from Pre-Raphaelite painters to the Arts and Crafts movement, yearned to retreat to an era before the Industrial Revolution, valorising the spirit of medieval England. And before the Industrial Revolution? Eighteenth-century artists, architects and philosophers strove to break with the Middle Ages, looking back to the apparent order of the classical past, while in the sixteenth and seventeenth centuries fierce battles over monarchy and religion continually rewrote the relationship between past, present and future. By the time we reach the 1530s, we find people nostalgic for a vision of home that looks very different to our own.

Nostalgia, as well as history, has often been the terrain in which political battles are fought in the present. The question of when the 'good old days' might have been is intimately bound up with the question of what the 'good life' looks like to people in their own day, and whether change is taking them closer or further away from it. Was the Industrial Revolution Britain's heyday of power and prestige, a tale of how ingenuity, grit and determination gave rise to the 'Workshop of the World', creating levels of wealth and comfort throughout society that earlier generations could scarcely have dreamt of? Or was it instead a story of how Britain's landscape was destroyed by factories and pollution; an age in which the rich grew richer at the expense of the poorest in society, who were forced to toil in unimaginable conditions and to live and work in overcrowded and unsanitary cities? Even if standards of living increased in subsequent years, did industrialisation inaugurate a process of widening inequality that has continued into the twenty-first century, as well as a culture of overwork and anxiety that we still deal with – or is it laughable to imagine that people might be happier without the benefits brought by industrial technologies? In turn, was 'medieval' a byword for barbarity and backwardness, the 'dark ages' of supposed ignorance swept away by the Renaissance and Enlightenment, or was it a more contented time before the rise of individualism, and the economic changes that would come to be known as modern capitalism? These are questions that have deeply preoccupied people over the past 500 years, as they weighed the gains as well as the losses of their age, and they are ones whose legacy we still debate today.

Why do we so often turn to the past at times of change and uncertainty? We know that life was far from easy, and yet we cannot help imagining that things were simpler than they are in the present. We yearn for times gone by, investing memories with a sense of completeness that the present can never have, even as we forget that no one experienced things that way at the time. Every generation, in their turn, has had to face unprecedented change and uncertainty, to accept that things might go wrong at any moment and that even in times of progress there will be things that are lost forever. Nostalgia offers us protection from our anxieties: the chance to escape our worries about what the future holds and recall a story that might tell us who we are and where it is that we are going. And yet we know that real life is always too complex to fold the truth into the comforting structure of a storybook.

So why are we still so tempted by the lure of life in earlier periods of history, to put on our rose-tinted glasses and revisit a time when Britain was truly 'Great', where everyone pulled together as a community and everybody knew your name? We often think of nostalgia as the stuff of cultural comfort food – something cosy and twee, and possibly even a little unseemly for full-grown adults to dwell on – and yet earlier generations understood how dangerously seductive the pull of nostalgia could be. In the seventeenth century, homesickness could be deadly, and physicians warned that people could succumb to nostalgia as if to a disease.

In 1688, a Swiss physician, Johannes Hofer, published a medical treatise on a mysterious new disease that seemed to be affecting Swiss soldiers fighting abroad, by combining the Greek word *nostos* – homecoming – and *algia* – pain. Separated from their homeland, soldiers seemed to be sick with longing; from 'the sad mood originating from the desire to return to one's native land.' Homesick soldiers were losing touch with the present, fixating on their faraway object of desire with single-minded obsession. They were confusing now with then, real and imaginary events, hearing voices of loved ones that weren't there; some were even wasting away, falling deeper into depression as their 'vital spirits' were progressively extinguished. The only cure was to return, to become a part of their home once more.[3]

Over time, the meaning of nostalgia would broaden from a potentially fatal disease to a milder and more common condition, encompassing, as it did so, the longing for a faraway time as well as place. As more and more people began to experience the waves of change that we think of as making up the process of 'modernisation' – as new technologies and industries developed over the eighteenth, nineteenth and twentieth centuries, as people moved around their countries as well as the globe in unprecedented numbers, and as landscapes were changed beyond recognition by growing towns, cities and suburbs – nostalgia came to play an increasingly important role in what it was to be 'modern'.[4] It was part of what it meant to experience a world of transformation, in which people felt increasingly cut off from the past, looking back and realising what had been lost as well as gained. No longer a specifically medical diagnosis, it moved into the realm of art and literature, as nineteenth-century Romantics drew on the bittersweet pull of this tantalising emotion that was sometimes achingly melancholy, yet sometimes sentimentally pleasurable, while they wandered through the countryside and gazed upon time-mellowed ruins, as in Wordsworth's 'Tintern Abbey', or else remembered what it had been like to experience the world as a child, before the cares and anxieties of adult life.

By the middle of the twentieth century, nostalgia had become part of common parlance – something that was being drawn upon by advertisers, consumer goods and leisure industries as people bought into enjoyment of the olden days. And yet nostalgia never entirely shed its pathological associations. In post-war Britain, it was to become intimately linked in the minds of social commentators, politicians, and many 'ordinary' men and women with Britain's dwindling role and power in the world, as decolonisation and deindustrialisation created an image of a shrinking island nation whose best days were all behind it, and where consumerism was seen to be creating a society of individuals who had lost touch with feeling part of their communities. What had started off as a curable disease had come to refer to an incurable affliction that individuals as well as whole societies were susceptible to, because no one, no matter how hard they desire it, can truly return to the past.

Britain's fixation upon the fading glories of the national past has been likened to a collective illness. 'Nostalgia,' announces journalist Doug Anderton in Jonathan Coe's tragicomic Brexit novel *Middle England*, 'is the English disease.'[5] The culture wars over Britain's history that rage in the national media over statues, stately homes, museums and university curriculums reveal a huge emotional investment in the meaning of Britain's past – at times, a sense that to re-examine our understanding of British history is an existential and political threat.[6] The idea that we should draw pride from Britain's story – or a particular version of it – carrying it as a source of inspiration into the present, is matched by the anger of those who infer they are being asked to feel shame instead. On the other hand, people who argue for a dispassionate reckoning with the myths we have been instilled with have often dismissed these culture wars as a distraction manufactured by elites to deflect attention from more important issues, a cynically populist campaign waged in bad faith rather than out of genuine sincerity. And yet we know, too, that it could only ever be a successful strategy because it taps into real and deeply felt emotions. It draws on the need we all share to make a home out of the past, to feel rooted in a beginning – a question that is always connected to what kind of a home it is that we are making in the present.

Nationalism has always been intertwined with nostalgia. The 'essence' of national identity is always located by nationalists in the past: a time when people were supposedly more bounded, more united, more purely and quintessentially 'national' than they are in the present. The nations people imagine reach back to misty, often mythic origins, linking people across time to those who shared their geographical homeland long ago – even when we know that centuries of migration, intermixing and cultural change mean that these origins are often fictions of the imagination.

I want to tease apart the Anglo-centric vision of Britain on which our current debates about nostalgia are centred. My focus is primarily on both England, and an England-heavy image of Britain, as these are the perspectives from which nostalgia for the *British* past is most often articulated, though I will also touch on nostalgias for Scottish and Welsh pasts that have shaped our understanding of Britain's history. (I leave aside entirely the complexities of nostalgia in – or indeed for – a wider UK, that at different times in its history has encompassed both Northern Ireland and Ireland.)

The yearning for lost greatness that a wide range of observers have seen as a cultural explanation for Britain's twenty-first-century malaise has been envisaged as a peculiarly English affliction – a post-imperial hangover that people in Scotland and Wales are generally seen to have moved on from. Indeed, people in Scotland and Wales have long drawn a sense of who they are from oppositional identities, as well as that of Britons: histories of their struggle against English domination. While I will at times explore the ways in which Scottish and Welsh observers historically framed their nostalgia *against* Englishness, I also want to shed light on a lesser-known story, as we travel back towards the England of the sixteenth century: how the Britain that we often think of as a more recent construction than England, Scotland and Wales was in the past the most mythically nostalgic nation of all.

This is not to say that either Britain or England is a uniquely nostalgic place, or that people who live there feel the weight of history more keenly than people do elsewhere. This is not a book about whether people in Britain have fallen victim to a nostalgia trap in a way that other people might have escaped from. But we can view Britain and its history in a new light through its changing relationship to the past. And I want to show, too, that there is nothing new about our current debates about history – these are questions people have been asking for centuries. By journeying backwards through British history over five centuries, we can trace the ways in which people wrestled with the changes and anxieties that defined their age; how they made sense of the transformations they were living through by looking back to the past. Each age, in turn, rewrote history in its own image: sometimes forging connections with distant ancestors, sometimes seeking to escape the mistakes of earlier generations, and at others reimagining the past as everything the present was felt to be lacking. Nostalgia might not give us an accurate perspective on the past, but it tells us a great deal about how people viewed the societies in which they lived.

By moving backwards in time through British history, we can harness nostalgia's perpetual backwards glance, taking us back to a past that is both strange, and strangely familiar. It is one of the ironies of history that while we can never entirely understand the past, in some ways we know it better than those who lived through it at the time: we can stand outside it and view it as completed, finished, a coherent process that we can begin to make sense of as a whole. We look back through the lens of everything that has happened since, creating timelines that trace developments from their origins, as we pronounce that some things were 'ahead of their time' and others were on the 'wrong' side of history. I want to unsettle this familiar framework of histories that have a beginning, a middle, and an end, and take us back to people who were rewriting their *own* histories, as they remade the past to make sense of their own unfinished presents.

Popular history has often been a way in which ordinary men and women claimed the right to take part in the life of their nation. By offering narratives in which people can feel part of their national story, a shared inheritance that reaches back through the centuries, Britain's history has often been both a source of pride to people in the present, and a way of articulating their stake in shaping their society's future.[7] At times, Britain's ruling elites have looked suspiciously upon working men and women's appetite for history, seeing it as harbouring a radically democratic impulse. In the wake of the French Revolution in 1789, for instance, which sent shockwaves through Britain's ruling classes as they feared the potential for uprising from below, politicians and intellectuals worried that people's growing interest in historical novels and stories of Britain's past signalled their dangerous ambition to take control of the national narrative. And yet Victorian educators increasingly came to realise that popular history could be pressed into the service of an imperial future, helping to raise a new generation who would follow their forebears' example in expanding and defending a global empire. Sometimes, the popular history that bubbled up from below could be explicitly anti-elitist, such as in the wake of the First World War, when books such as 1066 and All That took aim against the patriotic myth-making of Victorian empire-builders, rejecting the supposedly heroic histories people had been instilled with that had sent them into the trenches on the promise of glory.[8] But elites, too, have long realised that they could harness the power of popular history to shape obediently patriotic citizens. Even in the age of Shakespeare, enterprising playwrights were arguing that the history plays people were lining up to see were far from the ungodly entertainments that puritans raged were leading people astray: told from the right perspective, stories that showed how rebellions always failed and agitators were punished, while inviting audiences to marvel at the bravery of their leaders, could inspire people to allegiance, harnessing patriotic emotions in service of the state.[9]

History so often feels a more comfortable place to inhabit than the present – a time and place where we can take refuge from the uncertainties of our own age, and reacquaint ourselves with a familiar world. Yet as we travel back in time, we find people living through times that seemed worryingly unfamiliar to their eyes. Every age views its own as one of unprecedented change; each generation has seen itself as more 'modern', more mobile, more technologised than the last – a process that reaches back at least to the first great wave of rural–urban migration in the eighteenth century, and still further to the scientific revolution of the sixteenth and seventeenth centuries, and the Tudor voyages of 'discovery' that would give rise to global trade and empires. At any given moment, we find people looking backwards, looking forwards, celebrating changes as well as lamenting their effects; sometimes welcoming progress whole-heartedly, sometimes uneasily, and at others feeling their society was accelerating into catastrophe. Even people who embraced their age as one of progress and transformation could look back nostalgically upon a past that was forever out of reach and yearn to recapture its essence once more.

Nostalgia is such a powerful and timeless feeling because it is a yearning to be free from anxiety. We feel secure in the past because we know how things turned out: we cannot help imagining the past with the benefit of hindsight. As the historian David Lowenthal argues, what people are really nostalgic for is the condition of *having been*: the desire to inhabit a world that is imagined to have a sense of completeness and predictability that is always lacking in the present. The one thing that is always curiously absent from the pasts that nostalgics imagine is nostalgia itself – no one back *then*, we decide, needed to look behind them for comfort.[10] But people have always looked back with longing; forgetting, in turn, that the people they looked back to were doing the same.

I

Keep Calm and Take Back Control

2021–1979

In recent years, Britain's obsession with reliving the fading glories of former greatness has been likened to a national pathology. From politicians who draw on nostalgia for the 'Blitz spirit' or an imperial past when Britannia ruled the waves, to an endless array of consumer goods riffing off the 'Keep Calm and Carry On' attitude of wartime austerity, many have argued that these are the retrograde obsessions of a culture unable to face reality. Comparisons to the days of British imperial might and 'our finest hour' reached fever pitch during Brexit, and invocations of the Second World War were rearticulated with a new intensity at the outbreak of the coronavirus pandemic, as journalists, politicians and 'ordinary' people alike reached for familiar stories that could help make sense of a very different crisis.

Accusations of being stuck in the past have most often been aimed at the political right, but nostalgia cuts across the political spectrum. While Conservatives have articulated their visions for Britain's future by evoking images ranging from a nineteenth-century imperial heyday to an Elizabethan romance of swashbuckling 'free-traders', the future of Labour has at times been presented as a choice between the 1990s and 1970s. Just as Keir Starmer's leadership has been charged with having no new ideas beyond the 'things can only get better' assurance of the Blair years, Jeremy Corbyn was suspected of living in the political landscape of the seventies, unable to come to terms with just how much had changed.[1] In the wake of the 2007–8 financial crisis, as David Cameron was campaigning for a new era of economic austerity, Labour ran an election poster depicting Cameron as the extravagantly unregenerate detective Gene Hunt from the BBC drama *Ashes to Ashes*, perched on an Audi Quattro in snakeskin boots under the plea 'Don't let him take Britain back to the 1980s.' Yet as far as the Conservative Party was concerned, this was something of an own goal – many of their voters, they felt, would jump at the chance to transform Britain's economy as rapidly as under Margaret Thatcher. 'Fire up the Quattro,' they countered, with their own poster of DCI Cameron: 'it's time for change.'[2]

In the run-up to Brexit, Remainers, no less than Leavers, sought to marshal the 'lessons' of history in support of their campaigns; while protests for a second referendum confronted the kind of bullish military chauvinism of Nigel Farage with self-consciously old-fashioned expressions of British good manners. It was a cultural climate that produced fierce adoration for the cinematic revival of Paddington Bear in 2014 and 2017 – the master image of a Britain in which immigrants were welcome, and intolerance could be overcome with kindness, marmalade and the occasional hard stare.

More than anything, nostalgia has become weaponised in the recent 'culture wars', where British history has become a key battleground of national identity. On the one hand, politicians attempt to reshape an 'official' version of 'our island story', explicitly moulding the past to serve their agendas for Britain's future. On the other, controversies rage about the ways people consume history as a form of entertainment and leisure: how the ways in which the past is presented through period dramas, museums, art galleries, and even vintage posters and tea towels unconsciously shape how we understand the world, and Britain's place within it. Disputes over statues, stately homes, and the legacies of slavery and empire have provoked fierce debates over the ways in which Britain remembers its past, in which many feel that 'British values' and patriotism are under threat, while many, too, feel cut off from a sense of belonging. Those arguing for a recognition of Britain's multiracial heritage, and a greater understanding of the British Empire, are accused by cabinet ministers in the national media of waging a pernicious campaign to tarnish Britain's image of itself. Why are historians and heritage workers accused of 'trashing' the past, when it is their job to interpret it?[3] How have we ended up here? Let's start at the end.

WE'LL MEET AGAIN

Who wouldn't have felt nostalgic in March 2020? As countries throughout the world closed their borders, shuttered businesses, and imposed constraints on the lives of citizens that would have seemed unimaginable in the distant days of 2019, the very idea of normality began to take on the bittersweet appeal of a vanished golden age. With each day's news seemingly redefining the word 'unprecedented', as people were alternately confined to their homes and negotiating a world outside that was rapidly being cast as alarmingly unsafe, who would begrudge anyone the stuff of cultural comfort food? Social media feeds filled with throwback photos of happier times, streaming services registered sharp increases in nostalgia playlists and old TV programmes, and channels broadcast fondly remembered sporting victories. The BBC re-ran the 2012 Olympics opening ceremony – as one journalist wryly noted, 'widely acknowledged to be one of the best events where everyone came together before Everything Started Going A Bit Wrong.'[4] National shortages of flour, yeast, knitting wool and potting soil became topics of animated discussion, as people revisited the arts and crafts of their childhood or sought to bake, grow and make-do-and-mend themselves out of a crisis.

No one seemed quite sure of the spirit in which to do all this, caught between earnestness and internet-wearied irony. Was this an innocent distraction from a dreadful situation, a much-needed revival of older ways of getting by, or a kitschy refusal to engage with the horror of unfolding disaster? Or was it all of these things?

Irresistibly, comparisons were drawn, even before the first national lockdown, to the Second World War. After a decade in which ironical injunctions to Keep Calm and Carry On had launched a thousand tea towels, posters and sundry faux-historical novelties, comparisons to the 'Blitz spirit' were reached for reflexively in defiance of the oncoming pandemic. 'I'm 84. I survived rationing. I'm not scared of coronavirus,' wrote author Hunter Davies in the *Sunday Times* of 15 March, in protest at the prospect of elderly people being asked to shield themselves.[5] (Although survival was, of course, the point of rationing.) Throughout the following months, a number of elderly people who had lived through the Second World War as children became minor media celebrities through comments that held up their survival in wartime as an argument against lockdown restrictions – comparisons that seemed to have a widespread emotional appeal, despite the obvious counterclaim that living in a country at war had nothing to do with contracting a highly contagious illness. Infection-control measures were correspond-ingly envisaged as a surrender to Nazism. 'Plucky pensioner' Maureen Evans from Barnsley shot to (thankfully figurative) viral fame after a vox pop in which she told a BBC interviewer she 'didn't give a sod' about Covid, later telling MailOnline: 'I am 83 – I never thought I would feel like I was in Italy when Germany invaded. This is a free country for God's sake.'[6]

Yet as the scale of the pandemic became apparent over the course of March 2020, attitudes of wartime defiance were increasingly countered by wartime comparisons to the spirit of pulling together. 'Our generation has never been tested like this,' stated Health Secretary Matt Hancock, ahead of publishing the government's emergency Coronavirus Bill. 'Our grandparents were, during the Second World War, when our cities were bombed during the Blitz. Despite the pounding every night, the rationing, the loss of life, they pulled together in one gigantic national effort.' Two weeks into lockdown, the Queen's special address to the nation echoed 'forces' sweetheart' Vera Lynn's promise 'we'll meet again.' By the seventy-fifth anniversary of VE Day on 8 May, wartime experiences were overwhelmingly the lens through which people were trying to make sense of their own experience in the present, as thousands strung up bunting, sang along to Vera Lynn, crafted homespun Captain Toms out of yarn or papier-mâché, and danced socially distanced congas in their driveways.

Captain Tom Moore himself emerged from unexpectedly viral crowdfunding success as the national hero of the moment, seeming to pass the torch from military veterans to health workers as he raised £39 million for NHS Charities Together. Moore's enormous public appeal drew on a well of nostalgia for the kind of everyday heroism of ordinary men and women in wartime that, in received wisdom, was held to have decayed

Residents in Chester celebrate a socially distanced VE Day in 1940s clothing, May 2020.

in an age of individualism and consumer plenty. As the journalist Henry Mance observed, Moore's laps of his garden gave visual form to sacrifices that were being made away from the public gaze, both at home and off-camera in emergency wards. 'A smartly dressed veteran with three medals on his chest – this was heroism as we could understand it.'[7]

In many ways, this rather more benign epidemic of war nostalgia running alongside the actual one made sense. As supply chains broke down and supermarket shelves emptied, with purchases restricted on essential goods such as soap, milk, eggs and bread, it was hard not to recall images of rationing, while public drives to sew face masks and stitch scrub bags for healthcare workers evoked the ethos of make-do-and-mend. Adjusting to legally enforced restrictions on leaving the house, going to work and meeting others, it was entirely reasonable to look back to the last time in living memory that a government imposed such severe restrictions on daily life. It is a powerfully strange experience both to inhabit a world that is suddenly, terrifyingly out of control, in which people are dying, and also to find that day-to-day moments can still at times feel shockingly mundane. We all have a deep need for stories that make sense of these experiences, which provide a roadmap for how to act and how to feel, and the Second World War provided a story that was immediately recognisable: the tale of a nation pulling together in the spirit of collective, supposedly classless virtuousness, united in the shared experience of threat yet indomitably doing their best.

At their most hopeful, comparisons to the Second World War seemed to rewrite a story of modern Britain as a long decline from 'our finest hour'. For over half a century, the master narrative of British society was one in which deindustrialisation and decline as a world power had been paralleled by the breakdown of community, the rise of individualism and selfish consumer spending, and of generations of self-obsessed youngsters weaned on technology with no respect for their elders.

Opinion polls and media debates consistently framed the late twentieth and early twenty-first centuries as an age in which community spirit and neighbourliness were being irretrievably lost. A 2018 survey by the think tank Demos, for instance, identified nostalgia for lost communities, and a feeling of personal isolation, as one of the most salient factors through which people articulated the changes they had experienced over the course of their lifetimes, with 71 per cent of respondents feeling that their communities had been eroded. Changing experiences in British life were consistently expressed in terms of a yearning for a national sense of strength and unity; as one respondent felt, 'it's all changed. You go back to the Second World War and we were very resilient then, and the aftermath of the Second World War, we were quite resilient, but I think that's drifted out of society.'[8]

In the years preceding the pandemic, generational divides in particular had become the stock fodder of media clickbait – invariably framed as a battle for social consensus between avocado-eating millennials and 'woke warriors' on the one side, and avaricious boomers hoarding property wealth on the other. But the first months of the pandemic seemed to offer a much more hopeful counter-narrative: of young people prepared to put their lives on hold to shield the elderly; of people checking in on neighbours and delivering groceries to friends and relatives. Mutual aid groups proliferated to offer support to local communities. By March 2021, research by a coalition of charitable organisations and community groups suggested that over 12.4 million adults had volunteered during the pandemic, ranging from helping at food banks, community centres and tenants' associations to conservation projects, youth groups, sports clubs and cultural organisations. Within a few weeks of the first lockdown being announced in March 2020 alone, more than a million people had signed up as NHS volunteers, in what was widely reported as the biggest volunteer recruitment drive since the Second World War.[9]

On the other hand, easy invocations of the Blitz spirit did a real disservice both to questions of how to manage and understand a very different crisis, and of wartime experiences themselves. In the first weeks of lockdown, media discussion on 'what we can learn from the war generation' was matched by a raft of historians and commentators drawing attention to the ways in which these comparisons were not only unhelpful, but unhealthy. 'The horror of coronavirus is all too real. Don't turn it into an imaginary war,' argued Marina Hyde in the *Guardian*. 'I'm not sure who this register of battle and victory and defeat truly aids. We don't really require a metaphor to throw the horror of viral death into sharper relief: you have to think it's bad enough already.'[10] War metaphors created such an atmosphere of combative confusion that people sitting down in urban parks were branded 'traitors' as their photographs were circulated on social media.

Not only was Blitz nostalgia fuelling attitudes of carelessness towards people's difficulties in the present, it tended to trivialise real experiences of suffering in wartime and promulgate historical misunderstandings. The assumption that people living through the Blitz rallied around the call to 'Keep Calm and Carry On' has become so entrenched that it is impossible to override it with the fact that almost no one heard these words until the year 2000, when a surviving poster was found in a second-hand bookshop in Northumberland, because the poster was never approved for mass display.[11] There is a pervasive tendency to see the experience of war as broadly a good thing, something that brought out the best in people, and to ignore or even actively reject remembrance of its toll. Historians have been countering for more than half a century that the reality of being bombed night after night produced long-lasting psychological trauma – much of it untreated and unrecorded – that deeply affected people's lives for decades after the war, and have drawn attention to the class divisions, racial tensions, mass panics, thriving black market, and jewellery stripped from the bodies of bomb victims that existed in parallel to attitudes of resolve and plucky endurance. But the dominant public image of the Second World War remains much the same as the wartime propaganda put out by the government at the time: of people playing the role of character actors in a national production of muddling through, not of complex lives or deeply felt experiences of suffering. Refracted through myths of exaggerated stoicism, a reluctance to truly empathise with the complexity of people's lives in the past is matched by a refusal to engage with the complexity of the present.

With the worst death rate in Europe by far at several points in the first and second waves of infections, the UK government's repeated disinclination to accept that lessons could be learnt or comparisons made between the UK and other countries' handling of the pandemic, while drawing so heavily on distortions of British history to repeat the same mistakes all over again in handling the second wave, was perverse. When asked in the House of Commons in September 2020 why Italy and Germany had far lower rates of coronavirus, and whether the UK's failing test and trace system might be to blame, Boris Johnson responded that 'there is an important difference between our country and many other countries around the world: our country is a freedom-loving country. If you look at the history of this country over the past three hundred years, virtually every advance, from free speech to democracy has come from this country,' before going on to blame the British people's refusal to obey guidelines.[12] Few things could symbolise this dogged belief in British exceptionalism, articulated through wild misappropriations of history, more starkly than the government's decision not to take part in the EU's ventilator procurement scheme, in favour of what Johnson referred to as 'Operation Last Gasp' – breezily gesturing at wartime industrial efforts through a pun about suffocating to death.[13]

Though the prime minister did go on to reference Britain's history of international collaboration in the 'fight' against Covid.

In an op-ed for the *Daily Mail* in November 2020 that promised 'sunlit upland pastures ahead' over 'the last barbed wire', he avowed that 'armies of science are coming to our aid with all the morale-boosting, bugle-blasting excitement of Wellington's Prussian allies coming through the woods on the afternoon of Waterloo.'[14] Which was presumably a nod to the centuries-old trope that while pluck and love of freedom were unquestionably English possessions, science felt a bit German. Indeed, the *Mail* itself reported a marked divergence in different countries' use of scientific language and Second World War metaphors in their handling of coronavirus, noting that while the UK media drew heavily on analogies between pandemic responses and the 'Blitz spirit', 'German coverage meanwhile uses scientific words partly due to losing the war.'[15]

Amid this upwelling of Blitz nostalgia, conservative commentators at times seemed to forget that they were managing a respiratory pandemic, not a home front in an imaginary war. Eurosceptic former MEP Daniel Hannan, for instance, protested against school closures by recalling that, in the Second World War, boys from the City of London School had been evacuated to Marlborough College. 'The two schools shared premises, one set of boys doing games while the other was in class. Even at the height of the Blitz, no one missed a day of schooling,' he tweeted, perhaps underplaying the number of non-public schools that were destroyed in air raids, but thankfully stopping short of advocating putting London's children on trains to live with elderly people in the countryside. As if repeatedly dipping his hand into the nostalgia tombola, at one point Hannan wrote in the *Telegraph* of his hopes that 'if coronavirus has a silver lining' it would be that social distancing could bring about a revival of the curtsy.[16]

Even in its more benign forms, nostalgia can obscure the reality of history and human suffering, leading us to fetishise people we remember as struggling quietly, never complaining – seeing the good in people only when enduring in the face of adversity. It's an attitude that led former Conservative deputy chairman Lord Ashcroft, for instance, to dismiss social justice campaigns with a list of imaginary protests that 'generation woke' might have made during the Second World War. Hypothetical complaints included 'there are only male and female toilets in the air raid shelter and I don't identify as either', 'this respirator haversack has a leather strap and I'm vegan', and 'I find the term "black out" offensive' – mocking younger generations for things he had invented at their expense.[17] (In reality, the government did recognise that a substantial number of people in the 1940s didn't eat animals, issuing special ration cards for vegetarians.[18])

Nostalgia, here, performs a strange double service: we disdain comfortable twenty-first-century lives, and idealise the hardships of previous generations ('they didn't have much but they were happy', 'times were tough, but we didn't think anything of it'), even as we empty these memories of the pain and uncertainty they had at the time. Prince William's comments, as he praised community fundraising during the first lockdown, that 'Britain is at its best, weirdly, when we're in a crisis' tapped into a popular sense that there is a kind of nobility to the spirit of pulling together in times of suffering, in contrast to the inertia of modern consumerist ease. It is a paradoxical nostalgia for the 'good old days' when times were harder, a yearning for the struggles and hardships of previous generations, without giving up the benefit of hindsight about how things turned out all right in the end. It fuels a belief that the moral value of suffering leads to a happily-ever-after. But it is easy to mistake the stories we tell for reality itself. It is inevitable, in turn, that we will look back fondly on the heroism and bravery of life in lockdown, the moments of pride and simple pleasures, forgetting how it felt to teeter on the brink of a worst-case scenario in which 20-, 50-, 100,000 deaths would be an unimaginable disaster. If Prince William's comments lie at the gentle end of the hardship nostalgia spectrum, at the other extreme is the sadomasochistic 'satire' of Rod Liddle opining in

The Times in 2019: 'a peaceful, easy life hasn't made us happy. Perhaps it's time to give war a chance.'[19]

HISTORY WARS

Nostalgia, like history, is about the stories we tell ourselves. What gets forgotten, what gets remembered, and whose story it is that we are telling. People go to war over these stories, and sometimes they imagine themselves into one. Amid criticism of the government's handling of the coronavirus pandemic, and worldwide protests against racial injustice in the wake of the murder of George Floyd in Minneapolis, in June 2020 Downing Street's Number 10 policy unit was reported to be pushing the prime minister to shore up support by waging a culture war over British history.[20] Following the toppling of the statue of slave trader Edward Colston in Bristol, Johnson condemned calls to remove statues of historical figures, stating that Britain 'cannot photoshop its history' (though this was precisely what protesters had been arguing), and vowed to protect the statue of Winston Churchill in Parliament Square 'with every breath in my body.'[21] Government interventions in the way Britain remembered its history gained pace into 2021, as Housing Minister Robert Jenrick pledged to 'save Britain's statues from the woke militants who want to censor our past', while Culture Secretary Oliver Dowden summoned heritage bodies to a summit that Department for Culture, Media and Sport sources described as an attempt to 'defend our culture and history from the noisy minority of activists constantly trying to do Britain down.'[22] The National Trust became the subject of intense media attacks for research it was conducting into the links between historic properties and the legacies of slavery and empire, for which it was reported to the Charity Commission out of the feeling that exploring 'contentious' history was against the law. (It was not.[23])

We are in a strange position where each call for remembrance is recast as forgetting; every drive to shed light on the past is smeared as an act of censorship; and every attempt to re-examine the complexity of the past is denounced as simple-minded prejudice. Emotions run high, but are more often invented to discredit the positions of others – anyone arguing for a dispassionate understanding of history is liable to be branded as a guilt-ridden apologist driven by shame and hatred for their own country. For Johnson, 'it's time we stopped our cringing embarrassment about our history ... this general bout of self-recrimination and wetness.'[24] But you will be hard-pressed to find a historian or a heritage worker anywhere arguing that people should feel this way about their country or its history in the first place. On the other side, the drive to look only for the good in history frequently casts Britain's past as a source of pride, a deep emotional attachment that should be cherished and drawn on as a source of inspiration today. Yet while Britain's role in abolishing slavery, for instance, or in defeating Nazi Germany, are invoked as things we can be proud of in the present, this argument viscerally rejects the idea that a logical consequence would entail feeling shame about episodes of British history too. We are warned that holding 'heroic' figures to account for the atrocities of slavery and empire would be to judge the past by today's standards, and yet evidence that many people at the time also found these exact things abhorrent is ignored.

In such a climate, even mild pronouncements provoke intense anger: as David Olusoga writes of his experience as a public historian, 'if you want someone to call you a traitor or accuse you of hating Britain, try suggesting that Britain is a normal nation or that our history is remarkable but not exceptional.'[25] It has got to the point where even the word 'imperialist' provokes rage, if the suspicion is that the Empire is not being praised. 'Heroes of Rorke's Drift branded "imperialist" over links to empire', ran an article in the *Telegraph* critical of a review into the links between colonialism and the Queen's art collection.[26] But how else would you describe a painting created to celebrate colonial warfare?

A range of commentators have read this blurring of the lines between history, nostalgia and amnesia as the consequence of Britain's failure to fully confront its own past. Empire, in particular, is both everywhere and nowhere in popular consciousness. It is taken as given that Britain was 'great' because it once had a large and powerful empire, yet the realities of empire remain shrouded in myth and fantasy. There is a vague sense that it must have been better than other countries' empires; an insistence that even though the purpose of empire was to extract wealth from Britain's colonies, those colonies gained the residual benefit of things like railways that they are held to have been incapable of building themselves, if left to their own devices in subsequent centuries. Many people report having been taught little of empire at school – as the journalist Sathnam Sanghera writes, for instance, 'my education in British empire was almost non-existent . . . we explored both world wars at length . . . but I don't recall it once being mentioned that tens of thousands of brown people from across empire were fighting for Britain and that empire made great financial contributions too.'[27]

In turn, a lack of awareness about the history of empire compounds misunderstandings about British society itself. For Afua Hirsch, 'few who invoke the history of imperial greatness realise that the British Empire was the reason for post-war mass immigration from Africa, Asia and the Caribbean in the first place.'[28] The author, rapper and activist Akala has written similarly of post-war migration:

> No one explained that our grandparents were not immigrants, that they were literally British citizens – many of them Second World War veterans – with British passports to match, moving from one of Britain's outposts to the metropole. Nobody told white Britain that, over there in the colonies, Caribbeans and Asians were being told that Britain was their mother country,

that it was the home of peace and justice and prosperity and that they would be welcomed with open arms by their loving motherland.[29]

But the gaps in people's understanding are compounded still further by the nature of what *was* taught about empire. A number of commentators have emphasised that those in their sixties and over first learnt about British history between the 1930s and 1960s. It is a demographic that includes men who were conscripted into National Service between 1946 and 1962 – many of whom were pressed into colonial wars, in which people fighting for independence were the enemy.[30] Their earliest understandings of Britain and its history were shaped in the context of Britain having a global empire, and needing new generations of men and women to maintain it. And this education can operate unconsciously as much as consciously, being absorbed as much through culture and society as in formal schooling. It doesn't require explicit propaganda for people to be imbued with a sense that Britain's power and greatness are just the way it is; an inevitable result of superiority, something that doesn't need to be explained by looking into where it came from and why. For the journalist Adam Ramsay, this has fed into a widespread 'nostalgia for a time when life was easier, and Britain could simply get rich by killing people of colour and stealing their stuff', because the inextricable links between the two have never been adequately acknowledged. 'All of this is made possible by lies: the lies many of us were told about what our great-grandparents were up to in India, the lies we told ourselves when we decided not to look too closely, the lies we told the people we subjugated.'[31]

And this continues today. In recent memory, prime ministers from Gordon Brown to David Cameron and Boris Johnson have publicly called for the celebration of aspects of the British Empire, viewing it as something overall to be proud of, while explicitly arguing that we should wind down memories of imperial atrocities and move on. For disgraced former defence secretary Liam Fox, whose plans for the Department of International Trade were branded 'Empire 2.0' by civil servants, 'The United Kingdom is one of the few countries . . . that does not need to bury its 20th century history.'[32] An attitude that rested both on the frightening assumption that countries *should* try to bury unpleasant aspects of history to make themselves look better, and on a stunning disregard for Britain's twentieth-century history itself. As Ramsay writes, 'their nostalgia doesn't extend to the genocide [in Tasmania], forced famine [in India], concentration camps [in South Africa], castration with pliers, or rape with broken bottles [in Kenya], though the willingness to ignore all of these does tell us something important.'[33] Something has gone very wrong with how we think about Britain's history when the empire comes to be accounted for as a balance sheet of good and bad, as if any conceivable gains could make this a price worth paying.

This is more than just a debate about the past, important though that is. It is, fundamentally, about origins. Boris Johnson will defend his vision of Churchill with his last breath, because a challenge to traditional figures of heroism is a challenge to his entire worldview. Whose experiences are prioritised in remembering the past, and whose are disregarded or silenced, directly mirrors who is marginalised in the present. In the view of those who claim to 'defend' Britain's heritage, they are both just 'noisy minorities' gaining ground from the people whose perspectives count most. This is why, in a multicultural society that is home to many overlapping heritages and identities, nostalgia has become such contested territory, in which many feel that 'British values' and pride are under attack, while people of mixed heritage so often feel cut off from a sense of belonging.

Writers such as Afua Hirsch, Akala and Reni Eddo-Lodge have highlighted the savage irony that a country so invested in nostalgia for the national past has failed to acknowledge the realities of British history. As Eddo-Lodge asks: 'I needed to know why, when people waved Union Jacks and shouted "we want our country back", it felt like the chant was aimed at people like me. What history had I inherited that left me an alien in the place of my birth?' For Sathnam Sanghera, 'the defining political narrative of my lifetime' has been one that refuses to acknowledge the legacies of empire as a vital context for Britain's racial diversity, in favour of the ahistorical idea 'that black and brown people were aliens who arrived without permission, with no links to Britain, to abuse British hospitality.' 'Indeed', he writes, 'the narrative that brown people imposed themselves on Britain is so powerful that I absorbed it myself.' Growing up in Britain as the child of immigrants 'would have been significantly less agonising if, during my lifetime, Britain had not acted like we were aliens and interlopers but were here because of long-standing historical ties.' Eddo-Lodge writes similarly that 'I had been denied a context, an ability to understand myself.'[34]

There is, too, an entrenched narrative that immigration to Britain is a relatively recent phenomenon, dating from the second half of the twentieth century, so that portrayals of the multicultural past are seized upon as a distortion of history rather than an accurate reflection of it. Continual furores over casting diversity in period dramas are fuelled by the instinctive convictions of a section of the British public that its history is and should be *white*. The media was ready to give lavish prominence, for instance, to actor and professional grievance generator Laurence Fox's complaints that filmmakers were 'forcing diversity on people' by 'shoehorning' people of colour into historical dramas. Despite claiming to find the appearance of a single Sikh soldier in Sam Mendes's war epic *1917* to be 'great ... brilliant', Fox continued: 'but you're suddenly aware there were Sikhs fighting in this war. And you're like, "ok, you're now diverting me away from what the story is".'[35] Even while acknowledging that Sikh soldiers did indeed fight for Britain, this is a worldview that insists it is not part of *the story* of the

First World War. It insists that people of colour are incidental to the main narrative, even when their presence is fact.

These assumptions shape our understanding of history so powerfully that facts themselves can come as a surprise. Sanghera writes of learning as an adult about eighteenth-century writer, composer and social reformer Ignatius Sancho, and nineteenth-century Chartist leader William Cuffay, that 'if I had to guess when the first black activists became famous in Britain, I would have said it was the 1960s.' Despite his hometown of Wolverhampton's long multi-ethnic history, in local history groups and nostalgic studies such as *Wolverhampton Memories* the photographs show only white residents. Writing of Sake Dean Mahomed, the first Indian author in English and founder of England's first curry house in 1810, he emphasises that 'Mahomed's very existence challenged the idea that has been hammered into me my entire life: that brown people are relatively recent interlopers,' when in fact they have lived in Britain for centuries.[36] So insistent is this received narrative that when Classics professor Mary Beard pointed out on Twitter that there had been black people in Roman Britain – which should be completely unsurprising in an empire that colonised and recruited soldiers from Africa, still less when we have classical sources describing a Libyan emperor greeting an Ethiopian soldier at Hadrian's Wall – she faced a 'torrent of aggressive insults'. One social media commentator accused her of 'literally re-writing history'.[37] Which she was in fact doing, because that is her job – but the history she is writing here is one that puts facts back in after they were strenuously written out in the first place.

People do not react with anger like this unless maintaining the same old narrative is of deep importance to them. It is easy to dismiss the reactionary nationalism of the 'culture wars' over British history as a distraction manufactured to direct attention away from more substantial political issues, but we also need to consider that these things are deeply felt and sincerely believed.

And we need to consider why, and what this narrative is doing. We recognise instinctively, for instance, that Boris Johnson wrote a book about Churchill because he sees himself in the Churchillian mould, so that for us to approve of one is to approve of the other. As the historian Richard Evans notes,

> Johnson, as the subtitle of this book proclaims, is a firm believer in the 'great man' theory of history. Not for him the subtleties of the complex interplay of historical forces and individual personalities ... Winston Churchill alone, he writes, 'saved our civilisation' ... all this, he argues, confounds what he sees as the fashion of the past few decades to write off 'so-called great men and women' as 'meretricious bubbles on the vast tides of social history.' The story of Winston Churchill 'is a pretty withering retort to all that malarkey. He, and he alone, made the difference.'[38]

Historians, generally, manage to make room for both the importance of society as a whole and the contributions of its leaders, and do not experience this balance as personally threatening. But we are not really being asked to take seriously a philosophy of history in which Churchill is 'alone' responsible for every world event and development he had a leadership role in, because that would also entail giving him sole responsibility for the Bengal famine of 1943 – and when historians discuss even Churchill's partial contribution to this they are named and shamed in the national media and in starts pouring the abuse.[39] What we are being asked to do is to defend his status as 'hero' in the face of attacks by the complexity of reality.

Indeed, the cult of Churchill, and of heroising historical figures generally, has produced a climate in which anyone arguing for change is liable to be assumed to be tearing him down along with everything he stands for. Amid protests against police violence and for women's safety in the wake of the murder of Sarah Everard in March 2021, the statue of Churchill in Parliament Square was given a round-the-clock police phalanx even though no one had threatened it. The order, it was reported, had been to 'protect Churchill at all costs.' Two days later a bill passed its second reading in Parliament that would give a ten-year jail term for defacing a statue, which Policing Minister Kit Malthouse defended as a proportionate reflection of their 'emotional value'.[40] This is the danger of nostalgia in its most extreme forms: feeling so personally attacked by someone damaging a statue that hurting them back by taking ten years of their life feels like justice. And this *is* profound nostalgia: not something sentimental, or comfortable, or twee, but nostalgia with the pain in it, the fear and the rage that someone is threatening the home you had imagined, and the place you had hoped for within it. It is the anger of people who do not wish to confront the suggestion that the ideal they remember and are striving for might not be a good one, after all, for everyone; that the imagined homeland you long for is being rejected by people trying to make a new one, in which you and your values might no longer be welcomed.

STANDING ALONE

The desire to imaginatively resurrect war through the framing of political debate has long intermingled with nostalgia in British culture. Just as the pandemic was imagined through the lens of fighting on the home front, Brexit, both before and after the 2016 referendum, had been imaginatively transformed into a war against Europe. Reflexive invocations of the Second World War have been a stock trope of the British media at least since the Falklands War in 1982, peaking again with a surge of don't-forget-the-war Germanophobia surrounding German reunification at the turn of the 1990s. Decades of glib media jingoism about two world wars and one world cup or cheese-eating surrender monkeys or various blanket grievances culminated in comments such as Boris Johnson's likening of the EU to the expansionist ambitions of Hitler, or MP Mark Francois's pledge that 'my father, Reginald Francois, was a D-Day veteran. He never submitted to bullying by any German and neither will his son.' Eurosceptic billionaire and Brexit financier Peter Hargreaves declared that leaving the EU 'will be like Dunkirk again . . . Insecurity is fantastic', while Nigel Farage vowed that if there was a delay in triggering Article 50 he would personally 'don khaki, pick up a rifle and head for the front lines.'[41] And so on.

The substance of what actually happened in the Second World War was of little relevance compared to its symbolic value in conjuring a vague atmosphere of inevitable triumph and jingoistic rectitude. This was history hollowed out into a warm bath of antagonistic cheer and self-congratulation: what the writer James Cooray Smith has referred to as 'a culture that boils a vast and unimaginably complex conflict down to the title sequence of *Dad's Army* – an animation in which a Union Flag is forced off the European continent by a trio of Nazi triangles, and after returning home bobs around defiantly . . . It's the difference between those who remember war, and those who only remember war films.'[42] Indeed, at times Brexiteers could seem to be suffering from a kind of false memory syndrome, in which television was mistaken for historical memory. Ahead of the referendum, Leave.EU co-founder Arron Banks, for instance, claimed to have received a £30 donation in a letter from a Second World War veteran, whose animus was apparently directed against 'what we called the surrender monkeys' he had fought alongside on the Continent. As the columnist Fintan O'Toole noted, this seemed unlikely, as the earliest known use of the phrase dates to an episode of *The Simpsons*.[43]

From the 1990s onwards, Eurosceptic journalism deployed war metaphors to elevate ever more minor – and frequently invented – inconveniences over EU regulations about crisp flavour or banana straightness, and putative red tape, into a clash of epic suffering. This played into a broader culture in which memories of war, and particularly the Second World War, are consumed as a leisure activity, a form of entertainment that offers the comforts of moral clarity; of winners and losers, heroes and villains. Yet this nostalgia frequently blocks any real appreciation of the realities of war, even as it purports to honour it. For the historian Mark Mazower, observing the upswell of wartime nostalgia surrounding the seventieth anniversary of the outbreak of war in 2009, the 'pride and self-congratulation', 'the endless recycling of the same themes – Dunkirk, the D-Day landings, Churchillian greatness – starts to devalue the heroism of those times as much as to celebrate it.' Nuance can start to carry the murky whiff of collaboration and treachery; a sense that contemplating the horror of war outside of a staunchly nationalist perspective might look a lot like appeasement. For Cooray Smith, writing of Nigel Farage's 'oafish' fantasies of Dunkirk, this is barely even nostalgia: 'nostalgia requires an element of pain . . . for Farage and his ilk there is no pain in this behaviour, just the most extraordinarily banal comfort.'[44]

British history seemed to offer an inexhaustible well of trivial comparisons and bellicose optimism around the EU referendum. Brexit was likened by politicians and media commentators to any number of formative wars and historical dramas – the Reformation, the Napoleonic Wars, the Declaration of Independence, the Corn Laws, the 'buccaneering' spirit of imperialist free-traders. It obscured the reality of the past at the same time as hysterically distorting the view from the present. For MP Jacob Rees-Mogg, framing Brexit at the 2017 Conservative Party Conference, 'This is Magna Carta . . . It's Waterloo! It's Agincourt! It's Crécy! We win all of these things!' After an audience member bellowed 'Trafalgar!', Rees-Mogg replied 'and Trafalgar, absolutely.'[45] Writing in the *Telegraph* in 2018, Boris Johnson claimed – wildly incorrectly on a number of fronts – that Theresa May's Chequers plan for a softer Brexit would have been the first time that 'our leaders were deliberately acquiescing in foreign rule' 'since 1066'.[46] The journalist Anoosh Chakelian objected of this constant stream of 'sub-GCSE historical references' that 'the main problem' isn't even 'the inaccuracy' of the assertions, inaccurate as they are. 'The main problem is the sheer *basic*ness of the reference ... you wonder if they've just groped for the easiest bit they can remember from their textbooks, after running out of invocations of Winston Churchill's patriotic spirit'.[47] This is not history, nor even really nostalgia for a rose-tinted version of history itself, so much as it is a nostalgia for the gusto of imperial schoolboys learning about history – enjoying the glow of half-gleeful, half-solemn pride in a sweep of grand confirmations that Britons were not only the winners, but the goodies too.

This insistent vagueness in appeals to the glories of the past found its purest distillation in the Leave campaign's call to 'take back control'. As many commentators have observed, the message was deliberately vague as to what exactly had been lost, or what needed to be regained. Control of what? Back to when? It was a slogan that went through various iterations: early suggestions in conversations with campaign director Dominic Cummings had been 'get change', 'keep control', and then, at Cummings's suggestion, 'Vote Leave, let's take control' – which was indeed the version used when the campaign launched with an online video in October 2015. Yet this evolved, slightly but significantly over the following weeks, into 'take *back* control'. As Cummings explained, the crucial tweak in this message played into what behavioural psychologists refer to as the powerful human impulse towards 'loss aversion'.[48] People, he argued, were far more anxious about losing things than they were motivated to gain them. Taking 'back' control widened out the field of people's anxieties to suggest a whole realm of just rewards that might be regained; not only proclaiming, on the side of a bus, a weekly £350 million that could be recovered, but appealing to a host of inchoate yearnings about fading pride and glory that, it was promised, could be recaptured once more.

For many observers, this longing to recapture what was being lost was indelibly marked by nostalgia for empire. Liberal Democrat leader Vince Cable's remarks that Leave voters were 'nostalgic for a world where passports were blue, faces were white, and the map was coloured imperial pink' was emblematic of a widely held feeling that those who had voted for Brexit were stuck in the past, uniquely in thrall to a lost era of power and pride.[49] American commentators looked on the referendum from afar and saw Britain as 'cling[ing] to imperial nostalgia' and 'delusions of empire', interpreting the vote as the 'last gasp' of a country in the death throes of post-imperial decline.[50]

This narrative became received wisdom among many Remainers. The journalist Gary Younge, for instance, argued that 'Britain's imperial fantasies have given us Brexit', while Afua Hirsch has written that 'the ghosts of the British Empire are everywhere in modern Britain, and nowhere more so than in the dream of Brexit.' Among many others, the historian David Olusoga has highlighted just how out of step these rose-tinted images of the imperial past are with historical reality: 'the Brexiters ask us to "believe in Britain" but not the real Britain, with its flaws and contradictions and a history full of inglorious chapters as well as achievement. The Britain we must believe in is an unreal land of distorted memories and colonial amnesia.' Fundamental misunderstandings persist as to the source of Britain's historic wealth and power in the world, which perpetuate misunderstandings about Britain's place in the world today. As Olusoga contends, this is a 'dangerous nostalgia for something that never existed', mixing up Britain's formal empire and colonies with an informal 'empire' of global trading networks that, in reality, were much more economically significant. 'The empire, even at its height,' he writes, 'never came close to absorbing the majority of our exports or providing the bulk of our imports, and neither will the Commonwealth, no matter how good a trade deal we win.'[51]

Yet longing for the supposed glories of empire, while forgetting or misunderstanding the reality of much of its history, are not necessarily mutually exclusive. As the historian Robert Saunders emphasises, 'it is probably only possible to be *nostalgic* for empire if you *forget* most of its history.'[52] When charged with nostalgia, even the most staunchly rhetorical imperialists insist that their aim is not to restore a British Empire of ages past, but simply to inject the spirit that once made empire possible into ambitions compatible with twenty-first-century values. For Boris Johnson, writing in 2018, the goal of Brexit was '*not to build a new empire, heaven forfend,*' but simply to 'rediscover some of the dynamism of the bearded Victorians . . . to go back out into the world in a way that we had perhaps forgotten over the past 45 years: to find friends, to open markets, to promote our culture and our values.'[53] But this is the same Boris Johnson who recited Kipling's 'The Road to Mandalay' at a Buddhist temple in Myanmar, getting as far as 'the temple-bells they say—', before the British ambassador hurriedly cut him off from continuing with 'come you back, you British soldier.' The same Boris Johnson who wrote of Africa that 'the problem is not that we were once in charge, but that we are not in charge any more'; who referred to 'cheering crowds of flag-waving piccaninnies' with 'watermelon smiles' greeting the Queen on Commonwealth tours; and who extolled the virtues of the Foreign Office at the 2016 Conservative Party Conference by shouting '178 nations of the world we either conquered or invaded' to a cheering audience.[54] It is a nostalgia for the spoils of imperialism (both psychic and material) without the wish to run an empire – an insistence on having one's cake and eating it, taking moral credit for having decolonised while retaining the bullish superiority of an imperial power. It is a nostalgia that seeks to restore the attitude of a time when it was still possible to maintain the assumption that the default position of other countries, in their dealings with you, would be one not only of deference, but of *gratitude*.

In spite of the feel-good jingoism about invading other

countries, in spite of the Enoch Powellite rhetoric and the wistful quotations of Kipling, Johnson has referred to the end of empire as 'a profoundly good thing', and there is no reason to doubt his sincerity. In his words (but my italics), it was 'good for Britain and good for the world that . . . those *responsibilities* have been taken away.' In this reading, Britain retains all the benefits of a world power, without what Kipling would have referred to as 'the White Man's burden' of assuming the costs of administrating and controlling colonised people. 'Of course we don't want to wield our hard power,' Johnson continued. But Britain's previous military might was now 'dwarfed' by

> a phenomenon that the pessimists never predicted when we unbundled the British Empire and that is soft power – the vast and subtle and pervasive extension of British influence around the world . . . and up the creeks and inlets of every continent on earth there go the gentle kindly gunboats of British soft power captained by Jeremy Clarkson – a prophet more honoured abroad, alas, than in his own country, or J.K. Rowling, who is worshipped by young people in some Asian countries as a kind of divinity, or just the BBC . . . [55]

Even as this rhetoric congratulates Britain for decolonisation, it rests on imperialist mentalities played for humour in order to sustain a sense of implacable superiority and can-do optimism. We are asked to imagine Britain going out into the world as imperial conquerors revered like gods by credulous natives, through which we gain the emotional benefits of nostalgia for empire even as we benefit, too, from disowning its reality.

In the weeks following the referendum, a similar ideal was expressed by former Conservative Party chairman Grant Shapps as he set out his vision to restore Britain to its historic status as 'the world's greatest trading nation.' 'We need to rediscover the swashbuckling spirit of the nineteenth century when we practically owned the concept of free trade,' he proclaimed. For the former Brexit secretary David Davis, too, 'our history is a trading, buccaneering history – back to Drake and beyond. That's what we're good at.' While explicit references to empire are absent from such remarks, they emphatically rehabilitate the wealth that empire brought into simply a result of Britons' 'swashbuckling spirit' and derring-do.[56] The gunboats of nineteenth-century imperialism, which established free trade to Britain's advantage by threat of force, are imaginatively folded into a tale of Elizabethan romance, plucky privateers and heroic explorers. In turn, this story suggests that Britain today can somehow reap the rewards that came with imperial and naval supremacy if only people could summon up enough courage. If this is nostalgia for empire, it is not a longing for anything approaching a history that actually existed, but a yearning to give a tale of past triumphs real power to shape the future, if people could just believe in it hard enough. No one is seriously advocating that entrepreneurial Britons set out in the 2020s to sack enemy ports under armed force, or raid merchant vessels for plunder in the Spanish Empire. But they are sincerely suggesting that we imagine international trade in those terms, and cherish its emotional resonance, carrying it into our daily lives as a source of psychic inspiration.

What is being longed for, more than anything, by these nostalgic free-traders is a mentality propelled by a story of Britain and its history. It is nostalgia fuelled by a romantic sense of history as a grand sweep, bounding from one age to the other and into the present – but never stopping long enough to contemplate what is true or not, or what is being ignored – with the comforting sense that even as Britain changes, it remains the same, indelibly imprinted with the same enduring national character and bound to succeed, again and again, by force of historic inevitability. Yet it is a story that is only sustained by holding in balance two very different, opposing narrative threads. Alongside a story of Britain ruling the waves, amassing the largest territorial empire the world has ever seen, is a parallel narrative of plucky little Britain standing alone against overwhelming odds, punching above its weight and standing up to the oppressions of larger, rival powers. This duality has a long history that was already well-entrenched in popular consciousness before the referendum. Many of the events that loom largest in retellings of British and English history are of honourable retreats, characterful disasters and heroic failures: from the Charge of the Light Brigade to Scott of the Antarctic, the 'last stand' against the Zulus, the Somme, Dunkirk and beyond.[57] Popular memories of the Second World War, especially, become a way of *not* thinking about empire, denying the salience of imperialism in telling the story of Britain. This narrative of a plucky, underdog isle underplays both the role of empire in supplying wartime manpower and resources, and Britain's international allies, in favour of an image of an island nation standing alone against evil. It insists upon the right to enjoy the psychic benefits of being the underdog, at the same time as continuing to revel in the status of overdog, too.

There are several pressing problems, however, in reading this curious combination of imperial nostalgia, amnesia and Second World War fixation as the driving force behind Brexit. Many Brexiteers argued that – far from yearning for imperial power – they were spearheading an anti-imperial liberation movement. It was the EU, they argued, that harboured ambitions of imperial domination in Europe, and was treating Britain like a colony. The connections between anti-imperialism and Euroscepticism have a long history, not least because the expectation that Britain would lead Europe from within had often been presented in the 1970s as a way for Britain to retain its status as a world power in the wake of decolonisation. As one correspondent to the *Daily Mail* put it in 1975, 'the EEC [European Economic Community, a forerunner of the EU] must become the new British Empire.' Campaigning for a Leave vote in the 1975 referendum on EEC membership, the *Spectator* had attributed imperial nostalgia to *remainers*, arguing that 'nostalgia for the days when Britain was the greatest of the European powers' was making people all too ready to abandon their independence 'for part of the identity of something bigger.'[58]

People do not need to have a clear understanding of imperial history, or even knowingly feel nostalgic for certain elements of imperialism, in order to have had their worldviews unconsciously shaped by the legacies of empire. But why would this only have affected half the population? Why should it only be Leave voters who are apparently susceptible to imperial nostalgia? If nostalgia for empire, or for a sense of nationhood that came with it, are still at play in British society, this is a legacy through which all sides of the European debate comprehend their role in the world.[59] Moreover, it wasn't Britain that voted Leave as a whole, but English voters who swung the balance – and within England, voters who identified as English *rather* than British gave their strongest support to Leave overall.[60] The empire was, of course, a joint British project; in fact, at times, Scotland and Wales were overrepresented in colonial administration, emigration and the armed forces compared to England, relative to population size. 'Imperial nostalgia' becomes a blunt tool when it cannot explain why swathes of Scottish and Welsh voters, and people in England who felt more British than English, would be immune from its effects – still less why their apparent freedom from empire nostalgia would automatically translate into a vote for Remain.

Surprisingly little attention has been paid to the nostalgia of Remain politicians and voters. This is particularly remarkable given that in the past few decades a range of politicians who backed Remain, including David Cameron, Tony Blair and Gordon Brown, have argued that Britain should celebrate and draw pride from aspects of its colonial history, and – in the case of Cameron addressing the legacies of slavery in Jamaica – 'move on' from the atrocities of the past.[61] Similarly, Brown declared in 2005 that 'the days of Britain having to apologise for its colonial history are over', while Cameron maintained in 2013 that 'there's an enormous amount to be proud of in what the

British Empire did and was responsible for.'[62] According to the broadcaster John Kampfner, during the 1997 general election campaign, Blair was only at the last minute prevented from including the line 'I am proud of the British Empire' in a speech about foreign policy, and even then left shadow Foreign Secretary Robin Cook 'aghast' at the tone of pride in Britain's past military glories. By the lead up to the Iraq War in 2002, Blair's foreign policy guru Robert Cooper was arguing that 'a new colonialism can save the world' in an op-ed for the *Observer* headlined 'Why we still need empires'.[63] Attitudes such as these were shaping the terrain of public debate long before the referendum, irrespective of one's stance on Europe. A 2014 YouGov poll revealed that 59 per cent of those polled felt empire was 'something to be proud of', while 49 per cent thought that former colonies were better off for having been part of the Empire, and a full third of respondents agreed they would 'like Britain to still have an empire'. Though polling conducted by Ipsos MORI in August 2020 found that feelings of pride about the British Empire had fallen to 34 per cent, with half as many respondents answering 'don't know' as in 2014 – suggesting that prominent public debates about the nature of empire since the referendum *have* had an effect in increasing awareness and lowering positive perceptions.[64]

While in the run-up to the referendum Leavers were widely charged with being uniquely stuck in the past, or else pathologically attached to a glorious version of British history, both sides sought to marshal history in support of their campaigns. Even arch-Remainer Nick Clegg succumbed to Trumpian cravings for a lost golden age of power and pride, titling his 2017 manifesto *How to Stop Brexit (and Make Britain Great Again)*. Just as the Leave campaign drew on the testimony of Second World War veterans, who told voters 'please don't give away everything we fought for. Please give your vote to our great country', the Remain campaign found veterans who warned that Brexit could jeopardise the peace they had fought for. 'For me, Britain is stronger in Europe because it reflects the values my generation fought for in Europe,' argued one veteran in a campaign video. 'We sacrificed many, many men in both world wars and this was to establish a peaceful and prosperous union. We can't sacrifice this now.' Where Leavers were inclined to view the Second World War as an enduring lesson in being suspicious of Continental ambitions, the Remain campaign emphasised the EU's origins in the post-war determination never again to see Europe divided. David Cameron invoked Winston Churchill as an object lesson in reforming the EU from within, as he promised to 'stay and fight' Britain's corner in Churchill's image:

> At my office, I sit two yards away from the Cabinet Room where Winston Churchill decided in May 1940 to fight on against Hitler – the best and greatest decision anyone has made in our country. He didn't want to be alone, he wanted to be fighting with the French and with the Poles and with the others but he didn't quit. He didn't quit on Europe, he didn't quit on European democracy, he didn't quit on European freedom.[65]

More present-centred arguments in favour of Remain, too, drew on the appeal of a sense of belonging – a sense of being 'at home' in Europe – whose emotional resonance became all the more acute as the referendum threatened to re-establish the imaginative border between island and continent. Yet this often seemed incongruously at odds with sentimental appropriations of war and Churchill. In its most extreme form, this was sometimes a sense of feeling at home in European culture that cast Englishness in particular as something embarrassing, outdated, provincial. In its broadest terms, the charge of 'metropolitan liberal elitism' is just as blunt an analytical tool as 'imperial nostalgia', but there *is* a current of personal and cultural nostalgia among many Remainers that is only mildly connected to the European Union as a political and economic entity. Memories of foreign holidays, inter-railing, expanding cultural horizons; of good wine, varied European foodstuffs and sundry cosmopolitan pleasures. While seemingly innocuous, this nostalgia at times figured the EU less as a complex and imperfect group of institutions than as a repository of all that is nice on the Continental mainland – an attitude perhaps most succinctly encapsulated in the anti-Brexit rallying cry 'fromage not Farage'.

Yet this existed, too, alongside highly self-conscious articulations of British gentility. Alongside Europhilic slogans, signs at protest marches drew consistently on images of Britishness centred on gentle twee and unflappable good humour: 'this doesn't seem very well thought through'; 'more tea less Brexit'; 'I don't usually protest, but really?'; 'I'm British, I'm on a march, things must be bad.' Brexit-adjacent social media discussion drew on a seemingly bottomless enthusiasm for faux-archaic swearing: 'Cockwomble', 'Arsebadger', 'Wankpuffin'.[66] It answered the need for civility in political discourse by reaching for the moral universe of children's literature, in which lessons in politeness come from quaint eccentrics and woodland creatures, evoking a mid-century fantasy Britain where nothing had ever gone wrong before.

SECURE – IF SOMETIMES SLIGHTLY INSANE

There is a current of nostalgia that is not unique to, but often associated with Remainers: one that views 2016 or thereabouts as a moment of rupture, when everything started going a bit wrong in one way or another, and bathes the years before it in a false glow of consensus. It has become a cultural cliché to miss the 2012 Olympics as a time when everyone came together, a brief window where it felt uncontroversial to be fervently patriotic, and when many found themselves surprised at the pride and relief they felt in Britain doing things well while the rest of the world looked on. The Olympics opening ceremony has come to be viewed as the high-water mark of a post-imperial nation that understood, at long last, who it was again. Yet these memories tend to obscure and downplay the divisions of the preceding years – the pressing fear, for instance, that London 2012 was unprepared to meet the threat of terrorism, the riots in London and cities across England in August 2011, student protests in 2010, the upheaval of the financial crash and the beginnings of economic austerity. It is all too easy to look back still further upon New Labour as a gentler time for politics, forgetting how deeply divided the country was over war with Iraq, or the progressive hardening of debate around immigration, multiculturalism and civil liberties; but remembering the optimism of 'Cool Britannia'.

It is especially difficult to make room for these memories of how things looked on the ground at the time, because London 2012 itself is so strongly associated with its own narrative of British history. Danny Boyle's opening ceremony offered a romantic origin story for a modern, multicultural nation, pre-empting grandiose self-celebration with knowing outbursts of quirk in a way that seemed both somehow quintessentially 'British', and oddly unfamiliar. In many ways, this was the received narrative of modern Britain: a green and pleasant land home to literary and scientific genius alike, which gave birth to dark Satanic mills, and yet in doing so became the Workshop of the World, before going on to defeat the Nazis and rise again to become a cultural powerhouse.

If some of these developments were distinctly mixed bags – when, for instance, British ingenuity produced the horror of nineteenth-century factory conditions – these were swiftly countered by the inexorable rise of people power: of Chartists, suffragettes and Jarrow marchers. Yet the performance gave a new prominence within this grand sweep to the rise of the welfare state and the NHS; to the *Empire Windrush* as a metonym for a tolerant, welcoming, forward-looking Britain that had arrived in the twenty-first century with a renewed sense of faith in the inevitability of progress. Empire itself, of course, was

43

notably absent, not least because it would have been crass beyond belief to have portrayed a similar trajectory of hope emerging from the horrors of empire to a global audience. But why should we expect it to have been included? The opening ceremony was not and was never intended to be a balanced treatment of British history, but a partial account whose purpose was to celebrate Britain. The aim had not been to paper over the cracks in British history, but to emotionally connect us to a national drama unfolding through generations of people – sometimes banding together, sometimes galvanised by a brilliant leader – trying, struggling, failing better and succeeding. What we are nostalgic for, more than anything, in remembering summer 2012, is for a time when we were ourselves nostalgic.

Because the story of British history performed in the 2012 opening ceremony was so compelling, it gained its own momentum, influencing both how the rest of the world saw Britain and how Britain saw itself in ways that were mutually reinforcing. The *New York Times*, for instance, wrote that Britain had presented itself to the world as 'a nation secure in its own post-empire identity', if 'sometimes slightly insane' – a flattering verdict for a country that often likes to think of itself as wearing patriotism more lightly than in the American mode, confident enough to undercut its nationalism with eccentricity.[67] An Australian political theorist suggested that the image of Britain presented by the Olympics meant that many countries were now 'looking to Britain as an example of a dynamic multicultural society united by a generous patriotism.' Moreover, commentators reflected, this was changing how it felt to be British for the better. The journalist Yasmin Alibhai-Brown wrote at the end of the Olympics that 'these two weeks have been a watershed of true significance. There has been a visceral reaction among black and Asian Britons to what we have seen. For some, it has been perhaps the first time they have really felt a part of this country. For others, the promise of tolerance and integration has come true.'[68] It seemed, momentarily, to offer an answer to a question that had rattled along unresolved since the post-war years and into the twenty-first century: did Britain stand for anything outside of its history?

For others, though, with the benefit of hindsight, the festival of nostalgia and optimism around the Olympics lulled Britain into a 'false sense of security' that 'ill-prepar[ed] us for the bleak years to come.'[69] The Windrush scandal of 2018 certainly put paid to any national sense of self-satisfaction that Britain had been welcoming of Caribbean migrants, or that the state even recognised their status as British nationals. When weighed against the divisions of Brexit and beyond, it does feel like summer 2012 was a rare moment of relative consensus. For a few weeks, patriotic nostalgia felt more uncomplicated, and more compatible with a tolerant, forwards-looking optimism, than it did in the years before or since. And yet, even at the time, this story of Britain was met with an embittered reaction among those who felt a narrative was being taken away from them. Rupert Murdoch found the ceremony 'a little too politically correct', while the *Mail on Sunday* opted for full-throttle fulmination against its 'Marxist propaganda', lamenting that incorporating the NHS as 'an official strand of our island story' was 'a damaging and ultimately self-defeating national tragedy.' For the *Mail*, it was those who celebrated the growth of the post-war welfare state who were wallowing in misplaced nostalgia and 'sentimentality': 'Britons' misty-eyed myopia' was apparently blinding them to real failings within the health service.[70] The Conservative MP Aidan Burley found the ceremony 'more leftie . . . than Beijing, the capital of a communist state!', suggesting that its treatment of Britain since 1945 was little more than left-wing posturing and 'multi-cultural crap'.[71]

But for the television producer and future director of *Brexit: The Movie* Martin Durkin, this story of Britain was 'topsy-turvy' from start to finish, an 'extravagant display of dim-brained left-wing history' from a 'miserable northern socialist'. For every development Danny Boyle regarded as a source of pride, Durkin

saw shame; each defeat of wickedness and cruelty Boyle celebrated was, for Durkin, a turning point of a once-great nation
in decline. He looked 'in vain' for a paean to 'global free trade'
and found none. In his reading, the true story of Britain was the
'achievement of being the first proper capitalist nation, and
everything that went with it.'[72]

KEEP CALM AND CARRY ON
(AND ON, AND ON)

In the 2000s, when we might plausibly have been imagining the
look and feel of a new millennium, it could feel as though nostalgic visions of history were everywhere. Indie kids donned tea
dresses, beehives, satchels and winklepickers, drawing eclecti-
cally on Teddy Boy, Rockabilly and Skinhead influences as they
sung ironical ditties of post-war 'Albion', while the folk-rock
revival conjured up age-old images of pastoral Englishness.
Nostalgic nightlife became an unlikely growth industry, with
electro-swing club nights, prohibition-era speakeasies supplying gin in teacups, or Blitz-themed parties promising to 'escape
the drab safety of the modern world for a time when Londoners defied Hitler's Luftwaffe'.[73] Transatlantic conversations
emerged around the appearance of the 'hipster' – a figure who
was hard to define precisely, but whose various iterations might
be found riding a penny farthing, collecting vintage records and
film cameras, rehabilitating neglected brewing methods, or
raiding second-hand stores for modernist furniture.

Following the 2007–8 financial crash and the beginnings of
the economic austerity of the Cameron–Osborne years, the
modernist aesthetics of wartime and post-war Britain became a
way of articulating a changing national mood. The Keep Calm
and Carry On poster – though it was mass-produced for the
first time in 2008 – evoked a seemingly authentic mentality of
wartime Britain, an imagined attitude of stiff upper lips, stoicism

and muddling through in the face of adversity. In turn, it spawned an entire industry of tea towels, cushions, crown logos, Union Jack bunting, notepads disguised as ration books, and vintage-inspired novelties in Gill Sans font and muted colours that evoked a time of virtuous austerity and public-spiritedness. There seemed to be an inexhaustible well of nostalgia for the moral fibre and make-do-and-mend of wartime generations: 1940s booklets on domestic skills were reissued by enterprising publishers, cooking blogs and books provided recipes themed around the restrictions of ration cards, while Jamie Oliver's 2008 bestselling book and TV series *Ministry of Food* took its name from the actual wartime ministry that managed rationing and food economy.[74]

In many ways, these revivals of earlier ways of living answered a deep need in the twenty-first century. For many people, the global consumer economy was offering an at times bewildering variety of choice. Not only this, but an endless array of fast fashion and throwaway goods was perpetuating both horrific working conditions in the developing world, and contributing to an environmental crisis. Why not turn towards an aesthetic that eschewed plastic carrier bags in favour of canvas totes and netting shoppers (which really do *seem* like they would be better for the environment[75]); why not repurpose second-hand clothes and furniture instead of buying new ones? In the wake of the financial crash, amid rising unemployment, stagnating wages and spiralling housing costs, it was entirely understandable to look back to earlier generations who had also had to make do with less – and who had often excelled at it. A nostalgic attachment to analogue technologies such as vinyl, tapes and print photography was a way of holding on to the emotional value of *things*, in a digital economy where anything can be accessed on-screen almost instantly. Why not select the best things that might otherwise be lost from the past, and combine them with all the advantages of the present?

But sometimes, the aesthetics of the past can end up serving a very different agenda. The nostalgia of the Keep Calm and Carry On years of Conservative austerity, for instance, was deeply bound up with memories of the post-war austerity of the 1940s and early 1950s: years that had seen full employment, the construction of the welfare state, the NHS, comprehensive education, and a massive public housing programme as well as rationing and restraint. For the writer Owen Hatherley, the overlaying of this most recent austerity with the imagery of an earlier, very different era, meant that 'at times ... it felt as if parts of the country began to resemble a strange, dreamlike reconstruction of the 1940s and 1950s, reassembled in the wrong order.' [76] At a time when the Conservative–Lib Dem coalition was instigating some of the most severe cuts to public spending in living memory, people were summoning up the aesthetics of an age when the country had rebuilt itself into prosperity through massive government investment.

The Keep Calm and Carry On poster itself evoked nostalgia for a time when people had – apparently – trusted the government to tell them what to do, safe in the knowledge that those in power had their best interests at heart. But this was, in many ways, a fantasy. While we do not know how the British public might have reacted to the exhortation to Keep Calm and Carry On in wartime, because it never became an official propaganda poster, we *do* know that plenty of people were irritated by the determined cheeriness of the wartime propaganda they did see around them. Working-class diarists and interviewees in Tom Harrisson's 1976 study *Living Through the Blitz*, for instance, recalled being infuriated by the patronising tone of government messaging. They knew well that this classless image of Britain pulling together was far from the reality on the ground – not everyone was in this together in the same way. The state itself seemed genuinely to fear the working classes, rather than regarding them with benevolent paternalism. Whitehall had sought to avoid the use of large public air-raid shelters wherever possible, in favour of private Anderson shelters in back gardens, worrying that such concentrations of the working classes might create a shared 'shelter mentality' where people would, at best, lie around and avoid work, and at worst breed mass hysteria or even subversion.[77]

Our nostalgia is often for a time when we have an idea of class relations as having been more harmonious – of people across the social scale being united in the same shared goals and interests. Period dramas such as *Downton Abbey* invite us to admire the strong and struggling but always deferent working classes, who know their place, while imagining the ruling classes as well-meaning patricians who take care of their dependents. For Hatherley, this is the same attitude at work behind Keep-Calm-and-Carry-On nostalgia: a yearning for 'an actual or imaginary English patrician attitude of stiff upper lips and muddling through . . . it is *a nostalgia for the state of being repressed* – solid, stoic, public-spirited, as opposed to the depoliticised, hysterical and privatised reality of Britain over the last thirty years.' So what happens when we import these myths about history into the present, and deploy them in a very different context? We are asked to annex all the positive memories of an era with a powerful central state, national welfare and a strong public sector, and imaginatively sprinkle them over a set of completely opposing values.[78]

But is this too much weight for a vintage poster, a period drama or a heritage tea towel to bear? It is all too easy for our nostalgia to be co-opted into serving a political agenda, and perhaps one that we never intended, but is our nostalgia really the problem here in the first place? And our nostalgia isn't always for a time of deference to authority: our enthusiasm for *Downton*-esque tales of upstairs-downstairs harmony is matched by an appetite for dramas like *Peaky Blinders*, where working-class gangsters and card-carrying communists thwart aristocratic fascists and assassinate police inspectors. It is difficult to know how much any of this is just harmless fun, an escapist fantasy in which history is a form of entertainment and leisure, and how much this shapes what we understand of reality. Our understanding of what happened in the past will always shape what we understand to be inevitable, desirable and possible in the world today – which is, after all, why political energies are directed so concertedly towards shaping an 'official' version of history in curriculums and citizenship tests. Sometimes, it really does matter what kind of a story it is you are enjoying, and why you are being told it. But sometimes a tea towel really is just a tea towel. It is perfectly possible to enjoy the aesthetics of aristocratic period dramas, say, or the shabby charms of a less materially comfortable age, without endorsing the social relations that produced them and while celebrating their demise. Every generation, in its turn, has drawn stylistic inspiration from history – there is nothing inherently wrong with looking back and finding selective aspects to admire, while not wanting to trade in the social progress that has been gained since. And yet we can never entirely escape the fact that even the most harmless-looking nostalgias can often be a cover for something else entirely.

MARGARET THATCHER'S VICTORIAN VALUES

We've been here before. In the 1980s, the 'heritage wars' erupted in national newspapers and the pages of scholarly journals over the ways in which Britain was remembering its past. The popularity of anything from stately home visits and historical tourism to Laura Ashley, ITV's 1981 adaptation of *Brideshead Revisited*, or the chart-topping sales of Edith Holden's *The Country Diary of an Edwardian Lady* (1977) were pointed to as signs of a nation pathologically attached to its history, unable to face the realities of post-war decline and retreating into misty-eyed visions of a green and pleasant land. To its critics, the cult of the country house was symptomatic of a reactionary turn against collectivism and democracy, while nostalgic evocations of rural and village life were read as a 'Disneyfied' version of history, one that sanitised the past and was making possible the rise of a Little-England nationalism.[79]

At the start of the decade, nostalgia was held up as an explanation for economic decline. No wonder, ran this narrative, Britain had lost its industrial lead, when it had always been so in thrall to fields and hedgerows and bygone rustic pleasures, with the nation's best minds absorbed in pastoral poetry when they might otherwise have been drawing up science and innovation strategies.[80] In turn, it was argued, the more Britain's importance in the world diminished, the more people were turning to the past for emotional compensation. By the end of the decade, nostalgia was interpreted as the mood that had made Thatcherism possible: providing consolatory myths about British and English tradition, even as the last remnants of tradition were carved up by privatisation, financialisation and rapid technological change. Heritage, it was charged, was little more than Thatcherism in period costume. For the critic Tom Paulin, the British heritage industry was 'a loathsome collection of theme parks and dead values', while a journalist in the *Sunday Times* described the whole island as 'an escapist theme park that stretches all the way from Dover to John o'Groats.'[81] It didn't help that John Major was still promising in 1993 that Britain would always remain a country of 'long shadows on county [cricket] grounds, warm beer, invincible green suburbs' and 'old maids bicycling' to church on a misty morning.[82] So toxic was the word 'heritage' that by 1997, it was rumoured, Tony Blair's advisors were studiously arranging his photo opportunities out of sight of old buildings, lest any taint of elite tradition tarnish the New in New Labour.[83] The Department of National Heritage was swiftly renamed the Department for Culture, Media and Sport to minimise use of the H-word.

But why was this popular interest in history so strongly linked to the charge of a socially regressive conservatism? There was more than a touch of left-wing snobbery at play here, a sneering at people's taste for National Trust outings, Merchant Ivory films, and faux-antique gifts from Crabtree & Evelyn or Past Times. As the historian Raphael Samuel noted, taking a more kindly view on the popular history boom, there is a long tradition on the intellectual left of rebuking the masses for what the Labour statesman Ernest Bevin called the 'poverty' of their desires. For many on the left, the heritage industry served as a kind of opiate of the people, presenting a sentimental version of the past that obscured the realities of inequality in past and present alike. But as heritage workers were at pains to point out, many of their properties and attractions had little to do with country houses or the aristocracy, and still less a top-down vision of history – people were equally interested in the every-day lives of 'ordinary people', from farmers and cottagers to miners and ironworkers. And many of people's enthusiasms had obviously populist leanings: Morris dancing, for instance, or local history and folk museums.[84] Why should people's interest in history mean that they were unable to face the present?

Moreover, the Conservative Party's commitment to 'heritage' in the 1980s was frequently only skin deep – more about sustaining an idea of the national past than preserving its actual traces. Nostalgic appeals to the rural Shires were coupled with deregulation and development: a free-market stance that prioritised building and industrial farming over conservation. Thatcher herself denounced environmentalists as 'romantics and cranks', 'the enemy within', while Environment Secretary Nicholas Ridley dismissed conservationists as 'pseudo-Marxists' who failed to appreciate the rights of landowners to do as they wished.[85] Ridley himself declared that he had 'a recurring nightmare' that the countryside would be frozen in time by nostalgia, under 'some conservation order or another', leaving Britain with an 'ossified' landscape that would be little more than a 'green museum'. Instead, he offered a vision for change and transformation, in which he argued that the countryside 'has always been, and should always be, a product of the interaction of man and his environment as time goes by.' Those who opposed local building developments were labelled 'NIMBYs' (Not In My Back Yard) motivated by selfishness (though it was later revealed that Ridley himself had opposed a housing development that threatened the view from his rural bolthole in the Cotswolds).[86] As one critic remarked, 'there was no greater enemy of heritage than Nicholas Ridley at the Department of the Environment.'[87]

In part, this identification of heritage and popular history with the political right had seemed to have an instinctive truth to it, because it seemed to dovetail with the Conservative Party's own appropriations of history. For Margaret Thatcher, British history was a means of re-energising a country that had lost its way. Invoking the 'greatness' of Britain's past could be a way of reversing national decline. Casting herself in the role of Winston Churchill, the Falklands War was envisaged as a return to military might and supremacy. Those 'waverers' and 'faint-hearts' who had feared that 'Britain was no longer the nation that had built an empire and ruled a quarter of the world'? 'Well,' she said, 'they were wrong.' The 'lesson of the Falklands' was that 'Britain has not changed and that this nation still has those sterling qualities that shine through our history . . . we have not changed. When the demands of war and the dangers to our own people call us to arms – then we British are as we have always been: competent, courageous and resolute.' 'We have ceased to be a nation in retreat,' she declared in the aftermath of victory in 1982 – but why, she asked, had it taken 'a war to bring out our qualities and reassert our pride? Why do we have to be invaded before we throw aside our selfish aims and begin to . . . work and achieve as only we can achieve?' As prime minister, she pledged, she would bring this spirit back home. If Britain could keep alight 'that spirit which has fired her for generations past', it could 'achieve in peace what we can do so well in war.'[88]

Yet Thatcher, too, was prone to accusing her opponents of being stuck in the past; of giving undue weight to former glories in telling a story of Britain that was long-since outdated. Post-war Labour governments, she argued, had run the country into the ground by pursuing the same old solutions, dedicating themselves to maintaining obsolete labour practices and determined to keep producing uncompetitive goods out of a misplaced sense of tradition. It was leading, she felt, to national idleness and complacency. Britain, she had warned as Leader of the Opposition in 1976, was becoming a 'museum economy', where people were 'living in the nostalgic glories of a previous industrial revolution.' On the eve of the general election in 1979, she warned that if the nation didn't change 'our ways and our direction, our greatness as a nation will soon be a footnote in the history books, a distant memory of an offshore island, lost in the mists of time, like Camelot, remembered kindly, for its noble past.'[89] What was needed was a shake-up.

Yet this was a narrative that – even as it consigned Labour to a past that was thankfully being left behind – presented the Conservatives as the party of both history *and* future. Where Labour might have told the story of Britain as one of hard-won rights fought for by the people, of a nation that had pulled together in the Second World War and been honoured, in turn, with the welfare state, healthcare and social housing (a narrative that would later structure Danny Boyle's Olympic opening ceremony), Thatcher offered the romance of trade. Businesses became the prime movers in this new national epic, taking heroic decisions and conquering new markets in pursuit of private wealth and public glory. In her reading, it was not collectivism that had secured progress, but the entrepreneurial spirit. Post-war relics such as nationalised industries and a high tax regime were the worst kind of old-fashioned, but privatisation and monetarism, on the other hand, were at once the 'modern view', and a revival of the good 'old-fashioned laissez-faire' of Victorian industrialism.[90] It was a narrative that sold rapid change under the guise of tradition, a crusade that required Britain to shed its customary ways, where they had become ossified and sclerotic, in order to restore the purity of an earlier vision.

In particular, Thatcher offered 'Victorian values' as a medicine for the British people. Yet this was a very singular perspective on the meaning of 'Victorian' – one that had little to do with the Victorian era as it actually existed, and which one historian described as 'a Frankenstein monster of bits and pieces scavenged out of context for political purposes.'[91] As her critics observed, notably absent from Thatcher's vision of Victorianism was the nineteenth-century Tory Party itself, with its emphasis on the upper-class duty to care for the poor. Instead, this was 'the age of improvement', a liberal tale of self-help and individualism: of people who worked hard, pulling themselves up by the boot-straps and seizing opportunity through grit and discipline. In the face of what she described as 'a decadent, undisciplined society' (or what many conservatives feared was a slide towards moral anarchy), it promised a return to security; to family values and respect for authority. Against a background of riots and disturbances in inner-city areas such as Toxteth and Brixton, it offered the image of an older Britain where parents were strict, children respected their elders, and hooliganism was allegedly unknown. These were 'decent, fair, honest citizen values', she explained: 'you don't live up to the hilt of your income; you respect other people's property, you save; you believe in right and wrong; you support the police.'[92] 'Victorian' became a term that was interchangeable with 'traditional', the shining example of everything she felt people were failing to do and to be in the 1980s. It promised that once upon a time things used to be simpler, when there were clear boundaries between right and wrong, and hard work was always rewarded.

More than anything, Thatcher's 'Victorian values' drew on the experience of her childhood – of the moral lessons imparted by her father and grandmother in 1930s Grantham. 'I was raised by a Victorian grandmother,' she explained to a reporter for the *Evening Standard*: 'we were taught to work jolly hard. We were taught to prove yourself; we were taught self-reliance . . . You were taught tremendous pride in your country. All of these things are Victorian values. They are also perennial values.' As Raphael Samuel noted, it conflated her childhood experiences with that of an earlier national past, so that 'by a process of selective amnesia the past becomes a historical equivalent of the dream of primal bliss, or of the enchanted space that memory accords to childhood.'[93] It was a way of conjuring a sense of lost innocence that the nation might restore, with enough determination.

But this wasn't quite the primal bliss of comfort and ease – it was an ideal built upon struggle. Where many of her contemporaries were nostalgic for their memories of community – for the 'good old days' of neighbourliness and mutual help when in need – Thatcher's was an altogether lonelier vision. There was, after all, 'no such thing as society' for her, just individuals and families.[94] This was a severe kind of Eden, where times were hard, but scarcity had taught the value of self-control. Pain had a meaning. It had taught her to despise so-called 'soft' options and 'easy' answers, and never to shy away from taking 'painful' decisions and 'tough' measures, and it had worked for her. She would never again worry about being unpopular or seeming old-fashioned, because she had learnt what was needed for survival. 'Was she happy?' a journalist once asked in an interview. 'We didn't take happiness as an objective,' Thatcher answered. 'We did a lot. Our parents worked. Our home was always spotless.'[95] In turn, this stern nostalgia would be applied to the nation. Since the end of the Second World War, she felt, Britain had been decaying; its energies flagging through lack of determination. But she would reverse this decline, if only the nation could return to the mindset she had learnt in childhood.

Amid our current culture wars in the 2020s, which many have read as an outgrowth of the mentality that propelled Brexit in

2016, we can forget just how long these debates about history and nostalgia have been going on for. And we sometimes under-estimate for just how long people have understood British society to be lingering under a post-imperial, post-industrial malaise, unable to come to terms with the realities of decline. Our present-day debates over the 'story' of British history are not just in many respects a rerun of the 'heritage wars' of the 1980s – the terms of these debates about economy, society and empire have structured the political landscape throughout the late twentieth and twenty-first centuries.

Nostalgia has so often been read as an unhealthy fixation on a past that has vanished for the better: a regressive yearning for the class system, for empire, for a supposed time before immi-gration, and for a theme-park version of history that never existed in the way it is remembered. And yet this nostalgic vision of Britain's history has most often been invoked by the people arguing most vociferously for rapid and transformative change: from Thatcherite privatisation and financialisation to the deregulated 'global Britain' of Conservative Brexiteers. Nostalgia is rarely as backwards-looking as we often assume it to be. These calls for change have been both harnessed to and articulated through a grandly romantic story of Britain's past: a glittering background of triumphs and inspirations from which to press on into a shining future. But this tale of past and future glory depends, at the same time, upon the story of a nation that had lost its way somewhere along the road since 1945 – a nar-rative of decline that, as we are about to see, seemed to fly in the face of Britain's actual post-war history.

2

I Was Lord Kitchener's Valet

1979–1940

Had Britain been declining? Or was Margaret Thatcher's promised return to a neo-Victorian heyday in the 1980s a solution lacking a problem? Between the end of the Second World War and the end of the 1970s, Britain's power and influence on the world stage seemed to be locked in a downwards spiral that many worried was terminal – a country whose best days were all behind it, dwindling from a global power to a shrinking island nation. The British Empire, amassed over centuries, was dismantled in a matter of decades, while Britain's share of the world's manufacturing shrank precipitously, as anxieties over deindustrialisation and industrial decline generated gloomy forecasts for the future of the economy. While Britain's economy was still growing, it was growing at a much slower rate than in West Germany, France, Italy, Japan, the USA – countries that seemed to have taken over Britain's early lead in scientific and technological innovation, in which standards of living were racing ahead while British society seemed to be stagnant or decaying.

By the 1970s, out-of-control inflation, unemployment and industrial disputes were all contributing to a crisis mood, with dole queues, shuttered factories, crumbling Victorian terraces and prematurely aged housing estates seeming to symbolise a country in which the post-war settlement had failed. 'This really does look like a collapsing society,' reported *The Times* in 1975, while American journalists looked on and assessed that 'Britain is drifting slowly towards a condition of ungovernability.' Doom-laden warnings filled books aimed at the general reader: Tom Nairn's characteristic analysis in 1977 predicted *The Break-Up of Britain*, asserting that 'there is no doubt that the old British state is going down.'[1] These anxieties had been brewing for years. From the early 1960s, a steady stream of bestselling texts vied to outdo one another in grim foreboding about the state of the nation, with titles such as *The Stagnant Society* (1961) and *Suicide of a Nation* (1963), while Penguin commissioned a series of analyses simply titled *What's Wrong With Britain?* Nostalgia loomed large in these enquiries as to what had gone so wrong since 1945, for a country that in popular cliché was said to have won the war but lost the peace. The journalist Michael Shanks, for instance, had warned in *The Stagnant Society* that Britain was 'on its way to the embalming chamber', arguing that the greatest 'danger facing the British people today' was that 'we may bury ourselves under the rose-petals of a vast collective nostalgia . . . bathed in the glow of an imperial sunset' and 'lost in a sweet sad love affair with our own past.'[2]

Yet this was also the 'age of affluence': of new consumer goods, new ways of living, newly permissible pleasures, in which politicians confidently asserted that people had 'never had it so good.' In 1957, Prime Minister Harold Macmillan painted a glowing picture of Britain's economic future, optimistically predicting that 'you will see a state of prosperity such as we have never had in my lifetime – nor indeed in the history of this country.'[3] And in many ways he was right. Despite its high-profile troubles, Britain's economy grew faster between 1945 and 1975 than it had done between 1855 and 1945, at the height of industrial and imperial power.[4] New technologies heralded a future that would be radically different, and radically better. The welfare state, and the long post-war boom that had generated full employment for much of the period, had lifted millions of people out of poverty. Rising disposable incomes transformed everyday life. Luxuries and services that would have been unimaginable or unobtainable for the vast majority of Britons in the 1940s were ubiquitous by 1979, from spacious, secure housing to healthcare, cars, fridges, washing machines and televisions. Working hours were falling steadily, while paid holidays rose and then rose again – by the 1970s sociologists and media commentators were heralding the imminent arrival of the 'leisure society', a time of plenty and consumerist ease, in which labour-saving technologies and union power were combining to win an easier life for working men and women.

By the end of the 1970s, British society was more economically equal than it had ever been before, and more equal than it has ever been since. Huge cultural changes seemed to be ushering in a brighter, happier, more tolerant future: the rise of a 'permissive society' that placed a new emphasis on freedom and self-expression, where younger generations were throwing off stifling conventions and outworn traditions of class-bound deference. Progressive social and political movements – environmentalism, feminism, gay liberation movements, anti-racism organisations – were gaining ground. And while 'declinism' was fast-becoming one of the buzzwords of the age, people, it seemed, had never been more contented. A 1977 Gallup survey found that Britons considered themselves to be among the happiest people in the world, relatively unconcerned that other advanced countries were a little richer than they. A similar survey revealed that only a sixth of respondents felt 'very worried' that Britain was falling behind other nations, and almost half said they were 'not worried' at all.[5] And why should they have been, when so many of them enjoyed a standard of living that was unknown to their parents' and grandparents' generations, and were looking forward to a future in which their own children would be better off still?

OUT WITH THE OLD

After the upheavals of the Second World War, many looked firmly towards the new. This was the Atomic Age, the Space Age, an era of modern architecture and modern design, of futuristic dreams of a brave new world in which science would transform society almost beyond recognition. Cultural products from science fiction to children's cartoons envisaged a future of flying cars, robot butlers and protein pills for dinner, in which people would live in plexiglass bubbles, live on the moon. After the gloom and grey of the war-damaged 1940s, from the 1950s people's appetite for the new and the modern seemed inexhaustible. 'Old-fashioned' became a term of contempt rather than fond familiarity, evoking the tired, the dirty and outworn, while new synthetic materials were welcomed as excitingly futuristic innovations – Pyrex ovenware, Nylon sheets, Formica, Terylene.[6] The future was urban planning and redevelopment – modernist high-rises, streets in the sky, high-speed travel on motorways and flyovers, back-to-back houses cleared to make way for utopian ring roads and brutalist housing that would liberate people from an older world of want and toil. Yet by the 1970s, this promised new world was already being lamented as a failed experiment, the dream of a future that would never come to pass. Amid critiques of an atomised, polluted, consumer-driven world, one of the most popular programmes on TV was *The Good Life*, which relayed the mid-life crisis of a plastics designer who yearns to escape the emptiness of modern commercial life in favour of a nostalgic dream of homespun self-sufficiency.

We think we know this story – one in which the material gains of the post-war years were offset by the decline of community, the rise of selfish individualism and consumer greed. A tale in which the hubris of modernist architects and developers produced the failures of post-war planning, clearing away

Victorian slums only to create in high-rise flats and council estates the slums of the future. A country rebuilding itself from the ruins of the Blitz and the gloom of post-war austerity, giving way to the security and home-centred stability of the 1950s, with the bright future of the welfare state and modern consumer ease ahead. The colourful explosion of the 'Swinging Sixties', a youth revolution, that dissipated into the great grey hangover of the 1970s, the decade when the lights went out, which culminated in economic disaster and the 'Winter of Discontent', when people looked back and realised just how much they had lost. Then 1979: the year that Britain voted not just for new economic solutions, but for a backlash against 'permissiveness' and a climate of moral decline, longing for a return to 'family values' and respect for authority.

But is this true? Between 1940 and 1979, no one was untouched by change – dramatic, sweeping, often irreversible changes that transformed the ways people worked, lived, travelled, ate, and spent their leisure time. Urban and rural landscapes alike were radically altered, not just by modernist high-rises, office blocks and urban redevelopment schemes, but by newly expanding suburbs, New Towns, and by the mechanisation of agriculture that left little room for the preservation of the countryside. Yet not all these changes happened everywhere at the same rate, or for everyone at the same time. Nor were they experienced by everyone in the same way. At any given moment people were looking backwards, looking forwards, welcoming new developments as well as lamenting their effects, sometimes overwhelmed by the pace of change, and at other times complaining that some things were not changing nearly fast enough. And every new development brought with it intense debates over the meaning of change, in which the need for transformation and a widespread optimism that the future would be better than the past coincided with intense anxieties about upheaval, dislocation, and the decay of older ways of living.

More than anything, Britain was on the move. In the wake of

1945, when the largest ever swing in electoral opinion had brought a Labour government to power on the promise of building a 'New Jerusalem', many people were wondering, too, whether their future lay elsewhere. The end of war was supposed to mean the end of disruption, the return home to settled life, but a Gallup poll in 1948 found that as many as 42 per cent of Britons wanted to emigrate, leaving behind an old world that seemed damaged beyond repair and unlikely to recover its former glories, still in the throes of rationing and chronic housing shortages. Millions did – an estimated 590,000 people left the country during the late 1940s alone. Throughout the postwar decades, Britain remained a net exporter of people, most leaving for Commonwealth countries such as Canada, Australia and New Zealand; though this was a phenomenon far less remarked upon than immigration from Eastern Europe, Asia, Africa and the West Indies, and the ways in which an increasingly multicultural society was supposedly challenging British tradition. [7]

Within Britain, millions more moved around the country: from inner-city slums to overspill estates, commuter corridors and planned New Town developments; from 'traditional' working-class terraces to new-build flats and housing complexes; into cities in search of growing service-sector jobs and then out of them again in the suburban exodus; from the economically struggling North to the booming South-East, as well as to newly desirable rural retreats in the South-West and East Anglia. Between 1948 and 1958 alone, one family in every six moved into a newly built house or flat.[8] Even people who stayed put could find the places they lived in transforming around them, such as the inhabitants of the sleepy Hertfordshire settlement of Stevenage, population 6,000, once the setting of E.M. Forster's rural idyll in *Howards End*, who discovered in 1946 that they had been chosen as the site of Britain's first New Town, a planned development to house another 50,000 residents in a pioneering experiment in modern living.[9]

Welcome as many of these changes could be, they generated intense nostalgia for a past that was rapidly being left behind. Sociologists, policymakers and 'ordinary' people alike drew on rosy images of close-knit communities lost to an age of rootless individualism and suburban anomie. They welcomed the material gains of the post-war period, yet worried over a spirit of envy and materialism they felt was running rife amid this new affluence, and looked back to an older world of quiet contentment, a slower pace of life – a time before graffiti, vandalism, petty crime and inner-city violence. But should we take their word for it? After all, for every 1970s nostalgic looking back to the social heyday of the 1940s, when everyone had pulled together in the war and children respected their elders, we find people in the 1940s lamenting the loss of these exact same things. Were the 'good old days' a myth – did they ever exist?

SGT. PEPPER'S LONELY HEARTS COSPLAY

The old and the new mixed in surprising, often unexpected ways. At the Festival of Britain in 1951, modern design and technological innovations in the Dome of Discovery stood next to whimsical displays of English eccentricities, with the Lion and the Unicorn Pavilion telling a story of how the British 'national character' had developed over centuries, as visitors travelled between exhibits depicting a history of unfolding progress and liberty, landscape paintings by Turner and Constable, and celebrations of quintessentially British good humour. Promoted to the public as a reward for a nation rebuilding itself after six long years of post-war austerity, the festival has been remembered ever since for its optimistic, forward-looking ethos, heralding the arrival of new ways of living, new styles – substituting for rationing and greyness a bright future of cutting-edge design, scientific advances, clean lines and labour-saving devices. The Live Architecture Exhibition, for instance, showcased the functional modernity of the as-yet-incomplete Lansbury Estate in Poplar, with a brochure declaring 'here at Poplar you may catch a glimpse of the future London which is to arise from blitzed ruins and from the slums and chaotic planning of the past.'[10] Yet festivalgoers could also wander along the South Bank to the Battersea Pleasure Gardens, a nostalgic nod to Georgian and Victorian pleasure gardens at Vauxhall, Ranelagh and Cremorne, where Nell Gwyn-inspired orange sellers advertised the vanished delights of a much older London.[11]

This was history worn lightly, though – an opportunity for fun and entertainment, not a serious attempt to undercut the modernising bent of architecture and design. Winston Churchill was a lone voice when he waxed lovingly of Georgian grime at the tail end of the war, sighing in a cabinet meeting of the latest town-planning report that aimed to regenerate bomb-damaged centres: 'all this stuff about planning and compensation and betterment. Broad vistas and all that. But give to me the eighteenth-century alley, where foot-pads lurk, and the harlot plies her trade, and none of this new-fangled planning doctrine.'[12]

For the vast majority of Britons looking ahead to the post-war future, this would be an age of light, bright, functional design, shedding the decorative clutter, the dust-trap furniture and moth-eaten textiles of home interiors in favour of spaciousness and simplicity. Modernisation and home improvement became interchangeable terms, as DIY boomed in popularity for those with disposable incomes. Advertising promoted a new era of labour-saving appliances and man-made materials that would transform the home with the latest scientific advances. Interiors were systematically gutted of historic features: suspended ceilings covered up ornate Victorian cornices and mouldings; interior walls were knocked through to the front parlour, previously saved for 'best' and seldom used, but now increasingly widened out into open-plan living spaces. Home magazines offered recommendations for 'Disguising that old Fireplace', or provided tips on how to 're-surface your kitchen table with FORMICA ... a joy for years to come.' Just as 'modernisation' became synonymous with 'improvement', something to be pursued as a good in itself, so 'Victorian' and 'antique' were associated with the ugly and out of date, a heritage to be swept away in pursuit of progress.[13]

Amid this broad swing towards the new, by the 1960s an embrace of the old-fashioned could begin to seem daringly countercultural. Just as their twenty-first-century counterparts would express a swing in generational tastes through rehabilitating mid-century clothes and furniture, in Swinging London, a younger generation raided second-hand boutiques for ironic Victoriana, purchasing vintage finds from Granny Takes a Trip on the King's Road, which offered William Morris and Liberty print suit jackets to those in search of a flamboyant take on the fin-de-siècle dandy. For women, there were crazes for 'granny clothes' and crochet, while *Vogue* photographed Twiggy in a Victorian picture hat and ringlets, with a high lace collar, under the headline 'The Daring New Fashion Romantics'. On Portobello Road and Carnaby Street, the vintage boutique I Was Lord Kitchener's Valet sold an eccentric mix of fox stoles, feather boas, pith helmets and antique military uniforms to customers including Mick Jagger, Jimi Hendrix and John Lennon. As Robert Orbach, who worked in the boutique, explained of its name: 'it conjured up images of Edwardian smoking jackets, top hats and canes ... pure nostalgia.'[14]

While the 'Cool Britannia' of pop culture around the turn of the millennium would later look back for its inspiration to a 1960s heyday of cultural rebellion, the pop-cultural milieu of the Swinging Sixties was itself steeped in retro influences. But this was a very contemporary kind of nostalgia, less about a yearning for the past or genuine sentimentality than about kitsch, pastiche and parody. Bands folded the old and the new into irreverent combinations, playing around with

Vintage military jackets on display outside I Was Lord Kitchener's Valet boutique, Portobello Road, London, mid-1960s.

the incongruous and bizarre. The Kinks blended lyrics of teenage lust and sexual ambiguity with old-time cockney charm and images of wistful pastoral Englishness, veering between the late-night horniness of 'You Really Got Me' and semi-ironic, semi-earnest identification as 'The Village Green Preservation Society'; while The Beatles fused psychedelic rock 'n' roll with music-hall ditties in Edwardian military tunics. Peter Blake's cover for *Sgt. Pepper's Lonely Hearts Club Band* encapsulated this nostalgic-yet-contemporary mood of eclecticism, with The Beatles decked out in fluorescent frock coats and epaulettes, surrounded by a collage of Victorian imperialists, turn-of-the-century aesthetes, Hollywood icons and Hindu gurus, serried together behind a garden display pitched halfway between flower power and municipal bedding scheme.

In a decade defined by the fight for civil rights, the contra-
ceptive pill and the decriminalisation of homosexuality, history
was being appropriated precisely to cast it away in rebellion.
For a generation that was fast rejecting the customs and conventions of the past, subverting traditional sex and gender
roles and breaking free from the conformity of the class system, this fancy-dress spirit embraced the aesthetics of the past
at the same time as jettisoning its values. Donning a Victorian
dress or the uniform of an imperial conqueror was a way of
sending up the staunch masculinity, ladylike femininity and
class stereotypes of an age that had faded into obsolescence for
those in their teens and twenties, who had little memory of life
before the 1940s. In contrast to the repressiveness of the past,
dressing up in period clothes in the 1960s carried with it an
element of camp, an air of role play and fetishism at an ironic
remove from history itself. It treated history as a kind of sport,
where the past was a repository of stylistic inspiration, a
dressing-up box providing opportunities for personal expression.[15] This kind of wry playfulness and mock sentimentality
had only become possible because the history it drew on
seemed to have been safely consigned to the past – something
that was over, finished, having little bearing on people's lives in
the present.

Popular interest in history itself had been at a low ebb in the
1950s. For many people, after two world wars, they had
simply lived through too much history to want to immerse
themselves in more of it on the page, while many felt betrayed
by the nationalist narratives and patriotic 'lessons' that had
been instilled in them by historians and politicians, which
now seemed forever marked by memories of bloodshed. But
as time went on, this indifference or even hostility towards
history was giving way to more light-hearted enjoyment. As
the historian Peter Mandler writes, 'the disintegration of
myths of national destiny made it safer and easier for people
to forage in the past without feeling constrained or dominated

by it. So history began to look less like a burden and more like a funfair.'[16]

By the 1970s, this penchant for the antique and outdated was entering the mainstream. Synthetic fabrics and futuristic styles had become so ubiquitous that Laura Ashley peasant dresses now felt more contemporary, evoking a return to nature after years of plasticky consumerism. Modernisation in the home had now gone so far that fashion was beginning to swing the other way, embracing brickwork, wood and period decorations that the previous generation had studiously hidden away.[17] In part, this reflected a widespread disenchantment with modernism – a reaction against the utopian dreams of architects and planners that had promised so much and delivered such mixed results. In part, in an increasingly mobile post-war world, people were yearning to feel connected once again to the past. Along with a boom in antiques and older styles, there was a growing interest in local and family history.[18] For families who had moved to new flats, new houses, new towns, and brought their children up in a world of material comfort that their ancestors could scarcely have dreamt of, it was perhaps time to revisit their roots. But perhaps, too, it was now possible to feel fondly about period architecture because it was quickly becoming a rarity – something whose value was newly appreciated because its very existence was under threat. Victorian terraces and cast-iron fireplaces that had once been ever-present reminders of an older world of dirt, dust and industrial pollution, a domestic life of hardship and toil, could now be seen as miraculous survivals that had escaped the remorseless march of the modernisers.

BRING IN THE BULLDOZERS

The destruction of historic landscapes and environments had gone further in Britain during the 1950s and 1960s than any-where else in Europe. To a great extent, these transformations in the built environment had their origins in the pressing need to reconstruct towns and cities that had been damaged during the Second World War. Over 750,000 houses had been destroyed or severely damaged over the course of the Blitz, along with thousands more factories, schools, public services and historic landmarks. The damage had fallen unevenly: some areas had escaped relatively unscathed, yet many heavily industrialised areas, generally home to cities' poorer inhabitants, had frequently borne the brunt of aerial bombardment. In Bermondsey in south-east London, for instance, more than a quarter of the housing stock had been destroyed or rendered unusable, along with half of schools and more than 300 factories and warehouses.[19] In Coventry, the majority of the city's historic centre had been destroyed over the course of a single night.

Yet many urban problems had long predated the war. Slum clearances had been underway since the end of the nineteenth century, gathering pace in the interwar years, yet by 1945 swathes of inadequate, overcrowded and unsanitary housing still remained in towns and cities across Britain – decaying tenements and back-to-back terraces, the majority of which had been hastily put up by Victorian jerry-builders, and compounded by decades of neglect by landlords. By the end of the 1950s, despite post-war slum clearance programmes having been underway for more than a decade, 850,000 houses remained that had been declared unfit for habitation in England and Wales, most of them concentrated in large industrial inner cities. In the immediate post-war years, Britain's chronic housing shortage was one of the most pressing problems facing governments and policymakers. It was a daunting task, when hundreds of thousands of families were crowded into flats of just one or two rooms, many of them lacking their own access to hot water, let alone baths or indoor toilets. In Glasgow alone, it was estimated that 600,000 people – more than half the city's population – needed rehousing as an immediate priority.[20] But how could this be done, across the entire country and in a matter of years, and without dismantling forever long-standing communities? And how could people be redistributed en masse out of overcrowded towns and cities without destroying Britain's countryside in the process?

For many architects, planners and politicians, this was an unprecedented opportunity to build a brave new world free from the problems of the past. It was their chance to imagine a new kind of society that could combine the best of traditional, close-knit communities and neighbourliness with all the benefits of modern technology, a futuristic experiment in new ways of living. 'Stevenage will in a short time become world-famous,' the housing minister Lewis Silkin had proclaimed of plans for Britain's New Towns in 1946, at a packed public meeting. 'People from all over the world will come to Stevenage to see how we here in this country are building for the new way of life.' 'It is no good your jeering,' he declared, over cries of 'Gestapo!' and 'Dictator!' by residents furious they had not been consulted as test subjects for this daring new experiment, 'it is going to be done.' But though a little over half of residents declared themselves 'entirely against' the plans, fearing that the historic charms of a place that had been home to their families for generations would be destroyed almost overnight, others actively welcomed the proposals. When Mass Observation, a social research project that recorded everyday life in Britain from the 1930s to the 1960s, asked Stevenage residents 'How do you feel about it?', responses included 'it's time this town was woken up', and 'it's progress, and it's what we badly need here.'[21]

While a raft of plans were launched to disperse people into the spacious surroundings of once-rural areas, increasingly it was being argued that what was needed was to rebuild urban areas denser and higher. High-rise flats would replace sprawling suburbs and packed slums in inner cities, enabling people to remain in the same areas even if their neighbourhoods would be transformed beyond recognition – streets in the sky that would be furnished with the latest mod cons and surrounded by open green spaces. Historic centres would be redeveloped wholesale to make way for the car-powered future. By the early 1960s, the built environment was changing more rapidly than at any time since the height of the Industrial Revolution.

Much of it needed to go. Over a million families in London alone had been forced into sharing a house in the 1950s; as late as 1961 a third of houses still had no fixed bath. In the same year, 15 per cent of Birmingham's houses lacked their own toilet, while in Manchester almost a fifth of residents did not have access to a hot water tap. Years spent on waiting lists for council properties could run into double figures.[22] Many people were desperate to be rehoused – wherever they could find it and by any means necessary, whether it meant a prefab bungalow or a space at the top of a modernist high-rise. Yet these desperately needed transformations went hand in hand with the wilful destruction of historic environments and landmarks. Older housing that might have been repaired, and sometimes hadn't been damaged in the first place, was swept away under the same impetus as bomb-cratered ruins. While many inhabitants of working-class urban communities couldn't wait to get away, many, too, wished fervently to stay, and were deeply worried about whether or not they would find a similar sense of neighbourliness in their new residences.

But it was a period in which architects and planners displayed little fondness for old buildings. Anything Victorian, in particular, was likely to be vilified as symbolising an outdated age of industrial pollution, squalor and chaotically unplanned development. Critics wrote of the 'architectural tragedy' of the nineteenth century, with its 'sadistic hatred of beauty.' One of Britain's leading architectural historians, Sir John Summerson, wrote unsentimentally of the 'dreadful little Victorian villas' in Hampstead's Vale of Health, for instance, whose demolition had been proposed in favour of an ultra-modern block of flats designed by Ernő Goldfinger – houses that the architect himself described as having 'neither architectural nor aesthetic merit, nor charm in their own right.' Intervening in fierce public debate about town redevelopment schemes, one local newspaper, the *Wigan Examiner*, lambasted the Gothic red-brick townscapes that 'our Victorian grandfathers have inflicted upon us in such vast and nauseating quantities.' Amid these utopian dreams for the cities of the future, there was little room for wistfulness. 'Perhaps there is a little nostalgia', a town councillor reflected in Salford of local opposition to the impending demolition of its Victorian library and art gallery, 'but we cannot afford to have ancient monuments in Salford.'[23]

In the countryside, too, those who objected to development were liable to be dismissed as nostalgic diehards whose concern to preserve rural landscapes was standing in the way of much-needed change. Yet as the redistribution of urbanites from crowded inner cities gained pace, public debate increasingly turned to the preservation of the countryside, though the solution was far from clear. For every urban planner who argued that high-density flats were the only answer that could halt the endless sprawling of the suburbs, there was an opposing voice who countered that Britons were a garden-loving people, whose homes were their castles, and who dreamt of living in small-scale communities surrounded by rolling fields.[24] 'We thought our Planners would save our countryside,' observed one journalist in 1954, noting that 150 acres were being lost to development every day, 'but the bulldozers move over the farmland as relentlessly as ever. The new "estates" spread, like a rash, over the meadows.' The architectural critic Ian Nairn prophesied that at this rate, 'by the end of the century Great Britain will consist of isolated oases of preserved monuments in a desert of wire, concrete roads, cosy plots and bungalows,' in which 'the end of Southampton will look like the beginning of Carlisle.'[25] But for those who felt little fondness for their lives in Carlisle or Southampton, recalling not local character or geographical charm but wretched housing, poverty and industrial pollution, might this on the whole be a distinct improvement?

By the 1960s, as historic landscapes everywhere were threatened by ever more daring schemes for an entirely different future, the mood was starting to turn towards preservation. Perhaps the first sign of this growing appreciation for heritage under threat was the formation of the preservationist Victorian Society in 1958, whose founding members included the poet John Betjeman – later to launch a one-man crusade to save the much-hated Gothic facade of St Pancras Station. But the society's fondness for the Victorian was met by considerable resistance. 'Every time I leave it I wonder why as a whole it is so nauseating. I really don't think one could go to a Minister and say this is a great piece of architecture,' John Summerson concluded of St Pancras, initially turning down Betjeman's request to join the campaign to save the station. Even the group's name evoked suspicion. 'It had better avoid calling itself "Victorian",' remarked one architectural journalist after its first meeting. 'The word now has overtones of funniness.' (It was a cultural climate that would leave many, by the 1980s, baffled by how rapidly tastes had changed in looking back upon the Victorian era more fondly, from the popularity of neo-Victorian décor on sale in Laura Ashley to Margaret Thatcher's appeal to 'Victorian values'.) The Victorian Society suffered a major defeat in their campaign to save the Doric arch at Euston Station in 1961, when their pleas for a stay of execution were overridden by the Prime Minister Harold Macmillan. While some campaigns such as this were met by widespread local support, others were dismissed as reactionary old-fashionedness. 'It's a damned good job these houses are coming down,' railed the local MP, of Betjeman's campaign to save a row of period houses along the Thames at Rotherhithe. 'People come along trying to stop progress . . . just because they like the look of a few old buildings.'[26]

Often, the preservationists were fighting a losing battle. Town and city centre redevelopment schemes were increasingly hailed as the wonders of the age – a great leap forward in the progress of civilisation that would rival or surpass the best of historic architecture. Plans for a new precinct in Coventry were promoted as a visionary urban endeavour on a par with the Georgian triumphs of Edinburgh's Princes Street or Bath's Royal Crescent, while a Birmingham alderman proclaimed amid the emerging office blocks, tower blocks and inner ring-road system that 'in 20 years' time from now the future citizens of Birmingham will look back on this period of their city's history and will say: "This was Birmingham's finest and most courageous period".' Planners and tastemakers frequently saw their role as re-educating the public into an appreciation of modern architecture, countering what they perceived as 'public ignorance and apathy', 'morbid sentimentality' and 'aggressive retrogression' that compelled people's attachments to the cities they had. Writing for a popular audience, the Brutalist architect Basil Spence explained that 'not all this newness will succeed. But it is far better that some of it should fail and people should *try* than we should continue copying past styles paradoxically called traditional. Modern architecture is as exciting as any adventure in history for it looks straight into the future, not backwards . . . the future is bright.'[27]

For its critics, though, this was dangerous hubris. As historic landscapes were concreted over, centuries-old buildings were pulled down, and whole communities were relocated to the fringes of city centres into as-yet-uncompleted developments still lacking in proper amenities, more and more people were beginning to take pause and contemplate what was being lost. While historic streets were flattened to make way for Birmingham's inner ring road, a former lord mayor argued in the *Daily Telegraph* that it was far from 'a few nostalgic old fogies' who were having qualms about the scale of destruction – there was 'a deep, underlying resentment' among Birmingham's residents that their city had been handed over to developers more concerned with profit margins than with building a beautiful city that would work for its inhabitants. Amid the wreckage, the new city that was taking shape was beginning to resemble 'the vision of [George Orwell's novel] *1984*.' In Bristol, medieval and Georgian buildings alike were torn down, from a 900-year-old Norman townhouse in the city centre to Georgian villas in the suburb of Kingsdown that were cleared to make way for a 14-storey housing block; while in Coventry, timber houses that had miraculously escaped damage during the Blitz were demolished to clear space for a ring road. For one writer in the local paper in Blackburn, 'they say' the new town centre, with its concrete shopping precinct, will provide 'all the modern amenities and resultant civic pride.' 'All that will happen, however, is that Blackburn will be destroyed. The bulldozers will cut out its heart and replace a supermarket, tear out its soul and substitute escalators.'[28] It was a sentiment echoed in Philip Larkin's poetic tribute to Hull in 'Here' (1961), where the domes and spires of the Victorian cityscape, and the workaday grandeur of industrial activity, give way to the plate-glass shop fronts of high-street chains selling identikit clothes and electrical goods.[29]

For many who opposed the demolitions, this was about far more than an emotional attachment to historic architecture: however necessary it was to clear the way for better housing, workplaces and transport, the human cost was immense. The public was rarely consulted on the kind of homes and cities they wanted, and they frequently suspected that redevelopment schemes reflected the ambition of architects and planners far more than they engaged with the realities of people's everyday lives, or tried to understand their needs and desires. By 1969, an architectural guide to Coventry was lamenting that 'no attempt at human scaling appears to have been made' in the redeveloped centre, and 'the bulldozer has been given free rein among the terraces.' And however much people wanted better housing for themselves, better neighbourhoods in which their children could grow up in spacious, secure surroundings, the experience of watching old neighbourhoods destroyed could be intensely painful. Traumatic as the destruction of the Blitz had been, that had at least seemed unavoidable – it was something else entirely to see houses pulled down with deliberate, systematic intention. 'Bombing we can take,' reflected Betjeman, 'but the deliberate pulling down of a familiar street or building with associations, the felling of timber in a village and the destruction of old cottages is really playing about with part of ourselves. They are roots and home to somebody.' One observer looked upon 'streets and streets of devastation' in Liverpool, as slum housing was razed on a scale 'far worse than anything the German bombers could do even on the worst night of the May blitz.' It was worse still when the suspicion was that these homes didn't need to be destroyed in the first place. 'All these houses were well cared for and I think they would still have been in a good condition in 50 or 100 years', argued one letter writer to a local paper in Lancashire, of terraced streets in the process of being demolished.[30]

Poised halfway between an older world that was being dismantled, and a new one that had not yet taken shape, the outlook could be bleak. 'I saw a living community torn to pieces by the bulldozers and scattered,' recalled a Birmingham reverend of his parish in Ladywood, noting that space cleared for the inner ring road seemed to have started with some of the better housing. 'It could have been avoided.' Communities had been uprooted and dispersed across their cities in order for ground to be cleared, only for it to be left as waste ground for years before being redeveloped. Often, residents still remained when the demolition began; some hadn't wanted to abandon their homes and wouldn't leave until they were forced to, some were still waiting to be rehoused. Amid slum clearances in Liverpool, one journalist observed 'single families' living sometimes 'with a complete street to themselves', with 'acres of empty land all around them.' Many were elderly people who felt it was too late in their lives to begin again in a different community, or who simply had nowhere else to go. 'It's terrible living here while the other houses are being demolished,' explained an 82-year-old disabled resident in Bolton, as workmen pulled down terraces at the end of a row where homes were still occupied. Another elderly resident who had lived in the same street for 40 years 'stood watching the bulldozers pull down the house next door', regretting that 'they could at least have left the houses on either side standing until I moved.' Whether residents had wanted to move or not, they knew that when they said goodbye they would be leaving houses and areas that would soon no longer exist, moving on from places that could never again be revisited. When they closed the door on their old homes – their old lives – they were closing the door for good. Reporting on the redevelopment of Bethnal Green in 1959, *The Times* noted that 'whole streets have already been demolished', and 'again and again someone has chalked on the shattered walls "I lived here", with the dates.'[31]

NEW TOWNS AND 'GOOD OLD DAYS'

It has become a kind of received wisdom that 'community' declined over the second half of the twentieth century. Generations of observers from across the social and political spectrum have argued that close-knit, face-to-face communities, where everyone left their doors unlocked and where everybody knew you by name, were slowly eroded by modernisation and material progress, to be replaced by an age of privacy, isolation and hidden loneliness. Our image of the post-war period is often one which began in the spirit of pulling together during the war, yet ended with the individualism of the 1980s – ushering in a culture driven by materialism, self-interest, consumer greed and keeping-up-with-the-Joneses. While 'traditional' working-class neighbourhoods are remembered with rose-tinted fondness as places of easy sociability and mutual help when in need, suburbs and New Towns have come to symbolise a quiet life of domestic privacy and middle-class aspiration – 'dormitory' towns whose identity is defined more by their proximity to work than by any qualities of their own. Inner-city tower blocks and council estates, in turn, have often been seen to epitomise the failures of post-war planning: as places unloved by their residents, whose utopian ambitions were belied by the reality of social breakdown, in which prematurely ageing housing developments became nurseries of vandalism and crime.

But can the experiences of millions of people who made the transition to new homes and neighbourhoods over the course of the post-war period really be folded into this narrative – has this story ended up obscuring more than it reveals? Alongside this story of longing and loss, after all, runs a parallel narrative of an age of rising affluence, freedom and comfort; the decline of a repressively class-bound society, in which people threw off older conventions in favour of new forms of self-determination, personal expression and enjoyment. How can we square people's memories of the 'good old days' – when people, it is said, were happier for making do with less – with widespread celebration that people had 'never had it so good'? And does our nostalgia for more 'real' forms of community, lost to an age of individualism, depend on an image of a past that never existed?

Even for those in the closest-knit of communities, the lure of a better life elsewhere could be too strong to resist. Sociologists and researchers who visited working-class communities in cities across Britain, in the years following the end of the war, found that the majority of people they questioned were desperate to get out of their housing. Preferences were often mixed – a typical 1950s survey, of the Gorbals area of Glasgow, found that only 36 per cent of residents wished to stay in their current homes, given the choice, while a quarter hoped for new housing in the immediate area and two fifths wanted to move elsewhere entirely. A few years later in Leeds, researchers found 82 per cent of respondents keen to move wherever alternative housing could be found.[32] And very few who did make the move to suburban housing and New Towns regretted the decision. For many, the move could mean exchanging a tiny, overcrowded flat with communal sinks and toilet facilities for a house and garden; an indoor bathroom; domestic appliances; clean air and spacious surroundings. While they sometimes voiced pangs at having to break old ties and leave behind familiar neighbourhoods, they were overwhelmingly sure that moving out had been the best option for themselves and their children. 'Hitler did a good job when he blew up my parents' house,' was one respondent's feeling upon moving to Stevenage after the war, 'I wouldn't change this for anything.' At the beginning of the 1970s, researchers found that 87 per cent of people who had moved there in the previous decades still felt it had been the right decision, including an elderly couple who had relocated from Islington who declared 'this is like Paradise to us! It's as near to it we've ever been and are ever likely to get!'[33] Satisfaction in Milton Keynes was higher still – when the local development corporation conducted a survey in 1975 they found that only four families of the 290 questioned wanted to return to wherever they had lived before.[34]

As the historian Jon Lawrence emphasises, this is in many ways unsurprising – in contrast to estates housing those who had been moved in compulsory slum clearances, most people who had moved to Britain's New Towns had chosen to do so. And they were buoyed, too, by the sense that they were part of an exciting social and political experiment, pioneering new forms of community and new ways of living. Again and again, social researchers found the residents of New Towns expressing the sense that they had found a place outside England's class system, exchanging the conformity of an older world for modernity, progressivism and personal choice. 'Individualism' and 'community' were by no means mutually exclusive – exchanging the enforced proximity of crowded neighbourhoods for more spacious surroundings could enable more voluntary forms of sociability. Former Londoners in particular remarked that people in New Towns such as Stevenage were often friendlier: as one woman remarked of moving there in 1955, 'we're all close together here: we all depend on each other for help because relations are so far away. I hope to stay here for the rest of my life.'[35]

While the inhabitants of 'traditional' working-class communities who were questioned by social researchers had most often said that they would rather move into houses than flats, there were many people, too, who moved into flats and found that they loved them. In 1958, for instance, a letter writer in the *Daily Telegraph* intervened in a heated public debate between those for and against the building of tower blocks in Richmond for people rehoused from the East End, to say that – though he was no modernist – he was delighted with his new flat. 'I found myself at home,' he explained, almost despite himself: 'I hate rock 'n' roll, toneless music, abstract painting and all sculpture after Jacob Epstein. I am a cockney in exile. And yet I am content.' And while Glasgow's Castlemilk estate would later become notorious as an ill-planned scheme that was left in the following decades to deprivation and decay, residents who had lived there for thirty years or more by the 1980s looked back on their move in the 1950s and remembered not a sense of longing or loss for the older communities they had moved on from, but overwhelming excitement. 'I got it! . . . [we] were all delighted,' recalled one long-term resident of moving in, 'I had been on the housing list for twelve years.' Another resident explained that 'in the old tenement back-courts, everything was divided by railings and there wasn't much light because of the high tenement buildings. Here everything was so bright, clean and green.'[36]

What had life really been like in the tenements and terraces they had left behind? For the sociologists and researchers who interviewed working-class residents in new and old communities alike in the post-war years, new housing developments were the antithesis of the community spirit they found in older districts. Life in 'traditional' neighbourhoods and slums, they argued, was defined by friendliness, mutual aid and social bonding. They romanticised tight-knit communities, ignoring or minimising their downsides at the same time as creating a dystopian reverse image of suburban soullessness and alienation, drawing a picture of an increasingly 'affluent society' that was losing sight of the things of real value. But this was a view that was often shaped more by the researchers' assumptions than by the testimony of people who lived and worked in these communities themselves. Frequently, people explained that they *wanted* privacy, and the ability to keep themselves to themselves, not crowded living conditions in which everyone knew each other's business – often by simple virtue of the fact that they could overhear their neighbours. In Bermondsey and Bethnal Green, alongside those who drew a real sense of pride in living up to an image of cockney communalism and sociability, respondents detailed petty feuds and gossip-mongering, arguments raging through dividing walls, and conflicts over cleaning shared landings and negotiating communal washing facilities. For all their preconceptions about community ties, researchers found their interviewees explaining that closeness had its drawbacks.[37]

Looking back in hindsight on the earlier twentieth century, working men and women who wrote down their memories of slum communities in memoirs and autobiographies were often at pains to emphasise that, however much they could depend on their neighbours in times of need, the effect of lives lived at such close quarters could be oppressive. For the autodidact V.W. Garratt, who had worked on a factory production line before training as a journalist after the First World War, the slums of Birmingham in which he had spent his early years were 'areas where life is stifled into uniformity.' 'Individual development has little chance in hovels where all conversation can be heard by the next-door neighbour and local opinion sits in judgment on every movement,' he explained; 'the natural inclinations of people were continually checked.'[38]

Yet for all their acknowledgements of the everyday anxieties and irritations that came from living in such enclosed neighbourhoods, the working-class autobiographers and memoirists of the post-war period looked back on their early years as a heyday for community. 'They were happy days in that close-knit community,' recalled the septuagenarian Grace Foakes, writing down her memories growing up in London's East End around the turn of the twentieth century. 'The feeling of belonging outclassed everything else. There was poverty, disease, dirt and ignorance, and yet to feel one belonged outweighed all else.' 'Even as I recall the poverty and the squalor,' she wrote, 'the noise and the dirt, the narrow streets and dark alleyways, I feel a great sense of nostalgia for this unlovely place. For there as well were to be found comradeship and happiness.'[39] It was a view shared by the socialist activist Walter Southgate as he remembered his childhood in the East End in the 1890s, writing of the 'remarkable' spirit of resilience among his community: 'I experienced and witnessed numerous examples of the cockney's indomitable spirit in adversity ... Mutual aid was the keystone of existence.' Indeed, for Southgate, so strong was the sense of community that it could eclipse the appeal of social mobility – though it is perhaps not surprising that, as a lifelong socialist, he valued class solidarity over material aspiration. Reflecting upon why his parents had made no attempt to move out towards the growing suburbs, he imagined that

> The community spirit would be gone in any new effort to live aloof behind the suburban garden hedges, boarded fences and locked doors. My parents would have felt like fish out of water; the quietness, privacy and lack of neighbourliness would have

overwhelmed them and made them miserable. Gone would be the friendly chats at the street door on a summer evening, the mutual help when in need, the bustling street market stalls and the atmosphere of the public house.[40]

Echoing anxieties about the decline of community that were filtering into the media by the 1960s and 1970s, many autobiographers felt that they were spending their later years in an age of individualism and self-interest. For the 'old-time trade unionist' Arthur Collinson, 'the mass poverty' of the early twentieth century had 'united the victims in a way so different from that of the present day of so called affluence, which has transformed "each for all and all for each" into an "I'm all right Jack" society.'[41] Often writing down their accounts of life in an earlier age for the benefit of their children and grandchildren, autobiographers recounted their early experiences of poverty and hardship, emphasising just how much better things now were for younger generations. Yet they could be distinctly ambivalent about the effects of rising affluence. One autobiographer, including in his recollections a letter written to his adult daughter in 1970, considered that 'it is only in retrospect that one realises just how bad things were ... how far we have gone along the road from abject poverty to comparative affluence for everybody.' But 'maybe', he continued, things had now 'swung too far the other way due to the apathy of most and selfishness of the majority and an almost total disregard to consider anything other than the mercenary and superficial aspects of living, by so many folk.' Perhaps growing concerned that he was coming across as something of a curmudgeon, he added to his daughter: 'don't I go on ...'[42]

In their later years, immersed in media commentary about rising crime and anti-social youth, autobiographers instinctively linked the new-found affluence they saw around them with social breakdown. 'All in all,' reflected the 'Victorian Grandmother', Winifred Till, 'I think [mine] was a good age to grow up in,' when people had appreciated 'the simple things of life.' 'The horrors of violence and the greed for money and material things had not yet shown itself to any marked degree,' she felt, 'and our young ears were not subjected to "news of crime" and disaster as is churned out daily by our radio and television.'[43] In the early 1980s, one retired bus driver, Jack Jones, looked back on his childhood in Hoxton before the First World War and reflected upon how it compared to the youthful hooliganism he had seen around him in recent years: 'reading and hearing so much about the vandalism so rife today, I have racked and racked my brains in an effort to recall what type of vandalism we Hoxton kids indulged in, but without success. Nor can I recall the graffiti . . . which disfigures so many of our public buildings, as well as the tubes and buses, with what appears to be senseless exhibitionism.'[44] Time and again, the autobiographers tell us, in contrast to the individualism and carelessness running rife in younger generations, the world of their youth was a simpler, safer, more compassionate place, where children had respected authority, and people looked out for one another.

But should we take them at their word? Are these simply the age-old complaints of people late in life that everything was going downhill, looking back on idealised memories of the 'good old days' of their youth – or had something truly been lost over the course of the twentieth century? Certainly, levels of reported crime had been rising steadily. After an immediate spike following the end to the war, followed by a decline in the early 1950s, the growth of petty and violent crime alike had been consistently upwards. Perceptions, however, are not always bound to keep pace with statistics; moreover, the meanings writers ascribed to their experiences could themselves be highly variable. Indeed, autobiographers at times contradict their *own* experiences in lamenting how much worse things had become. The image of older working-class urban neighbourhoods that emerges from their own accounts is hardly one of obedience and security. After bemoaning the rise of youthful hooliganism over the course of his lifetime, for instance, something he maintained had been unknown in his youth, Jack Jones returned to his earlier memories and recounted that 'Hoxton was a wild, and sometimes violent, place in those days. Hardly a Saturday would pass without a riot call being issued . . . lads – yes, and lassies – just out of the pubs, laying into the police. Law and order would only be re-established when the number of heads cracked by police grew too many to bear.' The experience of witnessing these pitched battles, as a child, had been 'frightening', yes, but also 'exciting.'[45]

Even so, while levels of reported crime at the outset of the post-war period were remarkably low by twenty-first-century standards, the crime rate had quadrupled over the first half of the twentieth century.[46] While we might look back with our own retrospect on the years following the Second World War and see a world of relative safety, many people in the post-war years were – understandably – looking back themselves on a time that seemed safer still. When the Mass Observation project asked ordinary men and women throughout Britain to record diaries of their everyday lives, they found many people in the 1940s deeply worried over what they saw as an epidemic of criminality and social disorder. 'Meantime the crime wave spreads,' recorded Sheffield housewife Edie Rutherford in her diary in December 1945, 'I do feel that we are at fault in that our education system is wrong and we therefore send young folk into the world with such wrong ideas that we get all these social problems.' In the same month, B. Charles, an antiques dealer in Edinburgh, recalled receiving a letter from a Londoner that read 'honestly, London gets worse as the days go on. And it's so dangerous, you never know when you are going to get a knock on the head and robbed.' 'Who would have thought London would ever be dangerous before the war?' he reflected gloomily.[47]

It wasn't just crime that was heading in the wrong

86

direction – for Charles, this was one more sign that standards were slipping everywhere. The next year, his diaries reveal him ruminating about 'the complete decline of home life', 'the increase of divorces and the general "rottenness" of present-day society', and recording a conversation with his bank manager about 'how terribly "honesty" had suffered during the war. [The manager] continued that people who, before the war, would never have dreamed of doing anything dishonest, very often now seemed to think it was quite "in order" to pilfer and cheat if they got the chance. I am sure he is right.' And well before the boom in youth culture – and with it, a social outcry over teenage delinquency – that we often associate with the 1960s onwards, Mass Observation's diarists were deploring what had become of the youth of today. In May 1948, a retired engineer in Sydenham recorded in his diary:

> Mass Observation asks their members to say what their feelings are about the manners and morals and customs of the younger generation today (those born after 1918) about how they compare with those of the older generation. My own opinion is that they are very much worse in every way. Judging by the ones I come across, they have no manners at all, which may be due to lack of control by their parents, but from whatever cause, London children are absolutely crafty little liars and clever thieves, and think only what they can do for themselves.[48]

For all their complaints about the present, few people who remembered life in the nineteenth and early twentieth centuries genuinely wished to return to an earlier time. 'I don't believe that there ever were any "Good Old Days"', wrote the Sydenham pensioner. 'If you had lived then, it is fairly certain that you would have caught smallpox or died before you were five years old. I remember when I was a boy seeing men with their faces pitted all over with smallpox . . . No, the "good old days" are a myth for discontented people to talk about.'[49] It was a theme echoed throughout working-class autobiographies and

memoirs, as writers looked back on an earlier age and emphasised just how much had changed for the better. Despite
frequently idealising their own early experiences and bemoaning the state of the present, at the very same time, working-class
autobiographers wrote of their irritation with generalised
myths that life had somehow been better in the past. Whatever
the problems of the present, they hardly compared with conditions at the beginning of the twentieth century. 'In this year of
1975 with its problems of inflation and the dire times ahead,'
contemplated one memoirist, 'it is interesting for those like
myself to recall times when life was really tough. For those
born at the turn of the century . . . the present era of affluence
tends to make one cynical of the phrase Hard Times Ahead.'
'GOOD OLD DAYS,' he continued, 'Maybe for some . . . but
for most a life of hardship, struggle, and anxiety.'[50] 'How I
reached my present age is a miracle,' reflected a former public
health inspector, Jack Lanigan, in his private memoirs at 86, of
growing up in the slums of Salford in the 1890s. 'The thoughts
of those days still make a shiver run down my spine . . . My pen
cannot describe the heartbreak, the poverty and suffering.' 'Oh!
Those good old days?' he rhetoricised, with bitter irony – 'and
we kids even found time to be patriotic, why and what for God
alone knows.'[51]

What are we to make of all these contradictions? The very
same authors who looked back fondly on a vanished heyday of
community, and worried about what they saw as the individualism of the present, were also telling their readers how much
their society had changed for the better over the course of the
twentieth century. At the same time as lamenting what was
seemingly becoming of an 'affluent society', they emphasised
the immense suffering and injustice people had endured in an
age when they had been forced to make do with less. But perhaps these two impulses are not quite as paradoxical as they
first appear. Autobiographers took immense pride in how they
had made the best of it in difficult times, helping their

neighbours in moments of need and appreciating simple pleasures wherever they could be found. But they did not extend this
to approving of a social system that had seemed content to
leave so many people in lives of poverty. These sometimes contradictory narratives of past and present are how we all make
sense of the societies in which we live. We should not mistake
people's nostalgia for their memories of community for an
accurate reflection of how things used to be – and not least
when they themselves tell us, too, about the miseries that also
came with chronic financial insecurity – but the ways in which
they idealised aspects of the past *can* tell us something important. People were always in search of a time in the past when
people were seemingly happier, more contented with what they
had, more authentically connected to each other. With each
generation, the past became imagined as everything they felt
the present was missing. Their nostalgia was and is a way of
articulating the timeless desire for social connection, for belonging; the need to feel part of a whole.

THE MOTHER COUNTRY

While many people were reminiscing on life in a very different
Britain, Britain was increasingly becoming home to people who
looked back upon earlier lives far beyond its shores. For many,
this hadn't been a choice. In the aftermath of the Second World
War, millions of Eastern Europeans had been displaced or left
homeless, having fled or been expelled from their native
countries – 80,000 arrived in Britain as refugees, many of
whom had been recruited to rebuild post-war Britain amid
chronic labour shortages. Some had arrived having been rendered stateless: for many Polish immigrants, the communities
they had left behind were no longer part of Poland, but had
been absorbed into Ukraine and Belarus.[52] They had been irrev-
ocably cut off from their own pasts; literally having no homes

to go back to. At the same time, successive waves of voluntary migration from Eastern and Southern Europe, Ireland, India, Pakistan, the Caribbean, Africa, and countries throughout the world were transforming post-war Britain into an increasingly multicultural, multiracial society.

Whatever their reasons for arriving in Britain, all were changed by the experience, as pasts, presents and futures were realigned – each migrant to Britain had left their past behind and set out in search of a different, better future; whether that future would be the start of a new life in Britain, or the aim of returning one day to their country of origin. Just as millions of people had moved within Britain, leaving behind old, familiar neighbourhoods in search of new homes, new jobs and new communities, migrants to Britain looked both backwards and forwards, negotiating optimism and uncertainty as well as acute nostalgia. Change was to be welcomed with open arms, promising affluence, social mobility and new experiences. Yet at the same time they looked back to memories of a very different home, remembering distant homelands that – whatever their reasons for leaving had been – had offered a sense of belonging that could prove far more elusive in their new lives.

The *Empire Windrush*, which arrived in England in June 1948 carrying 800 West Indian and Caribbean migrants, has come to be remembered as the most visible symbol of the new multicultural Britain that would take shape over the following decades. But for the migrants who had left behind their homes thousands of miles away, this was, too, a kind of homecoming – after all, when their ship docked at Tilbury, the *Evening Standard* had heralded the new arrivals under the headline 'Welcome Home!'[53] What has come to be known as the Windrush Generation who came to Britain in the following years arrived as British citizens – making the journey from Britain's empire to the 'Mother Country'. As the author George Lamming, who left Barbados before coming to England after a few years working in Trinidad, explained: 'migration was not a word I would have used to describe what I was doing when I sailed with other West Indians to England in 1950. We simply thought that we were going to an England which had been planted in our consciousness as a heritage and a place of welcome.'[54] Or as Ivan Weekes, who would later become one of Britain's first black magistrates, remembered of moving to London from Barbados in 1955: 'I didn't feel I was coming to a place that was totally strange. I felt I was coming to a home away from home.'[55]

Indeed, many who settled in Britain in the late 1940s and 1950s had already spent time in Britain and found themselves at home. Imperial loyalties had been instilled since childhood in those who lived in Britain's Caribbean colonies, through education and colonial administration, and thousands had answered the call to volunteer as soldiers to defend Britain during the Second World War. Euton Christian, who joined the RAF in 1944, described how 'growing up in school [in Jamaica], we always regarded England as the mother country . . . as a parent who never often sees the children, but the children think of the parents abroad.' Caribbean soldiers who arrived in Britain during the war often found that their early sense of belonging was confirmed in the welcome they received. The Jamaican-born Cecil Holness, for instance, recounted how people 'went out of their way to do things for you, make you happy', when he arrived for RAF training in Yorkshire; local residents would 'invite you home for tea 'cos they say "Oh, we are all one. You're coming to England to help us."' 'They made us to feel as if we were at home. See, it was good,' he reflected sadly, 'not like what it is now.' After the war, 'all that changed.' The Guyanese actor, musician and writer Cy Grant reflected similarly that bonds which had been formed in war were suddenly withdrawn in peacetime: 'I must say, wearing an officer's uniform protects you and during the war people have a different sense of camaraderie. We were all in it together . . . but after the war you did notice attitudes were completely different out of uniform.'[56]

For many Caribbean migrants, the vast disjuncture between their expectations and the reality of life in Britain could provoke intense disillusionment. Homesickness was often painfully acute. Tryphena Anderson, who left home to answer the government's call for staff to join the new NHS at the age of 19, recalled how her intense nostalgia for Jamaica was made all the more unbearable not just by Britain's winter climate, but by the constant discrimination she endured. She described the experience of being alone, in an unfamiliar country, and sitting on a London bus as people one by one avoided taking the seat next to her:

> I came from such a bright place, so much sunshine, so much colour, and it was very depressing that time of year. They didn't know anything about us . . . I wish I could be back home so bad it hurts . . . One day I was on a bus, and I was upstairs and I was at the corner of Parliament Street, and I saw a black man . . . I just felt, if only this bus would stop, I would get off it and just run and hug him, and find out, you know, where he came from. Because you feel lost, you know.

While it had been hard to leave Jamaica, it was harder still to imagine returning prematurely. 'Can you imagine writing home to come back?' Anderson continued: 'what am I going back to? Where am I going to get the money from?'[57] Between sending money to family members back home, and having no other option than to pay extortionate rents for what were almost invariably inadequate housing conditions, migrant workers frequently found themselves living hand-to-mouth, deferring dreams for the future even as their pasts receded further into the distance.

The majority of Britain's post-war immigrants had envisaged that the move would be temporary. Throughout the following decades, people arrived from the West Indies, from Ireland, India, Italy, and countries all over the world, expecting to work in Britain for a few years, perhaps to send money back to their communities, and then one day to return. They had left home because they wanted a better future, but most imagined that this future would be back 'at home', not in Britain. As the historian Clair Wills writes, this placed migrants in temporal as well as geographical limbo, with their lives in Britain imagined 'as a kind of interregnum, a period to be endured or enjoyed because it would make possible a future that was envisaged, as often as not, as a return to the past made viable again.' Their nostalgia was simultaneously a form of anticipation, because they were investing in a future that was longed for as a better version of the past.[58] As MP Diane Abbott reflected of her parents' 'very strong cultural attachment to Jamaica': 'they came thinking they were going to go home. I mean, all their lives . . . all their lives, they talked about going home . . . I think for that generation – most of them die thinking they're going to go home the next year or the year after.'[59]

Yet the longer people stayed in Britain, the more a return to the past became an impossibility. The 'home' they dreamt of returning to was no longer the place they remembered – just as Britain was changing, the communities they had left behind had changed in the intervening years. As Rudy Braithwaite, who had worked as an activist in Notting Hill in the 1950s, explained after 44 years in Britain: 'there's no place like home. But [Guyana] is not the same country that I left. And I wouldn't be able to fit in, because nothing stands still . . . it's a different place.' He would have been returning to a 'different environment, different type of youth. Their values are different, you know, all over the West Indies. Everywhere, nothing goes backward, everything goes forward.' And migrants themselves were no longer the same people they had been, on the day they had left home. With the passing of years, people had been changed by the lives they had made in Britain. They had grown into new understandings of themselves, formed new communities, developed new kinds of belonging. 'Home' would now always be in two places. The writer and broadcaster Mike Phillips and his brother Trevor Phillips write of the Windrush Generation that 'in the old days . . . they used to say, "I don't want to leave my bones in this country."' But for those who did return to the Caribbean, 'even when they went back to live they left something of their hearts in London or Manchester or Leeds.'[60]

Of those migrants who chose to remain, many had raised children whose only memories were of life in Britain. For the children of migrants, their parents' homelands often became internalised as an idea of home, as part of their family's mythology. For Clair Wills, if this made a sense of 'belonging' – either to Britain, or to their parents' places of origin – complicated for the children of migrants, longing was more straightforward. 'We borrowed our sense of longing from our parents,' she writes of Ireland, where her mother had grown up before moving to Croydon at the age of 18: 'because they loved home, we did too.' But the longing she felt was not quite nostalgia, though it had much in common with it. She describes visiting her aunt and uncle's farm in West Cork as a child during summer holidays in the 1960s and 1970s, and the ritual homecomings that took place each year as she and her siblings were welcomed into a 'home' they had never lived in, playing in the fields with her cousins and 'even kitted out in scratchy Aran sweaters. It would be wrong to label this nostalgia. We were simply enacting the version of being Irish which was available to us, as people who were not quite at home.' But if this was a sense of belonging that had had to be 'forged', sometimes 'out of a kind of tourist brochure of styles', it was no less real for it. While some aspects of the way she and her siblings had enacted being 'at home' in Ireland had had to be faked, the relationships she built with her family were real.[61]

But for Wills, there is nothing unique about these experiences to immigrants and their children. This is perhaps 'the lesson that people find it hardest to learn, or to accept – that none of us securely belong.' When any of us leaves a home, she writes, 'we leave it for good. Even if we return, we cannot go back.'[62] No one is untouched by change, however welcome those changes; no one is immune from a sense of loss at being cut off from a past that cannot be recovered. Throughout the post-war decades, families who had only ever known life in Britain were living in places that had been, and were being, transformed. Families had moved to new houses, new communities, travelling back to visit friends and relatives in their old neighbourhoods and finding how much had changed there. Parents were consciously raising their children to have a better standard of life than they had known themselves, to entertain hopes of social mobility, while discovering that in some ways it took them further away from shared experiences – setting younger generations on the path to different ambitions, different anxieties, different pleasures. Those who stayed in the same place would carry memories of how things had used to be, in an earlier time: suburban streets where fields had been; housing developments that stood on the site of Victorian terraces; shuttered factories that had once been the heart of a community's identity; gentrifying neighbourhoods renovated by homeowners, which not long ago had been thriving working-class quarters. No one's 'home' remained entirely unchanged.

At the same time as people from all over the world were moving to Britain – many from Britain's former colonies or countries in the process of gaining their independence – the empire's colonisers were making the journey back to the mainland. As colonial administrations were dismantled, white settlers were moving to a Britain that, for many, felt very far from 'home'. In the wake of Indian independence in 1947, thousands of British expatriates were shipped back to Britain. Some were delighted to be returning, though many others felt their departure as a loss, remarking upon how cold, bleak and thin life in England felt by comparison. While adults living and working in the British Raj had generally had some experience of life in England, having been sent there to boarding school, when independence came many children were repatriated who had never been there before. As the journalist Brigid Keenan recalls of her family's journey back 'home' to England in 1948, when she was eight years old: 'it wasn't home in any meaningful sense. My sisters and I had never been there.' Members of her family had lived in India for five generations, including a French great-great-grandfather who had settled in Bengal as a silk weaver, Irishmen who had joined the British army in the nineteenth century, as well as grandparents who lived in Burma. 'I remember the pain and the loss and the homesickness of leaving India,' she writes, arriving in 'cold, grey, post-war, not-very-friendly Britain' to find that 'socially, the returnees were faintly despised. The feeling seemed to be that they had lived high on the hog, they hadn't suffered the Blitz or rationing or cold winters and so what could we expect now?' For the writer Lee Langley, who was 11 when she left India, England, too, struck her as a 'small, grey and cold place' upon arrival. 'India was fundamental to my thinking and attitude to life; to my sense of colour and smell and awareness of scale,' she continues, 'I never felt I belonged in England ... when I got here, I definitely felt alien.' But the lives they had left behind could never again be revisited. 'I can't defend the British Raj in India,' Keenan writes, 'no one ever feels any sympathy for those who are dispossessed of other people's possessions ... But I do, because I remember the heartache and the homesickness for the land we'd left.'[63]

How had those in Britain reacted to the rapid break-up of empire, in the decades following the Second World War? For one of England's most staunch erstwhile imperialists, the solution was to pretend it had never really mattered in the first place. Enoch Powell, whose 'Rivers of Blood' speech in 1968 is remembered as the definitive statement of post-war English racism and hostility towards immigrants, had once entertained hopes of becoming viceroy of India, having fallen 'hopelessly and helplessly in love' with the country while serving as an officer in Delhi in the 1940s. He took the news of independence badly, wandering the streets of London into the early hours in grief. 'One's world,' he declared, 'had been altered.'[64] Yet by the mid-1950s, Powell was claiming that the British Empire had been a 'delusion', a 'self-deception', a 'hallucination' all along. A few years later, he was asserting that England had 'remained unaffected through it all, almost unconscious of the strange fantastic structure built around her', and that the 'strange races' had simply 'fallen away' to reveal an ancient England in all its unsullied purity – all rolling fields and sturdy oaks, charming cottages and country churchyards. It was time, he argued, for the empire-builders to 'come home again from years of distant wandering.'[65] Britishness, with its shared project of empire, was dropped in favour of English nationalism; a nostalgic appeal to rustic delights and small, unchanging villages that he threatened would soon be swamped if immigration was not controlled. Britain, he determined, had been labouring under the delusion that big is great, expanding ever-outward, but after the shock of decolonisation had worn off he had decided that having an empire was overrated anyway. What was needed, for Powell, was to focus on growing a new English patriotism that would protect the purity of 'home'.

HISTORY IS NOW AND ENGLAND

The end of the Second World War was supposed to mean the return home – the longed-for return to normality after six long years of disruption. In the weeks and months following victory in Europe in May 1945, soldiers would return from combat; husbands would be reunited with wives; parents with children. Women who had worked in factories, in hospitals, as ambulance drivers or as land girls would resume their domestic lives; those who had spent time in the relative safety of rural communities would return to towns and cities – the continuation of millions of comings and goings that had taken place throughout the course of the war. But the prospect of 'normality' itself, which had been longed for so intensely during the war, could seem suddenly disorientating. For the writer and painter Denton Welch, whatever the inconveniences of wartime, it had at least become familiar; now all around him there seemed to be 'awful thoughts and anxieties in the air – the breaking of something – the splitting apart of an atmosphere that had surrounded us for six years.'[66] Yet even during the war itself, the satirical magazine *Punch* had predicted that future generations might look back fondly on the days of wartime hardship, with a cartoon depicting rationing in 1944. 'In about thirty years' time,' says a woman gesturing a towards a frantic queue of customers desperate to use their ration coupons, 'people will insist on describing this as the good old days.'[67]

All the same, as the novelist Sylvia Townsend Warner reflected in a letter to a friend in January 1946: 'no one in wartime can escape the illusion that when the war ends things will snap back to where they were and that one will be the same age one

"I suppose in about thirty years' time people will insist on describing this as the good old days."

Cartoon, *Punch*, 4 October 1944.

was when it began, and able to go on from where one left off.'[68] When the realities of peace began at last to take shape, many were now realising that a return to the past was impossible; too much had changed to simply begin again where they had broken off in 1939. For many, there was no 'normal' to go back to. People had lost relatives, colleagues, friends; been bombed out of their homes and workplaces; been changed by their experiences in wartime. In the two years it took to demobilise after 1945, servicemen and women returned to find that previous jobs were often no longer open, while the transition from the adrenaline of war to the mundane realities of peace was far from easy.

'Home' was not always the settled ideal that had been yearned for. For soldiers who had been traumatised by their experiences in combat, and the doctors and nurses who had treated them, support was rarely available – not least in a deeply repressive society where people were supposed to keep their emotions to themselves. Fathers might not have seen their children for years; but what they *had* been used to was an environment of discipline and hierarchy, where subordinates obeyed their leaders without question. For children, the experience of a father who was essentially a stranger returning home could be deeply unsettling, even damaging. In turn, wives who had experienced new freedoms and independence during the war found that their husbands returned expecting to resume their earlier roles as sole head of the household. The strain on families was sometimes too much to bear. Divorces rose sharply: from around 8,000 in England and Wales in 1939 to over 60,000 in 1947, a figure that would not be reached again until the 1970s.[69] And in many other ways, life was far from how it had been before the war. Rationing lingered into the 1950s, now extended to items such as bread that had never been restricted during wartime. Buildings and townscapes damaged during the Blitz could languish unrepaired for years.

It was all contributing to a sense of immense anti-climax, a benumbed adjustment to the 'new normal' of pinched, dull, shabby post-war austerity. Optimism and hope for a different, better future – encapsulated by Labour's landslide victory in 1945 and its promise of a 'New Jerusalem' – coincided, too, with widespread disillusionment. For Edie Rutherford, writing in her Mass Observation diary in August 1946, a year after the surrender of Japan, the end of war seemed to have 'passed unnoticed by most. The peace is so grim that it occupies all our time.' The general feeling seemed to be that the task of post-war reconstruction was so enormous, the depths of war-weariness so great, that things were unlikely ever to improve enough. 'Were I in my thirties, instead of my fifties,' declared fellow diarist B. Charles, 'I would, by hook or by crook, clear right out of Europe. Europe is completely finished.'[70] Returning to London from America, the novelist Christopher Isherwood was told that 'this is a dying city.' 'Several Londoners I talked to,' he wrote, 'believed it would never recover.' His visit was 'powerfully and continually depressing', as he wandered past plasterwork 'peeling from even the most fashionable squares and crescents', and dined in 'once stylish restaurants . . . reduced to drabness and even squalor.' London, he felt, 'remembered the past and was ashamed of its present appearance.'[71]

The inhabitants of post-war Britain dwelled with tantalising nostalgia upon the everyday luxuries and pleasures they had enjoyed before the war. Amid rationing and widespread shortages of once-obtainable ingredients, memories of food could be recalled with almost pornographic longing. 'Oh, those pre-war days!' rhapsodised one diarist for Mass Observation, 'June says that when she hears good, unobtainable food discussed now her mouth waters so much she actually dribbles. *Foie gras* . . . Pineapple cream made with real fruit. Strawberry meringue pudding made with whites of six eggs. A cake made with half a pound of butter,' she continued, 'a poached egg on a hot buttered muffin . . . Hollandaise sauce. Lobster . . . Veal cutlets . . . Asparagus. I'm dribbling, too, now.'[72] The food writer Elizabeth David found herself dreaming of the Mediterranean, as a succession of 'unspeakably dismal meals' were served to her in a hotel in Ross-on-Wye. 'Agonised' by a craving for the sun, and in 'furious revolt against that terrible, cheerless, heartless food', she began 'writing down descriptions of Mediterranean and Middle Eastern cooking . . . words like apricot, olives and butter, rice and lemons, oil and almonds.' Years later, she reflected 'that in the England of 1947, those were dirty words that I was putting down.'[73] Evelyn's Waugh's novel *Brideshead Revisited*, published in 1945, piled nostalgia upon nostalgia, as its narrator Charles Ryder looks back in the final years of the war upon the fleeting paradise of Oxford and country house life in the 1920s, epitomised by the teddy-bear toting Sebastian Flyte – a man, in turn, in love with his own childhood. As Waugh wrote of the novel, it was composed in 'a bleak period of present privation . . . and in consequence the book is infused with a kind of gluttony, for food and wine', and for the vanished 'splendours of the recent past'; confessing himself 'appalled' to revisit such extravagant prose when he revised the novel 'with a full stomach' in the 1950s.[74]

Not least because, in the words of one Mass Observation diarist in 1947, 'we seem infinitely worse off than at any time during the war,' post-war Britons could even feel nostalgic for the war itself.[75] 'The horrors of peace were many,' recalled Quentin Crisp in his 1968 autobiography *The Naked Civil Servant*. The war had been a time of 'death-made-easy', to be sure, but 'love-made-easy', too, had thrived in the atmosphere of 'shared danger'. There had been opportunities for friendship and camaraderie – not to mention the excitement of night-time liaisons with American soldiers.[76] For many, the heightened emotions of wartime had given life on the home front an intensity and a poignancy that had proved rare to experience since. When the Mass Observation founder Tom Harrisson collected the testimonies of Londoners describing their experiences of living through the Blitz, he found people expressing delight as much as anxiety. 'I wouldn't mind having an evening like it say once a week,' was one man's assessment of helping to put out bomb fires in his north London neighbourhood: 'ordinarily, there's no excitement, nothing to do or anything.' Even the experience of being bombed could be thrilling to some. A few days after the event, one woman described emerging 'blood-stained and covered in plaster dust' from the wreckage of a terrace that had suffered a direct hit, and sitting under a blanket in a neighbour's house

> feeling indescribably happy and triumphant. 'I've been bombed!' I kept saying to myself, over and over again – trying the phrase on, like a new dress, to see how it fitted. 'I've been bombed . . . I've been bombed – me!
>
> It seems a terrible thing to say, when many people must have been killed and injured last night; but never in my whole life have I ever experienced such pure and flawless happiness.

Thirty-five years later, the memory of that night still evoked intense nostalgia. When Mass Observation asked their wartime interviewees to revisit their memories in the 1970s, she looked back on it as a 'peak experience' in her life, 'as if the whole thing was somehow a gigantic personal achievement.' By then a grandmother, she put it on a par with 'the experience of having a baby.'[77] Even at the time, those who witnessed air raids could be deeply moved by the sense that they were living through history. 'I tried to fix the scene in my mind,' explained the same woman in 1940, of watching 'the red glow from the East, where the docks were burning,' in the minutes before she herself had been hit – 'because one day this will be history, and I shall be the one who actually saw it.' 'I wasn't frightened any more,' she continued, 'it was amazing . . . the searchlights were beautiful, it [was] like watching the end of the world.' One London factory worker, having been bombed out of his housing twice, explained why he and his wife had no interest in the prospect of being evacuated as non-essential personnel: 'what, and miss all this? . . . [not] for all the gold in China! There's never been nothing like it! Never! And never will be again.'[78] The intensity of their lives in the present could be heightened by the anticipation that one day they would look back on them as momentous, formative experiences. They were in the thick of the action, bearing witness to it. It was a feeling echoed by T.S. Eliot, as he reflected upon the unity of past, present and future, drafting *Little Gidding* while fire-watching from his post atop the London skyline – 'history is now and England'.[79]

It could of course be profoundly traumatic to watch familiar landmarks, homes, neighbourhoods destroyed by bombs. Tom Harrisson described how, among the residents of Coventry, who had endured near-apocalyptic devastation over the course of a single night in November 1940, 'suddenly, there was aching nothingness.' Residents were paralysed by the extent of destruction, unsure of what to do or where to go. 'Coventry is finished', 'Coventry is dead', were phrases heard again and again by researchers in the following days. Many were traumatised by the magnitude of the lives that had been lost, the injured, the streets flattened into rubble; 'many for a while showed no hope for the place. They could only survive as persons.' And yet, at the same time, the scale of it all – the sheer compression of damage around the cathedral and city centre – was undoubtedly impressive. Harrisson mapped out an emotional trajectory that was common in survivors in towns and cities everywhere: 'where social nuclei like cathedral and shopping centre were destroyed, there was a powerful dual impact: a first sense of drastic loss, closely followed by a quite passionate interest, growing readily to pride ... Meanwhile, the deadly effect would fascinate, even please.' By May 1941, researchers in London were noting the 'familiar ritual' of local residents gathering the morning after a raid to assess the damage wrought to monuments such as Westminster Abbey. On the morning in question, however, there was a distinct mood of anti-climax. 'What's happened to the Abbey?' one resident was overheard to exclaim, 'it doesn't seem to be touched.' As Harrisson noted, 'the standard for debris-watching had gone up' after eight months of continual air raids, 'so there was some disappointment.'[80]

For those who had fleetingly accessed new pleasures and opportunities during the war, the onset of peace could prove to be a period more of longing than relief. As Quentin Crisp reflected with an air of mourning, 'Londoners started to regret their indiscriminate expansiveness ... Emotions that had been displayed had now to be lived down.'[81] For a cohort of writers, the heady combination of danger, novelty and sexual tension that played out amid the darkened streets of London's blackout made the times 'an absolute gift' to the artist, as the novelist Henry Green wrote in a letter to fellow writer Rosamond Lehmann in 1945, reporting 'a frightful surge of power and ideas.'[82] Already accustomed to leading irregular, chaotic love lives, the atmosphere of danger seemed to serve as a powerful aphrodisiac for London's literary elite.[83] For Graham Greene as well as Henry Green, who served respectively as an air-raid warden and fireman during the blitz, the mood of 'tomorrow we die' was savoured as an opportunity for guilt-free adultery. 'War is a prolonged passionate act, and we were involved in it,' explained the novelist Elizabeth Bowen, who herself had spent the war first engaged in an extramarital affair with the Irish writer Sean O'Faolain, and then with 'the centre of my life', the Canadian diplomat Charles Ritchie, while also working as an air-raid warden.[84]

Not only this, but the aesthetic effects of bombing were often a stimulus to the imagination. For the poet Stephen Spender, the bombs crashing around his office in Bloomsbury gave one the sense of 'a little island of civilisation, surrounded by burning churches – that is how the arts seemed during the war.' 'London is extraordinarily pleasant,' Graham Greene informed the novelist Anthony Powell with deliberate unconcern, what 'with all the new spaces, and the rather Mexican effect of ruined Churches.' When Greene's own house in Clapham was destroyed in October 1940, there was little time for nostalgia. 'It's sad,' he wrote to Powell, 'because it was a pretty house.' 'But,' he added – perhaps reflecting on the possibilities it presented for his 'rather disreputable life' in London, with his wife now safely packed away to Oxford – 'oddly enough, it leaves one very carefree.'[85]

When the war was over, many writers felt that they never again lived with quite the same intensity. One by one, novels emerged that were infused with the sense of longing and love and loss, with titles such as Elizabeth Bowen's *The Heat of the Day* (1948) and Graham Greene's *The End of the Affair* (1951) – tales of all-too-brief relationships begun in war that were destined never to emerge unscathed in peace. And while not everyone had spent their war years in bohemian abandon, living out their own literary fantasies in bars and hotel rooms, this elegiac tone did in many ways catch the public mood. For many 'ordinary' men and women, the crisis atmosphere of war had been a chance to pursue romance, flirtations, affairs, that might otherwise have been denied – passions that would now have to be put away in the return to respectable, domestic, rule-abiding life. Amid millions of domestic reunions between husbands and wives, one of the most enduring depictions of duty and desire, *Brief Encounter*, was released in cinemas in November 1945. It was a bittersweet return to normality. In the film's final scene, which its viewers found almost unbearably moving, Celia Johnson's Laura has returned from her passionate affair with her lover Alec, denied the chance to say a final goodbye, and gone home to her family to find her predictable, dependable husband Fred where she had left him, reading the paper by the living room fire. Sensing that something has happened, he walks over to her and says, 'You've been a long way away.' 'Yes,' says Laura, and turns to him with a single, stifled sob, as he replies: 'Thank you for coming back to me.'[86]

In retrospect, the narrative of post-war decline has shaped our image of Britain between 1945 and 1979 as a time of retreat, in which people were felt to be increasingly susceptible to the impulse that the journalist Michael Shanks was already warning of in 1961: that 'the British people' were burying themselves 'under the rose-petals of a vast collective nostalgia' for a vanishing heyday of imperial power and pride. Given how entrenched our twenty-first-century narrative of imperial nostalgia has become, we might have expected to find people in the post-war decades convulsed by lament for Britain's global ambitions amid the rapid break-up of empire. But their nostalgias were so often more domestic in scope, centring on changes that were happening in Britain itself. Many welcomed these changes with open arms: very few people hesitated at the chance to move into a better home, or acquire newly affordable goods and labour-saving technologies; still less second-guess themselves about whether affluence was desirable in the first place. Yet people who had been longing in the 1940s for a time of plenty – for comfortable housing, better food, better wine; a time when purchases would not be restricted by shortages and queues and ration coupons – would by the 1970s be looking back nostalgically on a less materialistic time, when people had supposedly been content for owning less.

Rising affluence and materialism seemed to be wrapped up with the decline of community: a sense that people were becoming more and more fragmented. And yet nostalgia for its supposed loss was a constant. The 1970s nostalgics who yearned for the community spirit of the 1940s were looking back to people who had themselves, in reality, been mourning the decline of the 'traditional' communities of the turn of the twentieth century – feeling that already, in the 1940s, life in Britain was becoming characterised by individualism and social breakdown. Their nostalgia might not accurately reflect what pre-war British 'community' had actually been like, but it does reveal what people felt was missing in their society in the present: a deeply held feeling that Britain was pursuing wealth at the expense of social connection. But far less remarked upon was the rise of more voluntary forms of community: the expansion of people's social horizons beyond the neighbourhoods they had grown up in, their shunning of the restraints of class and gender, unconstrained by older social norms or fear of 'what the neighbours would say'; the undeniable fact that in the decades after 1945, more and more people were pursuing ways of living that they had chosen for themselves.

3

The End of the Garden Party

1940–1914

We often think of the years between the First and Second World Wars as a modernising age that dispensed with the corsets and conventions of the nineteenth century – from the Roaring Twenties to the mass development of cars, aeroplanes, telephones, the cinema and the radio. The generation that came of age after the Great War lampooned eminent Victorians, and debunking the past became a kind of national sport. Instead they looked ahead to new worlds of science, leisure and consumerism. At the same time, as we, along with generations of observers since the 1940s, look back on the interwar years with our own retrospect, we have often been tempted to bathe it in the glow of nostalgic innocence: the sentimental pull of a quiet, rural world that would be eclipsed by catastrophe in 1939. Yet as well as embracing the new, the men and women who lived through the 1920s and 1930s were similarly looking back upon their own pre-war pasts, and coming to terms with what had changed in the aftermath of conflict on an unprecedented scale. Those who lived through the First World War often yearned for the lost innocence of English rural life, as they remembered, or misremembered, it to have been, reimagining the Edwardian era as a long summer garden party free from anxiety and upheaval.

Stanley Baldwin became the prime minister of nostalgia, serving on three occasions between 1923 and 1937, endeavouring to regenerate the nation through the 'spiritual values' of the countryside, and extolling the wholesome virtues of rural life and tradition. '[I] wonder as to what England may stand for in the minds of generations to come if our country goes on . . . in seeing her fields converted into towns,' Baldwin ruminated, in a suburbanising age in which towns and cities were spreading further and further into the surrounding countryside; and rural communities, in turn, were being transformed as pylons, power lines and tarmacked roads were delivering new opportunities and new ways of living. For all these modernisations, Baldwin felt, the essence of national life could still be found in 'the tinkle of hammer on anvil in the country smithy, the corncrake on a dewy morning . . . the last load of hay being drawn down a lane as the twilight comes on.' 'To me,' he declared, 'England is the country, and the country is England.' And while the vast majority of Britons now lived in towns and cities themselves, Baldwin's hymning of England's vanishing pastoral charms seemed to have an enormous popular appeal. A collection of his speeches, *On England*, sold over 30,000 copies when it was released in 1926, and went through multiple editions in the following years, with six reprints needed to meet public demand within the first 12 months of publication alone.[1]

In many ways, this prime-ministerial retreat into rural nostalgia was a response to new threats. The 1920s and 1930s were filled with some of the most dramatic cultural and political developments of twentieth-century British history. As a traumatised population struggled to come to terms with the devastating losses of the First World War, the economic boom of 1919–20 seemed to promise an exhilarating future of growth and prosperity – only to collapse in a decade of stagnation, high unemployment, and then the most severe financial crash the world had ever seen in 1929, followed by years of depression and economic instability. The extension of the vote to all men over 21 and most women over 30 in 1918, and then to all women over 21 in 1928, heralded a new era of mass democracy and liberation; yet social and economic unrest, which culminated in millions of workers bringing the country to a halt in the General Strike of 1926, caused many upper- and middle-class observers to worry over a future of class conflict and revolution from below. More than anything, the rise of Bolshevism and fascism in Europe, as dictatorial regimes took hold in Russia, Italy, Spain and Germany, led many to conclude that the period they were living in was one of extremism and anxiety. Baldwin, like many Britons during the 1920s and 1930s, was left bewildered and dismayed by the uneasy character of the times, and by the disorienting pace of change. Might the solution be to reassure people that, underneath it all, England remained the quiet, unchanging, idyllic place it had always been, and that all would be well if people could just keep hold of these 'eternal values from which we must never be separated'?[2]

'THIS NEW ENGLAND IS LACKING IN CHARACTER'

Yet, as his critics observed, Baldwin was 'living in a landscape no longer to be seen from any window.' Prime ministers who had served both before and after Baldwin's terms in office criticised his backwards-looking rhetoric: David Lloyd George (prime minister from 1916 to 1922) thought he would have been better served doing something about unemployment, rather than invoking happy images of the rural workers of yore; while Winston Churchill, agitating against appeasement in the 1930s, felt he should have done more to counter the threat posed by Hitler instead of merely praising English decency and moderation. (And Baldwin's vision *was* an emphatically English ideal, for a British prime minister, one that had little to say about the place of Scotland and Wales in his vision of the national inheritance – as Baldwin alluded to in a speech given at the

Royal Society of St George in 1924, confessing his 'profound thankfulness that I may use the word "England" without some fellow at the back of the room shouting out "Britain".') While anthologies of Baldwin's rustic speeches sold in their tens of thousands, plenty of people, too, found them condescending and nauseating, and were unconvinced by his pose as the plain-speaking, pig-farming 'typical Englishman'. Intellectuals and industrial workers alike accused him of retreating into an escapist fantasy version of England, which completely ignored the ways in which people were actually living.[3]

To the eyes of many observers, their society had changed almost beyond recognition in the opening decades of the twentieth century. The country, they argued, had been taken over by a new mass culture – much of it imported from America – in which younger generations in particular had little interest in British and English tradition, or in the customs of the rural past. For many, these innovations were to be embraced whole-heartedly: consumer society was offering an unprecedented array of new opportunities for pleasure-seeking. The suburbs that were expanding into the countryside, aided by new and faster public transport, were enabling millions of people to live in cleaner air and more spacious housing, combining urban opportunities with greener surroundings, where previously they had had no choice but to live in overcrowded and polluted industrial centres close to places of work. Rising disposable incomes and newly affordable consumer goods, and new media such as the cinema and the radio, were offering everyday entertainments to people of all ages, while changing attitudes were enabling young people – and young women in particular – to socialise more freely. Dance halls, nightclubs and cocktail bars sprang up to cater to this newly relaxed atmosphere, while for those who spent their evenings at home, printed matter was becoming almost unthinkably cheap thanks to advances in technology, with a swelling mass market for newspapers, magazines and paperbacks.

But to anxious intellectuals, this was making the culture cheap, too. Mass democracy, they feared, seemed to be heralding a new kind of society, characterised by empty-headed enjoyment and dull uniformity. Workers, complained the novelist D.H. Lawrence in 1926, 'have got a new kind of shallow consciousness, all newspaper and cinema.'[4] The interwar intelligentsia railed against what they saw as a kind of collective dumbing-down, sneering at people's taste for mass-produced entertainments and the 'machine-made values' they believed came with it. For the writer and social commentator J.B. Priestley, touring by motor coach past shops and picture-theatres and suburban villas in his state-of-the-nation travelogue, *English Journey* (1934), the view from his window 'only differ[ed] in a few minor details from a few thousand such roads in the United States, where the same tooth-pastes and soaps and gramophone records are being sold, the very same films are being shown.' According to Priestley, England was becoming a land of 'glass and concrete and chromium plate'; 'arterial by-pass roads, of filling stations and factories that look like exhibition buildings, of giant cinemas and dance-halls and cafes, cocktail bars, Woolworths, factory girls looking like actresses.' British women, in particular, seemed to be the harbingers of this new Americanised culture in Priestley's ambivalent analysis, as he counterposed make-up and movie-star worship to romanticised images of the masculine working-class culture he remembered from his childhood in Bradford – where at least the 'old factories' had 'solid lumps of character in them', making 'substantial' things instead of 'potato crisps, scent, tooth pastes [and] bathing costumes.' Much as he celebrated that England had become a 'cleaner, tidier, healthier' place than it had been in the nineteenth century, he could not help 'feeling that this new England is lacking in character' – and sometimes it didn't look like his mental image of Englishness at all.[5]

For all these anxieties, at the same time as people were enjoying an entertainment culture imported from America, much of this new and distinctively modern mass culture was devoting itself to recreating the look and feel of olde England. In the new commuter towns, developers plastered Tudor roses and half-timbering onto the fronts of suburban semis, presenting a modern face of Merry England to the working and middle classes. On the radio, listeners could tune into a series of BBC talks on the 'national character', where the historian Arthur Bryant extolled the virtues of the yeoman farmer, explaining that 'most of us to-day are town dwellers, yet there are very few of us whose great-great-great grandparents were not country folk, and, even if we have no idea who they were or from what shire they hailed, our subconscious selves hark back to their instincts and ways of life.' Equally popular were the stories of 'Our Bill', a characterful Cotswold gardener who gave talks on the charms of village life and the beauty of the natural landscape that were radio favourites throughout the 1930s.[6]

While this growing interest in the rural past reassured observers such as Priestley, other intellectuals mocked the public's taste for manufactured 'quaintness' and 'picturesque bits' of Englishness, which seemed to be becoming a mass obsession by the 1930s. The novelist Evelyn Waugh launched a tirade against clichés of the olden days, infuriated by people's fondness for faux-historical country pubs calling themselves things like 'Ye Olde inne and the Kynde Dragon and Ye Cheshire Cheese', as well as mass hankerings for 'folk dancing . . . Wessex-worship, village signs . . . Devonshire teas . . . [and] anything the least tainted with ye oldeness.'[7] Like their twenty-first-century counterparts, who would be criticised both for their aspirations to own the latest technologies, and their nostalgic fondness for austerity-chic posters and tea towels, the masses were being chastised for the ways in which their consumerism looked backwards as well as forwards.

HISTORY IS BUNK

After the trauma of the First World War, many Britons were left feeling betrayed by the patriotic 'lessons' of British history that had been instilled in them by Victorian and Edwardian empire-builders. The drum-and-trumpet histories of military heroes and imperial adventurers they had been encouraged to put their faith in seemed to have led to little more than devastation on an unprecedented scale. Amid rising anti-militarist sentiment, a host of novels and memoirs appeared in the decade or so after 1918 that took aim against the futility of war, the failures of Britain's leadership, and the deceits people had been sold through war propaganda. Robert Graves's outwardly anti-nostalgic autobiography, *Goodbye to All That* (1929), for instance, was written in the author's 'bitter leave-taking of England' – bidding farewell not only to England itself, but to the passing of an old order marred beyond repair by the cataclysm of war, which had so brutally exposed the utter inadequacy of patriotism. There was no 'patriotism in the trenches', he wrote, 'that was too remote a sentiment, and rejected as fit only for civilians.' After the incompetence, the farcical stupidity and 'bloody balls-ups' of military leaders that had led to the casual, incomprehensible slaughter of his fellow soldiers, the only response possible seemed to crack jokes from a place of visceral rage and pain.[8]

It was a tone that was often matched in history writing during the interwar years, as former soldiers and conscientious objectors alike parodied the militaristic nationalism that had thrilled the previous generation with patriotic pride. The archetypically modern business magnate Henry Ford's aphorism 'history is bunk' was felt to sum up the attitude of younger generations towards the past. W.C. Sellar and R.J. Yeatman's mercilessly flippant caricature of history schoolbooks, *1066 and All That* (1930), skewered the stock conventions of jingoistic history education. Military and imperial triumphs, so often portrayed as a benevolent mission to bring civilisation to the world, were now rewritten as Britain's 'self-sacrificing determination to become Top Nation', and the hypocrisy of imperialism was exposed with lines such as 'the Roman Conquest was, however a *Good Thing*, since Britons were only natives at that time.' Relentlessly, hysterically absurd, mock exam questions included 'What is a Plantagenet? Do you agree?', while readers were treated to accounts of the Pheasant's Revolt, the Spanish Armadillo, and discoverer of the laws of gravity Isaac Walton. But this was more than just silliness for its own sake. For those who, like Sellar and Yeatman, had fought in the trenches, it was sending up a mentality that had led them into battle on the promise of glory – a way, perhaps, of anaesthetising pain with laughter, coming to terms with the trauma of war by making a decisive break with the past.[9]

This new spirit of irony and detachment was not just a product of war-weariness and disillusionment: it was part of a revolt against the whole culture of Victorianism, with its earnestness, its moral rectitude, its public repressiveness and private double standards. While some who remembered life in the nineteenth century might look back fondly on a heyday of peace and security, members of the bohemian-intellectual Bloomsbury Group, who ranged from writer and artist siblings Virginia Woolf and Vanessa Bell to the economist John Maynard Keynes, were launching an all-out assault against the bourgeois conventions of Victorian respectability. The critic Roger Fry, appalled by his more nostalgically inclined contemporaries' fondness for Victorian times – an era that could seem in hindsight so much more comfortable and stable compared to the uncertain present – lambasted in 1919 'the incurable optimism of memory' that built an 'earthly paradise out of the boredoms, the snobberies, the cruel repressions, [and] mean calculations' of the nineteenth century. The standard for interwar irreverence had been set by Bloomsbury writer Lytton Strachey, whose *Eminent Victorians* (1918) lampooned Victorian worthies with its biographical sketches of Cardinal Manning, Florence Nightingale, Thomas Arnold and General Gordon. Even before the war, Strachey was writing to Virginia Woolf that their Victorian predecessors 'seem to me a set of mouth bungled hypocrites.' But war had given his project a new urgency. A conscientious objector, Strachey was coming to the conclusion that the Victorian era's leading lights had not just been hypocrites, but had bequeathed a 'profoundly evil' legacy to his generation in seeking 'to settle international disputes by force.'[10]

Used to flattering and reverential biographical conventions, when *Eminent Victorians* appeared, many readers were shocked by its satirical and mocking tone. The educator Thomas Arnold was portrayed as an interminable moraliser, whose 'pompousness in the style of his letters home' even as a schoolboy had suggested to his relatives 'the possibility that young Thomas might grow up into a prig.' Florence Nightingale's achievements were undoubtedly admirable, but Strachey wrote that she was close to intolerable on a personal level, driven by a zeal for sanitation that amounted almost to demonic possession; while the archetypical imperial warrior General Gordon, 'though a hero', was 'a little off his head.' Writing of the national outcry after the General's apparent execution in the Sudan, which had led to public calls to 'avenge Gordon', Strachey noted with acid disdain that it 'all ended very happily – in a glorious slaughter of 20,000 Arabs.' The book was an instant commercial success, launching Strachey to both fame and notoriety almost overnight. To older readers, looking back nostalgically on the Victorian era and venerating its 'Titans', this was little more than character assassination; but to younger generations, who had borne the brunt of a militaristic culture that had culminated in the pity of war, it was an exhilarating exposure of some overdue truths. Strachey's biography spawned a mini-industry of irreverent histories, mocking character portraits and drum-and-trumpet parodies. The word 'debunk' itself was coined in the 1920s to describe this new attitude to uncovering the past. As one critic reflected in 1932 of the impact that *Eminent Victorians* had in the years following the end of the war, Strachey's achievement had been to 'take down once and for all the pretensions of the Victorian age to moral superiority.' But it wasn't just the Victorian era that had been taken down – it was a whole attitude towards British history as a roll call of battles, victories, glorious deeds and inspirational stories, and the ways in which historical figures had been put on pedestals for the edification of future generations. Since the book had appeared, he felt, no one had 'been able to feel quite the same about the legends that had dominated their pasts. Something had been punctured for good.'[11]

While many Britons were losing interest in traditional political and military histories, a new kind of history was booming in the interwar years. People's attention was turning to 'everyday life', and the ways in which ordinary men and women had lived and worked in times gone by. Popular historians, educators and local museums were seeking to shape a new understanding of national identity, one rooted in folk culture and customs, that celebrated people not for their heroism but for their very ordinariness. The husband-and-wife historians Charles and Marjorie Quennell 'toured all over England in the weekends' and on 'motoring' holidays in the countryside, picking up information about vanishing ways of life; items such as hand tools and clothing patterns borrowed from collectors; and on one occasion an old plough they had salvaged on a trip to Norfolk. Their series of four books on *A History of Everyday Things in England,* published between 1918 and 1934, became interwar bestsellers – richly illustrated volumes aimed at schoolchildren that illuminated old costumes, handcrafts and vernacular traditions. Meanwhile, historian couple John and Barbara Hammond issued widely read books such as *The Village Labourer* (1911) and *The Town Labourer* (1917) that were reprinted throughout the following decades, which focused on modes of work that had been swept away by the Industrial Revolution.

As an introduction to a new edition of *A History of Everyday Things* in 1937 argued, 'dates of kings and queens, the principal events of their reigns, and copious attention to battles, murder and sudden death – these formed the material of much school history down to a generation ago . . . distorted in outline, it furnished a sorry equipment of historical knowledge for the British citizen.' But for the historians of everyday life, children could learn far more about how people in the past actually lived by learning about the things they made. Moreover, it might help them to reflect on what they wanted to do with their *own* lives. 'We hope our book may help boys and girls to come to a proper decision as to what "job of work" they will take up later on,' the Quennells explained: 'the future belongs to the boys and girls of to-day, and they must alter things, improve them, and think of things other than money.' In contrast to how 'dull and dreary' and 'miserable the grown-ups look' while going about their business in the twentieth century, they encouraged their youthful readers to imagine the ways in which 'in the old days the craftsman enjoyed his job, or he would not have taken so much trouble to make quite ordinary things beautiful.'[12] As the historian Laura Carter has argued, it was the beginning of a turn away from celebrations of rulers, wars and military heroes and towards social history in schools that would, by the 1980s and ever since, see Conservative education ministers and newspaper columnists railing against the 'trashing' of 'our island story'.[13]

Local folk museums, too, tapped into a growing appetite for learning about vanishing industries and customs that had once given places their distinctive character. In Northampton, for instance, a centre of the shoemaking industry, the local museum reconstructed a traditional cobbler's shop, inviting visitors both to reflect on the origins of their community's identity – a trade that connected them with people who had lived there long ago – and to see how differently people had worked in a time before machines and factories. This was a nostalgia for bygone ways of life that was allied to a socially progressive agenda:

educating a mass public, for the first time, in the forces that had transformed their communities across the generations, and connecting them to a story of change. As one elderly visitor told the founder of the pioneering Highland Folk Museum, Isabel Grant – who had gathered together a vast array of items, from farming implements, tools and furniture to musical instruments, textiles, jewellery and photographs, as well as an open-air exhibit including a replica Inverness-shire cottage and live demonstrations of Highland crafts – she was 'helping people to feel their roots.'[14]

IN SEARCH OF ENGLAND

Charles and Marjorie Quennell, motoring about the countryside in search of the reality of British life in the past, were not the only ones on the move; the interwar period saw people across the social spectrum journeying around the country in unprecedented numbers. There were over a million cars on the road by the 1930s, a tenfold increase since the 1910s, while millions more people were accessing nearby countryside on trains, buses and motor coaches.[15] The period has often been described as one of the 'discovery' of the countryside, in which newly disposable incomes enabled town-dwellers to indulge as never before in their nostalgia for nature and quaint rural villages, aided by enormously popular handbooks such as the *Shell Guides* (compiled under the editorship of the poet laureate of suburban nostalgia, John Betjeman) as they set out in search of 'authentic' country experiences.

Writers and artists, too, were venturing in search of the 'real' England – looking for it, invariably, in rural locations. As the historian Alexandra Harris writes, by the 1930s 'it looked to many observers as if a whole concerted project of national self-discovery was underway.' Novelists and poets such as Virginia Woolf and T.S. Eliot, who had pioneered new experimental forms of writing, were now exploring themes of English history and village life. In an age in which avant-garde writers and artists were seeking new ways of exploring modern consciousness, depicting the swirling energy of cosmopolitan cities and engaging with cutting-edge industrial technologies, painters such as Paul Nash and John Piper were felt by their contemporaries to have 'betrayed the modern movement' in their turn towards rural landscapes. Anthologists collected pastoral poems and romantic writing in paperback volumes aimed at a mass readership, while guidebooks and travelogues with titles like *In Search of England* (1927) or *This Unknown Island* (1932) conjured nostalgic evocations of olde England, setting their authors up as discoverers of an unfamiliar land; inspiring tourists, in turn, to set out in pursuit of 'undiscovered' beauty spots, forgotten corners, and the 'lost secrets' of country life.[16]

Adding to the ranks of tourists voyaging in search of olde England, however, were many visitors who were enjoying the countryside in ways that had little to do with nostalgia. Historically, England's urban workers had taken their holidays by the sea, decamping en masse to seaside resorts that by the twentieth century were becoming crowded to bursting point on summer weekends. As policymakers and travel companies began to argue for the promotion of inland holidays, fashions for rambling, hiking, camping and youth hostelling caught on.[17] And as motor tourism became more and more popular, new restaurants, tea shops and roadhouses began to spring up to cater to urban visitors, advertising their delights with neon signs and roadside billboards; as did distinctly un-traditionalist bungalows and holiday shacks for those looking to establish a rural bolthole of their own.

To those who saw themselves as the custodians of rural life and tradition, the new-found popularity of rural leisure was deeply worrying. As far as England's social and intellectual elites were concerned, the urban masses had become a kind of invading horde, desecrating once-peaceful landscapes with litter and bad manners, and they set themselves up as defenders of the 'true' (by which they meant empty and 'untouched') countryside. The writer and broadcaster Cyril Joad – supposedly the 'Rambler's Friend' – complained of

> hordes of hikers cackling insanely in the woods, or singing raucous songs as they walk arm in arm ... people, wherever there is water ... grilling themselves, for all the world, as if they were steaks in the sun. There are tents in meadows and girls in pyjamas dancing beside them to the strains of the gramophone ... fat girls in shorts, youths in gaudy ties and plus-fours.[18]

If young people enjoying themselves was appalling enough, families were little better. With pained contempt, Joad described cars pulling up at picnic spots and seaside car parks to 'decant their contents of whining children, nagging mothers and bored fathers. The children play, the mothers sit and knit, and litter the beach with the debris of meals, and the father reads the paper on the rocks.' This in contrast to 'proper' country people, who knew that appropriate pastimes were hunting, riding and shooting, and whose only litter was cartridge cases and dead animals. According to Joad, 'the townsman let loose upon the country' was nothing short of a 'liability' and a 'blight'. *Country Life* magazine wrote similarly in 1936 that the 'townsmen seem to have the mentality of serfs. They act as uneducated slaves might be expected to act when suddenly liberated. They have no sense of responsibility towards the countryside.' In the face of what they saw as an invasion by the masses, rural social elites were presenting themselves as the guardians of natural beauty, casting nostalgic appeals to an older view of the countryside as their own privileged preserve as impartial environmentalism. More and more, it was being argued that – in the words of one local newspaper in 1933 – 'the only way to save the countryside for democracy is to keep democracy out of the countryside.'[19]

Even when not littering, there was a distinct distaste among the well-off and gentry classes for the populist urban culture that was spreading into the countryside in the tourists' wake. By the end of the 'roaring' 1920s, journalists were complaining that the car had made it possible 'for this generation to carry its villainous bad taste into every village', or of 'flashy couples who roar along the roads in supercharged sports models.'[20] Pausing for refreshment, they called at village inns that had been modernised to cater to this new audience, decked out 'to look like a night club with pink lampshades on the dining tables, [and] a constant racket of wireless and gramophone' – now filled, not with hearty locals nursing their ales, but smart young people drinking gin and tonic. The naturalist R.M. Lockley worried that these notions might be catching, insisting that 'the saucy nose-in-air mademoiselle of the city should not be allowed to give our unpainted local lasses an unjustifiable inferiority complex.' The implication was that a taste for urban pleasures risked unsettling simple country folk from their proper role of deference and modesty.[21] Writers were often conspicuously silent on the pervasiveness of rural poverty in the traditional villages and communities they romanticised, having little to say about the benefits that modernisations such as electricity were bringing. Their nostalgia was for a time when there had been not just clear boundaries between country and city, but clearly defined boundaries between social classes.

The city was encroaching on the countryside in ways that were far more permanent than passing motorists and holiday-makers. Four million houses were built between 1919 and 1939, the majority of them in the newly expanding suburbs that, in the space of a decade, could see once-isolated rural villages absorbed in the path of commuter belts, or joined into conurbations by ribbon development. Trees and hedgerows were cut down to clear the way for road widening, pylons and power lines were erected across fields, while an ever-increasing number of petrol stations, garages, road signs and advertising hoardings extended still further into the countryside, as if portents of oncoming development.

While post-war critics of urban sprawl such as Ian Nairn would predict in the 1950s that Britain would soon consist of 'isolated oases' of countryside squeezed out by 'concrete roads, cosy plots and bungalows,' this was in many ways the vision of Britain that interwar critics felt characterised the landscape of the 1920s and 1930s. Books appeared with titles such as *England and the Octopus* (1928) and *Britain and the Beast* (1938), in outcry against the relentless destruction of natural beauty. 'And still the destruction spreads like a prairie fire,' lamented the broadcaster Howard Marshall with apocalyptic warning: 'a gimcrack civilisation crawls like a gigantic slug across the country, leaving a foul trail of slime behind it.' One complainant to the *Daily Mirror* described the confusion of unregulated, low-cost jerry-building in Nottinghamshire, as people set up holiday homes and makeshift residences in the absence of planning controls: 'vans and sheds, dotted here and there, with no uniformity of spacing or design, with their accompanying wooden or corrugated iron outhouses, verandahs and extensions, which presents an appalling spectacle to anyone who sees beauty in rural scenery.' But even carefully planned developments that attempted to incorporate the look of village architecture were despised just as much as jerry-building. For one contributor to *Britain and the Beast*, the town planner Thomas Sharp, the 'new romantic villas and bungalows with their pebble-dash, their half-timbered gables, their "picturesque" lead lighted windows', so often favoured by urbanites who decamped to suburbia, 'were certainly in striking contrast to the terrace houses of their old congested quarters, but the contrast is merely between one kind of barbarism and another.'[22]

Amid this crisis atmosphere, a range of campaigns were launched to save what was left of Britain's countryside. New bodies such as the Council for Preservation of Rural England (CPRE), founded in 1926, joined the National Trust in aiming to protect the nation's rural heritage, while ideas were floated for green belts and stricter planning controls.[23] And yet there was a distinctly classed element, too, to these conservation efforts. In their drive to protect unspoilt countryside from the influx of the urban masses, the conservation movement was, in many ways, a class resistance, defending a vision of the countryside as a space for the privileged few. There was a real sense of anxiety among landowners and gentry that the traditional social structure of the shires was being irreparably weakened: a social world that had been regulated by the authority of country squires and parish churches, with clear boundaries between classes in which each had their part to play in keeping the system going – 'the rich man in his castle, the poor man at his gate', as the staple Victorian hymn 'All Things Bright and Beautiful' had it. It was a process that was being hastened by dramatic economic change. In the decade after 1918, a quarter of England's agricultural land changed ownership; between 1918 and 1920 alone, almost 8 million acres were sold, making it the largest-scale transfer of land since the dissolution of the monasteries. Its causes lay in a combination of agricultural depression, and the imposition of new and severe inheritance taxes, yet to many it seemed as if the First World War had wiped out a whole way of life, sounding the death knell of a centuries-old aristocratic order.[24]

Aristocrats and intellectuals railed against the urban masses and the claims they were laying to share in the privileges of rural England as they dispersed into suburbia, yet less remarked upon was the role of landowners in selling their acres to suburban developers. But where else were people supposed to go? As Thomas Sharp alluded to, people were spreading out into the suburbs because so much of their housing in cities was inadequate and overcrowded. Writers were intensely alert to the problems of housing in urban centres – indeed, books on English voyages into the countryside were matched by the impact of journeys such as George Orwell's *The Road to Wigan Pier* (1937), which unsparingly catalogued the miseries of urban poverty. But the social consciences of intellectual observers were markedly detached from an enthusiasm for feasible alternatives. For

the novelist E.M. Forster, reflecting upon Britain's housing crisis in the 1940s – something that had preoccupied him since his
uneasy description of the 'red rust' of suburbia creeping over
the horizon of Howards End in 1910 – 'people must have
houses. They must.' And yet with each new housing development, he could not free himself 'from the conviction that
something irreplaceable has been destroyed, and that a little
piece of England has died.' 'I cannot equate the problem,' he
concluded: 'it is a collision of loyalties.'[25]

Throughout the interwar years, a range of influential novelists generated gloomy state-of-the-nation diagnoses about what
was becoming of England. 'Doesn't it make you puke sometimes to see what they're doing to England, with their bird-baths
and their plaster gnomes, and their pixies and tin cans, where
the beechwoods used to be?' cries the protagonist of George
Orwell's novel of nostalgia, *Coming Up for Air* (1939), when
he revisits what was once the rural idyll of his childhood before
the First World War. 'And the newness of everything! The raw,
mean look! Do you know the look of these new towns that
have suddenly swelled up like balloons in the last few years,
Hayes, Slough, Dagenham, and so forth? The kind of chilliness,
the bright red brick everywhere.' While modernisation was in
many ways to be welcomed for the improvements it was bringing to people's lives, he could not help mourning that things
had simply been better before, in the happiness of the rural
past. D.H. Lawrence, having grown up in the mining communities of Nottinghamshire, had seen first-hand that the 'old things'
of rural poverty were part of the problem, knowing well that
'new things' were needed to improve the lives of workers. And
yet he, too, was visited by the uneasy sense that this new England which was replacing the old social structure of rural life
was hardly an improvement, writing of the world of the country house in *Lady Chatterley's Lover* (1928) that 'this is history.
One England blots out another. The mines had made the halls
wealthy. Now they were blotting them out ... The industrial

England blots out the agricultural England . . . And the continuity is not organic, but mechanical.'[26]

For Lawrence, it was not just the beauty of the countryside that was being lost, but a whole way of living and feeling that was rooted in the natural landscape. From a very different social perspective, Evelyn Waugh, too, looked upon the decline of country house and the rural social structure it represented, as aristocratic owners were forced to sell their estates or parcelled up land to developers, or else as new money took over dilapidated country piles. Over the course of the interwar period, Waugh turned from the biting satire of his early novels – in which, for instance, the appalling Margot Beste-Chetwynde in *Decline and Fall* (1928) tears down the 'awful' 'timbered Tudor architecture' of her Elizabethan country seat, in favour of a hysterically modern creation of Bauhaus 'ferro-concrete and aluminium' – to the aristocratic nostalgia that would culminate in *Brideshead Revisited* (1945). But as Orwell noted, these country retreats were something that only the privileged could enjoy. 'To live in the past is very expensive,' reflects his conflicted traditionalist in *Coming Up for Air*, as he weighs the temptations as well as follies of withdrawing from the modern world: 'you can't do it on less than two thousand a year.'[27] These were writers from different social backgrounds and with substantially different politics, yet all three set themselves up as chroniclers of the sorrow of a dying world, as well as the insufficiency of the world that was replacing it. In many ways, England and its landscape were changing too fast to know entirely how to feel about it, or what a better solution would be.

While those who argued for the preservation of the countryside reached wide audiences through popular books and essays that hymned Britain's natural beauty, or else in radio broadcasts about rural life and tradition, they had little political impact before the Second World War. The public, it seemed, had a boundless appetite for learning about natural landscapes and rural tradition, consuming nostalgic literature as a form of entertainment – but they had little interest in putting the brakes on the modern world, and still less a desire to actually return to older ways of living. In government, most politicians and civil servants regarded the preservationist lobby as a bunch of dreamers, cranks and snobs: the Town and Country Planning Committee reminded them tartly in 1937, for instance, that

> It is necessary to remember that the countryside is not the pre-serve of the wealthy and leisured classes. The country rightly prides itself on the fact that since the War there has been an unparalleled building development, a development which every Government has done its utmost to stimulate, and whose effect has been to create new and better social conditions for a very large number of persons.[28]

Preservationist bodies were well aware that the times were against them, and that their best efforts would be to mitigate rather than attempt to halt rural development. As the CPRE acknowledged in their Oxfordshire bulletin, 'any attempt to curb the development of the countryside' was 'doomed to futil-ity'; explaining to their readers that they would be pursuing the more modest aim of ensuring 'that development should be undertaken with due regard to local amenities.' Yet even so, public opinion was frequently hostile or unsympathetic to their cause. 'If the CPRE has its way,' thundered one letter writer to a local newspaper in the 1930s, 'the only thing people would be allowed to do with regard to enjoying the beauty of the scenery would be to look at it.' Or as another critic had it, writing in the *Brighton and Hove Herald* of social elites who sought to keep the South Downs as their own pristine retreat: 'ought we to preserve the Downs for the privileged few who enjoy the Downs because they have them to themselves?'[29]

And even the outright successes of preservationist campaign-ers seemed to confirm their powerlessness in the face of modern consumer capitalism. When the Town and Country Planning Act of 1932 restricted the spreading of advertisements and business signs in rural locations, companies throughout Britain were forced to remove many of their signs – including Shell oil, who took down some 18,000 advertisements; thereafter advertising this contribution to natural beauty as a measure of its environmental awareness.[30] Indeed, Shell became one of the foremost popularisers of the 'discovery' of the countryside, inviting its customers to 'see Britain first on Shell'. Launched in 1934, the *Shell Guides* to the counties of Britain, aimed at the new breed of motor tourist, recruited artistic and literary talents from John Betjeman to John Piper and John and Paul Nash to illuminate the ordinary as well as extraordinary delights of local areas (though, its critics said, it was the number of cars on the roads that was marring these delights in the first place). Advertising posters enlisted the leading artists of the day, such as Graham Sutherland and Vanessa Bell, to depict bucolic villages and market towns, historic landmarks, churches, castles and picturesque landscapes that could be reached by car. Yet while this was an advertising strategy that drew on people's nostalgia for rustic charms and pastoral scenery, it was also a distinctively forward-looking vision, conveying the look and feel of Britain through modern artistic styles. 'This is the nearest we have yet come in the modern world to popular art,' remarked the art critic Clive Bell, feeling it marked a refreshing change from tiresome clichés of 'old-world pageants' and 'dancing around the maypole' that saturated the prevailing popular image of the British countryside.[31]

Other companies were opting for full-throttle nostalgia in their appeals to urban consumers. While social commentators were lamenting English landscapes and ways of living that had been swept away by modern economic forces, modern enterprises were claiming to their consumers that they had bottled English history and tradition. Worthington beer ran a series of advertisements entitled 'This England' in magazines and newspapers throughout the late 1930s, declaring that 'the men of the cities ... yearn for the things of the country ... old turf, quiet

ALFRISTON

SEE BRITAIN FIRST ON SHELL

Vanessa Bell, *Alfriston*, 1931.

valleys and abiding peace.' Luckily for them, by cracking open a cold one at the end of the day, urban workers could dream themselves into a rural idyll of serenity and 'honest kindly things'. 'Worthington,' the manufacturers proclaimed, was 'brewed in the age-long English tradition, redolent of the countryside, friendly and shining clear as the English character itself.'[32]

YOUR BRITAIN – FIGHT FOR IT NOW!

Images of rural England had a huge appeal for soldiers fighting in the First World War. While government propaganda campaigns were slow to recognise this – issuing recruitment posters featuring bands of undaunted soldiers, or else a sternly pointing Lord Kitchener evoking memories of Victorian military glory – unofficial efforts recognised the potential for pastoral art and literature to act as morale boosters, and the emotional pull of

the countryside for soldiers and civilians alike. Editors such as
Ernest Rhys of Everyman's Library put together anthologies of
pastoral verse and classic literature to be distributed to
soldiers – as Rhys explained in the foreword to *The Old Country: a book of love and praise of England* (1917), 'as a reminder'
for those 'who were bound to be visited by home-thoughts.'[33]
War poets such as Siegfried Sassoon, Rupert Brooke, Edward
Thomas and Edmund Blunden contrasted the horror of the
trenches with images of pastoral bliss and ease, evoking the
countryside as a longed-for dream of peace, or else a stirring
symbol of patriotic pride. Organisations such as the YMCA
distributed posters of English landscape paintings to huts and
communal military spaces on the Continent, while Frank Pick,
who was usually to be found directing the graphic design of the
London Underground, commissioned artists to create nostalgic
images that would 'awaken thoughts of pleasant homely things'
in the minds of those fighting abroad.

Patriotism and nostalgia blended to create a very selective
image of 'home': one centred, above all, on the rural past.
Escapism was often explicit: as Arthur Yapp of the YMCA
felt of the average soldier in France, 'in imagination, he can
see his village home' – soldiers who, more often than not,
had their homes in industrial towns and cities. The 1911 census had classified 78 per cent of the population of England
and Wales as living in urban areas; yet it seemed that soldiers
themselves were just as moved by these villages of the imagination, and deeply identified with sentimental portraits of the
ideal they were fighting for. Periodicals like *Country Life*
were surprisingly popular in the trenches, meeting an appetite for images of idealised, happy ruralism that were about
as far away as one could get from the carnage, the mud of
the battlefield, and the mechanised destruction of modern
warfare.[34]

This role of the arts in rallying a people at war around images
of a green and pleasant land had come as something of a surprise.

At the outbreak of hostilities in 1914, the art world seemed to many to have been overtaken by modernist fashions for abstract styles such as cubism and futurism that had little, if anything, to do with ordinary people's lives. (While artists, in turn, had seemed to be increasingly exasperated with what they regarded as the philistinism of popular tastes – people's preferences for sentimental or pretty subject matter, their old-fashionedness and insistence that artistic skill lay in making things that looked lifelike.) To spend time on such inessential activities as painting and drawing while men were dying on the battlefield appeared to many to be 'fiddling while Rome burns'. Yet within a year of conflict, the arts themselves seemed to be mobilising, as artists, galleries and institutions began to rethink their social purpose, realising that they, too, had a role to play in a war of hearts and minds. Artists began to give up their peacetime careers, reconceiving their work as the embodiment of national identity, and rallying soldiers and the home front alike around unifying symbols of past and future peace. The 'peace picture' became a flourishing genre of nostalgic landscape painting, such as Benjamin William Leader's (now lost) landscape, simply titled *Peace*, which set a bucolic family picnic in a cornfield on a summer's day. At home, people purchased affordable prints and reproductions of peace pictures in their thousands; as one critic reflected, out of a yearning for 'a time of peace that felt so far distant in the past', that might momentarily transport them back to the 'happiness' of 'the days before the war', and to a contentment they had perhaps 'never enjoyed as it deserved' at the time.[35]

Yet if these images conjured the bittersweet draw of a pre-war world, they also suggested the hopeful prospect that this contentment might be restored. George Clausen's pastoral reverie, *A Wish*, which was distributed to soldiers by the YMCA, depicted a highly similar scene to Leader's, with a mother and child seated beneath a tree on a summer's day, before the thatched cottages and Norman church of an idyllic rural village. But while peace pictures consumed at home appealed to civilian memories of the past, *A Wish* was aimed at soldiers who were dreaming of a future back home. The mother and child, after all, were without a man. As the art historian James Fox writes, this was not so much an image of the past for soldiers abroad as a vision of the present, an 'idealised symbol of the nation as a whole' that they were fighting for, and to which they one day hoped to return. For one reviewer in the right-wing *Morning Post*, writing in April 1918, these very pictures of peace, paradoxically, 'suggest[ed] war. For are our soldiers not fighting that all the people of these islands may enjoy as freemen the tranquillity, the charm, and the romance' of these scenes that were 'so skilfully and feelingly represented?' This was pastoral art as military propaganda: as the reviewer recommended, 'the Minister of

George Clausen, *A Wish*, 1916.

Information's attention should be drawn to such pictures, which would far better serve propaganda purposes ... than misrepresentations of our heroic soldiers and of battle scenes on the Western Front.'[36]

At the same time, there is an otherworldly quality to these images of unbroken tranquillity, that was detached from the realities of past, present and future alike. Both explicitly and implicitly, the arts returned to a moment that was at once time-less and frozen in time: these images of pastoral England were often, very particularly, of early summer 1914. Leader, for example, added an inscription to his painting that, (mis)quot-ing a William Morris poem, read: 'Yellow the cornfields lay although as yet / Unto the stucks no sickle had been set.' Fox explains of this literary hint that 'the metaphor was clear: the picture did not just represent any peaceful scene; it recreated a precise historical moment that preceded the August harvest, as well as its tragic equivalent – the human harvest of the August war.'[37] Again and again, artists and writers set these enduring visions of the countryside on the very eve of war, a moment as well as an entire epoch that was eclipsed forever by the out-break of conflict. Edward Thomas's poem 'Adlestrop' (1917), too, conveyed a fleeting glimpse of the stillness of the English countryside, glimpsed from a train window as it pulled into a station in 'late June' 1914, before the author was sped away to a very different future. (As Philip Larkin would later put it in 'MCMXIV' (1964), of the way in which we look back upon an unsuspecting time, 'Never such innocence again.') It was as if there was a double emotional resonance to this nostalgia for a pre-war dream that was yearned for so intensely, and yet had never really existed – as we will see in chapter four, this vision of pastoral innocence is not how England had appeared to observ-ers in the years before 1914. People were nostalgic, really, for a time when they had themselves been nostalgic, when they had looked back on a still earlier rose-tinted past, unaware of the cataclysm over the horizon. Yet war had shattered this illusion so unsparingly that it transformed into a deeper yearning – a desire to return to how things had been, only this time to return with the benefit of hindsight, appreciating just how good they had had it.

Unsurprisingly, nostalgia was a recurring theme in soldiers' letters to loved ones back home. By 1917, the British army on the Western Front was dispatching 8,150,000 letters and over a million parcels a week. Lines of communication to families, friends, wives and sweethearts were a crucial front in sustaining soldiers' morale, in which the longing for home – both the comforting past, and the future promise of return – provided an emotional defence against the trauma of war. Nostalgia, too, could be a way of conveying the dreadful present to those at home. One soldier, Eric Chapman, wrote to his mother from the Somme in August 1916:

> All this area is one vast cemetery. Dead bodies taint the air wherever you go. It has robbed thousands and thousands of men of life, and thousands more of the things that made life seem worth living. I have come to look upon peace and quiet and home life as the Summum bonum [highest good]. I feel now that all I want is to be able to live quietly, and tend a garden, and study a bit.[38]

For another soldier, Matt Webb, his longing for home was articulated through dreaming of his parents' garden. 'I expect the garden is looking lovely again,' he wrote to his mother in 1915: 'when I think of what it was last summer + compare it with this war stricken + devastated country . . . it seems to me to be a little paradise in itself.' Throughout the war, young men promised to their loved ones that they would never again take for granted the goodness of their domestic lives, and were determined to return home with a true appreciation for their everyday pleasures, which after the privations of war would be enjoyed free from discontent or anxiety. 'I look forward very much to next summer when the war will end and everything and every one will begin to look fresh + happy again,' Frank

Merivale wrote to his mother and sister-in-law in December 1917,

> having been uncomfortable + miserable long enough to realize what comfort + happiness mean we shall really begin to enjoy life. We will have learnt how to enjoy just sitting in an armchair before a warm fire with all whom we care for either sitting beside us or not far away, our minds free from all fears of casualties for ourselves or others. Cheer up Mummy dear + buck up Blanche its bound to end some day.[39]

And yet the same nostalgic thoughts that offered comfort amid the horrors of war could also be a source of acute pain. As a tunneller, Jack Hickson, wrote, he longed to be returned to his wife and daughter; to a warm bed and a 'bright fire at home', but it was 'no use longing for impossibilities'. 'To dwell too much on home,' he felt, 'would drive one mad.' The longing for home, too, had to be counterbalanced by a recognition that he might not live to return. Appointing his wife as executor, and telling her that he hoped she would one day remarry if he were to die, Hickson wrote: 'I sincerely hope I shall be safely restored to you', but to pretend this was certain would be 'a fool's paradise'. The historian Michael Roper notes that soldiers and medical officials alike could be exasperated with the inadequacy of advice to remain calm and think of home. The psychiatrist W.H.R. Rivers, reporting to the War Office during an enquiry into shell shock, emphasised that when men had seen 'friends at their side with their heads blown off and things of that sort', it was no use telling them to 'put it out of mind, old fellow ... imagine that you are in your garden at home.'[40] While nostalgia could be a crucial coping mechanism, there were real limits to how much it could achieve in the face of severe trauma, injury and death.

With the return to peace in 1918, pastoral images conveyed an immense hope for rebirth and renewal. Laura Knight's painting *Spring*, for instance, completed between 1916 and 1920, visualised a new dawn of peace and optimism: a return to nature complete with apple blossom, birds, and lambs frolicking under storm clouds giving way to sunshine and rainbow – one of many artworks that symbolised the end of war as the happy changing of the seasons. As Knight described, images such as these were Nepenthe to a war-damaged people – a medicine to erase bad memories.[41] Yet traumatic memories frequently disrupted these idealised, hopeful visions. For war poets returning to civilian life, traumatic memories of war could shatter the idylls that had been longed for so intensely in the trenches. The narrator of Edmund Blunden's poem '1916 seen from 1921' sat in solitude in the English countryside, amid birdsong and flowers, but was drawn back compulsively to memories of battle, 'while life drags / Its wounded length from those sad streets of war / Into green places here, that were my own; / But now what once was mine is mine no more.' In Siegfried Sassoon's fictionalised autobiography, too, memories of the pre-war countryside had an intensely painful appeal in the wake of war: 'I cannot think of it now without a sense of heartache,' he wrote, 'as if it contained something which I have never quite been able to discover.'[42] For many, in the years after 1918, hope was giving way to disillusionment. Soldiers – who had so often idealised their gardens and firesides during the war, promising that they would never again fail to appreciate the privileges of peace – returned home to soaring unemployment, in which many felt deeply betrayed by a ruling elite that had conscripted them into conflict, but which now seemed content to return to a world of widespread poverty and inequality. After the trauma of combat, the sheer strangeness of what had once been familiar could be deeply unsettling. Civilians, in turn, could be fearful of the potential for violence among men who had returned home traumatised.[43] And the failure of the peace settlement, as Europe slid into political instability and chaos in the decades following the end of war, seemed to pose the awful question: what had it all been for?

As the Second World War approached, it seemed to many as if the nightmares of the past were returning to haunt the present with a vengeance. Siegfried Sassoon, like millions of others, despaired at the onset of what he called the 'Second Great War', lamenting 'all I want to do is forget – and forget.' In the face of this uncanny doubling of horror, he felt he was 'being reduced to an impotent absurdity.' When Neville Chamberlain declared war in September 1939, Sassoon recorded in his diary: 'it all makes me wish that the July 1918 bullet had finished me. I can do nothing now except endure this nightmare.' Sassoon had spent the interwar decades retreating into a nostalgic vision of rural England before the First World War, 'a world that seems now half Elysian with peace', drawn by the fantasy of 'giv[ing] the modern world the slip'. This was nostalgia as a curative response to trauma, reaching back into the remembered – or imagined – wholeness of a past that predated the losses of war. His retreat was secured by the purchase of a Georgian mansion in the Wiltshire countryside, from which he penned essays calling for the preservation of rural England; pastoral poetry and prose; and occasional reviews for the *Spectator* in the persona of 'Aunt Eudora' – a woman who was unashamedly Victorian in her tastes, with whom he poked light-hearted fun at the latest experiments of a younger generation of poets.[44]

Despite his desire to retreat and forget, at the outbreak of war in 1939 Sassoon found his impulse to withdraw chafing against a renewed sense of patriotism, returning to the national pride that had motivated him to volunteer as a soldier in 1914. His love for England, and especially for its countryside, was beginning to convince him that the war was both necessary and right; compelling him to revive his earlier identity as war poet with stirring appeals to the 'The English Spirit' (1940), in which 'The ghosts of those who have wrought our English Past / Stand near us now', as the nation braved the 'crusade of Teuton tanks'. Even Sassoon worried afterwards that he had 'overdone' it, with this 'grand style'; but this kind of transcendental emotional response to England's history was common, as the country geared towards the Second World War. Winston Churchill wrote of his conviction in similar terms, reflecting upon sitting in the House of Commons on the day Britain declared war on Germany that 'as I sat in my place, listening to the speeches, a very strong sense of calm came over me . . . I felt a serenity of mind and was conscious of a kind of uplifted detachment from human and personal affairs. The glory of Old England . . . thrilled my being.'[45]

But this was a much less bellicose appeal to British and English identity than had predominated during the First World War. Where First World War recruitment posters issued by the government had tended to depict heroic scenes of battle on the Western Front, or else rousing portraits of Saint George slaying a dragon – which had prompted astute observers to argue that leaders should be evoking the more bucolic imagery of 'peace pictures' instead – Second World War propaganda posters appealed to precisely this rural vision. Posters declared 'Your Britain – Fight for it Now' under scenes such as a rural village green, the rolling fields of the South Downs, and Salisbury Cathedral framed by trees. This was of course a very selective image of Britain; idyllic pictures of the nation that were felt to have a much more powerful draw than the urban and suburban landscapes in which the large majority of soldiers actually lived. Images of the English landscape such as the White Cliffs of Dover, too, became powerful symbols of national identity in popular consciousness, which served both on the home front as morale boosters, and as a promised return to soldiers fighting abroad. And while people were nominally encouraged to fight for Britain, Englishness was the dominant idiom in these appeals to nationhood: seeming to evoke a quieter, more introverted identity, associated with landscape, culture and home, rather than the images of national greatness and global ambition implied in the term 'British', with its project of empire-building.[46]

The historian Raphael Samuel observed that to follow the

First World War recruitment poster
depicting Saint George slaying a
dragon, 1915.

Frank Newbould, Second World War recruitment poster depicting
the South Downs, 1942.

popular culture of Britain in 1939 and 1940 'is to see a country in love with itself'. Patriotism was – naturally enough at a time of war – explicit, but it took on a very different form to celebrations of an imperial, conquering people that had predominated in the early years of the twentieth century. The English were re-envisaged as a race of amiable eccentrics who 'muddled through', keeping calm while the rest of the world went mad. According to George Orwell in his January 1941 essay 'England Your England', they were a private people, 'a nation of flower-lovers' and 'stamp-collectors', fond of their homes and gardens but averse to militarism and the worship of power – in implied contrast to the enthusiasms that had overtaken German culture. And yet, in Churchill's words, while the English were apparently 'peace-loving and ill-prepared' at heart, they had always been 'instant and fearless at the call of honour', willing to take up arms against the aggression of larger, rival powers. A huge amount of attention was devoted to espousing the virtues of the 'national character': the putative English love of tolerance and good sportsmanship; their kindness to others and protectiveness towards the underdog; their quintessential modesty and unflappable good humour; and, most especially, their steadfastly rural nature. The English, it was asserted over and over, might grumble or squabble on occasion, but they pulled together in times of trouble, drawing on centuries-old characteristics that could be called upon when they were needed once more.[47]

Amid this radical reworking of patriotism, the idea of 'national heritage' seemed to come into its own. While just a few years before, many had regarded preservationists as defending class privileges against the intrusions of democracy, the countryside now became envisaged as 'The People's Land'. The National Trust made a propaganda film of its activities with this title, released in 1941, commissioning a soaringly nostalgic score from Ralph Vaughan Williams to accompany the beauty of historic landscapes.[48] Addressing the nation in his regular Sunday

evening slot on the BBC, J.B. Priestley drew on a sense of timeless continuity and custom, declaring in June 1940 that the
sight of local volunteer forces manning the home front

> made me feel sometimes that I'd wandered into one of those rich
> chapters of Thomas Hardy's fiction in which his rustics meet in
> the gathering darkness of some Wessex hillside . . . There we were,
> ploughman and parson, shepherd and clerk, turning out at night,
> as our forefathers had done before us, to keep watch and ward
> over the sleeping English hills and fields and homesteads.[49]

The sense of a countryside under threat from enemy forces
gave a new poignancy to these images of rural tradition. In
1941, the art historian Herbert Read proclaimed that such
images conveyed 'a sense of the continuity of the English town
and village', showing 'exactly what we are fighting for', in
which 'every winding lane' was 'an expression of our national
character'. The emotional significance of an age-old landscape
under threat was the motivation, too, for Sir Kenneth Clark's
Recording Britain project, launched in 1939, which mobilised
the leading artistic talents of the day to preserve a 'pictorial
Domesday' of British life and landscapes that an enemy invasion might destroy.[50]
The Britain that was presented in this twentieth-century
Domesday book was, in many ways, unremarkable: churches,
barns, farmhouses and cottages; country lanes, high streets, shop
fronts, bridges over streams; Georgian terraces, market crosses,
stately homes, parkland; band stands, windmills, ancient ruins,
dry stone walls, fields and beaches. These were both historic
and timeless scenes that were celebrated for their gentle,
unchanging charm – depicting small-scale things in faded tints,
which seemed vulnerable in their quiet modesty. Indeed, the
Second World War seemed for some to have brought this older
Britain back to the fore, as it disrupted the rhythms of modern
life and land was reclaimed to 'Dig for Victory'. 'I love the war,'
remarked the artist and writer Olive Cook, who had worked

for Clark at the National Gallery. 'Agriculture flourished ... I can't tell you how beautiful it was in the war ... It was idyllic.' Yet it wasn't just the prospect of German invasion that was threatening these scenes. The idea had been to paint corners of Britain that seemed vulnerable not just to wartime destruction, but whose days seemed numbered in the face of suburban development and modern industry. The project built upon decades of anxieties about the destruction of the countryside, and the irreparable loss of tradition it represented, which had seemed to so many observers to characterise the new Britain that was emerging in the interwar period. 'Field by field and tree by tree our countryside dwindles,' mourned Arnold Palmer, the administrator of *Recording Britain*, 'and like a spendthrift heir we begin, too late, to keep accounts.'[51]

By the outbreak of the Second World War, a pastoral vision of the land as the shared inheritance of all Britons – a source of continuity that reached back through the centuries and linked people with their ancestors in timeless national tradition – was being rearticulated with a new intensity. Yet this was a landscape as well as a series of traditions that many people throughout the 1920s and 1930s had been arguing had changed beyond recognition, something they felt they were on the point of losing entirely. And it was a democratic ethos in stark contrast to the attitudes of social elites throughout the interwar years, who had looked uneasily upon the rise of mass culture and mass democracy, and argued for the need to keep both out of the countryside before its beauty was destroyed by invading urbanites and suburban sprawl.

The countryside that had been the subject of nostalgic lamentation at its loss became in wartime a source of nostalgic celebration, holding out the promise of an ideal that could be fought for and returned to once more. Just as people during the First World War had done, people in 1940 were looking back to a time before the outbreak of conflict and reimagining it as an idyll of peace and serenity – forgetting, too, that they had been nostalgic then as well, and anxious about the future. But as social commentators throughout the interwar period had acknowledged, the distinctly urban and suburbanised character of the Britain they were living in was the outcome of a long process of economic and social change; there was no going back to a world before cars, suburbs, mass-produced goods and modern industry. And modern industries themselves seemed to be becoming ever more adept at co-opting nostalgia for ways of life they were replacing: the suburban developers marketing a rural idyll through leaded windows and mock-Tudor timbering, the oil companies promising quiet country lanes and unpolluted scenery, the mass-produced beer adverts inviting workers to imagine themselves into a landscape without factories. As we are about to find, the foundations of this crisis mood about modernisation were being laid long before 1914, as people took stock of past, present and future after more than a century of industrialisation.

4

Never Never Land

1914–1880

We often imagine the late Victorian and Edwardian period to have been a time 'before' the modern world, in which the First World War serves as a convenient dividing line between old and new: on one side, the horse-drawn carts and corsets and Victorian repressions; on the other, mass democracy, the Roaring Twenties and the technological innovations that marked the transition to 'modernity'. But to twenty-first-century eyes, the speed with which the world changed in the years between 1880 and 1914 looks extraordinary.

While interwar observers looked back upon the countryside they felt had represented Britain before the First World War, feeling that their own age, in comparison, was one of urban sprawl and rural decay, it was far from the pastoral ideal they had imagined in hindsight. By the 1880s, Britain was the first predominantly urban society in the world, the first nation in human history to have experienced this scale of urbanisation. London was the largest city in the world by some distance, with almost five million inhabitants recorded in the census of 1881, rising to over seven million by 1911, the size of the next five largest cities – Paris, New York, Tokyo, Beijing and Mexico City – *combined*. In 1880, it was still just about possible to think of England as a 'green and pleasant land' of small villages and farms, with a few industrial towns marking blots on the

British landscape; by the start of the First World War, more than 35 per cent of the population lived in cities of 100,000 inhabitants or more.[1] Contemporary observers were as alarmed by the rapid expansion of cities and newly sprawling suburbs as they were, in turn, by the numbers of people leaving the countryside. The period marked the end of a long process of rural depopulation that had been underway since the eighteenth century, as people flocked to new lives in towns and cities, or else were driven from the land when employment opportunities dried up. By 1911, only around one in five inhabitants of England and Wales lived and worked in the countryside – roughly the same proportion as today. And the pace of technological change, too, seemed to be accelerating ever more rapidly, in a period that witnessed the invention of the wireless telegraph, the radio, the gramophone, cinema, the car and the aeroplane; discovered viruses, radioactivity, X-rays and the atomic nucleus; and put electricity and the telephone to widespread commercial use. By Edwardian standards, our own age does not seem very innovative at all.

Amid these transformations, many late Victorians and Edwardians expressed intense nostalgia for pre-industrial forms of work and community. Across the social and political spectrum, from conservative elegies for a vanished social order to left-wing critiques of industrialisation, and from the Gothic splendours of the newly completed Houses of Parliament to the homespun wares of the Arts and Crafts movement, many devoted themselves to making the new world look and feel as antique as possible. Technological innovations were celebrated as the wonders of the modern age, heralding a future that was scarcely imaginable to their ancestors, but many late Victorians seemed to yearn to retreat to an era before the Industrial Revolution, valorising the spirit of medieval England and calling for a return 'back to the land'. And yet these seemingly old-fashioned reveries were not always as backwards-looking as they first appear.

WE MODERNS

The closer we look, the more the years between 1880 and 1914 start to feel like several historical periods bunched together. Occupations that still existed unchanged since the Middle Ages coexisted with electric power stations and cutting-edge industrial processes. There had never been as many horse-drawn carts on the streets of London, but then there had never been as many lines on the London Underground.[2] Tennyson was Poet Laureate, penning High Victorian hymns to a vanished medieval paradise, and was then followed by the incurably outmoded Alfred Austin in 1896, waxing nostalgic about 'old England's washing days, home-made jams, lavender bags', but this was also an age of modernist art and literature, of post-Impressionism, cubism and futurism: aesthetic experiments that sought to throw off Victorian conventions and capture the excitement of a new, modern age. According to Virginia Woolf's famous observation, 'on or about December 1910 human character changed', a date that referred to the seminal exhibition of post-Impressionist painters organised by Roger Fry, which introduced British audiences to Manet, Van Gogh, Gaugin and Cézanne for the first time.[3] But the spirit of modernism had been brewing since the 1880s, as writers and artists broke free from traditional forms and realist techniques that sought to represent their subject matter as faithfully as possible, experimenting with new ways of conveying the 'feel' of modern experience.

Avant-garde artists and ordinary people alike expressed a sense of living in a new age of transition, characterised by dynamism, speed, and the boundless energies of capitalism. New communications technologies and faster modes of transport created a sense that the world was shrinking, forging connections between people and places formerly isolated at a distance. As people's mental horizons expanded to take in these new experiences, it started to feel, too, like the world was speeding up.[4] But life seemed to be taking on an uneasy character of fluidity, as if the modern world had spun away from its moorings. The optimism and confidence in the onwards march of civilisation that had characterised the middle years of Victoria's reign, as the British Empire expanded and the innovations of the Industrial Revolution began to create a sense of boundless possibility for the future, was giving way to a sense that progress was splintering into chaos – the goal everything was heading towards was no longer entirely clear.

While every age is inclined to think of its own as one of unprecedented change, the generation that came of age around the turn of the twentieth century was perhaps the first to really obsess over it. 'We moderns', they called themselves, proudly as well as anxiously.[5] Contemporaries celebrated the progress of the age, yet expressed a sense of grief for what had been lost in the processes of urbanisation and industrialisation, and they reacted against the ugliness of the industrial landscape and the social problems created by urban growth, worrying that society was being cut off from its historic roots. They looked back and felt that the past had become suddenly, completely inaccessible: that a gulf had opened up between the predictable, stable world of history and their own age of transformation. 'Consider, for example, how entirely in sympathy was the close of the eighteenth century with the epoch of Horace,' wrote H.G. Wells, with his eyes set firmly on the future in 1901, seeing little difference between the time of the French Revolution and the height of the Roman Empire. But technological change had swept away traditional modes of life and work – an entire social system had disintegrated at the hands of modern technology, and, for Wells, 'there can never be any return.'[6]

It was only recently that people had gained a term for the transformations they had witnessed. In 1881, the historian Arnold Toynbee gave a series of lectures at Oxford, swiftly followed by a whirlwind public tour, during which he introduced his audiences to the term 'Industrial Revolution' for the first time in the English language. He argued that, for the past century, the world had gone through 'a period as disastrous and as terrible as any through which a nation had ever passed.' New industrial machines, in the hands of factory owners, had destroyed traditional ways of life and older relationships between workers and masters, a process that had 'led to a rapid alienation of classes', enriching industrialists at the expense of the poorest in society, and creating ever more degrading jobs and living conditions.[7] Toynbee did also highlight the progress and improvements that had been made over the course of the Industrial Revolution, appealing to a national sense of pride at the technological advances that had made Britain the 'Workshop of the World'. But many of his contemporaries seized upon his critique of industrialism, painting nostalgic visions of the world they had lost, even as they conjured up gloomy predictions of the future. The period witnessed an explosion in the popularity of utopian and dystopian science fiction, from William Morris's time-travelling *News from Nowhere* (1890) to H.G. Wells's *The Time Machine* (1895) and the first film adaptation of *Frankenstein* in 1910, as writers vied with each other to dramatise the hopes as well as the anxieties of the age. Could industry be redirected towards the common good, enabling technological utopias where machines did all the hard work, leaving people free to enjoy lives of endless leisure? Or would technology come to control people's lives in ever more sinister, insidious ways, and was the solution to return to a simpler time of honest labour in the open air?

For the social campaigner and Liberal politician Charles Masterman, the dawn of the twentieth century was 'a time balanced uneasily between two great periods of change'. Modern civilisation was becoming 'ever more divorced from Nature and her ancient sanities', while urbanisation was creating a raft of social problems that only seemed to become more insurmountable with each passing year.[8] Hundreds of social enquiries were launched during the period into the condition of the urban poor, protesting the 'Bitter Cry of Outcast London', or else likening journeys into urban slums to a voyage into 'darkest Africa' – painting an alarming picture of a new 'race' of men and women that was allegedly being produced, as urbanites were cut off from the influence of nature.[9] Social elites, surveying the working classes from a distance, feared that urban life was breeding a new 'type' of person characterised by a predisposition to outbursts of excitability and hooliganism, and feared that these energies would one day interrupt into violent protest. But, for Masterman, the alternative was even worse: the idea that the working classes would simply accept the conditions being forced upon them by the new industrial capitalists, dividing their days between monotonous occupations and long commutes to featureless suburbs, sedated into the 'listless toleration of intolerable things' by the meagre comforts of modern consumer culture.[10]

Added to this was the apparent decline in religious belief that worried so many observers around the turn of the twentieth century. If the world was no longer following the divine plan, then what else was directing these social and economic forces, and what would replace the things they had destroyed? As the historian Jonathan Rose writes, of all the problems that troubled the intellectual classes, 'none disturbed so many people as the decline of Victorian religion'. This was not just an issue that affected intellectual observers, who had been so shocked by nineteenth-century scientific discoveries that seemed incompatible with the teachings of the Bible, from the theory of evolution to the age of the Earth. Ordinary men and women were drifting away from churches in unprecedented numbers – by 1901, only about a quarter of adults attended a weekly service, down from around a half in the middle of the nineteenth century; a figure which itself had already seemed alarmingly low to authorities in the 1850s. This left an enormous intellectual and spiritual vacuum behind. As Rose writes: 'without God, the universe lost all coherence and purpose in the minds of many late Victorians.'[11]

HOW STIFF WERE THEIR
UPPER LIPS?

It is hard to square these anxieties with our image of the late Victorian and Edwardian period as the heyday of the stiff upper lip: a time of stern, mutton-chopped patriarchs and not being amused, when hardy imperial adventurers, drunk with a sense of British pride and destiny, set out to turn the map imperial pink. But by the 1880s, the Victorian faith in progress was tempered by anxiety. The growing awareness of the social problems caused by industrialism was given further impetus by fears of national decline in the face of increasing international competition. The British Empire had never covered such a large area, and continued to be enlarged throughout the period, by 1913 ruling over a quarter of the world population and spanning a quarter of Earth's land area. But the economic rise of Germany and America was causing many to worry that Britain was losing its industrial lead, while the 'Scramble for Africa' undermined British complacency that it could continue its project of exploiting an entire continent unopposed, when other European nations, too, held ambitions to enrich empires of their own. At the turn of the century, Britain appeared to many as 'The Weary Titan', having exhausted its industrial and imperial energies, and set for a trajectory of relative decline.

These anxieties deepened further during the Boer War, fought against Dutch colonisers in South Africa between 1899 and 1902. Britain had assumed that the poorly armed Boers would be easily defeated, but as the conflict dragged on it proved far more difficult than anticipated, shaking confidence in the supremacy of Britain's imperial might. Fears worsened when statistics emerged showing that over a third of volunteers had been declared medically unfit for service, with the health of military recruits from industrial cities a particular concern. In Manchester, it was alleged that out of 11,000 would-be

volunteers, more than 8,000 were turned away due to malnour-
ishment and other physical disorders, prompting a national
panic that the population was no longer capable of defending and maintaining a global empire.[12] In an era in which
policymakers from across the political spectrum subscribed to
eugenicist beliefs in the 'survival of the fittest', statistics such
as these were ominously suggestive of the decline of an 'imperial race'.

'Degeneration' became one of the buzzwords of the age, as
concern grew that if humans had evolved to reach their present
state, so too might they start to regress backwards.[13] Scientists,
politicians and social commentators found a seemingly endless
list of evidence for humanity's retrogression, not just in the
health problems besetting urban dwellers but in social life and
culture too. Anything from mental illness, homosexuality and
social unrest to hedonistic lifestyles, racy novels, modern artworks, and even men liking flowers was liable to be labelled
'decadent' or 'degenerate', further evidence, to some, that without
urgent intervention, humanity was on course for irretrievable
decline.

For imperialists, the solution was to strengthen the shaky
foundations of British imperialism with stories that could offer
inspiration to a people whose national self-confidence was on
the wane. Historians, novelists and journalists retrofitted a narrative of British history, portraying Empire as the fulfilment of
Britain's historic mission – the consummation of its 'Anglo-
Saxon' destiny – shoring up an imperial master race with heroic
tales of 'our island story'. School textbooks and history primers
prepared a new generation to assume the mantle of imperialism, teaching children that Britain was the greatest nation in the
world – the birthplace of Anglo-Saxon liberties, first and best at
everything – and that as a uniquely freedom-loving people they
had a God-given mission to venture out and civilise the world,
whether the world wanted to be 'civilised' or not. 'Many countries are larger than England, none is more important,' ran one

schoolbook. The historian J.R. Seeley's enormously influential *The Expansion of England* (1883) aimed both to educate statesmen in the service of the 'mother country', and to build a sense of national unity by cultivating his readers' patriotism.[14] This was not so much nostalgia as living history: the past had clear lessons to teach, and those lessons were in how to maintain and enlarge the British Empire.

But for many, the blame was laid squarely at the feet of industrialism: if the health of the British people was being threatened by conditions of life and work in urban centres, the solution was a return to nature. The enthusiastic imperialist and former prime minister Lord Rosebery declared in 1900 that 'an imperial race cannot be reared' in 'the rookeries and slums' of Britain's cities, deploring the health problems, weakened statures and lack of stamina he believed were characteristic of the urban working classes.[15] If Britain was to be regenerated, it would be through the robust influences of the great outdoors. From public schools to the Scouting movement, imperialists asserted the need to bring up tough, strong, unsentimental boys through a regimen of outdoor contact sports and cold showers: imperial adventurers of the future who would develop their endurance free from the effeminising influences of modern civilisation.

The late Victorian and Edwardian period was not only marked by a growing awareness of urban problems, and fears of national decline in the face of international competition – there was also widespread anxiety about anxiety. Against this background of social and cultural turmoil, doctors and social commentators wrote of the increase of nervous disorders among their contemporaries, attributing these 'attacks of nerves' to the adjustments that the nineteenth century had imposed upon its populations. They blamed modern life itself for making people anxious, asserting that life in industrial cities was leading to an upsurge in mental illnesses such as hysteria and neurasthenia (a form of nervous exhaustion), as well as a worrying epidemic of headaches, neuralgia, heart palpitations, fatigue, muscle weakness, stomach troubles and assorted physical ailments, and was even responsible for an apparent increase in suicides. It was a condition felt to be affecting people throughout the industrialised world, wherever people were gathering into urban centres transformed by modern technology. The American physician George M. Beard created the diagnosis of neurasthenia in 1880, writing that 'modern nervousness is the cry of the system struggling with its environment'. The relentless pace of modern life in the industrial city, with its crowds and noise, the density of urban settlement, and the speed of travel and communications in the age of the railway and the telegraph were all thought to be contributing to an increase in anxiety.[16]

Anxious diagnoses such as these were not just confined to medical circles, or elite social critics grandly opining on the fate of civilisation: 'nervousness' was one of the defining idioms of the era. Anxiety spawned an entire industry, as people sought to purchase solutions that might soothe their fears and restore a condition of perfect health and ease. As standards of living rose for the more prosperous sections of the working classes, disposable incomes were becoming available to more people than ever before, and advertisers – for the first time – were beginning to realise that there were profits to be made in exploiting consumer emotions. A seemingly endless array of consumer goods proliferated, from patent medicines and tonic wines to cigarette brands, soaps, food and drinks, home exercise systems and even electric baths: all promising to alleviate the scourge of modern anxiety. Advertisers seized on consumer fears, realising that they could exploit and exaggerate anxieties in order to present their products as a remedy, creating bogus testimonials and dramatic before-and-after narratives to peddle materialistic cures for modern maladies. Patent medicine adverts, ubiquitous in magazines and newspapers, asked their readers 'what is this disease that is coming upon us?', asserting the ever-increasing prevalence of nervous disorders in society. Testimonials had users attest that 'my nerves got so bad I would shut myself up

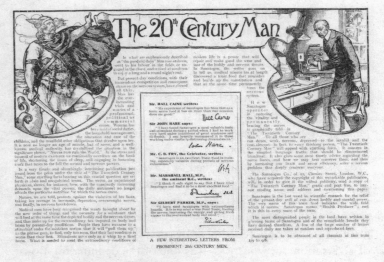

Advertisement for Sanatogen, *Graphic*, 7 November 1908.

and felt as though I never wanted to see or speak to anybody', or confess that 'I was always in an unfounded terror that something terrible was going to happen, and every little thing worried me for no reason whatsoever.'[17] 'IS THE FALL OF ENGLAND'S GREATNESS NEAR AT HAND?', asked the makers of Eno's Fruit Salt, somewhat hysterically, linking the perils of a sluggish gut to inability to defend a global empire, and vowing to regenerate the nation by curing it of indigestion.[18]

Because the majority of their consumers lived in towns and cities, advertisers appealed to rural nostalgia, promising to alleviate pathologies of urban life by endowing commodities with the supposedly health-giving virtues of nature. Manufacturers of tonic wine created a picture of the sickly clerical worker, enervated and wan from the artificiality of indoor toil. Sanatogen pushed the slogan '20th century man' to illustrate how pathological modern lifestyles were, contrasting an image of a robust ancient warrior, sword in hand, with a worried-looking man hunched over his desk and holding a pair of glasses. 'In what are euphemistically described as the 'good old days' the copy reads,

> Man rose at dawn, went to his labour in the fields, or engaged in the chase, and retired at sundown to enjoy a long and sound night's rest. But present-day conditions, with their tremendous competition and consequent strain on the nervous system, have altered all this. Man has the ever-increasing trials and worries of a professional, political or commercial career ... In the stress and turmoil of modern existence we continually overdraw on the bank of life.[19]

Advertisement for Sunlight Soap, *Illustrated London News,* 3 May 1902.

That the majority of consumers were the urban working and middle classes was rarely pictured in advertisements, outside of catastrophic 'before' images of miserable housewives or ailing office workers. Advertisements were set in rural villages, country cottages, ye olde market towns, medieval castles, classical antiquity – anywhere except the modern cities in which they were overwhelmingly purchased. The whole point of consumerism seemed to be that you could forget the problems of the present and enjoy the best of both worlds, imagining yourself into a past free from struggle or anxiety while enjoying the material benefits of the modern world. In a 1902 advertisement for Sunlight Soap – 'Not yet one and washing done' – a beaming housewife emerges from a thatched cottage to hang her linen out to dry in an incredibly idealised pastoral setting. No one in the history of the world has ever been happier to hang out their laundry. Puppies frolic on the lawn, in a garden enclosed first by a picket fence and then by a protective ring of trees, sheltering the family from the ugliness and competition of the industrial world outside. The benevolent sun, whose face bears the hands of a clock, weeps with joy – appealing to a more organic sense of time, measured by the changing of the seasons and the rhythms of night and day, in contrast to the clinical rationality of railway time and factory punch cards. In an era of tenement buildings and suburban terraces, picturesque country cottages were an idealised model of stability and order: the cottage and village community were charged symbolically with the preservation of older values in the face of capitalist transformation.[20] Modern commodities could guide the way forward, liberating housewives from hours of manual toil, while providing a reassuring sense of continuity through nostalgic appeals to history and tradition: ushering in a new mass consumer culture even as they appealed to remembered or imagined pasts.

These were secular, materialistic solutions to anxieties about the human condition in modernity. Doubtless many people bought into the nostalgic fantasies of advertising (how else would it have been such an economically successful strategy?), if only momentarily when hovering over a purchase. But many late Victorians and Edwardians were deeply worried about the materialist emptiness of all this. Commentators worried that consumerism was simply perpetuating the problems of industrialism, as people produced more in order to consume more, trapping society in an unending cycle of work and waste. The sociologist and pioneering town planner Patrick Geddes, who had begun his career renovating the tenement communities of Edinburgh's Old Town in the 1880s, was horrified by the vicious circle of production and consumption that exploited workers in unhealthy working conditions, leaving them to return each night to polluted and unsanitary dwellings. 'We make it our prime endeavour to dig up coals, to run machinery, to produce cheap cotton, to clothe cheap people, to get up more coals, to run more machinery,' he argued. 'But all this has been with no adequate development of real wealth, as primarily of houses and gardens, still less of towns and cities worth speaking of: our industry but maintains and multiplies our poor and dull existence.' For Geddes, the solution was not to wish these conditions away by retreating into nostalgia for a time before industrialism: 'I am no more seeking to return to the Mediaeval or the Roman past than to the Hebraic or the Hellenic order of things,' he wrote. 'I maintain return to the past to be impossible, its imitation to be undesirable.' Rather, the task was to improve the urban environment through better architecture and access to nature; to recognise people's fundamental need for beauty through establishing museums, libraries, arts and culture; and to redirect industrial machines towards the pursuit of happiness. A 'better future' was now dawning, he predicted at the outset of the First World War, in which scientific advances would be matched by 'new valuations of life, organic as well as human.'[21]

Geddes's optimism and hope for the future, however, and his faith that urban reforms could free people from their unhappiness, were not shared by all. By the end of the nineteenth century,

Victorian confidence in the ability of society to solve the problems created by the Industrial Revolution was evaporating, and was replaced by the uneasy awareness that many urban problems seemed more intractable than ever. It was giving way to a profound note of pessimism and despair that ran throughout Edwardian culture, a sense of disenchantment with the promises of modernity that caused many to mourn what they had lost. For Charles Masterman, writing in 1905, society was 'protesting through its literature a kind of cosmic weariness ... Faith in the invisible seems dying, and faith in the visible is proving inadequate to the hunger of the soul.' Time and again in his writings, he expressed his twin griefs for the loss of natural beauty and religious devotion that he felt had characterised English life since time immemorial. 'Beauty and the love of beauty, the old things, visions in the sunset, dreams by the fire light, are passing from the world,' he lamented. 'Comfort has been attained, and some security. But beauty has fled from the heart, and the hunger for it passed into a vague discontent. Religion has lost its high aspiration. Passion has become choked in that heavy air.'[22] Across the social spectrum, critics and policymakers, novelists and poets, and ordinary men and women alike shared his conviction that if hope was to be found amid modern despair, it lay in the spiritual values of the countryside.

FAR FROM THE MADDING CROWD

In 1901, Masterman gathered together a group of the leading young intellectuals of the day to tackle the problems of modern city life, in a collection of essays entitled *The Heart of the Empire*. The stated intention was to use the optimism of the start of a new century to lay out their hopes for the future of cities, and their visions for social reform. But for the contributors to the volume, and not least Masterman himself, it seemed as though the main problem with the modern city was that it was not the countryside. They worried especially for the fate of urban children, who had no memories of rural life to draw on, fearing that a new generation was being raised cut off from the pleasures and inspirations of nature. In his own essay, Masterman contrasted 'city up-bringing in twice-breathed air' to 'the spacious places of the old, silent life of England; close to the ground, vibrating to the lengthy, unhurried processes of Nature.' 'In former times,' he believed, 'the things of the earth were shot with spiritual significance.' Natural landscapes were suffused with a sense of meaningfulness that the man-made streetscapes of the industrial city could never have for Edwardian observers. Street after street of suburban houses seemed to have sprung up almost overnight, identikit red-brick terraces that had no history of their own. Variety seemed to have been replaced with sameness. As the historian G.M. Trevelyan wrote in his contribution to the volume, in the 'England of the past . . . each shire, each town, each village, had its own local piety, its customs, its anniversaries, its songs, its ethics, the indefinable but peculiar tone that marked it off from its neighbour.'[23]

One solution was simply to make these customs up again. The last quarter of the nineteenth century witnessed a series of attempts to reconnect with the past that have come to be known by historians as 'the invention of tradition'.[24] Many of the traditions and festivities that we think of as age-old British or English custom, perhaps dating from the Middle Ages or even rooted in older pagan beliefs, are often far more recent in origin, and can date their 'rediscovery' or even outright invention to the nineteenth and twentieth centuries. This is partly why the late Victorian and Edwardian period so often feels like several overlapping historical eras: these 'authentic' traditions weren't simply throwbacks or survivals, but were often new and distinctly modern responses to change. Forgotten folk songs were reconstructed and taught to schoolchildren, such as 'Scarborough Fair', blending new lyrics and melodies in 'ye olde' style with ones assembled from much earlier traditional ballads. May

Queens were crowned at fairs on newly established suburban commons. Morris dancing societies were founded to revive local folk dances that had been abandoned for centuries. At the same time, these revivals were presented as continuous, unchanging customs that linked people seamlessly from medieval, or even earlier pagan times, to their own day.[25]

Another solution to the problems posed by urbanisation was to find ways of getting city dwellers out into nature. Throughout *The Heart of the Empire*, the contributors stressed the need to organise visits to the countryside for urban children in particular, hoping to rekindle older emotions and ways of experiencing the landscape and its history in a new generation. 'Their life is a life lived in the present and for the present ... deprived of solid support in the Past,' wrote one contributor, Reginald Bray, in his chapter on 'The Children of the Town'. What worried him most was that, without instilling in them a love of nature, children might have no nostalgic memories of their own to draw on later in life: 'they have no memories of some idealised past and no hopes of some visioned future to lead them on. This loss of the inspiration of childhood is irreparable.' 'When our hearts grow weary,' he argued, 'we turn back and tread over again the paths of childhood's garden, now transfigured in the soft moonlight of memory, and find still growing there the old boundless hopes.' Without this bank of hopeful memories to draw on, he feared, people would be left powerless against the 'paralysing forces of modern life.' For Bray, the child's experience of nature was similar to the experience of religion: trees and plants, mountains and rivers, the sky and the stars could teach children to experience a sense of mystery and wonder so lacking in polluted streets and jerry-built suburbs. He felt that the sights, scents and sounds of nature would all combine to create an extrasensory experience, awakening children's 'consciousness of a "something beyond".' It was not a question of reading about nature in school books – the important thing was that children learnt to *feel* it. Even a weekend trip or

summer holiday in the countryside might make a world of difference. Bray praised the efforts of charitable organisations and
voluntary societies that had begun to organise trips to the countryside for urban children, writing that a holiday would mark 'a
break in the monotonous stream of the children's lives', helping
them to understand that a different way of life existed outside the
confines of urban poverty. 'The holiday actually does form an
epoch in their lives and stands as a landmark in their Past,' he
argued. 'To speak in this way may appear to be indulging in exag-
gerated language, but I appeal to those who have any knowledge
of the children to witness the truth of my statement.'[26]

Bray's faith in the transformative power of nature, and the
poignancy that nostalgic memories of the countryside would
hold for people later in life, is certainly borne out by the hundreds of memoirs and testimonies left behind by ordinary men
and women who experienced these visits as children. (It is a
distinct irony that these were men and women who – having
been encouraged by social elites in the pressing need to get out
into the countryside – would go on to live through an age in
which these efforts were so successful that it was a source of
considerable panic by the interwar years.) Working-class autobiographers, writing their accounts of life in an earlier age over
the course of the twentieth century, frequently wrote of their first
experiences of nature as a turning point in their lives, reminding them in difficult times that a happier life was possible. One
autobiographer, London-born Winifred Till, who wrote down
her memories of a trip to visit relatives in Surrey in the early
1900s, reminisced that 'every day was a delight, and I was completely happy. It must have rained sometimes, but my memory
is of warm sunny days' when she and her sister could 'run wild',
roaming fields and searching hedgerows for blackberries.[27]

For James Whittaker, who reflected upon his childhood in
the slums of Edinburgh and Leith before the First World War, a
summer spent in the Scottish countryside was an intoxicating
combination of pure, sensuous pleasure, spiritual awakening,

and almost overwhelming ecstasy; a kind of agony of joy. 'The memory of that summer,' he wrote in his memoirs, 'is to feel again one long, continual blaze of sunlight, and to remember one never-ending draught of sweet, sweet air . . . I met cows at Corstorphine; saw little rivers; discovered ferns and plants, reeds and rushes; smelled flowers and grass and herbs.' He reflected: 'for the first time in my life I knew beauty existed; and I have never forgotten to look for that priceless and painful thing since . . . the emotion I knew, swelling within my breast until it hurt and almost choked me, as I drank in the sweet-rankness of that dark grass.'[28]

But it was not always easy to square these memories of happier times with the realities of urban poverty. For another autobiographer, George Acorn, writing in 1911 of his childhood in an East End slum, nostalgia for the countryside brought the deprivation of his surroundings into sharper relief. Remembering a school trip he had taken to the Berkshire countryside, he wrote of these 'three glorious weeks' that it had changed his 'outlook on Nature and especially London. I had always looked upon open spaces as necessary stretches of green relief for the over-breathed air, but now I saw that the town was a blot upon the fair surface of a green world.'[29]

In writing their accounts of personal revelation and discovery, autobiographers were drawing not only on their own first-hand experiences of the countryside, but also upon a cultural tradition that was beginning to assign new meanings to the experience of nature. Historically, the idea of the countryside had stood for agricultural labour – of manual workers coming together as a community to harvest, sow and plough according to the changing rhythms of the seasons. But by the turn of the twentieth century, fewer than one in ten inhabitants of England and Wales were employed in agriculture (less than half the number who had worked the land in the middle of the nineteenth century), and the countryside was coming to signify a realm of rest and contemplation far away from the pressures of working life. Rural England belonged to the past. But at the same time, it began to function as a repository of nostalgic memories, in which certain ways of experiencing the countryside were becoming more important than the countryside itself.

In visiting and writing about the countryside, many late Victorians and Edwardians were seeking aestheticised, spiritual experiences that could help them feel connected to a bygone age – something that might compensate for what they felt had been lost in modern urban life. There was an explosion in the popularity of nature writing and pastoral novels and poetry, in which nature functioned as a pantheistic substitute for religion. Walking guides and pocket editions were bought in their thousands, as the urban working and middle classes took their church out of doors, and sought to enjoy personal spiritual experiences through words about nature.[30] Nature writers such as Richard Jefferies and Edward Thomas styled themselves as 'men of the fields', penning volumes like Jefferies's *Nature Near London* (1883) that provided descriptions of natural beauty spots within walking distance of the capital, enabling suburbanites to escape the world of work for the day in search of more meaningful forms of consciousness.[31] What their readers seemed to be looking for were intense, romanticised experiences: sensitivity to the beauty of nature, a delight in woodlands, flowers and animals; what the historian Lynne Hapgood describes as 'a desirable but unspecific meaningfulness that could fill a spiritual vacuum and provide an apparently traditional and stable framework for thought.'[32]

This sense of connection to an older world of tradition and stability was also what many readers of Thomas Hardy's Wessex novels seemed to be looking for. Much as Hardy drew attention to the darker side of rural life as well as the beauty of the countryside, his readers latched on to descriptions of happy peasant communities threatened by the blight of industrialism. Critics reacted furiously to the publication of *Jude the Obscure* in 1895, which unflinchingly described the miseries of financial insecurity amid the rural depression of the 1890s, in part because the countryside was conventionally supposed to represent an escape from the miseries of modern life. (Though inevitably, the sex scenes were a problem too.) But for Hardy, this was the irony of rural nostalgia: the shabby-chic picturesqueness of rural villages that so delighted urban visitors was actually a product of their poverty, not their supposed happiness. In a polemical magazine article, which charged the middle classes with indulging in a kind of poverty tourism, he argued that 'it is too much to expect them to remain stagnant and old-fashioned for the pleasure of romantic spectators.' The implication was that rural inhabitants were supposed to display the virtues of backwardness for the edification of wealthier and better-educated onlookers.[33]

As the Labour MP Henry Snell, whose own life was a rags-to-riches tale from agricultural labourer in the 1880s at the age of eight to party leader in the House of Lords, reflected in his autobiography: 'Romantic writers, politicians, and passing motorists, love to dwell upon the assumed delights of an agriculturalist's life,' and 'the thatched cottage with ivy clinging to its walls, is accepted as the symbol of ideal conditions. The people who are so thrilled by these artistic productions,' he warned his readers, 'know such places only from the outside.' For Snell, a life of 'grossly underpaid' manual work, without the help of labour-saving machinery, was 'a monotony of toil, broken only by tired and sometimes hungry sleep.'[34]

But an awareness of the harsh realities of rural labour did not dim people's nostalgia for the countryside. Indeed, it is significant that many writers who contrasted the disenchanting, stressful nature of urban life with the spiritualising beauty of nature themselves chose to live and work in cities. Edward Thomas – whose best-known poem 'Adlestrop' described the beauty of the English countryside on the eve of the First World War, with its 'willow-herb, and grass, / And meadowsweet' – styled his early writings in the model of Richard Jefferies's identity as 'Man of the Fields'. But Thomas was born and

brought up in suburban London, and published his first book of
nature writing, *The Woodland Life* (1897), while still a student
at St Paul's School. And while Jefferies grew up in the Wiltshire
countryside, he had no desire to work as an agricultural labourer
or farmer, and moved as an adult to the London suburb of Sur-
biton. Their writings are infused with a sense of the countryside
as an enchanted space *outside* daily experience – a space of
peace and meditation rather than one of manual labour in the
open air. Their countryside was transformed into a psychological
location that could be carried around as a private 'inner myth',
a utopian ideal with which to fight against the mundane realities of modern workaday life.[35] This was a nostalgia that was
not so much about wanting to get out of modern life altogether
as it was about enabling people to enjoy the virtues of nature
without losing any of the benefits of a modern urbanised world.

For the historian G.M. Trevelyan, who contributed an essay
to Masterman's *The Heart of the Empire*, this was the best
hope for the future. Whatever the problems of modern life
might be, it was impossible to wish away the technologies that
had brought about an urban and industrial world. Though he
lamented the disappearance of olde England and the loss of
rural modes of life, 'salvation' did not 'lie backwards in vain
regret'. For Trevelyan, if 'in the past life was naturally . . . beautiful and instructive; while to-day life moves in conditions
which tend to make it ugly and trivial,' the solution was to harness 'artificial' technologies to enable city dwellers to access
nature. Innovations such as electricity had the potential to
transform the polluted, smoke-laden atmosphere of industrial
cities that were currently dependent on burning coal, while
trains and omnibuses enabled town-dwellers, however briefly,
to access the pleasures of the countryside. It was not a question
of blaming modern technologies themselves for modern problems, but of redistributing relations of power: in the future, he
hoped, people would redirect these 'Titan forces' to serve 'the
best interests of the community.'[36] Again, it is hard to escape the

irony that these optimistic hopes would turn to nostalgic lament by the time they became a reality. The pylons delivering electricity from power stations, the expanding suburbs that offered people walking-distance access to nature, and the transport networks delivering urbanites into rural landscapes would come to be looked upon very differently by interwar observers, who saw them as the death knell of the countryside itself.

FORWARD TO THE NEW EDEN

For a small but influential handful of radicals, occasional visits to nature could never make up for what had been lost in Britain over the previous century of industrialisation. What was needed was to take the whole of society back to pre-industrial ways of living and working: to drop not just industrial machines and capitalist exploitation at the hands of factory owners but the whole structure of modern urban life, taking civilisation 'back to the land'. While voices from all sections of society decried the problems of urban poverty and overcrowding, and lamented the squalor of industrial landscapes, the vast majority of people assumed that the social and economic systems that had created them were here to stay. But a minority of social critics were arguing that these problems were so integral to industrial capitalism that the only solution was that the modern city itself had to go. Factories and industries needed to be dismantled, and the population resettled in hamlets and villages, returning the economy to workshops, guilds and an older culture of home-spun self-sufficiency.[37] Late-Victorian and Edwardian rebels started to drop out of modern life altogether: simple-lifers sought a return to subsistence farming in homemade clothing, middle-class experimenters formed vegetarian communes based on the works of Tolstoy, and left-wing intellectuals dreamt of utopias that would return Britain to a soft-focus version of the Middle Ages.

Seemingly paradoxically, this nostalgia for a romanticised medieval past was often an expression of revolutionary politics, and allied to radical socialist agendas that looked forward to utopian, egalitarian futures. While the writer and designer William Morris is best known today for his intricately patterned textiles and wallpapers, he was also a committed socialist activist who was passionate about democratising the experience of beauty. Morris was a founding influence on the Arts and Crafts movement, which intertwined aesthetic and social visions in advocating a return to the traditional craftsmanship of old English styles. Untreated oak furniture, hand-dyed textiles and simple earthenware were expressions of cultural dissidence: an aesthetic preference that proclaimed a rejection of machine-made products and all that the factory had come to symbolise. Arts-and-Crafts pioneers looked back consciously to old-fashioned styles, yet in doing so they laid claim to being the true experimentalists and modernisers of their age, rejecting not only disposable mass-made goods but the whole economic system that produced them.[38] 'Have nothing in your house that you do not know to be useful, or believe to be beautiful,' Morris exhorted his contemporaries, waging war not only on the clutter of Victorian interior design – the trinkets, ornaments, overcomplicated furniture, antimacassars – but upon modern civilisation itself. Industrial capitalism was forcing the working classes to toil in difficult and degrading conditions, to produce machine-made goods that failed to bring even the rich lasting happiness, and destroying the natural environment in the process. 'We must turn this land,' he urged his readers, 'from the grimy back yard of a workshop into a garden.'[39]

What was needed, Morris felt, was to return to an age where people worked together as a community, using their hands to produce beautiful things. In Morris's utopian novel *News from Nowhere* (1890), the narrator, William Guest, falls asleep after returning from a Socialist League meeting, and wakes to find himself in the year 2102. Yet this was a vision of the future that looked an awful lot like medieval England – if the Middle Ages were reimagined as a kind of pastoral communist Disneyland. A revolution has swept away the class structures of Victorian society, and the inhabitants of England have reverted to living in close-knit village communities, flourishing in harmony with the rhythms of the natural environment. To be sure, there have been some novel developments: freed from the repressions of Victorian culture, the inhabitants of utopia hold much more liberal views on crime and punishment, sex, love and marriage. (The weather, too, seems to have much improved on the typical British summer, with the sun shining day after day upon meadows and orchards and fields of happy workers.) But it was a decidedly retrospective vision of utopia, defined by craftsmanship and agriculture, in which 'machine after machine was quietly dropped under the excuse that the machines could not produce works of art, and that works of art were more and more called for.'[40] For Morris, a journey into the future was also a voyage back to the past.

At stake was the recovery of joy in a modern industrial age. The Arts-and-Crafts pioneer Charles Ashbee felt that the key task for modern civilisation was to enable people to regain a sense of fulfilment in their work. In the past, for Ashbee, craftsmen had taken pride in the products they made, but now that the factory system had become specialised through the division of labour, workers performed the same repetitive tasks each day on a production line, and were denied the satisfaction of seeing a project through to completion. 'We have now to find a means for man to labour again with his hands,' he argued, 'not mechanically, but inventively, imaginatively – to labour with the motive of joy.'[41] Ashbee and Morris were both heavily influenced by John Ruskin, one of the towering Victorian critics of industrialism, who had argued passionately for the redemptive pleasures of manual work. For Ruskin, by separating out creative and intellectual work from manual labour, the Industrial Revolution had dehumanised workers, seeing them as little more than cogs in a machine. While inventors and industrialists were praised as geniuses, their brilliant ideas depended upon delegating the actual work involved in carrying them out to poorly paid labourers, 'and we call one a gentleman, and the other an operative.' 'Whereas,' he argued, 'the workman ought often to be thinking, and the thinker often to be working, and both should be gentlemen, in the best sense. As it is, we make both ungentle, the one envying, the other despising, his brother.'[42] For Ruskin, creative work would bring dignity to manual labour, and vice versa, because the aesthetic was inextricable from the social: 'art' itself was simply the expression of people's pleasure in labour. For Morris, too, in an ideal society, workers would be considered artists: for 'what is an artist but a workman who is determined that, whatever else happens, his work shall be excellent.'[43] If capitalist forms of social organisation were dropped, and workers freed from the tyranny of a mechanical age, he hoped that people could return to work with the joyful spirit of play.

However, not everyone shared Ruskin, Morris and Ashbee's nostalgia for the supposed joys of manual labour. In H.G. Wells's 1905 science-fiction novel, *A Modern Utopia* – which was written in part in opposition to *News from Nowhere* – the central purpose of utopia was to free humanity from physical labour. For Wells, it was almost laughable to imagine that, given the right social conditions, the working classes might be made to enjoy their labour:

there is – as in Morris and the outright Return-to-Nature Utopians – a bold-make believe that all toil may be made a joy ... But indeed this is against all the observed behaviour of mankind. It needed the Olympian unworldliness of an irresponsible rich man of the shareholding type, a Ruskin or a Morris playing at life, to imagine as much.[44]

While the faith of Arts-and-Crafts idealists in the pleasures of good, honest hard work in the open air was no doubt well-intentioned, Wells was arguing that it carried more than a whiff of champagne socialism. He felt that only people who had ever really pretended at being workers could be naive enough to imagine this was preferable to letting machines do the heavy lifting for you. It was one thing to rough it in the countryside as a break from a life of middle-class luxury, quite another to toil for a living. For Wells, a utopian society depended on the mechanisation of industry, and 'the hope that all routine work may be made automatic.' The technological innovations of the nineteenth century were to be celebrated: he envisaged that it was 'becoming conceivable . . . that a labouring class – that is to say a class of workers without personal initiative – will become unnecessary to the world of men.' Wells shared his contemporaries' anger at the ugliness of industrial landscapes and the exploitation of workers, but railed against their nostalgia for a world without machines. It was 'the misfortune of machinery, and not its fault' that industrialists failed to recognise the value of art and beauty, but taking away modern technologies would hardly bring about an overnight revolution in people's values. 'Art,' he argued,

> like some beautiful plant, lives in its atmosphere, and when the atmosphere is good it will grow everywhere, and when it is bad nowhere. If we smashed and buried every machine, every furnace, every factory in the world, and without any further change set ourselves to home industries, hand labour, spade husbandry, sheepfolding and pig minding, we should still do things in the same haste, and achieve nothing but dirtiness, inconvenience, bad air and another gaunt and gawky reflection of our intellectual and moral disorder. We should mend nothing.[45]

In Wells's utopia, engineers, too, would be considered artists. There was nothing about industrial machines that required them to be ugly or to exploit the people who operated them: a truly ideal society would seek not to return to a time before scientific advances, but would ally art *with* science in the pursuit of happiness.

But a return to simpler and more 'natural' ways of living was not just a longing to retreat to a rose-tinted version of rural society in the past. For many simple-lifers, the relationship with nature they wanted to renegotiate was a new and unmistakeably modern one. The back-to-the-land movement was closely allied with vegetarianism, as campaigners advocated dietary reforms that could restore people's sense of connection to the natural environment. If modern civilisation exploited workers for profit at the expense of human happiness, and destroyed the natural landscape with polluting technologies in the process, its parallel was in the exploitation of animals. From the middle of the nineteenth century onwards, a raft of societies and organisations were set up to promote vegetarianism and oppose animal cruelty, championed by high-profile advocates such as the playwright George Bernard Shaw, along with magazines and periodicals with names such as *The Vegetarian Messenger*, or simply *Humanity*.[46] Satirists lampooned the worthiness and asceticism of perma-sandalled lentil eaters, but vegetarianism continued to grow as a social movement. By the Edwardian period, vegetarianism was virtually obligatory among those holding self-consciously advanced views about society.

The search for more 'natural' ways of life was closely connected, too, to reviving older ways of dressing. Social campaigners argued passionately for changes in dress, aiming to liberate people from the corsets and constraints of Victorian clothing and enable an easier, more natural relationship to the body. Women in particular argued the need for more 'rational dress' that would enable them to move freely through their lives, with dress reformers favouring looser styles that accommodated the natural shape of women's bodies. The dress reformer and Chaucer scholar Mary Eliza Haweis led the trend for 'artistic' and 'aesthetic dress' in the 1870s and 1880s, advocating free-flowing drapery inspired by the styles of medieval and renaissance gowns – available to fashionably bohemian customers in the new mock-Tudor department store Liberty.[47] Seeking inspiration in period costumes and vintage styles could be a way of protesting against the entire spirit of the age. For the simple-lifer and poet-philosopher Edward Carpenter – a passionate vegetarian, nudism advocate, and perhaps British history's most enthusiastic sandal-wearer – the task was to 'undo the wrappings and the mummydom of centuries' that had bound people up like a 'funny old chrysalis'. Houses were 'boxes with breathing holes', in which people had shut themselves off from the light of the sun and the open air, while shoes were 'leather coffins' for the feet. 'And who does not know the pleasure of grasping the ground – the bare earth – with his bare feet?' Carpenter asked his readers, arguing that if they found it impossible to imagine modern life without shoes, then something had gone seriously wrong with civilisation. If people found the prospect of 'brokers of the London Stock Exchange hurrying around' barefoot ridiculous, it was perhaps inadvertently revealing: 'because if the two things are really incompatible, it is quite possible that in the long run the Stock Exchange business may turn out to be the less important of the two.'[48] What could be more important, after all, than undoing the sense of shame that compelled people to hide from their own bodies?

The return to nature was particularly attractive to those for whom Victorian conventions and decorum seemed suffocatingly restrictive, preventing the expression of natural feelings and pleasures. Edward Carpenter was reacting not just against the petty rules and regulations of bourgeois respectability, but against the repressiveness of a patriarchal culture that forbade the free expression of sexuality – particularly same-sex attraction. At a time when male homosexual acts were illegal, and homosexuality was continually the subject of moral panics about 'deviancy' and 'degeneration' – particularly around the trial of Oscar Wilde in 1895 for 'gross indecency' – Carpenter was writing that same-sex attraction should be understood on the same terms as any human relationship: just as 'deeply stirring', just as 'ennobling'; one of the 'great human passion[s]'. It was 'tragic' to 'anyone who realises what Love is ... so profound, so absorbing, so mysterious' to see 'the fate of those whose deepest feelings' were condemned by the society around them.[49] Carpenter's pioneering gay rights activism was inextricably connected to his belief in the curative powers of nature: his faith that if only people could return to a simpler style of life and a more intimate relationship with the natural environment, then a new society based upon the free expression of emotion would be possible.

In 1882, Carpenter purchased a few acres of land at Millthorpe, on the edge of the Peak District a few miles to the south of Sheffield, hoping 'just to try and keep at least one little spot of earth clean.' 'I felt the need of physical work, of open-air and labour,' he explained, viewing his little piece of land as 'a sort of salvation.' When not tending the land or caring for his animals, he was writing, publishing books and essays to teach others how to adopt a simpler lifestyle and reconnect with their natural instincts. Mankind, he argued, needed to escape from civilisation: to find their 'way back to the lost Eden, or rather forward to the new Eden.'[50] Admirers and sympathisers began to make pilgrimages to witness first-hand Carpenter's experiments in natural living. Among his visitors were some of the leading intellectual figures of the day: a coalition of writers, researchers and campaigners whose interests lay somewhere between sex and nature, from E.M. Forster and Charles Ashbee to founder of the Garden City movement Raymond Unwin (who had begun with Letchworth Garden City in 1903 – a greener style of urban planning that would later inspire the design of Britain's New Towns), the novelist and anti-war campaigner Olive Schreiner, and the sexual psychology researcher Havelock Ellis. But the largest group of visitors were young gay men, inspired by Carpenter's openness in writing about his own sexuality. In 1898, Carpenter set up a household with his partner George Merrill, a young working man who lived with him for the rest of his life, tending their market garden together at

Millthorpe.[51] For Carpenter, free love was intimately connected to his love of nature: personal relationships, like all human life, should be free and joyful, healthy and creative, unconstrained by so-called 'civilised' strictures that had made people ashamed of their instinctive feelings.

For many late Victorian and Edwardian cultural dissidents, modern civilisation had quite simply ruined sex. Carpenter contrasted 'sexual embraces . . . under the burning sun or the high canopy of the stars' where 'their meaning can be fully understood', to shabby liaisons that took place in the 'stuffy dens' and 'dirty upholstery' of Victorian interiors.[52] D.H. Lawrence inveighed against bourgeois repressiveness for cutting people off from more 'earthy' forms of sexuality that he identified with the rural working classes, viewing pathological attitudes to love and sex as a bellwether for the diseased modern condition. For H.G. Wells, sex was a 'mighty passion, that our aimless civilisation has fettered and maimed and sterilised and debased.' 'Love,' he mourned, 'like everything else in this immense process of social disorganisation in which we live, is a thing adrift, a fruitless thing broken away from its connexions.'[53] This, too, was a kind of nostalgia, but it was certainly very different to a traditionalist yearning for thatched cottages or suburban Morris dances. Like Edward Carpenter, a growing number of novelists and cultural critics were beginning to argue that civilisation itself was a disease: that history, in the name of 'progress', had been one long march away from a state of primitive innocence and contentment. But modern civilisation might just be another passing phase of human development: the way back to a 'lost Eden' would also be the way forward to a new world.

DO YOU BELIEVE IN FAIRIES?

In 1910, Edwardian Britain was treated to an unprecedented display of primitive artwork. Used to the hyperrealistic portraiture and faithful landscape paintings of Victorian gallery exhibitions, visitors weren't quite sure what to make of the bright colours, expressive lines and half-naked figures set in unfamiliar tropical scenery. As one observer wrote in his diary afterwards in dismay, to call this sort of thing 'art' was 'either an extremely bad joke or a swindle.' To his eyes, there was no 'sense of skill or taste, good or bad, or art or cleverness' to be found in the paintings, but rather:

> The drawing is on the level of that of an untaught child of seven or eight years old, the sense of colour that of a tea-tray painter, the method that of a schoolboy who wipes his fingers on a slate after spitting on them . . . These are not works of art at all, unless throwing a handful of mud against a wall may be called one.[54]

Others had *arrived* at the exhibition with the intention of mocking the drawings. Fashionable ladies strolled through the gallery in fits of giggles, and one man laughed so hard at an artist's portrait of his wife that he had to be led outside for some fresh air.[55] Those who didn't find it funny, raged. To almost everyone who attended, it was an offence to civilisation that the show had even been organised in the first place – surely someone was having a laugh at their expense.

The exhibition was of the first post-Impressionist paintings to be seen in Britain, that had so captured the attention of Virginia Woolf, and the artists were Manet, Seurat, Gaugin, Van Gogh and Cézanne. What was so shocking to Edwardian observers was that the post-Impressionists were rejecting the very idea that art was supposed to represent its subject as faithfully as possible, and were instead choosing to evoke emotion. Style was now more important than subject matter, and the artists had found inspiration for new ways of representing the world in artistic movements outside the familiar canon of Western art history. Gaugin in particular had been inspired to take a new artistic direction after escaping the bourgeois taboos of fin-de-siècle Europe, in favour of a new life of colonialist child grooming in Tahiti. (Though he, of course, did not envisage himself in these terms, feeling that he had found in Polynesian culture a freer approach to sexuality – exotic pleasures that offered new imaginative possibilities to the open-minded artist, as he painted adolescent girls by day and took them to what he referred to as 'The House of Pleasure' by night.[56]) But to most viewers of the exhibition, these new experiments in bold colour and strange perspectives struck them as unreadable: even the supremely cultured E.M. Forster confessed that 'Gaugin and Van Gogh were too much for me.'[57]

Thankfully, an art critic from *The Times* – though he had ended up hating the exhibition just as much as the average viewer – was on hand to at least explain what the artists had been trying to achieve in their primitivism. 'It is the rejection of all that civilisation has done,' he enlightened his readers. 'It begins all over again – and stops where a child would stop . . . Really primitive art is attractive because it is unconscious.'[58] This was a kind of well-intentioned colonialist perspective: to praise indigenous and non-Western societies for the unconscious purity of their vision, viewing life beyond the confines of Western civilisation as possessing the same sense of enchanted innocence that was awarded to childhood. If modernity was defined by decadence and degeneration, then post-Impressionism was an attempt to escape the cul-de-sac of modern civilisation through the 'untrained' and 'primitive' vision of the child.[59]

Edwardian society was pervaded by an intense nostalgia for childhood. While avant-garde artists were mocked for making a virtue out of primitivism and childishness, a turn towards naivety can also be found throughout more mainstream culture. Not least in the booming popularity of children's literature, in a period that witnessed the creation of many of Britain's most enduring and well-loved stories, from *Peter Rabbit* to *Peter Pan*, *The Wind in the Willows*, *The Jungle Book*, *The Railway Children* and *The Secret Garden*. As more and more observers began to worry that modern civilisation had reached a dead end, in which progress seemed to be splintering into chaos, people started to wonder if the way out might be found in earlier phases of human development – children, after all, were the future. Victorian culture had elevated the middle-class family into the ultimate symbol of refuge from the anxieties of modern life. Stern Victorian patriarchs might be absorbed in the trials of more worldly considerations, but the sweetly smiling and tirelessly competent Victorian mother was the 'Angel in the House', sheltering the family from the ugliness and competition of the world outside. By the Edwardian period, attention was shifting onto children themselves: a growing number of writers began to imagine things through the mind of a child. If modern life was seen to be anxious, tired and disenchanted, then perhaps what was needed was to inject the modern world with some of the magic of a child's imagination.

As modernisation transformed people's lives at a seemingly ever-accelerating rate, readers could take refuge in worlds where good triumphed over evil, children never had to grow up, and Britain could always remain a place of secret gardens, enchanted woodland, and the myths and folklore of national tradition. It is telling that the setting of Edwardian children's literature was almost always pastoral. Edwardian children's writers were some of the fiercest critics of modern urban life, as if they themselves had not wished to grow up into the modern world. Britain's most beloved children's illustrator, Beatrix Potter, was a committed conservationist, and devoted much of her life to land preservation in the Lake District, seeking to preserve not only the unique hill country landscapes but to keep alive traditional techniques of fell farming. When not imagining the inner lives of woodland creatures, Potter was raising her prize-winning flock of Herdwick sheep, and was a key early influence on the National Trust. The Trust itself was established in 1895, and its founders were closely allied with socialist critiques of industrialism. Among them was Octavia Hill, who as well as pioneering the conservation of green spaces argued passionately for the need for urban reforms that could lift people out of poverty. The novelist Edith Nesbit, author of *The Railway Children* and *Five Children and It*, was a lifelong socialist activist, and was among the founders of the Fabian Society, which in its early stages attracted many simple-lifers who sought to advance the cause of socialist reform. Nesbit deplored the conditions of industrial capitalism that left workers in overcrowded urban slums. But she nonetheless found it difficult to accept that by far the simplest alternative was to rehouse people in the suburbs that were sprawling into the countryside and engulfing her cherished rural home in Eltham. 'Everything is getting uglier and uglier,' she grieved, 'and no one seems to care ... only the old people remember that things were not always ugly, remember how different things were – once.' Yet perhaps, if people were 'to show a child beautiful things', to 'charm and thrill [their] imagination ... to familiarise the child with beauty', there might be hope for the future.[60]

As well as their practical visions for a more equal future, many late Victorians and Edwardian intellectuals were susceptible to a touch of wish-fulfilment. A great many otherwise serious thinkers seem genuinely to have believed in fairies. Arthur Conan Doyle, whose creation Sherlock Homes so thoroughly employed logic, rationality and critical thinking to expose the inner workings of criminal mysteries, was to embarrassingly 'authenticate' photographs of the Cottingley Fairies taken in 1917, in which children had photographed themselves as if posing with real fairies, which were actually paper illustrations cut out from a story book. Doyle had a long-standing interest in mysticism and the occult, and was deeply curious about séances, telepathy and paranormal phenomena.[61]

There was a great deal of pantheistic spiritualism around the turn of the twentieth century, as people sought to find spiritual alternatives amid the contemporary crisis of religion – a spirit that made its way, too, into children's literature. In Kenneth Grahame's *The Wind in the Willows* (1908), neo-pagan spiritualism burst onto the page in 'The Piper at the Gates of Dawn' (a chapter that abridgers have been keenest to drop ever since, as it doesn't quite seem to fit in with the gentle tales of Ratty and Moley and Mr Toad – though it has had an influential afterlife as the inspiration for the debut album of Pink Floyd, those eclectic cataloguers of English tradition). In the chapter, Rat and Mole are greeted with a vision of the great god Pan, in an uncomfortable passage whose tone hovers somewhere between earnest religiosity and latent homoeroticism. 'Nature' seems to 'hold her breath', as Mole gazes upon the 'splendid curves' of Pan's 'rippling muscles' and 'parted lips'. The moment is 'breathless and intense, vivid on the morning sky; and still, as [Mole] looked, he lived; and still, as he lived, he wondered.' The next thing Mole knows, he has woken from a blissful dream he can no longer remember. Pan has gifted the creatures with 'forgetfulness' – because, if they could remember their joy in that moment, the memory of it might overshadow all that followed. The 'little animals' would be haunted with the knowledge that they could never be as 'happy and light-hearted' again.[62] The chapter is shot through with an extraordinary yearning for the intensity of religious experience, but this is paralleled, too, in nostalgia for the unselfconscious bliss of childhood. Was it a fool's errand to dwell on nostalgia for an enchanted happiness that was impossible in adulthood?

This same yearning was at the heart of a much more enduring vision of Pan: J.M. Barrie's *Peter Pan* – the tale of a boy who never has to grow up – first staged in 1904. Edwardian children's literature is haunted by the Victorian crisis of faith, and the search for more mystical forms of religion that might enchant the world once more. But whereas Grahame blessed his characters with forgetfulness, happy to let his readers go about their lives in the 'wide world' beyond the magic of childhood, for Barrie what was needed was to get his audience to wish for magic harder. Disbelief kills enchantment, but Tinkerbell insists that she could get well again if only children would

Paul Bransom, *The Piper at the Gates of Dawn*, in Kenneth Grahame, *The Wind in the Willows* (1908; New York: Charles Scribner's Sons, 1913).

believe in fairies. If people could just clap hard enough, drowning out the noise of doubt and cynicism, then all would be well in Neverland.

What people seemed to be looking for was undivided consciousness. In the Edwardian imagination, all that was wrong with the modern world seemed to be in how compartmentalised it was. People divided their days between the pressures of their careers in the city, and commutes back home to domesticated leisure in the suburbs. Cities were divorced from the countryside, urban dwellers had become disconnected from community and tradition, while intellectual life seemed to have become cold, mechanical, utilitarian – hived off from a sense of spirituality and from people's natural emotions. E.M. Forster's rallying cry in *Howards End* (1910) to 'only connect' – to reconnect people with nature; connect people with each other; connect the life of the mind with the life of the body – was emblematic of an entire cultural impulse: to recover a more organic, holistic way of being in the world, which might allow people to feel whole again.[63] Many Edwardians argued that they *did* carry within themselves the memory of a more harmonious time, before the anxieties of adulthood, when they had moved about the world more playfully. Childhood became envisaged as an Edenic state, a psychological paradise where people lived in the moment, alive to the joy and beauty of the world and the guardians of its mysteries, safe from the anxieties of both adulthood and modernity alike.

The theme of the ruined childhood paradise is common in Edwardian writings about adulthood. In his semi-autobiographical novel, *The New Machiavelli* (1911), for example, H.G. Wells recounted how he watched his childhood home of Bromley – or Bromstead in the novel – being ruined. 'All my childish memories are of digging and wheeling, of woods invaded by building, roads gashed open . . . hedges broken down and replaced by planks, of wheelbarrows and builder's sheds, of rivulets overtaken and swallowed up by drainpipes', recounts the narrator. 'The Ravensbrook of my earlier memories was a beautiful stream. It came into my world out of a mysterious Beyond, out of a garden . . . And after I was eleven, and before we left Bromstead, all the delight and beauty of it was destroyed.'[64] As we have seen, Wells was, in many respects, fiercely opposed to his contemporaries' romanticised nostalgia for rural olde England.[65] Yet his writings are infused with anger at the senselessness of unregulated jerry-building that permanently destroyed the beauty of the English countryside in favour of shabby suburban dwellings. In an age of unprecedented urban expansion, his experience of watching his semi-rural childhood home engulfed by suburban sprawl was typical.

There is a correspondence, here, between writers' nostalgia for the unspoilt countryside of the national past, and a more personal sense of nostalgia for their own memories of childhood. In remembering their childhoods, authors often reached not only for the mindworld of their childhood selves that was now inaccessible to them as adults, but for childhood memories set in physical environments that had in actuality been destroyed. There was thus a double sense of loss for authors who were never able to return to childhood landscapes and (re-)experience them as adults. Often, anxieties about the rootlessness of modern life were not just based on theoretical ideas about the alleged happiness of medieval peasants or 'primitive' societies. These ideas became intermixed with intensely personal emotions and experiences of growing up in landscapes that were no longer physically there. And often, in turn, the experience of childhood within these disappearing landscapes – characterised by undivided consciousness, sensory intensity and unmixed happiness – became identified with the lost landscapes themselves. Like Margaret Thatcher would later come to remember her childhood in Grantham as the model of an ideal society, it took the world as it appeared to a child for a reflection of what life had been like at the time.

For many late Victorians and Edwardians, to look back on the childhood worlds they had lost was almost unbearably poignant. Adulthood had required them to put away delight and joy, and wear a public face of emotional repression. The cultural ideal of the stiff upper lip made enormous psychological demands upon people, requiring men in particular to shun any hint of emotionalism in favour of an attitude of indomitable toughness and endurance. A society that required the maintenance of a global empire had little place for men who failed to grow out of their instincts of empathy and sensitivity. As the novelist George Gissing phrased it, of raising children in a seemingly ever more competitive world, 'our little crabs must grow their hard shells, or they've no chance.' In Rudyard Kipling's poem 'If', perhaps the seminal celebration of imperial stoicism, a boy would become a man only when he could

> Force heart and nerve and sinew
> To serve you long after they have gone,
> And so hold on when there is nothing in you
> Except the Will which says to them: 'Hold on!'

But most importantly, for Kipling, a real man would teach his son to 'never breathe a word' about his loss.[66]

And yet, as the historian Thomas Dixon notes, our present-day image of the 'repressed British male' of the period is an incomplete one. He reminds us that even the quintessential Edwardian military man, Lord Kitchener – whose resolutely moustached upper lip was to exhort millions of British men to fight in the Great War – was on occasion moved to a public outburst of weeping. According to the renowned singer Dame Nellie Melba, who met Kitchener in Melbourne in 1909, shortly after he had been discharged from his post in India, the general sank to his knees in front of her, imploring: 'Madame Melba, I've been in exile for eight years. Won't you—won't you sing me just one verse of Home Sweet Home?' And as she sang, Melba recounted that she watched 'two big tears' roll down his cheeks.[67] Nostalgia, it seemed, could move even the sternest of imperial warriors to tears.

Belying the public image of unflappable, armour-plated imperialists, children's fairy tales were particularly popular with soldiers returning from the imperial frontier. The playwright Walford Graham Robertson described the enormous success of his 1908 Christmas play *Pinkie and the Fairies*, with theatre stalls so packed with military men that they 'looked like a parade at Aldershot.' Robertson had intended that children would be his primary audience, but upon enquiring with a soldier friend as to how he had won such an unexpectedly devoted military following, he had been told that they had come in order to cry. It seemed that, although the soldiers had learnt to hide the trauma of war and put on a face of exaggerated stoicism, they were identifying in a way with the innocence of these make-believe childhoods. Night after night, as they sat in the theatre and watched children play with fairies in an enchanted glade, were they imagining themselves back into an earlier time in their lives, where a happy ending had felt possible if they just wished hard enough? According to the friend, what the soldiers had found 'most devastating' was the final scene, in which the fairies bid the children goodbye with a farewell song, and fade from their imaginations forever. At the end of each performance, Robertson recalled, 'the lights went up upon rows of bedewed shirt fronts', as, in the privacy of the darkened theatre, the soldiers had wept over Pinkie and their own lost fairylands.[68]

As the Edwardian era drew to a close, social observers were increasingly detecting a note of wish-fulfilment amid their contemporaries' dreams of lost innocence. For the writer G.K. Chesterton, there was a terrible irony to all this playful idealism, as the country geared towards the First World War. 'There really had been a sort of unearthly unreality in all the levity of those last hours,' he wrote of the mood on the eve of war, 'like something high and shrill that might crack; and it did crack.' Chesterton recalled how swiftly the mood had changed over the summer of 1914, as the realisation dawned that 'we've got to fight. They've all got to fight. I don't see how anybody can help it.' If the dreamers had been 'struggling to find their way back to Reality,' he reflected sadly, 'they found it all right.'[69]

Nostalgia for childhood and nostalgia for the rural past were both responses to the anxieties of modern life in the late Victorian and Edwardian era. In similar ways, both were driven by the impulse to seek refuge from change, retreating into imaginative worlds that housed memories of happier times. As social and economic forces transformed the landscape around them, late Victorian and Edwardian observers mourned the world they had lost, and expressed an intense yearning for a time when people's lives had seemed less divided – feeling their way back into periods that they remembered or imagined as being more stable, more complete, more uncomplicated in their happiness. But this was not so much a regressive impulse to wish away reality by escaping into the past. It was a constructive response, which aimed to revitalise the modern world: seeking inspiration in the past and infusing it back into the present.

And yet in retrospect, their nostalgia would come to be interpreted as a measure of how deeply people had been in denial about the danger of war looming over the horizon – a nation as well as a continent that had sleepwalked into catastrophe. As Chesterton reflected, the industrial and imperial anxieties people had been seeking relief from since the 1880s would culminate in the tragedy of 1914, as Europe's imperial powers faced each other in industrialised warfare on an unprecedented scale. At times, people ever since have looked back upon the years before the First World War and confused the imaginative worlds that late Victorians and Edwardians created with a reflection of how things had actually been at the time. We have often been tempted to reimagine the years around the turn of the twentieth century less as a time in which people were wrestling with what it meant to be modern – as they assessed the progress as well as the casualties of more than a century of industrialisation, and looked, in turn, to the transformations of the future – than as a pastoral dream of childish innocence.

5
Those Infernal and Damnably Good Old Times
1880–1789

Later Victorians and Edwardians would come to look back upon the course of the Industrial Revolution that had been developing for more than a century, and weigh the gains as well as the losses of their age with the benefit of hindsight. But how had these transformations appeared to the men and women who watched them unfolding? From the final years of the eighteenth century, it was undeniable to contemporaries that unprecedented social and economic changes were underway, as steam-powered factories sprang up, machines were invented to make goods at almost unthinkable speed, canals were dug, roads laid, and people poured into growing industrial centres to seek work in newly mechanised industries – a process that seemed to accelerate with each passing decade. The shock of the new was felt intensely by observers throughout the nineteenth century, as Britain's landscape was transformed by rapidly expanding towns and cities, smokestacks, railways, telegraph lines and engineering works; bringing with it extreme wealth, extreme poverty, and an entirely new pace of living.

No other nineteenth-century nation so thoroughly embraced innovation or saw its surroundings so profoundly altered, but this very commitment to progress generated an intense yearning for what was being left behind. The shock of Britain's rapid early industrialisation inspired intense ambivalence among the generations of men and women who lived through it; few other societies have combined such confidence and faith in progress with such nostalgic retrospection.[1] As the first country to industrialise on this scale, there was an enormous sense of national pride in British ingenuity and skill: a revelling in Britain's global pre-eminence as the 'Workshop of the World', as the future prime minister Benjamin Disraeli described it in a parliamentary speech in 1838. And yet many followed the poet William Blake in decrying the 'dark Satanic mills' that were scarring the landscape, forcing workers to toil in appalling conditions as they crammed into polluted towns and cities – before the factory legislation that would regulate working hours and safety, before the urban infrastructure that would develop to meet capacity, before they had even developed a vocabulary to explain the new phenomena that were being created around them.[2] This new Britain that was taking shape was a giant national experiment for which there was no roadmap.

While it would not be until the 1880s that people came to refer to the changes of the past century as one of 'Industrial Revolution', those who had lived through the late eighteenth and nineteenth centuries were aware that they were living through an age defined by revolution. To many of its contemporaries, in Britain as well as Europe, the French Revolution of 1789 marked a sudden transition into an entirely new political era. To some, it was to be welcomed that the people of France had risen up to overthrow absolute monarchy – 'in every province of this great kingdom the flame of liberty has burst forth', reported the *London Chronicle* in July 1789, an initial reaction that was far from untypical. 'Bliss it was in that dawn to be alive', remembered William Wordsworth of the Storming of the Bastille when he came to publish his autobiographical poem *The Prelude* in 1805.[3] Yet to others, particularly as violence in France deepened in the wake of the Revolution over the following months and years, it was a terrifying warning of the mob violence that might erupt at home. At a time when working

men were increasingly demanding the right to political participation, social elites looked uneasily on the potential for calls
for reform to spill into violent uprising from below. It was a
fear that was encapsulated in the Peterloo Massacre in 1819,
when armed cavalry charged into a crowd of 60,000 peaceful
protesters in Manchester who had gathered to demand the
reform of parliamentary representation, causing the deaths of
18 people and seriously injuring over 600 men, women and
children.[4]

Conservatives in particular feared throughout the following
decades that Britain's radicals might try to follow in the footsteps of French revolutionaries, issuing nostalgic defences of an
aristocratic *ancien régime* (old rule); fears that were periodi-
cally reinvigorated as waves of revolution swept throughout
most European countries in 1820, 1830 and 1848. These political upheavals compelled their contemporaries to look to the
past for reassurance. Politicians, historians and social commentators set out in search of historical confirmation that Britain's
political system could weather any storm – whether the lessons
of history showed that Britain could accommodate change and
reform without cracking at the seams.

CHIVALRY IS DEAD?

Shortly after 6pm on 16 October 1834, the Houses of Parliament burst into flames. The fire had been growing throughout
the afternoon, largely unnoticed, as warning signs were persis-
tently ignored. Peers began to note that the temperature in the
House of Lords was rising alarmingly. Tourists who had come
to view the Armada Tapestries found themselves squinting
through a haze of smoke. Curtains began to smoulder. By the
time the alarm was raised, it was too late: a huge fireball
exploded out of the building at around 6.30pm, burning 'with
such fury,' reported the *Manchester Guardian*, 'that in less than

half an hour, the whole interior presented one entire mass of fire.'[5]

The fire had been an accident waiting to happen. Experts had been warning for years that the building was a tinderbox, but no one could agree on how or whether to renovate it, not least because of the scale of the task before them. The ramshackle complex of medieval and early modern buildings that made up the Houses of Parliament had been joined over centuries into a warren of interconnecting spaces which had been added to and adapted by successive generations of architects, but by the early nineteenth century they were more or less unfit for purpose. The House of Commons chamber was crowded to bursting point, with space at such a premium that members had been rumoured to vote with the opposition sooner than give up their places.[6] The burning of Parliament, then, struck many as a decisive national moment: one that represented a turning point in the history of Parliament, and of a nation at a time of transition, poised between an older world and a new age of change.

For the thousands of observers who flocked to the streets of Westminster to watch the flames, this calamitous event seemed to confirm their viewpoint of the direction Britain was heading in. As the social critic Thomas Carlyle had it, crowds of working men and women cheered the fire on, seeing it as divine judgement for the Poor Law Amendment Act passed just a few months earlier, which had instituted workhouses for a nation in the grip of widespread unemployment. 'A man *sorry* I did not see anywhere,' he remarked afterwards. For conservatives, it seemed a fitting punishment for widening the franchise with the Reform Act of 1832, which had removed notoriously corrupt seats for 'rotten boroughs' with tiny electorates and created ones to give representation to new industrial areas; while for the radical journalist and politician William Cobbett, it could seem more like poetic justice – 'many appeared to consider it a well-merited visitation' that had put a torch to centuries of aristocratic misrule.[7] But whatever the viewpoint, the fire presented a historic opportunity, opening the way for the making of a new Palace of Westminster built for the needs of the nineteenth century. A Parliament fit for a nation at the height of its power: one that had reformed its political system at home and was rapidly growing its empire abroad, and in which life was changing dramatically under the sway of new inventions, innovations and industrial technologies.

Plans were launched immediately to find an architect who could realise a vision for Britain's future. In 1835, a Royal Commission was appointed to study the rebuilding of the palace, prompting a heated public debate about what style might best represent the nation. A year later, the commissioners organised a public competition, inviting architects to submit designs anonymously. The clear winner, the commissioners agreed unanimously, was an entry submitted by Charles Barry, which would incorporate the surviving buildings of the old Palace into a new complex lavishly covered with elaborate Gothic carvings, aiming to embody a vision of Britishness rooted in time-hallowed tradition. In doing so, they did much to establish Gothic Revival as *the* national style of architecture for the majority of the nineteenth century. In truth, the plans were actually something of a mishmash of architectural styles – Barry was a classical architect by training, more used to designing Italianate buildings inspired by Renaissance aesthetics (which had in turn looked back to the architecture of ancient Greece and Rome), but he developed his drawings in collaboration with Augustus Pugin, a 23-year-old architect who would pioneer the Gothic Revival in Britain. The resulting designs would take almost 30 years to fully realise, amid spiralling costs and delays, as the new building was constructed over eight acres of unstable ground, with a frontage facing the Thames a quarter of a mile long, and every inch of it covered with intricate Gothic detailing, from the carved stonework and lacelike tracery of thousands of arched windows to skywards-pointing towers and finials.[8] Taking its inspiration from the Middle Ages, it was a formula that would be repeated in thousands of buildings across Victorian Britain, in churches as well as secular buildings such as St Pancras Station – creating the architectural legacy that critics in the middle of the twentieth century would find so much in to deplore.

If the overall shape and symmetry of the building betrayed the classical influences of Barry's training, the detail was all Pugin's. Every aspect of the Gothic interiors, from the carving and panelling to furniture and even doorknobs, was meticulously designed by Pugin. This wasn't just the attention to detail of an architectural purist or obsessive (though he was, also, both of those things): Pugin was writing a story of Britain into the very fabric of the building. Wood carvings harked back to the faith and piety of the Middle Ages, paintings of Arthurian legends conjured up an age of virtuous heroism and chivalry, while murals of historical events depicted the ancient foundations of British liberty.[9] Britain's greatness, the building proclaimed again and again, was rooted in its history.

All this medievalism was, however, only skin deep. While Pugin's interior designs demanded the rediscovery of craftsmanship techniques not seen since the Middle Ages, the scale of the building required cutting-edge feats of engineering which made use of the scientific advances that were transforming Britain into the first and most advanced industrial nation. As an army of workers constructed a raft of concrete to shore up the Palace's foundations in the fast-moving currents of the Thames, steam-powered cranes hoisted girders high into the air to support the weight of a cast-iron roof. A host of schemes were floated for ventilation, lighting and sanitation arrangements that would ensure Parliament represented a rational, reforming organ of governance, one that was committed to the advancement of national science.

For many in the 1830s, these scientific advances were a source of national power and pride. Politics and science were closely interconnected: both moderate Whigs and liberal Tories shared the conviction that new technologies, innovations, and the spread of scientific knowledge throughout the social hierarchy would bring about social progress.[10] There was a widespread utopian hope that science would bring about the dawn of a new, more enlightened age. Technological innovations such as the steam engine were creating a sense of limitless possibility through projections of a future that would be powered by machines.[11] The opening of the Liverpool and Manchester Railway line in 1830, the first intercity railway in the world, in particular seemed to herald a new era – a steam-powered future in which the problems of the past would be solved by the inexorable progress of technology.

But why did Britain, at the height of its optimism and faith in innovation, choose in the Gothic Revival such a backwards-looking style? Why was Parliament doing all it could to put a medieval mask on a modern building? And what was a nation so proud of its Protestant history doing by deciding upon such a distinctively Catholic style of architecture – rebuilding the heart of government in an age of industrialisation with an aesthetic that evoked the spirit of medieval churches? A government that had just passed the most sweeping reforms of a British representative system since Oliver Cromwell's rule in the 1650s was now choosing to represent itself with a building that harked back to a feudal past of powerful aristocrats and deferential peasantry.

This seems especially puzzling given that, until the end of the eighteenth century, 'Gothic' had most frequently been used as a term of abuse. 'Gothic', a catch-all term for anything that wasn't classical in the wake of the fall of the Roman Empire, had been synonymous with a bygone age of medieval ignorance, cruelty, savageness and superstition – the supposedly 'dark ages' that had been swept away by the Renaissance and Enlightenment. The dominant architectural style of the eighteenth century had been inspired by classical Greece and Rome, as if to proclaim that Britain was the true successor of democracy and civilisation. While Gothic novels were booming in popularity as the eighteenth century drew to a close, and aristocrats were increasingly experimenting with the building of Gothic follies and stately homes, the whole point seemed to be that it was a chance to *escape* from the predictable, rational, modern world of progress. A taste for the Gothic might be indulged in by aesthetes, eccentrics and those swayed by literary fashions, but surely not by serious-minded legislators – for most people at the end of the eighteenth century, Gothic seemed to denote everything that modern, civilised Britain was not. Yet just three decades later, Gothic architecture had come to be seen as distinctively, quintessentially British – a style that seemed to embody the traditional values and ancient virtues that had enabled Britain's steady rise to greatness. What had changed?

Partly, this was a reaction against events that were happening abroad. The French Revolution had exerted a profound impact upon the thought of the time, creating the sense that nothing would ever be quite the same again. After 1789, the neoclassical architecture that had stood for the virtues of classical republicanism and enlightenment was increasingly associated with the violence of republicans in France who had turned the established order upside down. The Revolution prompted a conservative counter-reaction in Britain, as traditionalists sought to buttress the foundations of monarchy and aristocratic hierarchy against potential assault from below.

The politician and philosopher Edmund Burke famously declared that chivalry was dead, arguing that the spectacle of Marie Antoinette menaced by a mob of fishwives who had marched on Versailles heralded a descent into social chaos:

> I thought ten thousand swords must have leaped from their scabbards to avenge even a look that threatened her with insult. But the age of chivalry is gone. That of sophisters, economists, and calculators has succeeded; and the glory of Europe is extinguished forever. Never, never more shall we behold that generous loyalty to sex and rank, that proud submission, that dignified obedience, that subordination of the heart, which kept alive,

even in servitude itself, the spirit of exalted freedom. The unbought grace of life, the cheap defence of nations, the nurse of manly sentiments and heroic enterprise, is gone![12]

The fact that no one had rushed to defend the unprotected body of a queen against a violent mob seemed, for Burke, to represent an appalling dereliction of the social contract. This was more than just nostalgia for a vanished age of loyalty and honour: for Burke, 'the old feudal and chivalrous spirit of fealty' was, paradoxically, the very source of modern freedom. By submitting to one's place in the social hierarchy, he argued, Britons maintained their liberty – chivalry wasn't just an outdated custom of the medieval past, it was Europe's proud cultural heritage, a lubricant for the social order that kept chaos and tyranny at bay. He feared that people's demands for greater rights could only threaten the delicate balance of duty and deference that had kept Britain stable for centuries. While many of Burke's intellectual contemporaries ridiculed his conclusions, deriding his thinking as 'Gothic' – in the older sense of the 'dark ages' from which Britain had, thankfully, moved on – as the nineteenth century progressed, the concept of chivalry came to play an increasingly important role in the way Britons thought about themselves. This was the Gothic re-envisaged as the foundation of modern greatness: proof of Britain's age-old commitment to liberty as well as its unique political stability, in contrast to the absolute monarchies threatened by revolutionary upheaval on the continent; as in the jurist William Blackstone's description of the British constitution as 'an old Gothic castle, erected in the days of chivalry, but fitted up for a modern inhabitant.'[13]

RULE, BRITANNIA!

Throughout the opening decades of the nineteenth century, anxious patricians continued to worry that riots and mass

demonstrations over the right to vote, the replacement of workers by machines, and the removal of restrictions on religious
minorities (most notably the Catholic Emancipation Act of
1829, which put an end to centuries of legal restrictions against
Catholics, and was passed amid protests and threatened insur-
rection in Ireland), were revealing a nation on the edge of an
abyss.[14] The shadow cast by the French Revolution continued
to colour how those in power interpreted demands for change
or restoration from below. Protests, unrest and demands for
reform at home now seemed especially dangerous in the context of a fresh wave of revolutionary enthusiasms in Europe,
prompting the fear that tensions would spill over into mob violence that would attack Britain's ruling elite as outdated relics
of the past.

Yet Britain was recovering, too, from its own revolutionary
upheaval. The loss of the American colonies following the Declaration of Independence in 1776, finally accepted in 1783 after
eight years of war, had badly shaken British confidence, and
was viewed by many as divine punishment for the moral failings of slavery and empire. Not only had Britain been stripped
of the most valuable part of its empire, but a territory once
governed from London with which Britons had felt closest
emotional ties was now loudly proclaiming itself as not just
independent, but freer and more deeply committed to liberty
than the mother country.[15] This national crisis of confidence,
however, would not last long. By 1815, Britain had taken new
territories in India, southern Africa, South America and Australia, and was ruling over a fifth of the world population.
While the millions of men and women living in these territories
had been brought under British rule by armed force, this new,
Second British Empire, it was proclaimed, would be more moral
than the first, more committed to its role as a force for civilisation. Just a generation after defeat in America, a new narrative
was forming that traced a line of unbroken continuity between
Magna Carta and the abolition of the slave trade: England, it

proclaimed, was the birthplace of liberty, a nation destined by providence to abolish slavery and shine as a beacon of freedom and civilisation to the world.

The campaign for the abolition of the slave trade was closely bound up in the question of what it meant to be British. At a time when war with America had called Britain's commitment to liberty into question, anti-slavery could be a way of reaffirming national virtue. Opposition to the slave trade was increasingly embraced as a patriotic act – a way to redeem the nation, offering proof that British power and supremacy were founded not just on wealth and military might, but upon freedom, religion and high moral calibre.[16] While for most of the eighteenth century, the majority of Britons had seen little inconsistency in proudly declaring their love of liberty at home while profiting from the traffic of men, women and children into slavery abroad, by the end of the 1780s the British public were coming to regard the slave trade as a national embarrassment. In Manchester in 1788, for instance, as many as two thirds of the adult male population signed a petition demanding an end to the slave trade, sparking scores of similar petitions across the country that eventually amassed up to 100,000 signatures, making it the largest petition drive the country had ever seen.[17] In the same year, the writer and campaigner Hannah More argued that slavery was a 'shame' 'inscribed' upon the national character, one that threatened Britain's historic reputation as a land of liberty, asking her readers: 'Shall Britain, where the soul of Freedom reigns, / Forge chains for others she herself disdains?'[18]

This enormous popular upwelling of protest built upon decades of growing revulsion at the practice of slavery, but the timing of the drive was no coincidence – 1788 had marked the centenary of the Glorious Revolution, which had overthrown the Catholic James II and ensured Britain's Protestant succession. It was the first event in Britain's history to have a public centennial celebration, with processions, assemblies and festivities held across the country, in which people of all political stripes laid claim to the Revolution's legacy and memorialised it to serve their own visions for Britain's future. At a moment when Britons were revelling in their historic favour and good fortune, it seemed the perfect opportunity to call on the nation to honour its highest ideals.[19] Anti-slavery offered a way in which ordinary men and women could take part in their nation's history – a welcome chance to reclaim their freedom-loving heritage.

Grassroots anti-slavery campaigns continued to grow throughout the opening decades of the nineteenth century, culminating in 1833, the year Parliament voted to abolish slavery in most British colonies, when more than 5,000 petitions were signed by over one and a half million people.[20] (The reality in the colonies was considerably less hopeful than this optimistic popular narrative: slavery continued in territories administered by the East India Company, such as in Sri Lanka, and clandestine slave-trading continued within the British Empire throughout the following decades.[21]) This popular enthusiasm for abolitionism was part of a wave of wider campaigns for political reform, in which people power seemed to be becoming more important than ever before. More and more, ordinary men and women were laying claim to their right to take part in the political and cultural life of the nation – and arguing that this was not just their right, but a patriotic act that could spur the nation on to future greatness. And yet, as we will see, these new aspirations would take the form of an almost insatiable appetite for English history.[22]

In an age defined by revolutionary upheaval in Europe, from 1789 to 1848, the fact that Britain had successfully – and peacefully – effected widespread reform was held up by many as further, conclusive proof of British supremacy. After losing an empire in America, Britain had bounced back to victory over Napoleon in Europe in 1815, while avoiding revolutionary violence at home and amassing the largest and most powerful empire in the world. And as the nineteenth century progressed, there seemed to be ever more reasons to feel optimistic about Britain's future. The first and most advanced industrial nation had, by the 1860s, the highest GDP in the world and the highest per capita income.[23] Scientific innovations were transforming the world around them, suggesting dreams of a machine-powered future in which the problems of the past would be solved by the boundless possibilities of technological progress. Contemporaries were well aware that industrialisation was creating, too, a raft of new and distinctively modern problems – not least in the rapidly swelling towns and cities into which workers were pouring in search of new opportunities. But there was a general faith among those who saw their age as one of progress that these problems would be solved as technology grew more and more advanced. The weariness and disillusionment that would be felt by later Victorians and Edwardians – their anxiety that, despite all these advances, the problems of overwork and poverty remained as pervasive as ever – would only begin to crystallise towards the 1880s. As one author commented in 1852, 'no one can contemplate the unexampled progress of science within the present century ... without feeling that a new epoch has commenced in the history of our race.'[24]

It was an age of enormous pride and faith in progress. Of course, there were deep concerns over the ways in which industrialisation was disrupting traditional ways of life and work, and fears about unemployment and social disorder in sectors where human labour was being replaced with machines. But industrialisation also seemed to be bringing people closer together. Improvements in travel and communications meant that the whole country seemed to become smaller. Regions that had previously seemed remote and inaccessible could now be visited more easily. News travelled more quickly. Innovations in printing meant that books and newspapers were becoming cheaper, bringing them within the reach of more people than ever before at a time when literacy rates were rising dramatically. All these forces operated powerfully to create a new imaginative sense of the nation, making it easier to unite people in a common cause. Throughout Britain, ordinary men and women were increasingly demanding recognition as a unified body with a common identity, common habits, a common history and a common future.[25] There were many grounds for a sense of excitement and confidence that the future would be better than the past. Why look back?

THE CULT OF THE PAST

While many in the nineteenth century celebrated the scientific and technical progress of the Industrial Revolution, others lamented the smokestacks and machinery that were fast destroying a green and pleasant land. Pre-Raphaelite painters devoted themselves to depicting the chivalry and romance of feudal and mythical pasts, Romantic poets expounded upon the beauty of unspoilt countryside, and social critics across the political spectrum appealed to a vanished age of medieval glory and honour. Popular culture abounded with rosy images of 'England in the Olden Time' and the 'Merry England of Good Queen Bess', while historical novels by authors such as Walter Scott became runaway bestsellers – at their peak selling up to seven million weekly instalments, and endlessly copied, pirated, plagiarised, staged, and set to music. By the middle of the century, it was difficult to avoid historical themes and references in any corner of high or popular culture, as the craze for history boomed from a niche pursuit of intellectuals and antiquarians into a mass-market industry.[26] Debates about past, present and future raged in scholarly periodicals and the national press, as people sought to make sense of the changes they were witnessing. Intellectuals vied with each other to diagnose the 'Condition of England' or the 'Spirit of the Age', alternately decrying the failures of industrialism and pinning idealistic hope on technological innovations, and drawing upon lessons from history to ask what direction Britain might be heading in.

For the philosopher and historian Thomas Carlyle, the dawn of the Victorian era was 'The Age of Machinery'. There had been, he argued, 'a mighty change in our whole manner of existence': manual workers and artisans were being replaced by machines, horse power was rapidly being superseded by engines and railways, while oceans that had once taken months to sail across could now be crossed in days by steamship. 'For all earthly, and for some unearthly purposes,' he wrote, 'we have machines and mechanic furtherances ... We remove mountains, and make seas our smooth highways; nothing can resist us. We war with rude Nature.' Many of these developments were to be celebrated: Carlyle marvelled at 'how much better fed, clothed, lodged and, in all outward respects, accommodated men now are' thanks to technological advances. Yet he lamented that while 'wealth has more and more increased', it had, at the same time, tended to gather more and more into the hands of the already wealthy, 'increasing the distance between the rich and the poor.'[27] Despite Britain's considerable resources, swathes of the working classes were still living in acute deprivation. Indeed, in many areas industrialisation seemed to have led to a dramatic decline in the living standards of the urban poor. The rapid growth of industrial cities such as Birmingham and Manchester, which had seemingly sprung up from nowhere almost overnight, was creating a raft of social problems as arrangements for adequate housing and sanitation failed to keep pace with the demand for factory workers. Novelists, physicians and social campaigners alike produced deeply troubling accounts of the plight of urban inhabitants, contrasting life in Victorian cities with nostalgic accounts of a vanishing world. As one critic, the surgeon Peter Gaskell, had it (not entirely accurately), in the years before about 1760, 'the same generation' lived 'age after age on the same spot, and under the same thatched roof, which thus became a sort of heirloom, endeared to its occupier by a long series of happy memories and home delights.' But under the influence of the Industrial Revolution, people had been sucked into the anonymity of polluted and unsanitary cities, substituting home comforts for 'a system of toil continued unbroken by rest or relaxation', and leading not just to diseases of overwork and deprivation, but to 'the breaking up' of community and 'family ties'.[28]

But for Carlyle, the problem went deeper still. He believed that an increasingly mechanical society was changing the way people thought and felt, as if they, too, were taking on the character of machines. He argued that people were increasingly being used as a means to an end, while legislators had stood by and allowed workers to be exploited by the new class of industrial capitalists, in which moral principles seemed to have narrowed down to the law of money-making: 'public principle is gone; private honesty is going; society, in short, is falling to pieces.'[29] Only spiritual rebirth could save Britain from imminent self-destruction. Carlyle's account of the new industrial society was enormously influential, inspiring social critics from John Ruskin to Charles Dickens, Elizabeth Gaskell and the future prime minister Benjamin Disraeli, as novelists and reformers alike took up the question of whether the first industrial nation might have taken a wrong turning.

For many Victorians, the solution lay in the past. From across the social and political spectrum, a range of observers began to look back to the Middle Ages in a new light. Whereas in the eighteenth century the Middle Ages had often denoted the supposedly 'dark ages' of ignorance and superstition, by the Victorian era medievalism was taking on the misty-eyed appeal of nostalgic reverie. 'It was beautiful; it was human!' rhapsodised Carlyle of the feudal system, imagining a time of spiritual contemplation and contentment set against modern industrial alienation.[30] Instead of an age of brutality and violence, the Middle Ages became reimagined as a time of order and social harmony, of brave knights and generous hospitality in which everyone knew their place in the social hierarchy, where people were bound together in close-knit communities by ties of duty and deference – a vanished world that might serve as a protest against the spirit of the nineteenth century.

This was very much a pick-and-mix approach to the Middle Ages. Whatever their political and social views, medievalists could look back and find something to admire, while quietly passing over outbreaks of violence, plague, lawlessness and disorder. For conservatives, feudalism offered a model of a social order in which honour-bound aristocrats and deferential peasants thrived peaceably in a network of mutual rights and duties. Disraeli's 'Young England' movement, an aristocratic clique of romantically inclined Tories, advocated an idealised resurrection of the feudal system in the 1840s, arguing that the problems of industrialism could only be solved from the top down: by a strong monarchy and established Church, and a culture of aristocratic philanthropy. Even the radical journalist William Cobbett, horrified at the laissez-faire economics that allowed industrialists to profit without any regard for the welfare of their workers, turned to a lost feudal order as a means of improving the lot of the poor, writing: 'the days of the Veres and Percies, and Cliffords, and Nevilles, must return, and the glory of leading *vassals* into the *field* must once more be the responsibility of England's gentry.'[31] But for most radicals, the Middle Ages offered not a model of hierarchy, but a golden age for the dignity and rights of individuals, when wages were adequate and ordinary men and women were well-clothed and fed. In songs and poetry, Chartists articulated their campaign for working-class political rights through calls to restore a 'Merry England' defined by the hearty self-sufficiency of agricultural communities, when 'poverty and want were then unknown, / And the peasant seemed as happy as the monarch on his throne.'[32]

Idealistic as these visions of the Middle Ages were, this was more than just rose-tinted fondness for a golden age of plenty that never really existed. Chartist campaigners were conscientiously framing their political demands in the language of history, presenting themselves not as radicals or revolutionaries, but as restorers of British and English tradition. Drawing upon historic images of olde England, they could present themselves as patriots, arguing that it was they, and not corrupt politicians and parasitical aristocrats, who were the true defenders of the nation.[33] And many workers *did* nurture memories of a happier time. For workers in industries where mechanisation had, sometimes in the space of a single generation, replaced traditional modes of handcraft that had existed unchanged since the Middle Ages, they could look back to genuine memories of a time when employment was more stable, and work was dictated by the rhythms of the household rather than the behests of factory taskmasters. Nostalgia for a vanished social order was not necessarily regressive – many people looked to the past for inspiration, seeking solutions to social problems that were not unrealistic utopian dreams, but tried-and-tested ways of living that might be restored again because they had once existed. Progress and reform could be sanctioned by rooting calls for change in history and tradition.

It was one thing to want to look back to the past and recover positive aspects of life that might have been lost in the transition to industrialism, but it was all too easy to shade into romanticising vanished ways of living that had gone for the better. The novelist Henry James, for instance, travelling from Boston to Europe, wrote that London and Paris filled him with 'nostalgic poison' for the backwardness of an Old World that the United States had, thankfully, liberated itself from. Settling in England in the 1870s, he found himself lured by the temptations of nostalgia for an aristocratic heyday, penning lyrical essays on the retrograde charms of the English countryside. Visiting Warwickshire, James fancied 'that there was still a good deal of old England' to be found in rural villages, to the point where he almost found himself looking around for 'the village stocks ... I was on the point of going into one of the ale-houses to ask Mrs Quickly for a cup of sack.' For James, in 'this richly complex English world', 'the present is always seen, as it were, in profile, and the past presents a full face.' Visitors didn't need to be told that they were entering a conservative country – British Toryism was written in the very 'hedgerows' and 'verdant acres' of the English countryside. But the socially regressive features of the squirearchy weren't to be wished away; 'it deepens the local colour – it may be said to enhance the landscape.' Rhapsodising about the picturesque charms of historic England, James started to find that even local almshouses and asylums were 'so quaint and venerable that they almost make the existence of poverty a delectable and satisfying thought.' This was the kind of derangement that the American poet Walt Whitman had cautioned his readers against, warning Americans heading for Europe that 'there are germs hovering above this corpse. Bend down to take a whiff of it, and you might catch the disease of historic nostalgia for Europe.'[34]

As the cult of the past deepened, a number of observers were beginning to worry that Britain's obsession with history was becoming a little unhealthy. Diagnosing the 'Spirit of the Age' in the 1830s, the philosopher John Stuart Mill took aim against 'those men who carry their eyes in the back of their heads and can see no other portion of the destined track of humanity than that which it has already travelled.' Artists and architects worried that the country's infatuation with Gothic Revival threatened to deprive the Victorian era of any style or originality of its own. For the painter John Constable, all this medievalism was simply 'a vain endeavour to reanimate deceased art, in which the utmost that can be accomplished will be to reproduce a body without a soul.' Even George Gilbert Scott, one of the most prolific champions of Gothic Revival architecture, lamented that his contemporaries were 'content to pluck the flowers of history without cultivating any of our own', asking his readers 'shall we ever have an architecture of our own day?'[35]

But while medievalists were incurring the ire of their contemporaries in looking back to a world they had lost, others were looking to history and stressing continuity, not rupture, with present times. Whig historians and politicians, who emphasised the rise of constitutional monarchy, personal freedom and liberal democracy, were creating a new narrative that fused tradition with progress, and continuity with change, as they delved into the past in search of the qualities they believed had defined Britons since time immemorial. The historian and statesman Thomas Babington Macaulay declared that 'the history of England is emphatically the history of progress', arguing that to study the past was to trace 'the steps by which the England of the Doomsday Book, the England of the Curfew and the Forest Laws, the England of crusaders, monks, schoolmen, astrologers, serfs, outlaws, became the England which we know and love, the classic ground of liberty and philosophy, the mart of all trade.' For Macaulay, the lessons of history revealed that the British were 'a people blessed with far more than an ordinary measure of political liberty and of intellectual light' – Britain's ancient traditions were the foundation of modern greatness. This was to become an enormously influential narrative as Britain's role in the world expanded. The onwards march of progress suggested to many Victorians that Britain had not just the right, but the responsibility to bring civilisation to the rest of the world, establishing British institutions and British government throughout the Empire.[36] (It is a narrative that remains influential today, as Boris Johnson insists that 'virtually every advance, from free speech to democracy has come from this country', while imperial apologists maintain that the British Empire was a force for good that 'civilised' the world.[37])

While nostalgic medievalists expressed a sense of grief for ways of life that had vanished forever, Whigs joined Anglo-Saxon with modern times, stressing remote resemblances. The historian Edward Freeman traced the story of Britain back to before the Norman Conquest, arguing that these ancient origins 'were not mere matters of curious speculation, but matters closely connected with our present political being.'[38] As Freeman had it, the superior qualities of his countrymen had been in evidence for over a thousand years of history, with a taste for democracy that had evolved through the centuries into the British constitution. In this reading, one could trace an unbroken line of continuity between the Anglo-Saxon Witenagemot, or national assembly, and Victorian democracy. Freeman's national history was epic in scope, suffused with purple prose that heroised the English people as a whole – at one point during his account of the Norman invasion, for instance, a scene takes place at 'a spot doomed to be memorable and fatal above all other spots in ... history' – the kind of portentous tone that would later be satirised in Sellar and Yeatman's *1066 and All That*. But he had the knack of making his audience feel part of history, as if they too were participating in a national drama of progress unfolding on a grand scale.[39]

This wasn't just a preoccupation of political and intellectual elites: popular interest in British history was also bubbling up from below. Macaulay's *History of England*, published in five volumes between 1848 and 1861, sold in the tens of thousands in its early years of publication, figures that put him almost on a par with book sales of Charles Dickens and Walter Scott.[40] His works reached a wider audience still through lending libraries and mutual improvement societies, which were becoming ever more numerous throughout the Victorian era. Among his readers were the members of a working-men's club, who wrote a letter thanking Macaulay 'for writing a history which working men could read.'[41] Throughout the country, ordinary men and women were developing a voracious interest in British and English history – not just for weighty volumes of historical non-fiction, but for historical novels, illustrations, costumes, tourism, pageants, plays and festivities. Serialised in weekly instalments, Walter Scott's heroic tales of Scottish and English history could reach audiences in their millions. There was a

growing fascination with antiquated habits and outdated practices that, by the nineteenth century, seemed far out of reach.
Victorian artists such as Charles Leslie and W.P. Frith found wide
audiences with paintings depicting 'May Day Revels in the Time
of Queen Elizabeth' or 'A Coming of Age in the Olden Time',
hoping to reach the popular market through mass-produced
engravings. They were knowingly drawing on people's nostalgia for the gaiety and charm of the 'good old days', conjuring
up images of an age – as in Frith's *A Coming of Age in the
Olden Time* – when aristocrats had supposedly rubbed shoul-
ders with their tenants at communal celebrations and ensured
no one went hungry, and hearty peasants, in turn, gathered to
cheer the benevolent lord of the manor. As one reviewer of the
painting reflected: 'we, in our days of commercial activity and
enterprise, can scarcely realise such a scene of festive enjoyment
as this,' asking his readers: 'are we, with all our boasted advancement in science and civilisation, really a wiser and happier people
than our forefathers of three centuries ago?'[42]

COMING OF AGE IN THE OLDEN TIME.

Wood engraving after W.P. Frith, *A Coming of Age in the Olden
Time* (1854).

Yet the effect of this popular interest in history was not necessarily backwards-looking. History could bolster a growing
sense of national pride, by claiming justification in ancestral
achievements. It provided a way for ordinary men and women
to feel part of their national story. As the historian Peter Mandler writes, 'by giving people a long pedigree of blood and
culture, reaching back many centuries, history conveyed to the
powerless and disenfranchised a tremendous sense of entitle-
ment and potential for the future.' Intellectual elites had initially
been suspicious of this new appetite for history, worrying that
it suggested a rising nationalism among the lower orders that
might lead to social and political agitation. The fact that this
appetite had particularly taken the form of historical novels
prompted complaints from the pages of high-cultural journals
that popular history was degrading and falsifying what should
be a serious and scholarly undertaking. But increasingly, the
ruling elite was coming to realise that national history could be
a crucial glue for social and political cohesion – far from being
subversive, popular history had proved to be a useful tool for
cultivating patriotism.[43]

ROMANCING THE NATION

The popular appetite for history was, above all, *romantic*. It
was part of a new wave of romantic nationalism, which understood nationhood not as something imposed from the top
down by monarchs or governments, but as an organic development unfolding from people's shared languages, religions,
cultures and customs. There was a growing interest in myths,
folklore and vernacular traditions, as people sought to find
romantic origin stories for English, Welsh and Scottish national
identities. In Wales, there was an unprecedented surge of interest
in Welsh culture, as scholars and patriots rediscovered linguis-
tic and literary traditions – and sometimes, where traditions

couldn't be found, making them up again. Societies such as the Gwyneddigion (taking its name from the Gwynedd region of North Wales) were established, combining poetry readings and literary criticism with communal singing and harp music, while antiquarians popularised tales of heroic bards and ancient druids, drawing on history and myth to create new (though supposedly age-old) traditions.[44] The fifteenth-century leader Owain Glyndŵr was elevated to the status of national hero: a figure whose valiant but doomed resistance to medieval English rule – not to mention his mysterious disappearance into the mists of time – perfectly matched the romantic-nationalist mood.

In Scotland, Walter Scott led the way in rekindling people's interest in their national past. In novels and poetry, Scott reimagined Scotland as a land of Celtic romance and sublime landscapes. While eighteenth-century observers had derided Highlanders as barbarians at the fringes of Scottish society, the romantic imagination re-envisaged the Highlands as a place rich in ancient customs, noble ideals and rugged mystery. Traditional Highland dress had almost fallen out of use by the 1780s – not least as it had been outlawed between 1746 and 1782 in the wake of Jacobite rebellions – but in the final years of the eighteenth century the upper and middle classes began to take a new interest in tartanry, seeking new ways of expressing national pride that were rooted in apparently ancient tradition. Scott was enormously influential in popularising this new image of Highland culture, serving as president of the Celtic Society of Edinburgh, where he described members dining together 'kilted and bonneted in the old fashion, and armed to the teeth.' The cult of the Highlands found a wider audience still in 1822, when Scott designed a pageant in honour of George IV's state visit to Scotland, which drew on old and invented traditions alike in what one historian has since described as 'a bizarre travesty of Scottish history.'[45] Half the population of Scotland was drawn to the capital for the visit, with Scott stage-managing a procession of clan chieftains to pay homage to the King, who himself was clad in a kilt of the Royal Stuart tartan – itself a recent invention, part of the nineteenth-century 'authentication' of clan tartans that Scott had been instrumental in promoting.

This was a new image of Scottish history: one that was now elevating Highland culture to stand in for the whole of national identity. Despite hailing from the Scottish Lowlands himself, Scott seemed to have been carried away by nostalgia for a supposed golden age of Celtic romance that ignored Lowland culture altogether. Even Scott's devoted son-in-law and biographer, J.G. Lockhart, felt that this national mythologising was approaching the status of a collective 'hallucination', arguing that 'with all respect and admiration for the noble and generous qualities which our countrymen of the Highland clans have so often exhibited . . . they had always constituted a small and almost always unimportant part of the Scottish population.'[46] But, in a way, this was part of the appeal. Especially since the Highland Clearances of the eighteenth and nineteenth centuries had seen landlords instigate widespread evictions of tenants in favour of more profitable sheep farming, Highland culture was taking on the romantic appeal of a proud but vanishing way of life, menaced by the encroaching forces of modernisation.[47] (This was even, perhaps, a form of cultural appropriation, with socially and financially privileged Lowlanders and Highland landowners cosplaying as 'Heilan' laddies and lassies – sometimes the very same people who were contributing to the breakup of Highland communities by clearing farmers from their land.)

As well as playing a leading role in the creation of a new, romantic vision of Scottish history, Scott was also to have a significant influence on English national mythology. While Scott's early novels had focused on formative moments in Scotland's past, the publication of *Ivanhoe* in 1819 saw his attention turn increasingly to England. These novels of English and Scottish history dramatised clashes of values at crucial moments of transformation, from the dying Anglo-Saxon world of *Ivanhoe* after the Norman Conquest, to Roundheads and Cavaliers in the aftermath of the Civil War, or Jacobites and Hanoverians fighting over the succession to the British throne. This was a crucial aspect of Scott's enormous popular appeal – as well as indulging their appetite for the adventure and romance of times gone by, his readers could find useful reflections for their *own* age of transition in the changing societies that the novels brought to life. Readers didn't have to choose between dreaming of a heroic and romantic past, or focusing their attention on the present: for a generation who had lived through an age of violent revolutions and war in Europe, Scott's dramas of historical conflicts offered a way in which people could think through the defining issues of their own age while appearing to escape them.[48]

More than anything, though, Scott's readers came to be entertained. While social critics such as Carlyle and Disraeli looked back to the Middle Ages in search of remedies for the problems of the present, readers of historical novels were more likely to look to the past simply for enjoyment. Plenty of people enjoyed history without wanting to return to it, as an object of entertainment and curiosity. History offered up the charm of the exotic – the 'olden times' could be celebrated and indulged in precisely because they were *past*. While Scott himself dreamed of vanished ages of heroism and chivalry on the page, writing in his baronial mansion of Abbotsford in the Scottish Borders, among collections of medieval relics, ancient manuscripts and suits of armour, his general faith was in the forces of progress and innovation – indeed, Abbotsford was Scotland's first home to enjoy the distinctly modern convenience of gas lighting.[49] In turn, his readers could momentarily throw off their modern sensibilities and imagine themselves into romances of history without giving up the benefits of the present, safe in the knowledge that they lived in an age of modernisation and progress. These romantic national histories were emerging in the context of a widespread acceptance of change: as glittering origin myths for unmistakeably modern nations.

THE BAD OLD TIMES

By the middle of the nineteenth century, a number of writers were beginning to lose patience with their contemporaries' romanticising of the past. The poet Elizabeth Barrett Browning took aim against Scott's medievalism, writing that she distrusted 'the poet who discerns / No character or glory in his times, / And trundles back his soul five hundred years' in search of inspiration. Her epic poem *Aurora Leigh* (1856) skewered male writers who complained about the present while idealising selective aspects of the past, arguing that 'every age / Appears to the souls who live in it ... Most unheroic' – even Queen Guinevere, she reasoned, was probably bored by King Arthur on occasion. For Barrett Browning, if there was 'room for poets in this world', their 'sole work' should be 'to represent the age, / Their age, not Charlemagne's – this live, throbbing age.' George Eliot, for one, was glad not to have lived 'when there were fewer reforms and plenty of highwaymen, fewer discoveries and more faces pitted with the small pox.' Like Barrett Browning, she scorned writers who praised the selective idealised merits of the past, while pronouncing the present trivial and vulgar, arguing that

> perhaps they would have had the same complaint to make of the age of Elizabeth, if, living then, they had fixed their attention on its more sordid elements, or had been subject to the grating influence of its everyday meannesses, and had sought refuge from them in contemplation of whatever suited their taste in a former age.[50]

Charles Dickens vented misanthropic rage against his contemporaries' reverence for the past, writing to a friend that 'if ever I destroy myself it will be in the bitterness of hearing those infernal and damnably good old times extolled.' He explained that he was compiling *A Child's History of England* (1851–3), which thoroughly debunked the stock heroes of history education

(Henry VIII, for instance, was 'a most intolerable ruffian, a disgrace to human nature'), hoping to inoculate future generations against politicised visions of a rose-tinted past. 'I am writing a little history of England for my boy,' Dickens continued to the friend, 'for I don't know what I should do, if he were to get hold of any Conservative or High Church notions; and the best way of guarding against any such horrible result is, I take it, to wring the parrots' necks in his very cradle.'[51]

A Child's History of England seemed to go out of its way to emphasise the worst aspects of history. Far from the 'Merry England' of nostalgic medievalists, for Dickens the Middle Ages were a litany of cowardly kings, 'wicked nobles', 'bad landlords' and selfish clergy, who 'had gone on very badly indeed.' The feudal system was a time of 'suffering under great oppression' for the common people, who 'were still the mere slaves of the lords of the land on which they lived, and were on most occasions harshly and unjustly treated.'[52] England under the Tudors was little better, in which 'people were constantly being roasted to death', the executioner's axe 'fell through the necks of some of the bravest, wisest, and best in the land', and 'the national spirit seem[ed] to have been banished from the kingdom.' The Stuarts were dismissed as 'a public nuisance altogether.' No monarch since Alfred the Great escaped Dickens's censure, but even Parliament 'were as bad as the rest', and would have been better advised, he felt, 'to avoid long speeches, and do more work.'[53] Conforming to popular opinion about the 'Merry England of Good Queen Bess', the only period of history that came in for praise was Elizabethan England, which Dickens pronounced 'a great reign for discovery, for commerce, and for English enterprise and spirit in general', with 'many improvements and luxuries . . . in the general manner of living.' But even here, he reminded his youthful readership, 'cockfighting, bull-baiting, and bear-baiting, were still the national amusements, and a coach was so rarely seen' that even the Queen herself was forced to navigate roads on horseback.[54]

But if Dickens's childhood readers were supposed to reflect on how lucky they were to live in an age of civilised values and modern conveniences, they were not encouraged to be complacent about British pride. In discussing the War of American Independence, Dickens reflected that the United States, having been left to its own devices, had grown to become 'one of the greatest nations of the earth.' It was, he argued, 'honourably remarkable for protecting its subjects ... with a dignity and a determination which is a model for England. Between you and me,' he confided in a stage whisper, 'England has rather lost ground in this respect since the days of Oliver Cromwell.'[55]

Writing for an adult audience, Dickens was similarly equivocal about whether the injustice and cruelty of the past was preferable to the injustice and cruelty of the present. His historical novel of the French Revolution, *A Tale of Two Cities* (1859), famously declared that

> It was the best of times, it was the worst of times, it was the age of wisdom, it was the age of foolishness ... In short, the period was so far like the present period that some of its noisiest authorities insisted on its being received, for good or for evil, in the superlative degree of comparison only.[56]

This was a view that challenged both the pessimism of Victorians who were nostalgic for the glamour of times past, and the optimism of those who felt that things were always getting better thanks to the modern forces of progress. Yet even this ambivalence proved too much for some readers, who were more used to hearing their forebears discussed in reverential terms, with their achievements invoked as a yardstick which the present hoped to measure up to. As one furious critic of the novel had it in the pages of the *Saturday Review*, Dickens was taking 'a sort of pleasure, which appears to us insolent and unbecoming in the extreme, in drawing the attention of his readers exclusively to the bad and weak points in the history and character of our immediate ancestors.' For the reviewer, this was personal: these weren't just abstract historical figures Dickens was talking about, but 'the grandfathers of the present generation', who were, he felt, being caricatured as 'a sort of savage, or very little better ... cruel, bigoted, unjust, ill-governed, oppressed, and neglected in every possible way. The childish delight with which Mr. Dickens acts Jack Horner and says What a good boy am I, in comparison with my benighted ancestors,' he thundered, 'is thoroughly contemptible.'[57]

These were positions in a culture war not far removed from those we see today in the twenty-first-century press, in which debates over social injustice spilled into the terrain of history, pitting those who drew pride from Britain's heritage as a storehouse of inspirational role models against those who re-evaluated historical figures and events, in pursuit of what their critics saw as little more than virtue-signalling.

Yet Dickens, too, was susceptible to idealising the world of 'the grandfathers of the present generation' that was beginning to pass just out of reach of living memory. Many of his novels are suffused with sentimentality and nostalgia for the world of his boyhood. Looking back fondly on the leisurely days of stagecoaches, country inns and warm hospitality was a way of critiquing the inequality and upheaval of the age of the railway and the factory. By the time *A Christmas Carol* was published in 1843, many people who were deploring what they saw as the new, selfish spirit of industrial capitalism were looking back wistfully on a time of jollity and communal celebrations by a blazing fireside. Despite her decidedly un-nostalgic attitude towards the days of 'highwaymen' and 'small pox', George Eliot similarly reflected with fondness upon the turn of the nineteenth century (20 years before her birth) from a 60-year retrospect, writing in *Adam Bede* (1859) that 'ingenious philosophers tell you, perhaps, that the great work of the steam-engine is to create leisure for mankind. Do not believe them.' For Eliot, industri-alisation had led to a more rapid pace of living, not only ushering in faster modes of transport and ways of working, but bringing with it ever more books and newspapers to read, scientific discoveries and theories to keep on top of, letters to reply to, things to do and to see. 'Those old leisurely times' of country walks and quiet contemplation, she felt, were gone – 'gone where the spinning-wheels are gone, and the pack-horses, and the slow wagons.'[58]

In an age in which industrialisation was uprooting people physically as well as psychologically, the very idea of being 'at home' in the world was beginning to take on a new and intensely nostalgic appeal. In an era of mass migration, when moving from country to city in search of employment – or even travelling from Britain to the far reaches of the empire – was becoming an increasingly common, shared experience, the meaning of home was taking on more and more importance. This was not so much nostalgia for a historical period that was passing out of living memory, as a yearning for personal memories and stages within each person's life cycle. Homesickness, and how to find one's way back home, became one of the defining themes of Victorian literature, reaching its extremity in the figure of Cathy in Emily Brontë's *Wuthering Heights* (1847), whose ghostly figure pines to be let in to her old house, crying 'let me in – let me in! . . . I'm come home!'[59]

Of course, moving house was not an experience new or unique to an industrialising nation; the emotional pangs of missing an old home while trying to put down roots in a new one were age-old. On the face of it at least, the lives of Jane Austen's characters appear untouched by the Industrial Revolution, yet the experience of moving house is one of the great themes of her novels. In *Sense and Sensibility* (1811), for instance, Marianne Dashwood falls physically ill through excess of regret and reminiscence, when her family are forced to move out of her beloved childhood home of Norland Park. She wanders throughout the house on her last evening there, wailing histrionically: 'Dear, Dear Norland . . . when shall I cease to regret you!—when learn to feel a home elsewhere!—O happy house!' Yet Marianne is cured of her nostalgia once she begins the process of accepting that, one day, she will come to feel at home elsewhere, and form an attachment to another place, another house. Throughout Austen's novels, plots hinge on the drama of characters needing (and wanting) to build a new home for themselves, while at the same time missing what they have left behind – and, finally, coming to terms with it. The story can only be resolved once her protagonists have ceased to feel nostalgia as a traumatic, painful loss, and come to look back on their earlier lives with fondness and acceptance. As Elizabeth Bennet counsels Mr Darcy in *Pride and Prejudice* (1813), 'you must learn some of my philosophy. Think only of the past as its remembrance gives you pleasure.'[60]

Where male writers were prone to wax nostalgic about a medieval world of beauty and chivalry destroyed by modern industrial ugliness, female novelists were often far more accepting of the changes brought about by industrialisation. In *North and South* (1855), for instance, Elizabeth Gaskell offered a much more optimistic picture of industrial life and work than accounts such as Carlyle's, which asserted that the Industrial Revolution degraded and dehumanised its workers, and generated material wealth at the expense of physical and spiritual wellbeing. Moving to the industrial town of Milton-Northern, a fictionalised Manchester, Margaret Hale initially feels intense nostalgia for her old home of Helstone in the countryside of southern England. Shocked by roughness and dirtiness of the industrial North, and appalled by the treatment of factory workers, she at first pines for life in a country village, dwelling on 'thoughts of home with all the longing of love.' Margaret's image of Helstone closely matches the romantic nostalgia of social critics who deplored the spirit of industrialism – she describes it in Edenic, even fairy-tale terms, 'like a village in a poem – one of Tennyson's poems.' Yet she begins to realise that her rural idyll is in fact not so idyllic for all its inhabitants: while factory workers toiled for their wages in difficult and dangerous conditions, agricultural poverty was an even more pervasive problem. Later, she discourages her friend Higgins from travelling south to find work, warning him 'you could not stand it . . . The mere bodily work . . . would break you down . . . You would not bear the dullness of the life.'[61] Margaret comes to realise that, for all the problems of urban and industrial life, it had its advantages, offering wages to be spent amid the bustle and excitement of city streets, and the promise of wider cultural and intellectual horizons.

Indeed, the historian Susan Zlotnick has argued that women writers more readily welcomed the new industrial world than did their male counterparts, because it seemed to point the way forward to a better world for women. While writers such as Gaskell and the Brontë sisters were undoubtedly concerned by the problems of industrial poverty, ill-health and inadequate housing, they were also excited by the changes industrialisation was bringing, in part because they recognised that such changes might offer the possibility of women's freedom and economic independence. The spectacle of working-class women labouring alongside men in factories, earning their own wages – which had suggested to so many male observers a world turned worryingly upside down – seemed to carry the promise for middle-class women that they, too, might one day gain financial liberation, and expand their horizons beyond the confines of home and family. Charlotte Brontë, for instance, who had grown up in the genteel poverty of her father's parsonage at Haworth, considered financial dependency to be 'the one great curse of single female life', and felt that working for wages in a factory would be preferable to a life of domestic confinement over which she had little control. Money could act as the great equaliser, giving a woman power to do as she liked. As she wrote to her sister Emily in 1839: 'I could like to work in a mill. I could like to feel some mental liberty.'[62]

This was, of course, a decidedly middle-class perspective on the supposedly liberating potential of factory labour. But what about mill workers themselves – how did the millions of working men and women who made the transition to industrial life and work feel about the changes they were living through? The working-class poet and power-loom weaver Ellen Johnston, for one, treasured the economic freedom that mill work brought her as a single mother with a child to support in the 1850s and 1860s, declaring: 'a thousand times I'd be a factory girl!' Not that the work was easy – the polluted atmosphere of the mill greatly damaged her health, and she described factory life in her autobiography as one of 'incessant toil'. But Johnston's identity as a skilled worker was just as much a source of pride and self-worth as her status as a poet. She proudly related her skill at the loom and the praise she received from her employers, and wrote of the excitement of living and working in Glasgow's industrial centre, amid the 'clink' of 'anvils', and workers gathering to drink their 'hard-won pleasure' after their shifts – the 'joy that springs from wealth of daily toil.'[63]

Accounts such as Johnston's present a stark contrast to Victorian writers on the 'Condition of England', who surveyed the urban working classes from a distance and asserted that industrialisation had degraded and exploited workers by depriving work of meaning. The historian Emma Griffin argues that autobiographies and memoirs written by ordinary men and women present a very different picture to the poets, novelists, philosophers and social commentators who decried industrialisation and romanticised older agrarian ways of life. Many people who wrote down their life stories wholeheartedly embraced modernisation, and flocked to towns for new opportunities, excitements, and the promise of self-development and social mobility. For Griffin, 'attention has been focused for so long upon the way change destroyed older and valued ways of life that historians have largely failed to notice the gains that many working men wrought for themselves out of the turmoil.' Throughout the nineteenth century, she argues, the men and women who made the transition to industrial life and work frequently wrote of their choices in terms of pride and empowerment, sounding 'celebratory notes of improvement and progress' as they reflected on the course of their lives.[64]

Wages in factories were often higher, and more stable, than in rural occupations, offering the promise not just of economic independence, but of enhanced social status and self-worth. As one anonymous writer recalled of his apprenticeship in a Lancashire factory, he was 'never as happy as I was at that time'. Very few rural–urban migrants chose to return to the countryside later in life. Industrial towns and cities offered excitement, and new people to meet, but also more cultural and educational opportunities than could often be found in rural areas. Night schools, Sunday schools, lending libraries, reading clubs and mutual improvement societies were proliferating in towns and cities throughout the nineteenth century, providing opportunities to acquire new skills and passions, as well as a route for the self-taught and self-made into carving out a better future for the working classes through participation in local politics and trades unions.[65]

This is not to say that autobiographers always enjoyed factory work. Many accounts describe difficult and dangerous working conditions, industrial accidents, illnesses, and periods of unemployment and extreme poverty. Thomas Wood, for instance, described starting work in a mill at the age of eight in the 1830s, working six days a week for as long as 15 hours at a time, and enduring the 'brutal' treatment of overseers – which, 'had a fair record been kept' of their behaviour, he felt, 'would read more like the doings of a West-Indian slave driver than a sober record of English life.' He recalled that 'the mortality among millhands was very great . . . we could count whole families of children who worked with us who had gone to an early grave.' 'Poverty' and 'keen want' had 'upheld a system of supplying victims.'[66] Autobiographies, then, can only give us a partial story. We cannot hear the accounts of the Industrial

Revolution's casualties: the men, women and children who did not survive to reflect on their life stories in old age.

Nor is it to suggest that all workers welcomed the transition from agricultural and hand labour to factory work. As we have seen, Chartists framed their campaigns for working-class political rights around images of a vanished 'Merry England' that had supposedly been a golden age for the dignity of the working man. In the early nineteenth century, Luddites, an underground organisation of textile workers, attacked factories in protest against the replacement of workers by machines, and the ensuing unemployment that was caused as traditional modes of labour were left unable to compete with industrial economies of scale. The decision to look for work in industrial towns and cities was not always a free one – many people simply had no other choice, in industries that were being transformed by mechanisation, and where traditional employment opportunities had dried up. Thomas Wood remembered his father, a handloom weaver, 'clinging to a doomed trade. Doomed to be crushed out by remorseless machinery.' He reflected on the terrible irony that his parents had sent him to work, first in a textile mill, and later to be trained by a power-loom maker – an industry set to make his father's profession obsolete. Wood wondered if his family had thought about it in these terms: 'perhaps my father accepted the inevitable, or, more likely still, I was sent there because there was no other opening.'[67]

Yet, of the workers who wrote down their autobiographies and reflected on the changes they had witnessed over the course of their lives, very few were nostalgic for an earlier time. Rather, they marvelled at the progress and improvements they had lived through. For Wood, it was 'a misanthrope indeed who would wish the old days or customs back again'. Writing from the perspective of 1880, he praised factory legislation that had 'throw[n] the protection of the law over those who cannot protect themselves', and reflected of the cruelty and abuses he had witnessed at work as a child that 'the memory of these things is passing away'. Many working-class autobiographers, who often wrote their accounts for the benefit of children or grand-children, invited them to reflect on how much had changed for the better. John Bennett, a carpenter born in the Wiltshire countryside in 1787, asked his children in the 1850s to 'look back and see what troublesome times we had during my bringing up ... The working classes, in my opinion, was never so well off' as they were now. The autobiographer Isaac Anderson's 'only wish' was that his parents 'had each lived to enjoy and to see the improvements I see', while Benjamin North, who had been born to agricultural labourers in 1811, reflected at the age of 70 that if his parents and ancestors could 'revisit the earth ... and see the domestic alterations, commercial improvements, and the wonderful and astonishing activities of life', they would not be able to 'believe their own eyes'.[68]

Throughout the nineteenth century, working-class writers consciously rejected narratives of decline they encountered among their contemporaries, and argued against cultural myths of the 'good old days' – or, as one autobiographer described them, 'the bad old times.'[69] As the carpet weaver and poet Noah Cooke wrote in the 1870s, 'some folks are apt to sigh that the former days were better than these. In some things,' he allowed, 'that may be true; but it certainly does not apply to the hours of labour, and the opportunities for rest and recreation. The working classes never had better times than now.' When Cooke had begun work as a boy, he had been working 14-hour days for little pay. But thanks to the mechanisation of his trade, 'upon the introduction of the power carpet loom, I was one of the first employed – the hours of labour being much shorter – I found more time to devote to self-culture.'[70] George Mallard, who worked as a farm boy in the 1840s, reflected in his memoirs that 'when I hear people talk of the good old days ... they must be ignorant of what did happen in those days. I know it was hard times where I was.'[71] James Hawker, who was born in Northamptonshire in 1836 and supported himself as a poacher, scorned the idea that agricultural labourers 'seemed a Deal Happier' in the days of his youth. In his opinion, he 'was merely a Serf.'[72] For the former 'beggar boy' James Dawson Burn, who wrote down his account in the 1850s, the Reform Act (of 1832, which had widened the franchise and tidied up abuses in the electoral system) and a host of legal and political improvements, had led to 'a new era in our national history', reflecting with a sense of pride 'that every step the Legislature has taken in the right direction has resulted in the renewed energy of the people.' 'When we take a quiet, retrospective view of the state of affairs in Great Britain in the early part of the present century, and compare it with the present,' he wrote, 'I think it will be admitted that as a nation we have much cause to feel grateful.'[73]

'EVERY SELF-RESPECTING CASTLE HAS A LEGEND OF BLOODSHED'

Yet there were perverse pleasures to be taken, too, in recalling the 'bad old times'. In an age of progress and improvement, many were beginning to crave a little taste of barbarity. From the 1790s, there was an explosion in the popularity of Gothic novels and stories, a boom which continued throughout the nineteenth century, as readers were drawn compulsively to tales that exhumed the skeletons in history's closet and presented the spine-chilling possibility that the past might, after all, prove to be undead.[74] Gothic writers were fascinated by the ruins of the past, creating imaginary landscapes of crumbling castles, decaying abbeys, and sinister primal forces. Novelists such as Ann Radcliffe and Matthew Lewis twisted and perverted nostalgia for the Middle Ages, offering to their readers the pleasurable terrors of ancient feuds and family secrets, or else subverted yearnings for chivalry with gruesome tales of corrupted monks, vicious nuns, ruined maidens and cruel aristocrats. This was a

fascination quite different from nostalgia for the alleged harmony of medieval communities. The Gothic imagination looked
back precisely to images of disorder, superstition and decay,
even as it conjured up threatening images of the ruins of the
future.

The fashion for the Gothic was the dark underbelly of the Age
of Enlightenment. In an age that had supposedly done away
with superstitious beliefs in magic, witchcraft and the supernatural, and which sought to use science to explain everything,
people were left with a hankering for the mysterious and inex-
plicable. At the same time as people were putting their faith in
a future of rational progress, Gothic fictions reacquainted their
readers with the sinister pleasures of uncertainty, in which the
past they thought had been safely left behind came back to
haunt the present with a vengeance.[75] This was horror as entertainment: readers could enjoy the terrors of the past vicariously,
at a safe remove from reality in the pages of fiction. Gothic
novels were frequently set in faraway locations on the Continent, featuring tyrannical Italian nobles or bloodthirsty Spanish
inquisitors, creating a reassuring sense that such horrors could
never unfold in a moderate Protestant nation like Britain; or
else plots hinged on sceptical protagonists who, at last, debunk
seemingly supernatural occurrences through the explanatory
power of science and rationality.[76]

In Ann Radcliffe's enormously popular novels, happy end-
ings were brought about by revealing rational explanations for
previously frightening phenomena. In *The Mysteries of Udolpho*
(1794), for instance, the young protagonist Emily is plagued by
a series of seemingly supernatural terrors in the castle in which
she is imprisoned, yet by the end of the novel these have been
revealed as the deliberate machinations of the scheming Count
Montoni, part of an elaborate ruse to gain control of her aunt's
estate. Like in *Scooby Doo*, this was a plot formula where villains would have gotten away with it if it weren't for those
meddling protagonists. But, increasingly, readers didn't want

their supernatural explained away, and were demanding that the horror feel real, at least in the world of their imagination. In Matthew Lewis's bestselling horror *The Monk* (1796), the devil himself burst onto the page in a scandalous tale of incest, rape, murder and sorcery, which provoked intense condemnation from critics in literary magazines but proved no bar to its commercial success. Readers seemed to be left unsatisfied by stories that reassured them of the solidity of their rational, modern world of progress, and were clamouring for tales that transported them back to the terrors and superstitions of the past, while novels such as Mary Shelley's *Frankenstein* (1818) imported age-old fears right into the heart of cutting-edge science.

This popular appetite for the gory and the gruesome spilled over into a fascination with the darker episodes of English history. The contents of history books written for use in schools testify to this interest in the macabre: after the Norman Conquest, the Black Death, the Plague and the Great Fire of London were often given the most attention. There was a growing interest in the victims of history, as school children were invited to sympathise with the plight of Lady Jane Grey ascending the scaffold, or imagine the terror of the little princes murdered in the Tower of London.[77] The implication was clear: youthful readers were encouraged to look back on a roll call of ghastly episodes and atrocious misdeeds, and reflect upon how lucky they were to live in a more enlightened age. But, as in Dickens's *A Child's History of England*, this was also childhood suffering served up as entertaining melodrama: for Victorian audiences steeped in sentimentality, the pathos of two innocent, unsuspecting young princes being led to their untimely ends by that 'boldest, most crafty, and most dreaded nobleman in England', their evil uncle Gloucester, proved an irresistible spectacle.[78]

The Tower of London itself was being rebranded as Britain's premier destination for the macabre. The middle years of the nineteenth century saw the growth of a new branch of the history industry – a boom in popular tourism. Visitors were flocking in their thousands to sites such as Westminster Abbey, Hampton Court, Windsor Castle, and especially the Tower of London, in search not just of national heritage, but of historic spectacle, led by guidebooks that sought to illuminate the cruel fates of past inhabitants.[79] In the eighteenth century, the chief attraction at the Tower had been the royal menagerie, which was moved in 1835 to a new home in Regent's Park. Visitors had come 'to see the lions', not to appreciate a medieval castle – which, at any rate, was falling into decay. By the dawn of the Victorian era it was an architectural mess of old buildings, modern brick offices, warehouses, storehouses, taverns, workshops, soldiers' barracks, and mouldering basements filled with explosives. In many ways, this reflected the history of the Tower, which had variously been used as an armoury, a treasury, a royal palace, Royal Mint, prison, and public record office.[80]

But in the Victorian imagination, the story of the Tower was transformed into one in which the imprisonment and torture of history's great and the good assumed a starring role – a fascination that continues today, with ghost tours promising the headless spectres and ghoulish screams of illustrious victims. Public interest was fuelled by writers such as William Harrison Ainsworth, whose *The Tower of London: A Historical Romance* (1840) painted a vivid picture of subterranean torture chambers, forced confessions and brutal executions. Light on plot and narrative, his readers seemed unsure whether it functioned as a novel or a guidebook. On the one hand, Ainsworth suggested to his readers how fortunate they were to have escaped the plagues and racks of the past, the religious intolerance and social disorder. On the other, the high dramas of earlier ages, the life-or-death struggles and dashing personalities, seemed to hold a glittering allure in comparison to the drabness and comparative stability of the nineteenth century.

Such was the effect of accounts such as Ainsworth's on the popular image of the Tower of London that one visiting Frenchman wrote of his excitement to experience this 'sinister necropolis' of 'melodramatic fame' in the 1850s. 'The historical monuments of this country, I notice, are popular in proportion to the horrors committed within their walls,' he reflected of English culture; 'every self-respecting castle has a legend of bloodshed and murder.' Yet it was hard to resist the charms of this national enthusiasm for the macabre, as one followed in the footsteps of prisoners through the heavy door of the Traitors' Gate, or wandered into the 'ominous-looking' 'Bloody Tower, where the little princes were murdered by the savage Gloucester', or the adjoining room 'where Henry VI was done to death . . .'[81]

George Cruikshank, *The Execution of Lady Jane Grey at Tower Green*, in William Harrison Ainsworth, *The Tower of London: A Historical Romance* (London, 1840).

This was about as far away as one could get from taking solace in nostalgia for the 'Merry England' of yore, or the hearty social order of the 'Olden Time'. The past was offered up as an exotic spectacle, a barbaric era out of which the modern world had safely, thankfully, emerged. Such gory history could only be enjoyed as entertainment because it was over, finished, no longer a threat. But even here, there was an element of nostalgia for what had been lost – a rueful sense that, though the dangers of the past had been greater, the rewards had been greater, too. And yet the popular appetite for history suggested a way in which Victorians could both have their cake and eat it: if something had been lost in the transition to their modern world of relative safety and progress, it could still be indulged in at a safe remove. As the essayist William Hazlitt reflected of Walter Scott's novels: 'they carry us back to the feuds, the heart-burnings, the havoc, the dismay, the wrongs, and the revenge of a barbarous age and people.' Readers were carried along in the excitement of it all, as they immersed themselves in a vanished world, with 'a wild cry of joy, at being restored once more to freedom and lawless unrestrained impulses.'[82] No one in their right mind would seriously exchange modern civilisation for a return to 'havoc' and 'heart-burnings' – the point was to vicariously savour the thrills of the past, consigning them to the realm of the imagination.

This fascination with both the violent passions and rose-tinted jollity of the past originated in the same impulse. It was their very embracing of change and innovation that spurred so many people throughout the late eighteenth and nineteenth centuries to look back with nostalgia. For the large majority of men and women, progress was to be embraced wholeheartedly. The compensation for what they had lost along the way was to enjoy nostalgia as a form of entertainment and leisure – sometimes bittersweet, sometimes straightforwardly pleasurable. And in time, nostalgia was being yoked to these same forces of change: if people lamented aspects of a world they had lost to industrial capitalism, they were doing it, more often than not, in the pages of mass-produced commercial media; or travelling to heritage sites on modern transport networks, on days off from mechanised occupations. And it was not just this that they would share in common with later generations of modern nostalgics. For the ordinary men and women who were taking more interest than ever before in Britain's history, the past had provided narratives of tradition through which they could safely, successfully make demands for their right to take part in the life of the nation. And yet social elites were realising that they, too, could shape popular history to buttress the status quo, cultivating popular patriotism through appeals to share in a glorious inheritance of progress and liberty. If, at the outset of the nineteenth century, social elites had worried that the popular appetite for history signalled workers' dangerous ambitions to take control of their national narrative, by the height of the Victorian era they knew that, under the right circumstances, it could make for pliantly patriotic citizens.

6

Decline and Fall

1789–1688

While Britain's nineteenth-century traditionalists would feel
that the French Revolution of 1789 had suddenly hurtled them
into a new era of upheaval and disorder, issuing nostalgic
defences of an aristocratic *ancien régime*, their predecessors
had spent the past century worrying that their own society was
being turned upside down. Far from the calmly elegant Georgian heyday that later generations would come to look back on,
throughout the late seventeenth and eighteenth centuries people
felt that their society was witnessing some of the greatest and
most disorientating transformations of all.

In many ways, Britain had never been more stable. The Glorious Revolution of 1688, which had deposed the Catholic
James II and secured Britain's Protestant succession, tipped the
balance of power firmly in favour of Parliament over monarchy. The fact that this had been achieved with little bloodshed
in England (though it led to significant loss of life in Scotland
and Ireland) was celebrated as a testament to Britain's superior
good sense; the just rewards of liberty and moderation. Britain
itself became a political reality with the Act of Union in 1707,
and social and political commentators on both sides of the border argued that Scotland and England now looked together
towards the rewards of a shared future – not least in Britain's
expanding empire abroad. The economy, too, was changing in
profoundly important ways: successive waves of revolutions in

politics, society and the economy – glorious, financial, industrial, commercial, agrarian – were felt to be transforming Britain into the envy of other nations, and were trumpeted at home as proof that Britons were a people uniquely blessed with divine favour: a land of liberty and prosperity, the inheritors of civilisation. Yet to many observers, this growth contained the seeds of its own destruction, and they looked to history in search of a remedy for the nation's latent disease.

But why were people so concerned that the nation's imminent decline lay just over the horizon? While Britain's power and prestige were increasing on the world stage though trade and colonisation – especially in North America, the Caribbean and India, as Britain sought to expand on its seventeenth-century gains – this rapid enlargement was felt to be straining the historic identity of a bounded island nation. The global free-trade, free-market capitalism that was emerging over the course of the eighteenth century seemed to many to be incompatible with national identity – it appeared to be unsettling society in new and disconcerting ways.

People were unquestionably growing rich through international trade, as companies imported goods such as sugar and tobacco from the New World, and tea, textiles and porcelain from Asia in ever-increasing quantities. It was all combining to create a consumer revolution, as demand for newly available and newly affordable luxury goods skyrocketed; yet the effects of this increased prosperity became the focus of intense national debate, as traditionalists warned that Britain was succumbing to a dangerous greed for luxury, and anxious aristocrats began to fear that their role and power were being challenged by the upstart ambition of newly moneyed men of trade, who sought to enter politics and lay claim to shape the future of the nation. In turn, both middle- and upper-class observers worried that even the poorest in society were beginning to climb the social ladder – risking the disruption of a clearly defined social hierarchy that people felt had kept their society stable through the ages. By the 1750s, it seemed to many as if the country was on the brink of crisis. While many intellectuals were taking stock of the ways in which these developments were changing Britain for the better, arguing that they were to be celebrated as welcome signs of progress, a new and exciting identity as a global trading nation, many of their contemporaries looked uneasily behind them, feeling that the lessons of the past showed that this appetite for luxury would lead them to their ruin.

INVENTING BRITAIN

How can we square these fears of decline and disorder with our image of the age as one of patriotic pride and bombast? Patriotic anthems such as 'Rule, Britannia!', 'Heart of Oak', and indeed the national anthem all date from the middle years of the eighteenth century. But these celebrations of national spirit were often founded as much on anxiety as pride. In the 2020s, amid media controversies about whether it is still appropriate to sing songs like 'Rule, Britannia!' at national events, given their alarmingly imperialist lyrics about inspiring 'dread' in foreign nations, we often imagine them to be simply a reflection of 'how things were' at the time, interpreting them as proudly patriotic celebrations of Britain's historic status. And yet they were written in a climate of real uncertainty about Britain's place in the world. In the case of 'Rule, Britannia!', the song's refrain to 'rule the waves' was intended more as an urging for Britain to succeed than a glorification of Britain's achievements when it debuted in 1740. The Royal Navy had not yet established itself as the dominant force at sea – it was only in the nineteenth century that the lyrics would be subtly transformed into 'rules the waves' as a statement of fact. In the 1740s, it was a song that looked to the future, with the hopeful anticipation that Britain would 'rise' 'still more majestic' through commerce and military victories abroad.

In one important respect, Britain itself was a new invention in the eighteenth century. The Act of Union of 1707, which joined the Scottish and English Parliaments, had prompted outbursts of nostalgia on both sides of the border at the erosion of older national identities. For some eighteenth-century Englishmen, union with Scotland threatened to destabilise an older English nationalism founded on supposedly Anglo-Saxon liberties, and they looked on Scottish ambitions with an uneasy sense of mistrust. The fact that, in 1715 and 1745, Jacobite armies marched into England from Scotland in attempts to regain the British throne ensured that older memories of cross-border hostilities remained alive throughout the eighteenth century.[1] One English observer recalled Robert the Bruce's advice 'never to enter into any Truce or Agreement of Peace with the English', reiterating the conviction that the past continued to act as a powerful force in conditioning how the English and Scottish viewed one another in the present.[2] In turn, many Scotsmen lamented the loss of Scotland's ancient independence, and expressed acute nostalgia for the days of medieval Scotland's resistance to English rule. Such nostalgia could also shade into the stock tradition of mocking England's less than glorious ancestry, that came from being repeatedly invaded by Romans, Angles, Saxons, Jutes, Danes and Normans. As one Scottish poem had it:

> For our Heretage was ever Free,
> Since Scota of Egypt tuik the Sea,
> Whilst ye have ever Conquered been:
> Thus four times thirld and overharld
> You're the great refuse of all the Warld.[3]

Increasingly, though, observers throughout the early eighteenth century on both sides of the border were arguing that it was time to move on from the memories and identities of the past, and look forward to the rewards of a joint future. (Although distinctions between English and British identities, in particular, are complicated by the fact that many English observers began to use the terms 'English' and 'British' interchangeably – a confusion that persists to this day.)

The novelist and social commentator Daniel Defoe wrote a *History of the Union*, which sought to place the Acts of 1707 within the national histories of both England and Scotland, but his ultimate aim was 'removing national prejudices' that had animated past hostilities. 'Time should now race out of the remembrance of these things,' he concluded: 'it seems strange that the seeds of that ancient strife should remain, now the generations concerned are removed out of the way.'[4] What was more, he argued, English nationalists who sought to draw on images of national purity were misremembering their own history. As he argued famously in his satirical poem *The True-Born Englishman* (1701):

> A true-born Englishman's a contradiction,
> In speech an irony, in fact a fiction.
> A banter made to be a test of fools,
> Which those that use it justly ridicules.
> A metaphor invented to express
> A man a-kin to all the universe.

For Defoe, the English had always been a 'mongrel race', a 'heterogeneous' population, that 'betwixt a painted Briton and a Scot . . . betwixt a Saxon and a Dane' had 'received all nations with promiscuous lust.'[5] These were provocative conclusions for some, but Defoe was making a broader point about the futility of basing national pride on misguided notions of ancestry. There was no glorious and independent past of national purity to return to in the first place. For Defoe, the true purpose of the nation lay in trade and commerce, and he exhorted both England and Scotland to look forward to a new age of British power and prosperity.

This was a theme that was echoed in the Scottish Enlightenment, as a coalition of philosophers, historians and economists sought to vindicate both the new commercial society and Scotland's place within it. For Enlightenment historians, as William Robertson explained, the task at hand was to show how society had advanced from 'barbarism to refinement', emerging from the ruins of a Roman Empire through the 'superstition' of the Middle Ages and towards 'the full splendour' of modern civilisation, which had subordinated the older social forces of church and nobility to the secular powers of law and central government.[6] Projecting this trajectory into the future, David Hume argued that Britons now looked forward together to a new phase in human development: one in which older militaristic virtues and traditional ways of living were giving way to a world in which commerce was encouraging people to entertain hopes and dreams that would have been unthinkable in the societies of the past, as 'the spirit of the age . . . carr[ied] improvements into every art and science.'[7]

Progress was in the air. 'Who even at the beginning of this century', asked the radical pamphleteer and philosopher Richard Price in 1785, 'would have thought that, in a few years, mankind would acquire the power of subjecting to their wills the dreadful force of lightning, and of flying in aerostatic machines?' From scientific inventions and innovations to the growth of trade and commerce, it seemed to many as if 'the progress of improvement will not cease till it has excluded from the earth most of its worst evils.'[8] More and more, people were arguing that this spirit of improvement was an important part of being British. Yet for every optimist about the future of civilisation, there was a detractor who saw in modern society the growth of corruption, a culture under the sway of new tastes and new pleasures that were eating away at the country's prized traditions. Throughout the eighteenth century, British men and women were reflecting self-consciously on the losses as well as the gains of their age, as they debated what it meant to live in a new epoch of civilisation.[9] For many observers, the society they found themselves in was a terrible betrayal of their nation's history.

THE DOWNFALL OF OUR STATE

With impeccable timing, in 1776 Edward Gibbon published the opening volume of his seminal history, *The Decline and Fall of the Roman Empire*. In the year of the United States Declaration of Independence, at the exact moment when the revolt of the Thirteen Colonies was threatening to destroy Britain's empire in America, the reading public was presented with an account of how a great and powerful empire might fall victim to its own success. In Gibbon's account, the Roman Empire had fallen because it was overextended abroad, with territories so vast that they could not be controlled without relying on an army of mercenaries that sapped the strength of their economy; while Rome's citizens, in turn, began to abandon the civic and military virtues of their forefathers, leading despotism to creep in at home even as they were menaced by invading hordes. The story of its ruin was 'simple and obvious': 'the natural and inevitable effect of immoderate greatness.'[10]

While Gibbon avoided explicit or hasty parallels between the British and Roman empires, many of his readers interpreted *The Decline and Fall* as a dire warning to the eighteenth century – a parable that suggested if Britain did not change course soon, then she too would fall inexorably into chaos and barbarism.[11] The 'lessons' of ancient history were a crucial way in which people made sense of their own age, through which they viewed and interpreted the political, economic and social developments that were happening around them. And yet people were also beginning to ask: were they living through an age of such transformation that the past could no longer be their straightforward guide – did the 'wisdom of the ancients' no longer apply in quite the same way, in their distinctively modern times?

By the end of the seventeenth century, Britain was at a watershed between the older agrarian nation and a new commercial one. Society was changing dramatically under the influence of new money, as more and more people sought to join in the wider circle of commercial improvement. The very experience of exponential economic growth was a new and bewildering one: there were intense debates over the meaning of change, as people asked what direction the nation was heading in, and what exactly was being left behind. On the one hand, in the heyday of Enlightenment, many interpreted Britain's trans-formation as a welcome sign of the powers of reason and improvement, heralding the birth of a new phase in the pro-gress of civilisation. On the other, a range of observers doubted whether such apparent wealth was genuine, or if economic growth could be sustained.

The South Sea Bubble of 1720, in particular, which had seen fortunes made and destroyed through rampant speculation on the stock market, seemed to suggest that this new wealth was an illusion, a house of cards that might bring about the collapse of the nation. The government had granted the South Sea Com-pany a monopoly in the trade in slavery with South America, and the company, in turn, had underwritten a chunk of the national debt. Insider trading, bribes to MPs, and hugely exag-gerated predictions of the profits that might be made from enslavement wildly inflated the company's value. Share prices soared as investor confidence built to the point of hysteria – 'when the rest of the world are mad, we must imitate them in some measure', reasoned one latecomer to the party – and then crashed.[12] It was Britain's first modern financial crash: the col-lapse of a system that people had assumed was too big to fail. Thousands of people were ruined financially, especially those who had already spent the money they assumed they were raking in. Throughout the following decades, traditionalists warned that, like Rome, Britons were fast abandoning their supposedly time-honoured virtues of moderation, painting a picture of a nation swamped by new money and new consumer pleasures that they argued betokened a dangerous greed for luxury, an abandonment of the public good in favour of selfish ostentation.

Britain's experience in war, too, seemed to suggest that she might fall victim to her own success. Britain was at war with France for much of the eighteenth century, necessitating huge government spending, and prompting many to worry about the ballooning national debt. Funds for war were increasingly being raised not just through taxation, but by the selling of debt to private investors in the rapidly expanding financial sector, occasioning frequent complaints by landed gentlemen about the way in which they were being taxed by the government to finance the national debt – a debt now held by new city men and merchants, whose increasing power seemed to threaten the aristocratic hierarchy and leadership they felt had kept Britain stable for centuries.[13]

Yet even peace seemed to come with costs of its own. The Seven Years War (1756–63), which had pitted rival coalitions led by Britain and France into conflict on an unprecedented global scale, ended in decisive victory for Britain with the signing of the Treaty of Paris in 1763 – a victory that marked Britain's rise to imperial and naval supremacy. After a dramatic struggle that had started badly for Britain and threatened at times to precipitate a national crisis, they had gained further territory in America; conquered much of Canada; captured Manila and Havana from Spain (which were then exchanged for Florida); and driven France out of territories in India, West Africa and the West Indies. But as the historian Linda Colley writes, 'it was the quality and extent of the victory itself that subsequently inflamed the peace. The success had been too great, the territory won was at once too vast and too alien.' While Britons had enormously inflated their power and prestige on the world stage, 'they were left wondering if they had overstretched themselves, made nervous and insecure by their colossal new dimensions.' How could a nation which had historically prided itself on liberty, secure in its self-image as a benevolent, trading empire, justify an empire that was now raised on conquest and maintained by force of arms?[14] The lessons of history seemed to suggest that empires that swelled in this way were in for a fall.

For many, the loss of the American colonies in the War of American Independence between 1775 and 1783 was a gloomy confirmation of Britain's future trajectory. For abolitionists campaigning for an end to the slave trade, this was divine punishment for a nation that had lost its way, a judgement for Britain's failings in the sight of God. The abolitionist and former slave Ottobah Cugoano argued that 'loss of territories and destructive wars' and 'national debt and oppressions' were 'tokens of God's judgment against the British empire.'[15] The narrative of decline-and-fall was a powerful way of imagining Britain's place in history: the writer and politician Horace Walpole cast his eye forward and predicted that one day 'some curious traveller' from the New World would 'visit England and give a description of the ruins of St Paul's.'[16] (It was a taste for imagining ruins that was also in evidence in his novel *The Castle of Otranto* (1764), the first Gothic novel, setting in motion a trend that would inspire so many later generations to seek inspiration in medievalism.)

Throughout the eighteenth century, moralists and social commentators met military crises with the same set of answers as to where it had all gone wrong: their countrymen had abandoned the ancient virtues they had apparently once possessed. In the wake of early setbacks in the Seven Years War, the popular moralist Reverend John Brown subjected the state of the nation to a wildly hysterical – though widely repeated – diagnosis. 'The honest pride of virtue is no more,' he bewailed; 'the character and manner of our times' was instead a '*vain, luxurious, and selfish* EFFEMINACY.' People had been infected with a 'lust for gold', amid the 'trifling and unmanly' pleasures of consumer capitalism, and were abandoning their militaristic virtues and sense of public duty.[17] This was to become an enormously influential narrative, as a raft of observers contrasted the gaudy display of luxury goods they saw around them to 'the ancient Simplicity of their Forefathers.'[18] As the *London Magazine* complained in 1756,

> The same virtues that dignified the Roman name once glowed in the breast of Englishmen: plain, frugal, honest and brave, they withstood the tyranny of papal oppression, and the ambition of their own princes; their valour and their piety founded our liberties ... But alas! I fear the comparison will prove equally just between the degenerated Romans and the Britons of later times. Our riches may be greater than formerly, but I am sure our virtue is less.

According to the author, this orgy of spending and pleasure-seeking had 'spread its baneful influence so wide' that it threatened to undermine the constitution and lead to 'the downfall of our state.'[19]

VIVA LAS VEGASHIRE

We often think of the English country house as embodying the virtues of timelessness, visiting stately homes that seem to merge authentically with the landscape, but we could just as easily read neoclassical architecture as a kind of eighteenth-century Las Vegas: faux-historical pleasure grounds for the newly enriched elite. Aristocratic improvers tore down medieval and Tudor halls, with their timber frames or fortress-like walls, and rebuilt their estates as neoclassical palaces, replete with Corinthian columns, Roman follies and Arcadian grottoes. Britain's growing prosperity was reflected in a wave of building, as aristocrats and upwardly mobile merchants and gentry alike invested their accumulating wealth in country estates. Over 150 country houses were built in the late seventeenth and first half of the eighteenth century alone – among them the twenty-first-century heritage attractions of Chatsworth, Blenheim Palace

and Highclere Castle, also known as ITV's Downton Abbey –
and still more were enlarged and remodelled, as part of a wave of
'improvement' that continued apace as the century progressed.[20]

While the ownership of land continued to be a hugely important source of economic and political power, there were, too,
new opportunities for money to be made in trade, commerce
and industry – and aristocrats took advantage of both, investing in rapidly growing sectors such as mining, canal-building
and urban development; banking and finance; and participating in merchant ventures such as the East India and South Sea
companies. Not least of all, there were fortunes to be made
through sugar and slavery. The sugar business alone represented about £50 million of capital invested in estates during
the century, enough to build Blenheim Palace 160 times over.
The Lascelles family, for instance, who had invested in the
Caribbean from the later seventeenth century, built the sprawling Harewood House in West Yorkshire from the proceeds of
plantation and slave ownership in the 1760s. The upwardly
mobile Beckford family extracted such vast wealth from plantations in Jamaica that they both erected the Palladian mansion
Fonthill Splendens, one of the largest country houses of its time,
and then demolished it in favour of the colossal Gothic monument Fonthill Abbey just 40 years later. Even as William
Beckford, inheriting the newly completed Fonthill Splendens
from his father in 1770, set about styling the interior in neoclassical fashions over the following decades, he was penning
Gothic novels and beginning to dream of realising his fantasies
in architecture – contributing to what would grow into a full-
scale Gothic revival in the nineteenth century.[21]

These brand new edifices, though expressions of new-found
wealth and power, were rooted in the aesthetics of the ancient
past. The columns and porticoes of Palladian architecture (a
double revival, in fact – a seventeenth- and eighteenth-century
revival of the Renaissance architect Andrea Palladio, who had
reinterpreted classical proportions and symmetry) were designed

to proclaim the British aristocracy as the true inheritors of the classical world, a ruling elite carrying the torch of civilisation for the benefit of those they governed. Gardens and grounds were landscaped into mini-paradises of pastoral nostalgia – evoking the arcadian idylls people had read about in classical myths and poetry, where people whiled away the hours in an atmosphere of bucolic innocence, far away from the pressures of the urban world. In the seventeenth century, gardens had been laid out in geometric, formal styles, expressing the owner's wealth and status through the labour it took to tame nature into symmetry: shrubs cut into man-made shapes, elaborate hedge mazes, herbs and flowers kept within the lines of square borders. But under the sway of new tastes for classical fantasy, over the course of the eighteenth century formal gardens were giving way to enclosed arcadias where visitors might stumble upon mock ruins, whimsical follies and grottoes, classical temples or rustic hermitages – sometimes complete with their very own resident hermit for a touch of atmospheric authenticity. This was nostalgia served up as a self-consciously cultured form of entertainment: as the landscape gardener and poet William Shenstone explained, to the educated visitor ruins were a kind of memento mori to the grandeur of past civilisations, which could 'afford that pleasing melancholy which proceeds from a reflexion on decayed magnificence.'[22]

Ruins could also convey a sense of pedigree for families who could trace their lineage back through the generations. Authentic ruins traced a family's lineage to before the Reformation, as England's oldest nobility had been awarded much of their land after the Dissolution of the Monasteries in the sixteenth century, when monastic lands had been redistributed into private ownership. Indeed, while the dominant fashion of the eighteenth century was for classical architecture, vestigial traces of medieval heritage could still be displayed in interiors as a badge of pride. Heraldry and decorative references to older architectural styles could be ways of proclaiming links with former

where the Hermit hangs his straw-clad cell

Sketch for the frontispiece to Reverend Gilbert White's *The Natural History and Antiquities of Selborne,* 'The Hermitage at Selborne' (1777), by Samuel Hieronymus Grimm, with the author's brother, Henry White, dressed as a rustic hermit.

royal dynasties, or ancient honours, titles and offices that had accumulated over the centuries.[23] In the second half of the eighteenth century, a handful of tastemakers began to experiment with medieval architecture in earnest. The eccentrically inclined Horace Walpole led the way with Strawberry Hill, begun in 1749, a Gothic fantasy that seemed wildly exotic at the time, replete with towers, battlements and elaborate carvings that sought to convey what he called 'the gloomth of abbeys and cathedrals.'[24] The Duke and Duchess of Northumberland, who, as Walpole explained, lived 'by the etiquette of the old peerage', commissioned a series of Gothic interiors at Alnwick Castle in the 1760s, wishing to make it clear through their surroundings that the blood of the ancient Percy family – renowned for their role and power in England's Middle Ages – ran through their veins.[25] But for the newly moneyed, mock ruins could draw on this aesthetic pedigree in announcing that one had 'arrived' – imitating the crumbling castles and ruined abbeys of the old aristocracy (albeit on a smaller scale) could be a way of creating the suggestion of an illustrious lineage and conveying an air of legitimacy. And if the building of a great estate was beyond one's financial reach, historical fantasies could still be recreated in miniature. As the century progressed, Thames-side classical villas and luxury cottages – thatched and timbered in charmingly homespun style for those who preferred a deluxe take on ye olde rusticity – were increasingly being built on the outskirts of the capital for an expanding class of successful professional men, who lived and worked in the City of London but wanted a taste of arcadian leisure or Merry Old England close at hand.[26]

For the older aristocracy, the rise of a nouveau riche with ambitions to live like nobility in country houses was deeply threatening. From the final years of the seventeenth century, as country Tories saw it, an aristocratic social and political order was being undermined by new money and new financial institutions; the newly prosperous middle ranks of merchants, bankers, industrialists and tradesmen were unsettling the traditions and stability of a hierarchical society rooted in the land.[27] On the one hand, the ownership of land was still hugely important in determining a gentleman's status and power. In an age in which only about 200,000 property-owning men (less than 5 per cent of the population) had the right to vote, it was a prerequisite for political participation. While people were starting to pour into towns and cities on a scale not seen before, the large majority of the population was still dependent on the land for work or associated with it. For the aristocracy, landed gentlemen provided vital leadership in sustaining the balance of this social order, presiding over a hierarchy in which everyone knew their place in a network of interconnecting rights and duties, underpinned by the age-old rhythms and traditions of the agricultural calendar. As far as they were concerned, the people owed their allegiance to the land: as landowners they were the cultivators of patriots who could be relied upon to defend the soil on which they depended. On the other hand, the economy was changing in ways that were challenging the customary authority of patrician society, as men of trade began to argue that it was *they* who were the true muscle and soul of the nation; the people who were powering Britain's economic growth and increasingly financing its expansion abroad.[28]

Anxious statesmen decried what they felt was a growing corruption at the heart of a society jittering with financial instability and greed, as a new breed of gentleman sought to climb the social ladder in pursuit of political power. The key figure in this power struggle between old and new was the Whig Prime Minister Robert Walpole (father of Horace), whose premiership spanned more than two decades, between 1721 and 1742. He was mercilessly satirised in John Gay's enormously popular *The Beggar's Opera* (1728) as the grasping 'Bob Booty', whose administration, it was held, was steeped in financial corruption that mirrored the wider corruption of society at large.[29] Having risen from the ranks of the minor gentry, Walpole's designs for a great house at Houghton Hall in Norfolk seemed to demonstrate the dangerous scale of his ambition: a Palladian mansion and landscaped grounds of such hubristic proportions that they necessitated a whole village to be swept out of the way in pursuit of an 'authentic' country vista. Following a high-profile falling out with Walpole, the Whig statesman Viscount Cobham designed an architectural rebuke of his own in his garden at Stowe. Steeped in nostalgia for the political heroics of the ancient world, a pristine Temple of Ancient Virtue stood across a miniaturised river Styx from a Temple of British Worthies, filled with busts of luminaries from Alfred the Great and Elizabeth I to Shakespeare, Milton and Isaac Newton. Exemplars of ancient virtue were joined with figures who Cobham felt represented the Whig history of progress and constitutional liberty. Juxtaposed to these were the ruins of the Temple of Modern

Virtue, fallen through corruption, with a headless statue of Walpole at its centre.[30]

In the face of these anxieties about a shifting political and social landscape, country houses were both a physical expression of landed power, and an imaginative retreat into a bounded fantasy world of stability and order. As new political challenges confronted the aristocratic hierarchy, the elaborate world of the country house could be stage-managed as a performance that kept up the illusion of unchallenged power and influence.[31] Increasingly, patricians were looking to set their houses in landscapes that conveyed an idyllic vision of timeless peace and tranquillity. The master planner of this fashion for pastoral fantasy was Lancelot 'Capability' Brown, perhaps the best-known landscape architect of the eighteenth century. The ambitions of the landscape garden spilled over from the immediate surroundings of a house to encompass swathes of parkland and broader vistas. As one contemporary observer noted,

> Every Man now, be his fortune what it will, is to be doing something at his Place, as the fashionable Phrase is; and you hardly meet with any Body, who, after the first Compliments, does not inform you, that he is in Mortar and moving of Earth; the modest terms for Building and Gardening. One large Room, a Serpentine River, and a Wood, are become the most absolute Necessaries of Life.[32]

While earlier gardens had sought to express man's mastery of nature with geometric shapes and precision topiary, Brown's aim was to transform nature into a picture, in which man-made efforts created a highly idealised, but apparently organic landscape. His stock formula was undulating lawns, encircling trees, ornamental temples or ruins, meandering streams and an expanse of water in the middle distance; creating an imagined or nostalgic landscape for his patrons – a picturesque arcadia such as they would have admired in landscape paintings, which were becoming an increasingly important art form in the eighteenth century, as artists reached for ever more romanticised evocations of nature's beauty.[33] Concealed ditches and perimeter fences created the illusion that the house merged seamlessly with its surrounding landscape, while keeping livestock and unwanted visitors at bay. More and more, gardens were appealing to the psychological ideal of an innocent past; nature as a place of purity and serenity, where everything could be found in its right and proper order, in contrast to the change and corruption of the urban world – the roots of a romantic vision of the countryside that would take on an increasingly central role in the way Britons' thought about their landscape over the following centuries. There was a growing emphasis being placed on the importance of simple communion with nature, inside the safely enclosed grounds of country estates: solitary walks and meditative contemplations, or else communal activities such as

Richard Wilson, *Croome Court*, Worcestershire (c. 1758–9), with grounds landscaped by 'Capability' Brown.

hunting and sport that re-enacted the rituals and traditions of a hierarchical way of life.[34]

And yet, for all these visions of timelessness and stability, the role of the country house in society was changing. Where once great houses had served as a focal point for the whole local community, Horace Walpole lamented that they now sat in 'pompous solitude' as private playgrounds for the elite. His nostalgia was for the 'bustling jollity of the old nobility.' Visiting the fourteenth-century Drayton House in 1763, the seat of Lady Elizabeth Germain, who was a notable collector of antiquities, he rhapsodised that 'the old furniture and customs' of a medieval seat of power had been 'kept up most religiously' in the 'most perfect order and preservation'. Amid the vogue for neoclassical renovations, he imagined there could scarcely be 'a House in England so entire in the old fashioned manner.' For Walpole, this was not just an admiration of its antiquity, but for the sense that an ancient estate was still beneficial and integral to its community.[35] Country seats had once represented a medieval ideal of hospitality: a system of public hierarchy where lords and ladies had entertained tenants and visitors alike in ancient ceremonies, rituals and communal festivities, and people of all social ranks were drawn together around hearths and dining tables. By the eighteenth century, shared festivities were dwindling, and servants and visitors on business were being kept out of sight via hidden back stairs; great houses were no longer settings that displayed how different social ranks might be bound together by loyalty to the lord of the manor. Increasingly, contemporary observers complained that patricians were preferring to stay in London at Christmastime to enjoy the pleasures of polite society, rather than taking the lead in traditional festivities alongside their dependents.[36]

By the middle of the century, country houses seemed to many to have taken on the sole functions of the public display of wealth, and the private enjoyment of luxury. Indeed, many critics linked this to the hubris of aristocratic 'improvers', who altered the landscape for their own enjoyment instead of the public good. William Cowper's poem *The Task* (1785), for instance, attacked the landscape designer 'Capability' Brown as an 'omnipotent magician', who commanded that 'woods vanish, hills subside, and vallies rise' for patrons who were simply indulging in another form of aristocratic extravagance and excess.[37] For the poet and playwright Oliver Goldsmith, the creation of extensive parks and grounds on what had often previously been arable land was contributing to the break-up and decay of rural communities, forcing workers away from a traditional way of life and into the anonymity of the city.

A range of observers launched damning condemnations of an aristocracy they believed were fast abandoning their sense of social duty. For all their sprawling ostentation, country houses were increasingly being left empty in favour of the temptations of the capital, or burgeoning Georgian spa towns such as Bath and Tunbridge Wells. This was also the great age of urban entertainments and pleasure gardens; of gambling, balls, theatres and coffee houses; when areas such as Bloomsbury and Mayfair were being redeveloped as models of architectural elegance. The Reverend John Brown raged in 1757 that 'instead of the good of others, or the happiness of the public', aristocratic efforts had sunk to 'the vanity of dress, entertainments, equipage, furniture.'[38] Moreover, their obsession with imported French fashions and fancies was tantamount to fraternising with the enemy. As Brown saw it, a selfish and degenerate aristocracy was leading the nation to the edge of a precipice. But Daniel Defoe, for one, nurtured the *hope* that the nobility's luxury would destroy them, enabling the transfer of wealth to more productive members of society. Aristocrats who burned through their fortunes in the pursuit of pleasure might one day be forced to sell their estates to newly prosperous tradesmen, who could in turn gain political power – if, that is, they did not succumb to luxury and greed themselves.[39]

THE VAST TORRENT OF LUXURY

If aristocratic spending sprees were prompting anxious assessments of the direction Britain was heading in, more worrying still to traditionalists were the ways in which an appetite for luxury was spreading throughout the social hierarchy. 'Luxury' became one of the defining debates of the eighteenth century: a way in which people could think through and make sense of the interconnecting social, cultural, economic and political changes that were happening around them. As colonisers and merchant ventures set out in search of new markets to conquer from the Elizabethan era onwards, creating global trading networks that were coming to play an increasingly important role in Britain's economy, new consumer goods imported from Asia and the New World such as tea, sugar and tobacco were coming within the reach of more people than ever before. From the late seventeenth century, new fabrics such as Indian chintzes and calicoes were enabling people of modest means to imitate the costly silks and brocades favoured by the aristocracy. As the economy expanded and incomes rose for an expanding group of middle-class consumers – many of whom had gained wealth through trade and commerce, and were seeking, in turn, to demonstrate their rising status – there were more and more opportunities to display their taste through the purchase of clothes, books, clocks, silverware, fine porcelain and furniture.

In an age in which towns and cities, and London in particular, were growing to accommodate a rising national population, as well as agricultural workers who were increasingly leaving the land for jobs in trade and industry, there was an unprecedented number of shops and taverns presenting new opportunities for entertainment and pleasure. By the end of the eighteenth century London had almost doubled in size since the start – at nearly one million people, housing about a tenth of the population of Britain. Industries were expanding and proliferating to meet rising consumer demand: the wheels of the economy itself seemed to be turning ever more quickly as people sought to keep pace with continual changes in fashion.

And fashions themselves seemed to be changing at a new and bewildering speed – as Oliver Goldsmith felt by the 1770s, 'the follies of the town' had once 'crept slowly among us, but now they travel faster than a stage coach.'[40] Must-have obsessions appeared seemingly out of nowhere and snowballed into roaring trades, such as Georgian society's unlikely love affair with the pineapple. This exotic fruit, imported from the tropics at great expense, had been one of Charles II's favourite status symbols in the late seventeenth century, with England's gardeners vying with each other by the turn of the eighteenth to try and grow hot-house pineapples at home, catering to the very wealthiest of patrons in search of extravagant displays of their purchasing power. Over the following decades, pineapple-mania was becoming a nationwide frenzy, giving rise to a mini-industry of entrepreneurial opportunities. The Earl of Dunmore commissioned an entire folly in the shape of a pineapple to tower over the hothouse in his estate in Stirlingshire. Pineapple rental shops sprang up for the aspiring beau monde, who lacked the funds to buy their own, but who might borrow one for a night to display as a centrepiece at their parties. So expensive were they that a pineapple in transit sometimes merited the hiring of its own security guard. By the 1760s, the enterprising pottery magnate Josiah Wedgwood was making pineapple-themed ceramics marketed within the financial reach of the middle classes, as an aristocratic fashion spilled into a mainstream trend – 'pineapple ware' that itself became part of a popular spin-off craze for ceramics themed around all things fruit and vegetable. But already, by 1770, pineapple ware seemed to be moving from status symbol to so last season, as Wedgwood expressed his relief that piles of unsold stock had been shipped to the colonies, where Britain's émigrés were thankfully a few years behind the latest trends in London.[41]

While Britain's growing prosperity was for many a source of national pride, for a raft of observers this was a worrying sign of a society grown lax: of the social order distorted through an unhealthy appetite for frills and extravagances. The jurist and novelist Henry Fielding wrote of 'the vast torrent of luxury, which of late years hath poured itself into this nation', which he believed had changed the manners, customs and habits of his compatriots almost beyond recognition, and contributed to an increase in crime. Moralists spoke of a population that had become 'diseased', 'infected', 'consumed' by luxury and pleasure-seeking, which had 'swept away' traditional ways of living and penetrated even to the 'dregs of the people'.[42] For the critic John Dennis, luxury was a 'spreading contagion', 'the greatest corrupter of the public manners, and the greatest extinguisher of public spirit.'[43] These anxieties would give rise to a growing backlash against the new spirit of capitalist acquisitiveness that was felt to be swamping the nation, as traditionalists issued nostalgic defences of an older Britain where life, they felt, had moved more slowly, and people had lived in an atmosphere of virtuous simplicity.

As more and more people sought to spend their wages on new consumer luxuries and decencies, anxious patricians were quick to conclude that those below them were trying to climb the social ladder by aping their 'betters'. As a journalist complained (with more than a touch of exaggeration) in the *London Chronicle* in the 1760s, 'dress, fashion, and affectation have put all upon an equality, so that it is difficult to tell the milliner from her ladyship, my lord from the groom, or his grace in Pall Mall from the tallow-chandler at Wapping'.[44] Social commentators worried that the social fabric would be torn apart amid an orgy of consumer spending: journalists, essayists, novelists and dramatists alike issued unrelenting prognostications of the horrors that awaited the nation if people did not mend their luxurious ways. Looking back to a putative golden age when everyone had accepted their place in the social hierarchy, and everyone had worked together as a nation, they perceived in the consumer economy a new vision of society in which selfish individuals were held together solely by envy and competition. In their view, luxury was not just a private indulgence or personal failing; it was a national calamity that threatened full-scale collapse.

Much as moralisers tried to paint a picture of disaster, their contemporaries pointed out that their society would barely function without the trade in luxury goods. Flying in the face of the moral rule-of-thumb that vices did not lead to virtue, the philosopher Bernard de Mandeville argued provocatively at the beginning of the eighteenth century that luxury was a 'private vice' that also brought 'public benefits', enabling the circulation of wealth throughout society.[45] If people abandoned consumerism, it would lead to mass unemployment and the collapse of the economy almost overnight; who would give the poor their wages if no one wanted to buy the goods they made? It was a tension that was difficult for his contemporaries to reconcile – nostalgia for a time when people had bought and made fewer things simply didn't pay.

The question of luxury was central to Enlightenment discussions over the nature and progress of society, as philosophers and economists sought to answer the question of whether history was a story of growing vice and corruption, or the upwards march of trade, industry and the 'civilising process'.[46] But these debates were not restricted to philosophical circles: they spilled down the social hierarchy and raged among the populace, as people tried to make sense of the changes they were witnessing. During the height of the luxury debates, a 1757 play, *The Tryal of the Lady Allurea Luxury*, put the titular protagonist in the dock on the charge of conspiracy to destroy the nation. As the prosecution alleged, 'for nearly a century past', luxury 'hath most wickedly and maliciously plotted and conspired the destruction of this land, by corrupting the morals of our people.' Making use of 'the most diabolical arts', she had apparently 'betwitch[ed] the people to their ruin – to make them in love with sloth and idleness … to give themselves up entirely to empty amusements' and 'false pleasures'. Yet the defence maintained that, quite to the contrary, Lady Luxury's 'whole life seems to be devoted to the welfare, the ease, and the happiness of mankind … she has refined our taste, enlarged our commerce, and perfected our politics.' And as the jury concluded, perhaps luxury herself was not to blame after all. No one was forcing the rich to spend their fortunes on pleasure, and leave wealth to trickle down through job creation, when they might otherwise be investing directly in building canals, roads and public improvements.[47]

For many traditionalists, however, luxury consumption was simply incompatible with national identity. They worried about the loss of older relationships of duty, deference and cooperation that seemed to have been rejected in favour of unbridled hedonism. 'Were they the sons of tea-sippers,' raged the travel writer and much-mocked pioneer of the men's umbrella Jonas Hanway, 'who won the fields of Cressy and Agincourt?'[48] Men who indulged in such effeminising pleasures as drinking suspicious foreign leaves in tiny cups, he felt, were a poor reward for their battle-hardened forefathers – a complicated bugbear for a man who was jeered in the street for protecting his head with what looked like a ladies' parasol.

As the older agrarian nation was giving way to the newer commercial society, a group of consumers who came in for particular condemnation were farmers – those sturdy yeoman who were supposed to be the last line of defence in sustaining images of English tradition. The novelist Tobias Smollett disapproved of wealthier farmers' changing ways in the 1760s, describing their wives and daughters dressed 'in their jewels, their silks and their satins … their clumsy shanks like so many shins of beef, new cased in silk hose and embroidered slippers.' This in contrast to misty-eyed remembrances of the rural maids of yore, as he waxed nostalgic about the 'buxom country lasses' of his youthful memories, who 'in their best apparel delight, their white hose and clean short dimity [cotton] petticoats.'[49]

Poorer farmers, too, were felt to be succumbing to a ruinous taste for luxury. As the rural world was being transformed by these new economic forces, enquiries into the causes of rural poverty lambasted those who worked on the land for their apparent improvidence. The agricultural writer Arthur Young insisted in 1768 that 'there are numerous families that are completely clothed by the parish [who] will let their clothes drop to pieces, without being at the trouble of ever mending them, at the very time they have every day drank their tea sweetened with nine-penny sugar.'[50] Tea had first been imported to Britain in the seventeenth century and had been an expensive rarity, but by the late 1760s when Young was writing, over 3,000 tonnes were being imported each year (considerable quantities were also being smuggled in illegally to avoid paying heavy import duties). Prices were falling rapidly, bringing it within the reach of workers' budgets: a cup of sweetened tea was beginning to become a staple of a poverty diet, staving off hunger and providing much-needed energy to labourers.[51] And yet to wealthier observers it still seemed an unnecessary extravagance that the poor could do without.

A generation later, Young's fellow social investigator Sir Frederick Eden blamed the rural poor for *buying* their clothes, opposing 'respectable persons' who made all their own clothes to 'opulent farmers', whose crime seems to be little more than wearing 'cloth, purchased in the shops.' Yet even as Eden asserted the superior moral as well as practical qualities of homespun fabrics, he was forced to concede 'that articles of cloathing can be purchased in the shops at a much lower price, than those who make them at home can afford to sell them for.'[52] As the first textile factories began to spin yarn, and then weave cloth on an industrial scale from the 1780s, prices were falling, and those who relied on selling hand-made textiles for income were finding it harder and harder to compete – a process that would accelerate into the nineteenth century as the Industrial Revolution gained pace. But at this early stage, elite observers who surveyed the lower classes couldn't quite let go of their older image of things: that 'homespun' meant prudent, and shopping meant 'luxury'. The new industrial economy that was beginning to emerge seemed to work in a way that was counterintuitive. (It is a reality that still seems counterintuitive to twenty-first-century capitalists, as middle-class critics issue admonitions to time-poor workers on benefits about swapping out convenience foods for slow-cooked 'austerity' meals that make the most of humble ingredients.) Behind condemnations of the seeming extravagance of the rural poor were economically rational consumer choices, but these were choices that sat uneasily with critics' nostalgia for the nation's poor's modest past.

GLOBAL BRITAIN

Increasingly, though, contemporary observers were arguing that returning to an alleged golden age of homespun goods and self-sufficiency would be an act of national self-harm: Britain had gained a global empire through trade and commerce. Horace Walpole mocked his countrymen's instincts to complain about modern improvements 'and [bring] us back to the simplicity of ancient times.' To those who wondered 'how we did before tea and sugar were known', he replied: 'better, no doubt; but as I did not happen to be born two or three hundred years ago, I cannot recall precisely whether diluted acorns, and barley bread . . . made a very luxurious breakfast.' For Walpole, critics of consumerism were ignoring the ways in which trade overseas was expanding Britain's wealth and power in the world – in their obsession with returning to the national past they 'thought on nothing but reducing us to our islandhood.'[53] More and more, people were arguing that trade and commerce was the very essence of the nation, a symbol of progress and a source of celebration, which would lift the country into a new era of hope and prosperity. Britons were beginning to absorb the experience of commerce into their self-understanding. For Daniel Defoe, the source of British and English greatness was in their identity as a trading nation – trade was the very lifeblood of civilisation, which 'like the blood in the veins, circulates thro' the whole body of fraternities and societies of mankind.'[54] As long as Britain could maintain its competitive advantage against other nations, commerce would guarantee British supremacy on the world stage.

In the Scottish Enlightenment, philosophers, economists and historians sought to turn the traditional view of the economy on its head, seeking to legitimise free-trade, free-market capitalism as heralding a bright new future for Britain. Many people were still subscribing to an older, 'mercantilist' image of the economy, in which people were supposed to be producing and exporting more than other countries were, not wasting their own money on foreign imports and useless fripperies. By the turn of the eighteenth century, observers like Mandeville had begun to argue that people were underestimating just how crucial consumer demand was in keeping the economy going. But these ideas took decades to trickle into received wisdom, not least because so many elite observers worried that encouraging people to buy as many luxuries as they could afford would lead to social climbing and social disorder, and ultimately to decline and fall – a shameless giving in to vice at the expense of virtue. By the middle years of the eighteenth century, economists and philosophers were setting out, in turn, to show that wanting to own things was hardly a sign of moral weakness in the first place. Adam Smith argued in *The Wealth of Nations* (1776) that the consumption habits of the lower orders did not stem from their selfishness or moral corruption, but from the 'constant and uninterrupted effort of every man to better his condition.'[55] David Hume contended that – far from having degenerated from a supposed golden age of virtue – modern commercial societies, with their 'innocent' indulgence in luxury, were the happiest and most virtuous communities in history. People were hardly pursuing sensual gratification at the expense of everything else in life; they were learning to 'cultivate the pleasures of the mind as well as those of the body.'[56] Their arguments chimed with moral reformers who were arguing that, far from causing sloth or idleness among the labouring poor, those who sought money to purchase tea, sugar and fashionable clothing would be encouraged to be *more* industrious, enabling even the poorest in society to join in the wider circle of commercial improvement.[57]

Where traditionalists might look back to the discipline of Sparta and Rome and argue that modern citizens, by comparison, were enslaved by indulgence and vice, Hume saw the development of gentler commercial virtues. For Hume, the pursuit of luxury had actually stabilised society. 'When the tempers of men are softened as well as their knowledge improved,' he argued, 'humanity appears still more conspicuous, and [this] is the chief characteristic which distinguishes a civilised age from times of barbarity and ignorance.' Commerce, in short, was leading to 'an increase of humanity.'[58] For Hume, people who depended on trade and commerce rather than conquest for security simply behaved better around each other. In contrast to the violent tempers that had regulated more warlike societies, the modern economy depended on trust and reliability: in the commercial marketplace, people had to convince each other that they could be depended upon to make good on lines of credit, fulfil orders by post, or attract the right sort of customer. They were buying beautiful things, stimulating the arts, at the same time as cultivating scientific knowledge in search of new ways to produce them. It was all combining to create a culture in which being polite and respectable, knowing how to present yourself at your best while facilitating social interaction, was becoming more and more important.[59]

(Though as recent media attention has highlighted, Hume had no qualms about 'humanity' when he encouraged his patron to purchase a plantation worked by enslaved people in Grenada in the 1760s. This was a modern economy that increasingly depended for its wealth upon outsourcing barbarity on a seemingly ever-growing scale to plantations and slave traders beyond Britain's borders – a fact that Enlightenment thinkers dealt with either by ignoring how integral it was to their society, or justifying it by creating new theories of racial superiority. It was racism that they were criticised for in their own time – something that is often forgotten in our present-day culture wars about Britain's imperial history. The Scottish philosopher and poet James Beattie, for instance, forensically demolished Hume's assumption that black people were 'naturally inferior' to white when he published his 1770 *Essay on Truth*, stressing that it was imperative people stop deploying shoddy reasoning as a justification for slavery. The essay became a bestseller, prompting a furious reaction from Hume.[60])

Yet even among Britain's most enthusiastic celebrants of trade and commerce, nostalgia for traditional ways of life could lead to condemnation of developments that were in fact integral to the economic growth they welcomed. Older views of the economy remained a powerful way of making sense of change. For all Daniel Defoe's celebration of expanding trade and commerce, he remained intensely ambivalent about the consumption of luxury goods. Young people weren't saving their wages 'against a rainy day' like they used to, even servants were becoming 'puffed up with pride' and neglecting their duties, and it was leading to all manner of awkward social situations for the author, such as greeting the ladies of a house and accidentally kissing 'the chamber-jade into the bargain, for she was as well dressed as the best.'[61] But for Defoe, the worst of it was that people's taste in fashion was fundamentally unpatriotic. There had been a broad swing in fashion away from heavy, durable English-made woollens towards imported Indian cottons, French silks and laces. As far as Defoe was concerned, the sizeable English woollen industry had been 'the fund of our whole commerce', 'the spring and fountain of our wealth and prosperity for above three hundred years', 'the life and blood of the whole nation, the soul of our trade.' Dependable English broad cloth had been 'the ancient glory of England', but English manufacturers, he felt, were now 'despised by our own people' – in their preference for flimsy foreign textiles, people had 'ruin[ed] our own manufactures . . . we weakened our own country.'[62]

This kind of economic nationalism was common in the first half of the eighteenth century. The traditional view of the economy saw Britain as engaged in a zero-sum game with other nations, where the purpose of trade was to sell surplus goods abroad and amass bullion in return. The idea of choosing to import luxury goods rather than making them at home created a worrying image of the nation haemorrhaging gold and silver to Asia and France, in exchange for little more than trifles. The economist Malachy Postlethwayt worried whether England could maintain commercial and military parity with France while being 'Frenchified out of more . . . than half a million per Annum in our balance of trade.'[63] Merchant ventures such as the East India Company had grown enormously rich through the trade in foreign luxuries, but had this come at the expense of domestic industries? Anxious observers painted a picture of a liberal metropolitan elite who were damaging their country through cosmopolitan tastes and their refusal to buy British.

However, not only did Britain's predicted economic ruin not occur, but imported luxuries seemed to be contributing towards Britain's commercial expansion with each passing year, spurring the economy to new levels of growth through the power of consumer demand. But the arguments of free-traders were slow to gain wider acceptance, not least because they were out of step with traditional views of society. The traditional, mercantilist view of the economy – which understood the nation to be working together as a whole, in the joint project of selling surplus goods abroad and maintaining a favourable balance of trade – seemed to complement perfectly an older vision of society, where each social rank had their part to play in the order of things, regulated by a ruling class who guided this national project in the right direction.[64] On the other hand, free-market capitalism seemed to transfer these powers of regulation to the market itself. Where an Adam Smith might have seen luxury consumption as part of people's universal desire to 'better' their condition, anxious patricians saw a future in which the ties of community would be pulled apart by greed, acquisitiveness and economic competition. While twenty-first-century conservatives yearn to resurrect a patriotic history of free-trading Britain, setting out in search of new markets around the globe, for many eighteenth-century observers, free-market capitalism was creating problems of its own, in ways that were straining the historic national identity they remembered with such pride. Even Britain's most impassioned advocates of free trade could find themselves lamenting its effects upon society, struggling to accept the fact that the production, import and trade in goods that they welcomed could not be separated from the spirit of consumer acquisitiveness, and the destruction of domestic industries and traditional ways of living that they worried would undermine the country.

THE DESERTED VILLAGE

At the same time as commerce was transforming life in towns and cities, the rural landscape itself was being transformed by the forces of capitalism, as landowners took up new scientific methods for drainage, crop rotation and selective breeding, and enclosed open fields and common land into privately owned farms. The catch-all term for both enclosures and new farming methods was 'improvement': by privatising farms, landowners argued, they could ensure that their land was used as efficiently as possible. To agricultural improvers, these innovations were bringing much-needed modernisation to the countryside. Improvement was increasing agricultural yields, bringing wastes and marshland under cultivation through better drainage and fertilisation, and producing a crucial surplus to feed the ever-growing urban population as well as to export abroad for profit. But while the innovations that were making the countryside ever more productive and profitable were for many a source of national pride, there was also deep anxiety over the upheaval it was bringing to rural society.

Enclosure became the subject of furious nationwide debates, as its critics accused landowners of increasing their own profits at the expense of rural workers. For centuries, English agriculture had depended on common land, where people had shared rights to plant crops, graze animals, forage and collect wood for fuel. The enclosure of common land had been taking place on a smaller scale since Tudor times, but from the 1750s the number of enclosures began rapidly to gain pace, and were increasingly performed through parliamentary acts that many felt were open to abuse by powerful landowners, leading to intense debates about the nation's past, present and future. In some areas, landowners doubled or even tripled the rents they charged after enclosing their land. Opponents of enclosure argued that landowners were 'erecting private benefit on public calamity', careless of the upheaval it brought to rural communities, and forcing people away from the land they had maintained for generations into the anonymity of urban life and work.[65]

At a time when more than half of England's workers were employed in agriculture – 55 per cent in 1700, falling to 35 per cent by the end of the century; a trend that would accelerate into the nineteenth century, with only a quarter of workers farming the land by 1851 – this had huge implications for national identity.[66] And for those that remained, the decline of open-field farming and rise of large, privately owned farms transformed generations of independent smallholders into agricultural labourers working for wages. A range of social observers protested that the people were being robbed not just of their land, but of their very identities. Most dramatically visible of all, enclosure was fundamentally changing the look of the English countryside itself. The patchworks of small fields and hedgerows that we think of today as a timeless natural landscape were in many cases eighteenth-century creations, overwriting an older landscape of open fields and commons, shared pastures and meadows – the image that people had had in mind for centuries when they imagined their nation. In Wales and Scotland, too, enclosures and clearances reshaped the landscape as tenants were evicted from their land. In Scotland, in particular, many small settlements were torn down, and their occupants forcibly displaced by landlords to purpose-built villages on the outskirts of new large-scale farms, or else to newly created crofting communities on poorer-quality ground. Would the nations people remembered be lost forever amid the destructive forces of capitalism?

Oliver Goldsmith's polemical poem *The Deserted Village* (1770), much discussed and debated amid the controversy over enclosure, conjured up a lost paradise of village life, as he railed against a parasitical system that funnelled capital away from communities in decline to fund the 'silken sloth' of aristocratic excess. Like many of enclosure's fiercest critics, he believed that England's expanding economy was leading to widening social inequality – economic growth had helped cities flourish, and had enriched landowners and the urban middle classes, but this had come at the expense of the poorest in society.[67] In particular, the capitalisation of agriculture was sapping rural villages of their resources. Whether the result was that smallholders were transformed into wage-labourers, or people were forced to seek work in towns, cities or even overseas in British colonies, the outcome was the same: people, he argued, were being made into exiles in their own land. Goldsmith's poem opened with an idyllic account of life in a rural village, the 'Sweet Auburn' of the speaker's youth, creating a profound sense of the importance of people's emotional ties with place and landscape:

> How often have I paused on every charm,
> The sheltered cot, the cultivated farm,
> The never failing brook, the busy mill,
> The decent church that topt the neighbouring hill,
> The hawthorn bush, with seats beneath the shade,
> For talking age and whispering lovers made.[68]

But under enclosure, 'all these charms are fled.' Worse still, men of 'wealth and pride', bent on enlarging their estates, were claiming 'a space that many poor supplied; / Space for his lake, his park's extended bounds, / Space for his horses, equipage and hounds' – for Goldsmith, the result of all this enrichment and pleasure-seeking at the expense of those who worked the land could only be a mighty 'fall' that awaited the nation.[69] Widely read and reprinted, it became an influential image of the unhappy changes that were being wrought upon rural communities – though one poet, George Crabbe, penned a riposte in *The Village* (1783), feeling that Goldsmith was being laughably sentimental in imagining the charms of the rural past, when life for the rural poor had always been characterised by backbreaking toil.[70]

And yet rural workers themselves were constructing idealised images of the past to serve as a protest against rising inequality in the countryside. English radicals emphasised people's historic right to common ownership of the land: as Thomas Spence, one of the foundational figures of English socialism, argued, enclosure was an attack on the traditional rights of the people. Sharing Goldsmith's feeling that workers were being exiled in their own homes, 'today', he declaimed in 1775, 'men may not live in any part of this world, nor even where they are born, but as strangers.' For Spence, a golden age of freedom and independence had once existed for working men, but private interests were now depriving them of their rights in a betrayal of the nation's history. This was nostalgia as a political weapon, pitting memory against capitalism, and presenting those who fought for the rights of workers not as agitators, but as custodians and restorers of national tradition.[71] Popular songs and ballads also drew on the importance of memory in arguing that enclosure had impoverished rural communities while the rich 'reap[ed] the gain'. Circulated orally within communities and across the generations as well as in writing, these songs were an important way through which people imagined their communities (both local and national) across time. As one ballad written down around the end of the century recalled:

> In old times I have heard 'tis true,
> That a poor man kept a pig and a cow,
> Their commons and places to feed them on,
> That a poor man might live happy then.[72]

Much as agricultural improvers might insist that enclosure was for the good of the nation as a whole because it increased agricultural productivity, songs and ballads avowed that the common people would remember a very different story. 'There may be rich men,' ran another ballad,

> Both Yeomen and Gentry,
> That for their owne private gaine,
> Hurt a whole Countrey
> By closing free Commons;
> Yet they'le make as though
> 'Twere for common good,
> But I know what I know.[73]

Politicised workers drew on a strong tradition that reached back through the generations in popular memory, in which the people's ownership of common land was not simply based on the expectation that its abundance could and should support them – it was '*the* land', conveying an important sense of belonging and connecting them symbolically to the national past. It gave people both a sense of having a stake in the nation, and a sense of identity rooted in a specific place and community that had a history of its own. In working-class politics, enclosure undermined crucial aspects of people's identities. Loss of access to common land did not just come with severe economic implications: it had been part of a culture of neighbourliness, mutual aid and gift exchange that shaped the life of communities. With wage labour came enforced mobility, as workers increasingly needed to travel to different farms, villages, towns and cities in search of enough work to support them throughout the year. And for men who had historically prided themselves on independence, self-reliance and their ability to support a family, becoming dependent on wages instead of land for subsistence could mean the loss of a traditional form of manhood.[74] All this combined to create a powerful narrative of dispossession in rural working-class culture. For many, whatever the hardships of rural life, their right to 'the land' had once provided a better social structure and more self-determination than agricultural wage labour or factory work.

It wasn't just the rural working classes who were concerned about being dispossessed of their identities as well as their land: a number of middle-class and aristocratic observers also felt this had worrying implications for the nation's future. Looking back to the past, they noted the historic relationship between military strength and social stability, on the one hand, and people's deep-rooted connection to the land on the other. Using the model of ancient Rome, they argued that classical republicanism had depended on a class of independent, armed citizens whose virtue was guaranteed by the ownership of land. This was a kind of military patriotism in which, in times of threat, morally upstanding warrior citizens who had skin in the game would be prepared to take up arms to defend their land and their liberties alike. Transferring this logic to England, opponents of enclosure argued that what was needed were independent yeomen and smallholders who were willing and able to go to war for the state.[75] Under enclosure, however, the ownership of land seemed to be concentrating into large-scale farms owned by the already wealthy, who had the resources to buy out smaller proprietors. If those who were hired to work the land were now motivated purely by economic need and self-interest rather than a shared investment in the land, where would the country recruit its soldiers of the future? For one anonymous 'Country Farmer', writing in 1786, it was 'no wonder' that 'British arms were so unsuccessful' in the War of American Independence (1775–83), not least because so many small farmers who had been driven from the land had themselves migrated to the colonies – migrants who had then fought against British soldiers. The only solution, he felt, was to open up enclosed land once more, and return to the wise policies of 'our forefathers'.[76]

Tradesmen and industrialists countered this wistful vision of military patriotism rooted in the land, arguing that it was an increasingly outdated way of understanding society. Urban dwellers, they affirmed, felt just as much a part of their nation and were just as likely to answer the call to defend their way of life – if not more so, because their communities weren't dependent on able-bodied men being available at times such as the harvest.[77] Like the economist Sir James Steuart, they contended that 'it is from the free hands, the manufacturers and artificers, that our armies are recruited, and not from the cottager and small farmer.'[78] The nation, they argued, drew its military strength from present-minded patriots, not by nostalgia for a vanishing agricultural ideal. Philosophers and historians of the Scottish Enlightenment drew attention to the differences between ancient and modern societies, emphasising that it was a good thing that the harsh militaristic spirit of past societies had declined in proportion to older ways of organising the rural economy. David Hume, along with Edward Gibbon, agreed that the liberty of the ancient world had rested on a joint foundation of arms and agriculture, but they maintained that the 'virtue' of Sparta and Rome had been so unforgivingly harsh and violent that it hardly deserved the name.[79] The rise of commerce had been worth the trade-off: for Hume, ancient Romans themselves would have been amazed at 'the degree of clemency, order, tranquility, and other social virtues' that had been 'attained in modern times.' Though even here, there was a wisp of nostalgia for the ancient past – as Hume confessed, the statesmen and warriors of the classical world 'have a grandeur and force of sentiment, which astonishes our narrow souls.'[80] But his faith was firmly in the forces of modern improvement; a view shared by Gibbon, as he wryly noted that even ancient Romans had displayed that age-old 'propensity of mankind to exalt the past, and to depreciate the present', in failing to fully recognise the commercial improvements of their own age.[81]

THE TRADE OFF

Yet even the most enlightened optimists could reflect with melancholy regret on what had been lost in the transition to modern ways of living. For all their celebrations of progress, Enlightenment thinkers were distinctly ambivalent about the compromises this entailed. No theory of human progress could be constructed that didn't seem to suggest that something vital, too, had decayed. As the philosopher and historian Adam Ferguson argued in 1767, it was to be celebrated that the 'savage', violent passions that had animated ancient Greeks and Romans had been superseded by a politer and gentler culture, in which people had been 'softened' by the experience of living in a commercial society – where, at least in theory, people were motivated by the need to co-exist peacefully, rather than by codes of vengeance and rivalry. On the other hand, at least ancient passions had provided an outlet for bravery and heroism, where people were driven by loyalty and life-or-death struggles to defend their homelands, not by shabby concerns for profit margins and fashionable consumer luxuries. A Gaelic speaker who was intimately familiar with Highland culture, Ferguson felt that commercial society had cramped the 'character' of modern citizens, in ways that not only compromised their public spirit and honour, but endangered their happiness.[82]

Even Adam Smith – who, more than anyone in the eighteenth century, vindicated the new phase of capitalism that was emerging – worried about the insufficiency of commercial culture. One might spend a lifetime in the pursuit of wealth and luxury, but materialistic lifestyles threatened at 'every moment to overwhelm the person that dwells in them'. Like an impractical designer coat, consumer pleasures 'keep off the summer shower, not the winter storm, but leave him always as much, and sometimes more exposed than before, to anxiety, to fear, and sorrow.'[83] Commerce, they felt, had brought relative comfort and safety to more people than ever before, but it could not entirely compensate for what had been lost.

Even medical opinion was not immune from nostalgia for a less acquisitive time. The physician George Cheyne had diagnosed consumerism as part of *The English Malady* (1733), contrasting a time 'when mankind was simple, plain, honest and frugal', and 'there were few or no diseases', to the prevalence of 'spleen, vapours, lowness of spirits, hypochondriacal and hysterical distempers' among his contemporaries.[84] It would become an influential explanation of the ills people felt were running rife in Georgian society (though his contemporaries pointed out that prosperity was leading to the reduction of older ills, like famine). But why was Cheyne convinced that these nervous maladies – what we would now classify as symptoms of depression and anxiety – were a characteristically *English* disease? For Cheyne, and for generations of ambivalent capitalists after him, these were the diseases of modern civilisation: England seemed to be racing ahead of other countries in transforming its economy and expanding trade overseas, but it seemed to be creating, too, new forms of unhappiness. 'Since our Wealth has increased,' he argued, 'we have ransacked all Parts of the Globe', gathering up its 'whole Stock of Materials' simply to end up with a social addiction to 'excess'. Consumerism, he felt, was making people sick.[85]

In this new phase of modern capitalism that was developing from the later years of the seventeenth century and into the eighteenth, people were increasingly facing a dilemma that has preoccupied generations ever since: for all its material improvements, did capitalism really make people happy? It wasn't a question that was easy to answer – how could you disentangle the progress of science and knowledge, the rise of a more peaceful society in which more and more people were better clothed, better fed, and expressing themselves through new goods, new tastes and pleasures, from the corresponding forces that were destroying older ways of living and working, disrupting and sometimes tearing apart communities, and concentrating more and more wealth at the top of society? Would the workers who had never chosen to take part in this transformation ultimately be better off for it? While people in post-war Britain and into the twenty-first century would later come to debate the corrosive effects of an 'affluent society' they felt was characterised by individualism, consumerism and the decline of community, these were also questions on which people felt the future depended more than two centuries earlier. Very few people felt that this trade-off had been a mistake, or wanted to roll back the clock entirely: Britain's growing wealth and power were a huge source of national pride, progress that was to be celebrated as long as people felt it could be sustained.

And yet many social commentators held on to a contradictory mix of nostalgic ideas about how the lower classes, in particular, should be going about their lives in the new economy. The undeniable fact was that as land was enclosed and agricultural productivity increased, while profits were channelled mostly to landowners, people were going to move into towns and cities in search of work – some voluntarily, in search of new opportunities, new excitements, new ways of living, and some having no other choice. Because they increasingly lacked access to common land and shared resources, and worked long hours for wages, they were going to need to buy things instead of making them; purchases that were also contributing to economic growth. Consumer demand was creating, in turn, new jobs in production and supply: an inseparable process that was laying the foundations of the Industrial Revolution. But much as socially and economically privileged commentators were benefiting from this process, they regretted that Britain's workers were no longer sustaining an image of virtuously homespun self-sufficiency, issuing nostalgic laments about the changing face of Britain's once-humble 'poor'. The economy was bewildering people in ways that it continues to do today. People argued that growing international trade could only be a good thing, at the same time as lamenting the upheaval it brought to British manufacturing. Even as Enlightenment optimists praised how much more civilised and gentle people were becoming in a commercial society, their contemporaries were railing against the ways it depended upon exploiting people's resources and labour abroad, outsourcing slavery beyond Britain's borders. These are modern problems, but they are modern problems with a long history.

7

The Committee for the Demolition
of Monuments

1688–1530

If we journey back in time in search of an age of contentment and stability, a society in which people were not convulsed by change or reeling in the wake of transformation, it is a hard sell to alight in the sixteenth and seventeenth centuries. Between 1530 and 1688, England broke with Rome and forged a new Protestant nation; reverted to Catholicism and then to Protestantism once more; descended into civil war; abolished the monarchy and then restored it again. The Reformation, Civil Wars, Interregnum and Restoration continually reforged the relationship between the nation's past, present and future in ways that were intensely fought over by successive generations. History had continually to be rewritten to bring the story of England into line with these social and political revolutions, and the past was weaponised as never before. Protestants and Catholics, royalists and parliamentarians alike formed rival visions of history-as-propaganda to sanction their causes.

Amid these conflicts, nostalgia itself could be dangerous. Protestant and republican iconoclasts sought to destroy traces of the nation's Catholic and monarchical heritage, as they outlawed religious practices, tore down statues and defaced churches; aiming to physically wipe out memories of the recent past, lest the material traces of an earlier time tempt people back into their former ways. People were deeply divided about what should be done with the physical evidence of a problematic history, from religious images and statues to books and even buildings. Was it better to re-contextualise this heritage by defacing it, leaving it as a monument to the errors of the past and a warning to future generations against the dangers of back-sliding? Should it instead be destroyed forever so that the nation could start afresh? Or was it important to preserve records of the past in archives, before its memory was lost forever?

The story of this period that we look back upon today is often one in which the Britain as we know it emerged from these conflicts – between Catholics and Protestants, Crown and Parliament, Church and State. Observers ever since have cele-brated the development of constitutional monarchy and parliamentary democracy that unfolded in the wake of the pol-itical and religious battles of the sixteenth and seventeenth centuries. Paradoxically, the nation that emerged from these upheavals would begin to pride itself on its very stability: for centuries afterwards, historians, politicians and ordinary men and women would hold up the Glorious Revolution of 1688 as proof of the unique moderation and continuity of Britain's pol-itical system, with its time-hallowed laws and liberties, an ancient constitution that could weather any storm. Protestant-ism and patriotism would become fused in a narrative that celebrated the nation's steady upwards trajectory; a people who were uniquely blessed with divine favour, and destined to spread their influence around the globe. But Britain's future dir-ection was never a foregone conclusion for the people who lived through the sixteenth and seventeenth centuries, experi-encing successive waves of change and uncertainty.

In many ways, Britain itself had to be invented before it could be remembered. England completed the annexation of Wales under Henry VIII in the mid-sixteenth century, and then in 1603 the Stuart James VI and I joined the thrones of Scotland and England under a single monarch for the first time, as the contours of a united island nation began to take shape. While many resisted these developments as an unwelcome imposition that was swamping their own national histories and identities, a range of Tudor and Stuart observers, from poets to politicians, saw in them the resurrection of a long-mythologised past. Could this, in fact, be the rebirth of Britons as a once-united people, an island that a thousand years before had stood together against Saxon invaders? It was a promise that sent antiquarians scurrying into the archives to establish whether the blood of King Arthur ran through the veins of Tudor kings, in the hope that history could give the present the stamp of authenticity; or else sent sceptics in search of evidence that might debunk Arthurian tales as little more than patriotic myth-making.[1]

These efforts to sanction present developments by joining them with the distant past were crucial, too, to vindicating religious change. In the sixteenth century, while Catholics argued that Protestantism was a new-fangled religion, and that their church was bolstered by almost a millennium of English tradition, reformers retorted that they were returning to the Christianity of biblical purity, before it had been corrupted by the church of Rome. Insisting that their aim was restoration rather than innovation, reformers looked for evidence in the historical record that Christianity had first arrived in Britain not with a papal mission in the seventh century, but – it was said – when the biblical figure Joseph of Arimathea had visited Glastonbury.[2] To claim antiquity for one's views was to claim their authority and authenticity, in an age that viewed history as a source of timeless wisdom and knowledge, which could provide clear lessons for the present and future. As one seventeenth-century letter-writer, the gentleman Henry Oxinden, advised his son upon his studies: 'if you be desirous to know what shall be, read & observe histories . . . for all things in the world at all times have their very encounter with the times of old, there being no new thing under the Sun.'[3] The relationship between past and present; between tradition and innovation; between restoration and reform, was one of the defining questions of the age. The drive to create a dialogue between the present and the distant past was the character of the Renaissance itself, in its 'rediscovery' of the learning of classical Greece and Rome – and with it came the corresponding impulse that cast more recent history as the 'dark ages' of supposed ignorance and error, from which people had thankfully emerged into the light.

While this chapter in Britain's history comes to a close with the Glorious Revolution of 1688, with the arrival of the Protestant William of Orange and the deposition in exile of the Catholic James II and VII, 1688 was also a crucial moment in the history of nostalgia. It was the year that this curious malady was first coined by the physician Johannes Hofer to describe the pains of homesickness among Swiss soldiers fighting abroad. But people were experiencing nostalgia long before there was a word for it. Almost everywhere we turn, in the sixteenth and seventeenth centuries, we find people expressing a sense of being suddenly, entirely cut off from the past. At different times and in different ways, people looked back upon recent events that some celebrated as the birth of a new phase in the history of their nation, and others lamented as a catastrophic loss of their shared identity; as well as on times that everyone seemed to agree had been a golden age they could never quite recover.[4] And with that sense of rupture came anxiety as well as intense nostalgia, and a drive to make sense of their history.

THE BATTLE FOR THE PAST

When was the 'golden age', exactly? Who was innovating, and who was restoring? Did the course of history reveal that the English were a brave and freedom-loving nation, destined to throw off the constraints of papal and monarchical tyranny alike? Or could one trace a thread running through the pages of history, from Magna Carta in 1215 to the Restoration of the monarchy in 1660 and beyond, that showed the English to be a polite and moderate people, divinely ordained to balance monarchical rule and parliamentary democracy? These were questions that deeply preoccupied historians, no less than rulers and politicians, in the sixteenth and seventeenth centuries. During times of conflict, the stakes were extremely high. History was a powerful force of political propaganda: one that could be harnessed both to lend weight to the status quo and act as a tool of protest or rallying point for resistance. But as people tried to tease out narratives that could explain their society's course between past, present and future, the unpredictable twists and turns of political and religious change could threaten at any moment to leave them stranded on the 'wrong' side of history. In such a charged climate, nostalgia, as well as history, could be dangerously subversive.

Tudor and Stuart monarchs frequently presented themselves as the restorers of a golden age of peace and security. Henry VIII, future instigator of radical innovation, cast himself at the start of his reign from 1509 in the light of a pious restorer of tradition. Commemorating Henry's coronation in verse, the philosopher and statesman Thomas More (of course unknowing that he would later fall victim to the king's reforming agenda) prophesied that 'order' would be 'restored in him' once more, expressing his faith that the king's 'virtues' would equal those of 'any of his ancestors.' 'The golden ages first return to you, prince,' More continued extravagantly, with a reference to ancient philosophy that told of a long-lost age of primordial peace; 'o! Plato may thus far be a prophet!'[5] Just a decade before Henry would begin the process of separating the English church from Rome, his treatise the *Defence of the Seven Sacraments* (1521) had mounted a defence of papal authority in the face of Martin Luther's attacks on the corruption of the Catholic church's powers, presenting himself as outraged by Luther's contempt for 'the ancient Doctors of the church', and the time-honoured 'laws' and 'customs' of the Catholic faith.[6] Yet while he had earlier persecuted Protestant reformers as agents of corrosive novelty, by the 1530s Henry was presenting his own reforming agenda as a restoration, propelled by what one historian describes as 'weaponised nostalgia'.[7] The key legal foundation of the English Reformation, passed in 1533, cited for its authority 'divers sundry old authentic histories and chronicles' that – it was claimed – 'manifestly declared' that England is, and had always been, 'an Empire'. The implication was that the Pope's authority in England was a symptom of the nation's decay from its 'natural' condition of independence, free from foreign laws and intrusion, presenting religious reform as a liberation movement that would throw off imperial domination from Rome. (Just as Brexit would be imagined five centuries later, this was an imperial nostalgia that asserted England's historic status as a proudly independent power – the wrongful sense that a country which should be free to do as it chose was being treated by Europe like a colony.)

Yet there was considerable resistance to the idea that Protestantism represented the oldest, truest form of Christianity. While many embraced the new reforms – some enthusiastically, some under threat of execution, and most falling somewhere between these two ends of a complicated spectrum – Catholics would continue to refer to theirs as the 'old religion', taunting their enemies with the mocking question 'where was your church before Luther?' After two decades that had witnessed successive waves of reform under Henry VIII and Edward VI, the Counter Reformation that was briefly imposed by the Catholic Mary I, from 1553 until her death in 1558, revealed that many people had simply hidden away the church images, objects and texts that they were supposed to have destroyed by law – hoping for the day when the Catholic faith would be restored, even as they mourned the world they had lost since Henry's reforms.[8]

In turn, England's return to a Protestant monarch in Elizabeth I was celebrated by many as a new golden age for England. Military victories over Catholic enemies, especially the defeat of the Spanish Armada in 1588, were celebrated as seminal moments in a patriotic Protestant history. Martyrs to the Protestant cause who had been executed under Mary were held up as national heroes. John Foxe's *Actes and Monuments*, popularly known as *Foxe's Book of Martyrs*, was first published in 1563, and rapidly became one of the most widely read texts in the country – a status it would sustain well into the nineteenth century. This was a new version of history: one that traced a line of continuity between men and women who had been persecuted as heretics over the centuries, from medieval Cathars and Lollards who had opposed Catholic teachings to those who had been burned at the stake under Mary; an eclectic band of true believers who had kept the torch alight, and whose heroic example might provide a source of inspiration to his readers, strengthening their pride in having thrown off the tyranny of Rome. These were distinctly rose-tinted martyrdoms, in which victims invariably met with brave and noble deaths, steadfast and unwavering in their faith to the very end. Understandable lapses of fortitude in the face of persecution and torture were quietly glossed over, while those who had been momentarily tempted to recant under pressure, such as the Archbishop of Canterbury Thomas Cranmer, were transformed into shining examples of how the godly could overcome the moral weaknesses inherent in human nature.

Foxe wasn't one to let facts get in the way of a good execution story, even when the pedigree of centuries-old heretics as pioneering proto-Protestants was dubious at best. Material that might tarnish an image of Protestant courage and unity against the enemy was censored or rewritten. Foxe's opponents accused him of airbrushing history, and telling lies on an unprecedented scale. But the point had been to create a useable version of the past, one that could provide an inspiring origin myth for sixteenth-century Protestants as they looked back with the benefit of hindsight.[9]

Individual men and women who had survived religious

persecution under Mary also found themselves re-examining their experiences in a new light when they returned to safety as Elizabethans. Many who had escaped punishment by partially conforming to Catholicism carefully rewrote their life stories to align with the sacrifices made by those who had fled into exile or chosen to embrace death at the stake. The gentlewoman Rose Hickman, who *had* gone into exile, re-envisaged what, in reality, had been a comfortable stint with her husband in the Protestant haven of Antwerp as a wilderness of heroic suffering, when she sat down in later years to write her memoirs. It was a process of retrospective editing that would be repeated across many people's life-writing – indeed, memoirs left behind by parents or grandparents could be revised by their reformed descendants, who wished to avoid embarrassment by removing suggestions of their forebears' Catholicism. Compiling his family's history in 1607, the Yorkshire landowner William Wentworth rewrote an account of his own conception during Elizabeth I's reign in 1561 that his mother and father had passed down to him, deleting mention of a pilgrimage to a shrine that his parents had credited with curing their infertility. Not a good origin story, he felt, for a Protestant gentleman. In time, family histories would be amended and enhanced still further, as people's memories of their Tudor ancestors passed into family legend, in multiple rose-tinted retellings down the generations.[10]

Nostalgia for the days of Elizabeth's reign seemed to get underway almost immediately after her death in 1603. The poet and playwright Ben Jonson tried to galvanise collective enthusiasm for her successor James I, taking poetic advantage of his entrance into London on the Ides of March by hailing him as a new Caesar Augustus, who would usher in 'those golden times . . . returned again.'[11] But for many in England, the romantic memory of a flame-haired warrior queen, who had presided over an age of exploration, discovery and military glory, proved in the long run to be a far more irresistible imaginative spectacle. Already, at the outset of the seventeenth century, the image of the Elizabethan era as the 'Merry England of Good Queen Bess' that would be celebrated by Victorians and twenty-first-century free-traders alike – a heyday of swash-buckling privateers and buccaneering explorers; a time when 'this sceptred isle' was extolled in plays and poetry by Shake-speare and his contemporaries – was beginning to take shape.

But while landmarks in England's Protestant history such as the victory over the Spanish Armada, and later the discovery of the Gunpowder Plot against James I in 1605, would in later years be celebrated again as uncontentious anniversaries in the national calendar, in the first half of seventeenth century they had the power to create deep division. When the church began to reintroduce previously prohibited images, ornaments and ceremonies under Charles I in the 1630s, part of a new wave of 'beautification' in church interiors, it sparked widespread out-cry; seeming to confirm the worst fears of many that the king and the clergy might be attempting to smuggle Catholicism into the country again by the back door. Archbishop William Laud, the key opposition figure for those who favoured a plainer style of worship, took a particular dislike to depictions of the defeat of the Armada, which in some churches had replaced the images of saints and religious figures that had been destroyed by sixteenth-century iconoclasts.[12]

For many Protestants, images celebrating Elizabethan mili-tary victory over a Catholic enemy had seemed more acceptable than these earlier images – where those had been associated with the Catholic past and the sin of idolatry, depictions of the Armada were celebrated in an unmistakeably national and Protestant context. But by Charles I's reign, amid public con-troversy over the king's choice of a Catholic wife in Henrietta Maria of France, these images seemed suddenly divisive again. Nostalgic remembrances of landmarks in England's Protestant history came to be viewed in a newly contentious light, in the years when the fault lines that would later be entrenched in civil war from 1642 were beginning to take shape. By loudly and enthusiastically celebrating these Protestant anniversaries with bonfires and merry-making, people could publicly proclaim their opposition to the king's policies. Throughout the following years, the authorities looked on uneasily as Guy Fawkes's day celebrations spilled over into defiance and disorder, such as a crowd of revellers in Chelmsford in 1641 who turned to iconoclastic destruction and smashed the stained-glass windows of their local church.[13]

By 1635, the church was issuing new directions to the clergy for services to be delivered on 5 November, urging them to tone down the mood of anti-Catholic vitriol now that memories of the Gunpowder Plot were fading out of immediacy. For the more conciliatory-minded among the clergy, the feeling was growing that 'we were not so angry with the Papists now, as we were about 20 years since' – and that it might be counterproductive to 'exasperate' those with Catholic sympathies with further hostility, and instead try to 'win them to us by fairness and mildness.' Yet to the hotter sort of Protestant (as puritans and dissenters have been labelled), this was all part of a sinister conspiracy to obliterate the memory of the nation's proudest moments in its epic fight against the papacy – fears that were frequently linked to the suspicion that Charles harboured ambitions of tyrannical rule, in an age that instinctively connected Catholicism to absolute monarchy. The puritan polemicist William Prynne, one of the most outspoken campaigners against crown and church policies, railed against the attempts of officials to censor commemoration of these 'icon events' in England's history. One church rector, Henry Burton – who had been dismissed from his position in the royal court under Charles for his puritan sympathies – refused to tone down the homily to his congregation on 5 November, as he accused bishops such as Laud of launching a 'Popish plot' with their 'innovations' in churches, for which he was sentenced to lose a portion of his ears. For his own criticism of the king, queen and church, Prynne would be charged with sedition and lose first part, then all of his ears on two separate occasions.[14]

Throughout and after the civil wars, royalists and parliamentarians developed rival versions of the recent past that might vindicate their causes. History was given 'spin' – the battle to control the memory of events following the outbreak of war in 1642 was underway even as its earliest episodes were unfolding.[15] For parliamentarians, the Protestant nation had been increasingly imperilled from the start of Charles's reign in 1625, as they painted a picture of a king who had sought to do away with the power of Parliament, levying unjust taxes against his people and forcing through unpopular religious changes under the sway of 'evil counsellors' such as Archbishop Laud.

Parliament's cause could be bolstered still further by reaching far into the distant past. The controversial theory of the 'Norman Yoke' held that Norman conquerors had from 1066 imposed a yoke 'upon the neck of England', casting English history ever since as a struggle between rulers who had inherited power from the Norman oppressors, and the champions of supposedly Anglo-Saxon liberties. The monarchy, wrote Lucy Hutchinson, whose husband would sign Charles I's death warrant, was founded in the spillage of 'the people's blood' by William the Conqueror, a tyrannical bloodbath 'in which it hath swum' ever since.[16] Key constitutional documents such as Magna Carta became re-envisaged, not as gracious concessions to nobles granted by the Crown, but as the reassertion of ancient freedoms. This built upon an idea that had been developing in legal circles, which argued that the foundations of England's laws had already been laid down in the pre-Conquest period – implying that, as the common law had grown out of the centuries-old precedents and customs of the people, it was ultimately Parliament, as representatives of the people, and not the Crown, who had the power to take measures such as raising new taxes.[17] While Charles I had felt that it was in his power to dissolve Parliament and rule alone from 1629, parliamentarians argued that this was a tyrannical perversion of English history.

For royalist writers and historians, the story of England's descent into civil war was instead a tale of a once-happy nation overwhelmed by unexpected calamity. They conjured nostalgic images of a golden age destroyed by conflict: King Charles's 'fortunate islands', a 'land flowing with milk and honey' that had been 'the envy of all Europe', which had cruelly fallen victim to 'horrid distempers'. This narrative, established during the civil wars, was elaborated still further during the Interregnum in the 1650s, as royalists, looking back on what they fondly remembered as a gentler way of living, continued to make the argument in defeat that England's order had been overturned by upstart puritans who had seized control of Parliament.[18] Royalists who lived through England's republican decade frequently presented Charles I as an innocent victim of history. The poet Sir John Denham described him as 'the late great victim ... a sacrifice to quench the raging thirst / Of inflam'd vengeance' – one of a collection of elegies for Charles's execution in 1649 by some of the leading poets of the day, including John Dryden and Andrew Marvell. (Its contributors dodged the problem of implicating those who had signed the king's death warrant, and who were now running the country, by presenting the volume as a nostalgic tribute to a young aristocrat who in the weeks following Charles's execution had died tragically of smallpox on the eve of his wedding.)[19]

But one former royalist, the poet Abraham Cowley, who had been writing a history of the conflict during his wartime exile on the Continent, argued that under Oliver Cromwell's rule it was time to let go of this narrative and adapt to the new reality. Explaining in the preface to a new volume of poetry in 1656 that he had abandoned his earlier epic poem of civil war and burned the drafts, he wrote that it was time to 'submit to the conditions of the Conqueror', and 'lay down our Pens as well as Arms.' 'We must march out of our Cause itself,' he continued, 'and dismantle ... all the Works and Fortifications of Wit and Reason ... by which we defended it.' Instead of nostalgic laments and literary resistance, Cowley felt, to live in republican England called for 'The Art of Oblivion.'[20]

The example set by Cowley indicates just how complicated it could be to navigate the unpredictable sequence of events that people found themselves entangled in during the middle of the seventeenth century – and the perils of rewriting history to make sense of what was unfolding. When the monarchy was restored with Charles II in 1660, the lines Cowley had written just four years earlier would become a source of considerable embarrassment. Graciously pardoned by the king, Cowley employed 'The Art of Oblivion' all over again, deleting his premature pledge of submission to Cromwell when he released a new edition of the poems in 1667. Once again, in an entirely different context, it was time to forget the 'division' of the previous decades and move on – an imaginative feat that required him to rose-tint even the memory of civil war itself, as he described 'the enmities of Fellow-Citizens' as having been like that of a 'quarrel' between 'Lovers', who should now kiss and make up with the 'Reintegration of their Amity.'[21]

After the Restoration of the monarchy, Charles II's regime took an intense interest in the way his subjects were remembering the past. On the one hand, state policy in the 1660s was directed towards efforts similar to Cowley's: to tell people that it was now time to forget how divided they had been, and start afresh united. Forgetting became official policy: an Act of Oblivion in 1660 forgave past loyalties and forbade people from making any comments in speech or print upon a person's conduct during the previous two decades, in a state-mandated display of amnesia. The political philosopher Thomas Hobbes argued that forgetting was the basis of a just state, and amnesia should be the foundation of the social contract – the 'evil past' had to be suppressed for the sake 'of the good to follow.' For many in the aftermath of conflict, the only way to move on was to forget – or pretend to. On the other hand, contradicting the official instruction to forget, there was a renewed effort to shape a story of the recent past that could portray the Restoration as the natural and inevitable conclusion of a regrettable but short-lived episode in England's history; a return to the good old days before what were often described as 'the late troubled times.'[22] It was both a step forward into a more secure and tolerant future, and a return to an idealised past.

In the wake of the Restoration, history writing could only be published with state approval: Charles appointed a Historiographer Royal, and then a Surveyor of the Press, in a concerted attempt to shape what it was that people remembered. Works that were critical of the established order were censored – almost no work of history by a former parliamentarian or republican was published during the early years of Charles II's reign. What *was* allowed to be published invariably highlighted the sufferings of royalists over the course of the puritan Long Parliament during the 1640s and 1650s. State-sanctioned histories painted puritan leaders as little more than rabble-rousers, zealous political agitators who had posed as pious men of god. As far as the writer William Winstanley was concerned, compiling a *Loyall Martyrology* of royalists who had died for the cause, the suggestion that puritans had genuinely wanted to reform England's government was merely a cloak for their 'pride, envy, covetousness and ambition.' Oliver Cromwell consistently emerged as the arch villain of the piece: his trajectory rewritten from that of a leader who had initially been reluctant to assume the mantle of power, to a man who had harboured dangerous ambition from the start to rule like a tyrant. Historians created a kind of 'dishonour roll' of the regicides who had signed Charles I's execution warrant – in which, for instance, the politician Henry Marten was characterised as 'notorious for his ill life' – in the hope 'that they may stink to future generations', as the writer John Davies explained to his readers in 1661. It was a seductively straightforward explanation for recent events, one that allowed historians to evade questions of the legitimacy of parliamentary opposition to Charles I's policies and focus instead on their personal qualities – playing to readers' appetites for character assassination and public scandal. Histories such as these would sometimes skip over the Interregnum entirely, hurrying straight from regicide to restoration, or else treated it as a kind of waiting room for the nation that was barely worth remembering.[23]

And yet the state, much as it tried to censor rival versions of history, was never in complete control of what people remembered of the civil wars, nor of how they felt about the current regime. Printed pamphlets often evaded the efforts of the censors, while manuscripts could circulate underground – part of a thriving literary culture of critique and resistance, one which was increasingly taking aim at those in power through biting political satire. The poet Andrew Marvell, having written a number of royalist elegies early in his career, had in the 1650s taken a job in Cromwell's government and switched literary sides. By the 1660s, he had avoided punishment for cooperating with republicanism; been re-elected in the Cavalier Parliament under Charles II; and was covertly circulating a satirical poem in manuscript, in which the ghost of Charles I returns to warn his son of the fatal consequences of relying on bad advisors. This was a history of the recent past that implied a pointed critique of Charles II, as Marvell depicted the royal court – in carefully coded burlesque – as a place of notorious appetites and debauchery, whose sexual corruption mirrored the political corruption that its critics argued was characteristic of the new regime. While Charles II might present himself as the 'Merry Monarch', restoring a happier time before the civil wars, his opponents accused him of restoring little more than royal extravagance and thirst for power.[24]

Ordinary men and women, too, could draw on the history of the civil wars to express their continued opposition to Charles II, and later to his successor James II. The inhabitants of Taunton in Somerset, for instance, a parliamentarian stronghold which had withstood three sieges in 1644–5, continued to hold a three-day festival to commemorate the anniversary on which they had defeated their royalist besiegers, drinking and dancing their way around a bonfire as they chanted 'rejoice you dogs, 'tis the eleventh of May, the day the cavaliers ran away.' In 1671, a disapproving onlooker to the festivities reported back to the Privy Council that the locals appeared to 'glory in their rebellion (so far are they from repentance for it).' By the 1670s, memories of their resistance during the civil war were themselves passing into the stuff of nostalgic celebration. As the onlooker described, 'men, women and children throughout the whole town' were taking part in this collective 'rejoicing', 'many of which were not then born when the siege was raised.'[25] For the people of Taunton, as the immediacy of conflict faded into nostalgic remembrance, war stories were becoming transformed into a source of collective pride. But this was nostalgia with a subversive edge – one that insisted that as much as the authorities tried to persuade them to move on and forget the recent past, they would keep it alive in memory.

ICONOCLASTS VS ANTIQUARIANS

What was it that compelled so many people throughout the sixteenth and seventeenth centuries to destroy so much of their heritage? What was important to preserve and remember, and what was it better that they forget? By the end of the sixteenth century, successive waves of religious reform under Henry VIII, Edward VI and Elizabeth I had left the landscape of England a very different place to the one that had existed in 1530. With the advent of Protestantism came the obliteration of much of England's medieval past.

For reformers, the Catholic church had corrupted Christianity, hoodwinking people into obedience through mystery and superstition: the impenetrable masses delivered in Latin; the sensuous pleasures of incense, bells and music; the shrines and relics of saints that were said to have healing powers, or statues to which miraculous feats had been attributed. Images of saints and religious figures, reformers believed, were temptations to the sin of idolatry – of worshiping images themselves, as opposed to the word of God. Beautiful images and objects, and the stories of saints and miracles that surrounded them, were seen as insidious distractions from the biblical teachings people were supposed to be focusing on. Both officially and unofficially – sometimes by royal or parliamentary decree, sometimes undertaken spontaneously by local communities – reformers set out to dismantle the material world of Catholic worship from the 1530s, in waves of iconoclasm that continued into the civil wars and Interregnum of the 1640s and 1650s.

Images of saints and religious figures were defaced or destroyed in churches, by smashing stained glass and tearing down statues or chipping away at carved faces; altar tables were stripped of decoration; books and manuscripts were burned or repurposed; vestments were confiscated; crucifixes removed and smashed to pieces. At times openly admitting the Crown's need for 'a masse of money', Henry VIII and Edward VI expropriated church wealth on a colossal scale, much of it to fund war against the French throughout the sixteenth century – itself a nostalgia-saturated quest to regain England's lost empire in France. Gold and silver plate was melted down and transferred to the treasury, while lead bells and roofs were converted into guns and ammunition, or else sold by the shipload to the continent along with confiscated statuary. It amounted to the loss of an incalculable quantity of medieval sculpture, stonework, glass, painted panels and murals, tapestries, wood-carving, jewellery and metalwork, illuminated manuscripts and the learning they contained.[26] And the effects of iconoclasm extended far beyond the bounds of church interiors. Over 800 abbeys, nunneries and friaries were destroyed with the dissolution of the monasteries between 1536 and 1541 – a process that saw approximately a third of England's land transferred from church to crown, then sold off to aristocratic and gentry families who sympathised with Henry VIII's break with Rome. Perhaps 12,000 monks, nuns and friars were displaced from their homes and their vocations; people who had themselves been landlords who had powerfully shaped the life of their local communities.[27] Iconoclasm spilled still further into the countryside, in an age in which religion was written into the landscape itself; with wayside crosses that had once marked the bounds of local parishes, and traditional pilgrimages to shrines and holy sites that had given particular places their special character. Throughout England, as well as in Scotland and Wales where parallel Reformations were taking place, people found their lives and their landscapes changed profoundly.

Many ordinary men and women enthusiastically welcomed these acts of iconoclasm: assisting, and at times pre-empting, the image-breaking of appointed officials. There were many who did not look back upon Roman Catholic traditions with fondness. Contemporary observers recorded riotous youths throwing snowballs at priests, disrupting masses with mocking games, and profaning chapels with drunken merry-making. An agent dispatched by Thomas Cromwell, perhaps the most notorious state architect of the Reformation, described how he had handed over an ornate crucifix to 'the rude [unlearned] people and boys' who had come to assist his efforts at Boxley Abbey in Kent, who had then delighted in smashing it to smithereens. Elsewhere, holy objects were defaced and then given to children to play with, in the hope of instilling contempt for outdated superstitions in the next generation of reformers.[28] These instances of iconoclasm were not mindless acts of destruction and disorder. As the historian Alexandra Walsham writes, to watch or collaborate in the destruction of abbeys, church statues and crucifixes, was to acquire palpable proof that they were, after all, simply objects; not the vessels of miraculous power people had been taught could not be profaned without incurring the wrath of

God. 'To see a great abbey reduced to rubble or to cast an image on to a pyre without disaster striking was to be convinced that these structures and artefacts were indeed lifeless.' It was a concerted attempt to expose the centuries-old traditions they had been taught to revere as little more than a fraud.[29]

For a minority of diehard reformers, what was needed was *more* destruction. Religious radicals called for the demolition of parish churches, arguing that they must be left 'desolate' and 'laid on heaps' like the abbeys had been, because they could 'never be cleansed' of the historic taint of superstition and error. Few were prepared to go quite so far; yet this was simply a more extreme form of the logic behind many acts of iconoclasm. The aim had been to wipe out the traces of the nation's Roman Catholic past, so that 'no memory remained'. There was a widespread fear that to remember too much of the past would be to risk returning to it again. At times, reformers could fear that even the empty spaces and voids left behind in churches where images had been taken down might become a focus for wistful veneration – one bishop in the 1560s gave instructions to workmen that the niches where statues had once stood should be filled in 'so as if there had been none there.'[30]

Yet for other reformers, this attempted memory sweep ran the risk of writing out their own hard-won efforts from the historical record. The mutilated remains of images and pictures, they argued, should be left in place as 'monuments' of their righteous 'indignation and detestation' of popery. To look upon the broken statues and scarred walls of churches would be to be continually reminded of their achievements in breaking away from the corruption of the past. In order to avoid repeating the mistakes of past generations, they felt, it was necessary to remember. In the seventeenth century, the puritan chronicler Nehemiah Wallington lovingly preserved fragments of stained glass that he had witnessed broken in his church in the 1640s, 'to show the generation to come what God hath done for us.'[31]

Amid intense national debates in the 2020s about what

should be done with statues of people who historically profited from slave-trading and imperialism, such as Edward Colston and Cecil Rhodes, it is hard not to draw parallels with Reformation iconoclasm. Twenty-first-century debates hinge on questions of what should be done with the physical traces of a time when attitudes were very different to our own: should we pull these statues down, contextualise them with a plaque, or do nothing at all? Should Colston's statue have been left to rust at the bottom of Bristol harbour where he was cast by protestors, or is his legacy as well as his toppling best remembered within the walls of a museum? And who gets to make these decisions – should we let protestors and communities decide what to do with this heritage themselves, or make a case through appointed committees and legal channels? We would do well to remember that these debates do not originate with 'woke' activists in the present day, but are questions people have been asking for centuries. And yet, while our present-day culture wars over Britain's history share many similarities with those of the sixteenth and seventeenth centuries, the role of the state could hardly be more different. While right-wing newspapers and politicians consistently interpret calls to remove statues and decolonise our understanding of British history as an unpatriotic campaign to 'do Britain down' – or what Boris Johnson has termed 'a kind of know-nothing, cancel culture iconoclasm' – the Tudor state had argued that iconoclasm was a means of *reclaiming* a proudly independent history, for a nation that looked towards a future free from Continental control.[32] It is hard to escape the irony that the national history conservatives celebrate today rests on a Protestant origin story founded on the iconoclasm they deplore.

While many ordinary men and women as well as state officials in the sixteenth century enthusiastically welcomed iconoclastic reform, there were many people, too, who felt intense grief at the destruction that was taking place around them, and yearned for the material and spiritual culture of their pasts. The very ruthlessness of England's Reformation shocked its contemporaries into a sense of loss. Setting out in 1589 to demonstrate that the present time was a vast improvement on the days before the Reformation, the Lincolnshire minister Francis Trigge recorded with some disappointment the

> weeping & bewailing of the simple sort, and especially of women, who going into the Churches, & seeing the bare walls, and lacking their golden Images, their costly copes, their pleasant Organs, their sweet frankincense, their gilded chalices ... lament in themselves & fetch many deep sighs, & bewail this spoiling and laying waste of the Church as they think.[33]

Iconoclastic destruction was not just an assault against the papacy, far away in Rome – it was an attack on local memory itself. Parish churches had been shaped by generations of community efforts: people who had banded together and saved what little they had to raise funds for church decorations, donated items in memory of family members, or else left bequests in their wills and ensured that their legacy would be preserved in the memories of the congregation; who would, in turn, light candles and give prayers for the passage of their souls to heaven. This culture of remembrance extended beyond the bounds of the church and into the landscape, with wayside crosses and boundary markers that had been walked around in annual commemorations that shaped the life of their communities. Reformation had profound implications for a community's identity, creating an often painful sense of rupture between people and the remembrance culture that had, until recently, bound their neighbourhoods together.[34]

While some parishes welcomed the efforts of reformers, others were prepared to take a stand. In 1536–7, a popular uprising that had begun in Lincolnshire spread throughout northern England in defiance of the policies of the king's chief minister, Thomas Cromwell. In Lincolnshire alone, some 22,000 protestors were estimated to have risen in protest against Henry VIII's declaration of supremacy over religious matters. Localised rebellions continued throughout the following decades, amid successive waves of reformation, such as the Western Rising of 1549, which claimed the lives of 5,500 people. Others hid away prohibited items before they could be destroyed or confiscated by officials, patiently waiting for the day when Catholicism might be restored again. As Alexandra Walsham notes, one of the ironies of the Reformation was that it made holy objects and relics *more* rather than less accessible to ordinary men and women, now that priests, monks and nuns were no longer their custodians. Holy objects were preserved within the walls of people's homes, or else they wore the relics of saints close to their bodies, concealed beneath layers of clothing. In turn, these cherished items would be passed down as heirlooms to their descendants, keeping the faith alive by preserving it in memory. Throughout England, quiet acts of rebellion were taking place in the secrecy of people's homes, as Catholics composed ballads of the world they had lost 'to show our grief in song', even as they looked forward in the hope that God might one day 'redress our country's misery.'[35] In this way, nostalgia, too, could be a force of rebellion and resistance.

Particularly evocative was the dissolution of the monasteries. This was the cause that the leader of the northern rebels, Robert Aske, had gathered his followers around in 1536, protesting that the abbeys were 'one of the beauties of this realm'. The spectacle of watching these great houses – among the largest and oldest structures in the country – systematically demolished by hundreds of workers could be intensely traumatic to those who witnessed it. 'It would have made a Heart of Flint to have melted and weeped to have seen the breaking up of the House,' reflected one Elizabethan clergyman later in life, upon the destruction of Roche Abbey that he had seen as a young boy. 'It would have pitied any Heart to see what tearing up of the Lead there was, and plucking up of Boards, and throwing down . . .

and the Tombs in the Church all broken, and all things of Price, either spoiled, carted away or defaced to the uttermost.'[36]

With the passing of time, even committed Protestants were increasingly coming to the conclusion that the destruction of the monasteries had been a national calamity. For the seventeenth-century antiquary William Dugdale, it was 'the greatest blow to Antiquities that ever England had.' It must have been a 'barbarous generation' that had torn down 'these goodly structures . . . wherewith England was so much adorned'; a sentiment echoed by the historian Thomas Fuller in 1644, as he described Henry VIII's officials as 'cruel cormorants, with their barbarous beaks and greedy claws', who 'rent, tore and tattered these inestimable pieces of antiquity'. 'I wish the monasteries had not been put down,' lamented the antiquarian John Aubrey, on a quieter and more personal note a generation later: 'what a pleasure 'twould have been to have travelled from monastery to monastery.' More than a century on from the dissolution of the monasteries, by the later seventeenth century Aubrey described their ruined shells as scattered over the landscape 'like fragments of a Shipwreck, that after the Revolution of so many years and governments have escaped the Teeth of Time and the hands of mistaken zeal.'[37]

For historians and antiquarians, it was time to mobilise: to record and preserve in writing these traces of the past before they were lost forever. The antiquarian John Weever felt that if action wasn't taken soon, then 'nothing will be shortly left to continue the memory of the deceased to posterity'. Tormented by the scale of what had been lost, for three decades he travelled around the country documenting the tombs and commemorative inscriptions that had been damaged by iconoclasts, a feat which was eventually published as a book of *Ancient Funerall Monuments* in 1631. A similar impetus sent John Aubrey and many others on journeys around the country to document what remained of England's medieval heritage. In many cases, it was a race against time. On the eve of the civil wars, William

Dugdale journeyed frantically around England, on a one-man crusade to document the churches and memorials he feared – rightly – would be destroyed in the ensuing conflict.[38]

For other scholars, the greatest loss of all had been the destruction of books and manuscripts held in monastic libraries, whose walls had housed a large proportion of the nation's bibliographic heritage. Almost from the start, this purging of religious texts – and, along with it, the histories, chronicles, poetry, administrative records, and philosophical and scientific works that were caught up in iconoclastic destruction in the 1530s – were lamented as a 'calamity' and 'most horrible infamy' by conservative and evangelical writers alike.[39] Monasteries, churches and universities were ransacked of their collections. Medieval texts were burned, thrown in rivers, sold in bulk to wholesalers and repurposed as scrap, and put to countless other uses: as firelighters, wrapping paper, 'some to scour their candlesticks, & some to rub their boots', as well as 'nailed up upon posts in all common houses of easement' to be used as toilet paper. Still more were simply cast to the winds. 'The second time we came to New College after we had declared your injunctions,' one official reported triumphantly to Thomas Cromwell from Oxford in 1535, 'we found all the great quadrant court full of the leaves of Dun [Scotus, a thirteenth-century philosopher and theologian], the wind blowing them into every corner.' Watching this process unfold, the historian John Bale could not find words strong enough to decry these losses to the nation's learning. A former monk turned writer and controversialist, Bale was a seasoned critic of the monastic system, and had found favour with Thomas Cromwell for his religious stance early in the Reformation – but nothing, he felt, could excuse the 'desolation' of England's libraries. These texts had been 'memorials of our nation'. 'This is highly to be lamented,' he raged, by anyone who 'hath a natural love [of] their country ... I scarcely utter it without tears.' It had been a 'wicked age', he reflected in 1549, 'much given to the destruction of things memorable.' A century later, the historian Thomas Fuller was still finding it hard to come to terms with this 'irreparable loss of learning' in which so many texts had been 'massacred'.[40] For generations of scholars after the 1530s, they could only guess at what it was that might have been lost forever.

And yet even as seventeenth-century scholars and antiquarians were lamenting the incalculable heritage they had lost since the 1530s, others were coming to the conclusion that another wave of destruction was necessary. The process of church 'beautifica-tion' that had been undertaken under Charles I in the 1630s, spearheaded by Archbishop Laud, had sparked a renewed back-lash against church images; a backlash in which opposing decoration in churches was closely connected to parliamentary opposition to the Crown. For the poet and civil servant John Milton – a puritan in religion and republican in political sympathies – bishops like Laud who had returned decoration to churches were instituting nothing less than 'a new-vomited Pagan-ism of sensual idolatry', which had replaced 'the plaine and homespun verity of Christ's gospel' that had been so hard-won by Protestant reformers with 'all the gaudy allurements of a whore.' Amid civil war, during the 1640s and 1650s, both parliamentary legislation and unofficial acts of iconoclasm by parliamentary sol-diers would attack these Laudian 'innovations' – a process that would spill into the destruction of medieval images that had sur-vived the efforts of sixteenth-century reformers.[41]

Appointing a Committee for the Demolition of Monuments of Superstition and Idolatry in 1643, Parliament issued orders for successive waves of iconoclasm over the following years, ordering the removal of altars and communion tables, candle-sticks, crucifixes, crosses, pictures, superstitious inscriptions, organs, fonts, vestments and many other church items. Several MPs took pains to oversee in person that their orders were car-ried out to the letter – among them the chair of the Committee, Sir Robert Harley, who was reported in his zeal as tearing down images in Westminster Abbey with his own hands. Other accounts described Harley as ordering a church cross not only to be removed, but 'beaten in pieces, even to dust' with a sledge-hammer, and then sprinkled over the footpath 'to be trodden on in the churchyard', forcing the congregation to profane it still further as they filed in to worship; or else commanding that the glass in church windows be first demolished, then the shards 'broke with a small hammer', and then personally trampled upon by himself while 'dancing a jig to Laud'. While the historian Julie Spraggon explains that testimonies such as these were often compiled by hostile observers who may well have been exaggerating for effect, Harley's own wife, Brilliana, remembered him as having destroyed a picture of God found by one of his tenants with such thoroughness that he was satisfied only once he had 'flung the dust of it' into a nearby body of water.[42]

Throughout the 1640s, parliamentary soldiers engaged in spontaneous acts of destruction in churches and cathedrals – sometimes restrained by their commanding officers, but at other times given active encouragement by superiors who shared their sympathies. Cathedrals were ransacked in what contemporaries described as a 'carnage . . . of furious sacrilege'; acts of destruction that could widen out from specific targets of religious iconoclasm, and into an attack upon the authority of bishops and monarchs represented in these structures. One bishop wrote of his grief at the damage wrought to Norwich Cathedral: 'what clattering of Glasses, what beating down of Walls, what tearing up of manuscripts . . . what demolishing of curious Stonework that had not any representation in the World, but only the Cost of the Founder and Skill of the Mason . . . what Tooting and Piping upon the destroyed Organ Pipes' there had been, he bewailed. There were reports at Wells of soldiers breaking 'all such monuments or pictures they espied, either of religion, antiquity, or the Kings of England'; while at Winchester, soldiers were alleged to have attacked statues of James I and Charles I, and had to be prevented from defiling the bones of Saxon kings. When soldiers attacked images in Canterbury Cathedral – a process that local inhabitants appear to have also taken part in – destruction was so extensive that their superiors stepped in only when the fabric of the cathedral itself became 'threatened with ruin'. Despite his puritan beliefs against religious images, the commander in charge of soldiers at Canterbury, Sir Michael Livesey, later apologised to the Dean and declared himself 'ready to faint' when he saw the damage that had been done. Elsewhere, however, soldiers were permitted to proceed without restraint. At Lichfield, images that could not be reached by ropes were shot at with guns, and an estimated 12,000 feet of glass was broken down, leaving 'the whole fabric of [the building] exceedingly ruinated', as a survey concluded in 1650.[43]

By the end of the civil wars, many cathedrals were in such a state of disrepair that a parliamentary committee in 1651 was suggesting they might productively be demolished. There was little enthusiasm for the prospect of costly restorations of what many felt were outdated relics of a past they had at last defeated. The committee's recommendation was that, wherever possible, 'all Cathedral Churches, where there are other Churches or Chapels sufficient for the People to meet in for the Worship of God, be surveyed, pulled down, and sold.' According to the Venetian ambassador, a start was about to be made on Canterbury, before city authorities and leading local figures began to petition Parliament that they very much wanted to keep their cathedrals. In Norwich, however, the city's mayor and aldermen had already in 1650 been petitioning Parliament for the demolition of their *own* cathedral, so that it 'may be given to the City for a stock for the poor'. The corporation of Great Yarmouth, hoping that they would also benefit from this sell-off, enthusiastically agreed with the Norwich governors, describing it as 'that vast and altogether useless Cathedral', whose dismantling might pay for the repair of their pier.[44] Like the bomb-damaged historic centres that would be demolished in the post-war years of the twentieth century, it was a financial climate in which many felt they could hardly afford to be nostalgic about old monuments in need of repair – still less when the architectural heritage in question was of an era they felt had vanished for the better.

But for a minority of puritans, economic considerations were far from the primary motivator behind the drive to demolish England's material heritage. The puritan preacher Hugh Peter wanted to pull down Stonehenge, lest people be tempted into a return to paganism. In the 1650s, one godly woman, Mary Netheway, was moved to write to Oliver Cromwell about the dangers of having statues of classical gods and goddesses in the gardens of his new residence at Hampton Court, feeling that these were not so much innocent garden ornaments as 'cursed monsters' of idolatry, whose continuing existence would incur the wrath of God. (There is no evidence that Cromwell was interested in considering the case for their removal.) A few years later, a Quaker cook crept into the grounds with a hammer and tried to smash them to pieces.[45]

Just as they had lamented the iconoclasm of sixteenth-century reformers, seventeenth-century antiquarians deplored the destructions of the civil wars. And yet it was this very process of destruction – which had spurred so many people to grief and nostalgia – that had, in turn, been galvanised into a drive to preserve their heritage. Throughout the sixteenth and seventeenth centuries, the scale of iconoclasm and reform had shocked its contemporaries into a sense of loss at the buildings, images, objects, books, traditions and customs that were being destroyed around them. Their awareness of what had been lost was giving rise to a growing movement to study and record the traces of the past. By 1628, contemporary observers were noting the new-found phenomenon of the antiquary: who, 'strangely thrifty of Time past', would travel 'forty miles to see a Saints Well, or ruined Abbey'. The historian Margaret Aston has written that, by the end of the seventeenth century, 'long-felt regrets for the losses of the monastic past had matured into some of the best early fruits of English historical scholarship' in the writings of William Dugdale, John Aubrey and many others. Nostalgia had merged with and stimulated the study of history.[46]

In time, the painful sense people felt, while gazing upon ruins, of a past now largely irrecoverable, would spill out from the works of historians and antiquarians and into art and literature – into the fascination that ruins would come to hold in the Gothic and Romantic imagination. There is a poignant irony to the fact that the ruined abbeys, which were a source of shock and grief to so many people in the sixteenth and seventeenth centuries, would be celebrated by later generations who enjoyed their nostalgia at leisure. As the shells of gutted abbeys and monasteries aged into time-mellowed ruins, they would come to be enjoyed as 'picturesque' relics by eighteenth-century aristocrats wandering through the grounds of country estates, offering to them pleasingly melancholy reflections upon decayed magnificence. By the turn of the nineteenth century they would become sources of inspiration to writers and artists who set out in search of the spooky or sublime, and later by Victorians seeking an antidote to industrial ugliness – an aesthetic that would, in the Gothic Revival, be rehabilitated as the architectural style of a Protestant nation. Yet to observers for at least a century after the dissolution of the monasteries in the 1530s, there was nothing mysterious, or beautiful, or sublime, in these shattered husks of buildings. The immediate effect of the dissolution had been to make England appear a much less magnificent place. And the loss had been not just of beautiful buildings, but of a social world and way of life: the holy relics, the religious services, the sacred songs, the familiar sound of bells ringing across the landscape; the monks and nuns who were remembered in hindsight as having been good and kindly landlords to their communities, who had offered hospitality to travellers and pilgrims. As Francis Trigge observed in the 1590s, 'many do lament the pulling down of the abbeys, they say it was never [a] merry world since.'[47]

MERRY ENGLAND

In the wake of the Reformation, many were nursing memories of a more harmonious, gentler time, looking back to an England defined by its Catholic identity. Both in secret and in public, a range of observers expressed intense nostalgia for a landscape marked out by abbeys, monasteries, shrines and pilgrimages, holy statues and miraculous relics; and a vanished time of saints' days, May games and communal festivities. Amid sixteenth-century reforms that sought to do away with these Catholic and pagan hangovers in the religious calendar, many followed the physician John Caius in mourning the loss of what he called 'the old world, when this country was called Merry England.'[48]

As people looked back upon the waves of change and disruption that had made up the Reformation of the mid-sixteenth century, there was a growing sense that they were now inhabiting a society markedly different from that of their ancestors.[49] The interlinked religious, political and economic changes people were living through became contrasted with what was remembered as an unchanging time of yore, before the break with Rome. The dissolution of the monasteries, in particular, became linked in people's imaginations with a new spirit of individualism, greed and money-making they felt was starting to take over the country. Gone, they felt, were the days of charity and hospitality, when church authorities had cared for the poor and shared their abundance at communal festivities; in its place had come men who thought of nothing but lining their pockets with the wealth they had expropriated from churches, who had created an epidemic of homelessness by expelling monks and nuns, and who had taken over their role as landlords and set about extracting every penny they could from their tenants. Where once landowners had entrusted that the boundaries of the land people farmed would be maintained in local people's memories, now they were employing professional surveyors to take exact measurements to calculate their rents. It became a common complaint that 'the world was merrier, before measurings were used ... A tenant in these days must pay for every foot, which is an extreme matter.'[50] It seemed to epitomise a new attitude to the land that prioritised money-making for the already wealthy over the traditions of the common people, leading to a widening gap between rich and poor – a process as well as a protest that would later accelerate amid the enclosures of the eighteenth century. For those who protested these changes, the past became reimagined as a golden age of merriment and plenty: the perennial olden days of nostalgics who remembered a time when prices were lower, neighbours were friendlier, people were less greedy, and everyone had looked out for each other as a community.

By the later sixteenth century, it was a well-worn cliché that elderly people who had grown up before the Reformation looked back fondly to a time when 'the poor people got a good living', and aristocratic luxuries like venison were supposedly 'no greater a rarity in a poor man's kitchen than mutton is now'. Protestant reformers, impatient with their contemporaries' nostalgia for the pre-Reformation past, took aim against a stereotype of the elderly simpleton who blathered on about the days of their youth and blamed religious reforms for everything they disliked in the present, insisting that they used to be able to buy 'twenty eggs a penny' in the 'plentiful a world as when Abbeys stood.'[51] The seventeenth-century churchman John Favour sarcastically relayed the complaints of 'the old superstitious people of this land' who claimed – he alleged – that there were 'fewer Salmons up their river, since the mass went down: for they were wont to come up when they heard the [altar] Bell ring.' In connecting Protestant reforms to developments (real or imagined) that had nothing to do with them, Favour argued, 'they do measure religion by their bellies ... the pretence is still, that the former way was the Old way, and that the Old way was the best way.' For another critic, the nostalgics who told

THE COMMITTEE FOR THE DEMOLITION OF MONUMENTS

him about the Merry England of the past were tellingly vague
about when exactly the 'good old days' had been in the first
place: 'they say it was merry before ... but they tell not what
time it was, with whom, nor wherein it was merry.'

Reformers set out to debunk these nostalgic myths and clichés
about the olden days, feeling that they harboured a suspicious
nostalgia for Catholicism itself. 'There is greater cause of good
mirth and joy, in these days, than was in those you spoke of,'
argued one Elizabethan writer against an imagined audience of
old-timers: 'we have the light, and freedom of the Gospel', and
a queen who as God's 'instrument hath all the time of her Reign
preserved us from wars, spoils, and heavy taxes. If your meaning be that smallness of rents, and cheapness of victuals make a
merry world', he suggested, gesturing at the kind of person who
complained about how many eggs they used to get for a penny,
they should take it up with inflation, not Protestantism.[52]

The 'Merry England' nostalgia that we think of today as a
source of shared national tradition was, in the sixteenth century, a terrain of religious and political division. Nostalgia for
the merry past was sometimes deployed as a protest against
reform, even as a rallying cry for rebellion and resistance. Nostalgia, in the wrong circumstances, could get the speaker
arrested. Between 1568 and 1601, nine people were indicted by
courts for 'seditious' or 'scandalous' references to the 'merry
world' – imagined both as a past they had lost, and a utopia
that might be regained once more. In 1597, for instance, one
man was charged for attacking Elizabeth I's rule, claiming 'it
would never be a merry world till her majesty was dead or
killed ... but we must not say so'. Rebels counterposed the
'merry world' to a present in which 'poor men could get nothing among them' thanks to the machinations of the Crown and
nobility, and expressed their hope that 'the Spaniards would
come' or priests rise up against the queen so that 'we would
have land cheap enough and a merry world' again.[53]

As time went on, references to the 'merry world' of the past became attached less and less to Catholicism and sedition, and were coming to be seen in a more gentle and unthreatening light. What had at first been a contentious subject of divided memory – a painful loss for some, a past thankfully discarded for others – would increasingly become a source of pleasure and shared remembrance. Towards the turn of the seventeenth century, more and more people were looking back fondly on a pre-Reformation world that was beginning to pass out of the reach of living memory. And, as it did so, 'Merry England' would be transformed into a cosy, ahistorical time of yore: a land of fables, adventures and legends; of knights and maidens; outlaws and their merry friends; good fellowship and good eating. In popular plays and ballads, happy tales were set among scenes such as Shakespeare's Forest of Arden in *As You Like It* (1599), an imaginary version of a real setting that incorporated hunters, shepherds, hermits and 'brothers in exile' living contentedly by the 'old custom'. Above all, it was a place of leisure – a hidden arcadia in which 'to lose and neglect the creeping hours of time.' It was one of hundreds of stories that conjured the romance of a merry medieval past, including tales of King Arthur and the Round Table, Robin Hood and his Merry Men, which had circulated for centuries but seemed to be becoming ever more popular genres of entertainment in the commercial marketplace; as well as various local legends of outlaws who had defied the powerful and looked out for the common people, transmitted from generation to generation through oral ballads and 'old wives' tales'.[54]

These stories of Merry England didn't attempt to be realistic depictions of the past, but a fantasy of timeless stability: what the historian Harriet Phillips describes as a 'fundamentally unhistoric collage' of stock tropes about 'merry monarchs, green forests and grateful tenants.' They offered to their audiences 'a version of the past which could be imaginatively inhabited . . . a narrative of origins which was effective precisely because it did not and could not rehearse this past with any accuracy.'[55] The merry-world nostalgia that had once seemed so politically and religiously subversive was being transferred into a secular culture of plays, stories, ballads and songs, cultivating nostalgia as a pleasurable experience that people could enjoy in their leisure time. By the seventeenth century, many Protestants were enjoying escapist tales of the 'merry world' before the Reformation, even as they warned people against returning to it religiously.

For more hard-line Protestants, however, these secular stories and merry entertainments were just as worrying as the Catholic tales of saints and miracles they were replacing. The bishop Hugh Latimer, who would be burned at the stake under Mary I in 1555, inveighed against people who 'prefer Robin Hood to God's word', while the Elizabethan clergyman Edward Dering raged against the 'spiritual enchantments' of Arthurian legends and folk tales, fearing that 'we have multiplied for ourselves so many new delights that we might justify the idolatrous superstition of the elder world.' By the late sixteenth century, puritans were waging a culture war on 'mirth', decrying people's ungodly fondness for cheap prints and ballads, stage plays, inns and alehouses, and festivities at Christmas and May Day – launching campaigns to purge popular culture of entertainment and merry-making, and to observe holidays as times of holiness and prayer; efforts that intensified throughout the first half of the seventeenth century.[56] Merry England might have been passing from a subject of divisive religious lament to one of shared, secular celebration, but for England's most enthusiastic evangelicals, a shared culture of merry-making was also leading their countrymen astray from God's light.

And yet one actor and playwright, Thomas Heywood, argued in 1612 that the historical plays people went to see in theatres were a force for social good. It wasn't just fables of a mythically merry past that audiences were lining up to see: in the age of Shakespeare, plays that dramatised historical kings and queens, battles and wars, were an increasingly important way in which ordinary men and women were learning about their nation's history. 'What English blood,' he asked, 'seeing the person of any bold English man' on stage, could fail to marvel at 'his fame' and 'valor'? 'So bewitching' was it for audiences who gazed 'wrapt in contemplation' upon scenes of English history, that 'it hath power to new mould the hearts of the spectators and fashion them to the shape of any noble and notable attempt.' It was an early argument for the power of popular history that elites in the nineteenth century would increasingly come to harness: that a version of English history, told from the right perspective, could buttress the status quo through the lessons it imparted to people. 'The theatre can use strong feelings to fashion good citizens,' Heywood continued:

> to teach the subjects obedience to their King, to show the people
> the untimely ends of such as have moved tumults, commotions
> and insurrections, to present them with the flourishing estate of
> such as live in obedience, exhorting them to allegiance, [and
> deterring] them from all traitorous and felonious stratagems.

Popular entertainments, Heywood argued, had the power to shape the public understanding of history – and to shape it in service of the state, by channelling people's 'strong feelings' into obedience.[57]

Merry England, too, could be channelled into the making of merrily obedient citizens. Anticipating the Restoration of the monarchy, in 1659 the courtier William Cavendish (husband of the philosopher and polymath Margaret Cavendish) wrote to Charles II of the importance of reintroducing 'Country recreations': 'all the old Holidays, with their mirth,' he argued, should be 'set up again . . . May Games, Morris Dances, the Lord of the May & Lady of the May, the Fool and the Hobby Horse, must not be forgotten.' This was nostalgia for Merry England leveraged for Machiavellian ends. 'These divertissements,' Cavendish explained, 'will amuse the people's thoughts and keep them in harmless actions, which will free your Majesty from Faction, & Rebellion.' To revive old English folk customs and festivities, which puritans during the Interregnum had tried to suppress as sinfully superstitious enjoyments, was sure to be a populist crowd-pleaser. Increasingly, in the seventeenth century, nostalgic celebrations of the merry past were becoming a way of drawing people together, through which people could harmlessly imagine their national community.[58]

THIS OTHER EDEN

But how much of this nostalgia was really about England's history itself, when it was so often nostalgia for a time that never really existed in quite the way it was remembered? Or was the point of imagining a nation precisely that it was a nostalgic fantasy? Historians of nationalism emphasise that the nations people imagine have always been carved out of an immemorial past, and projected, in turn, into a limitless future.[59] To imagine a national community has always required a series of imaginative feats: that the past lives on in the present, even when it is felt to be lost; that the 'they' who lived long ago are also a part of 'us'; that the nation of the past was more truly, quintessentially 'national' than the nation that exists in the present, because the past itself is rewritten to embody what the present is felt to be lacking. The idea of the nation requires people to feel authentically connected to others across time, who shared their geographical home, but whose customs, politics, worldviews and even language were often wildly different.

The Tudor period has often been seen as the time in which English identity as we know it today began to take shape: an age in which the Reformation shaped a sense of England as a proudly independent nation, when Elizabethan explorers set out on voyages that would give rise to a global empire, and when Shakespeare's history plays articulated the feeling of what it was to be English in ways that have resonated throughout the centuries. And yet, as the historian Philip Schwyzer argues, 'there is no doubt' that these developments shaped a growing sense of 'national consciousness in England . . . and that we find this consciousness expressed in Shakespeare's plays. The question is whether this national consciousness was in fact English.'[60]

Where is the 'England', for instance, that John of Gaunt describes in Shakespeare's *Richard II* (1595) – so often quoted in modern reflections on Englishness:

> This royal throne of kings, this scepter'd isle,
> This earth of majesty, this seat of Mars,
> This other Eden, demi-paradise,
> This fortress built by Nature for herself
> Against infection and the hand of war,
> This happy breed of men, this little world,
> This precious stone set in the silver sea . . .
> This blessed plot; this earth, this realm, this England . . .

As Schwyzer notes, 'this England' is an island; and, both in 1595 and in the fourteenth century in which John of Gaunt is speaking, the island it describes was ruled by two different monarchies, in Scotland and England. If the isle itself is 'sceptred' as a single 'royal throne', then the nation Gaunt and Shakespeare are imagining in their mind's eye must be that of the pre-Anglo-Saxon era, when the ancient Britons were thought to have been ruled by a single monarch – most famously, in the persona of King Arthur. And who is 'this happy breed', if not the Anglo-Saxons? (Who were, in fact, held in very low esteem in the Tudor era – not least as they were the people who had first embraced Catholicism in England – before the centuries of retrospective rehabilitation that would later elevate them into archetypically 'English' predecessors.) Partly, these references to islandhood were evidence of the perennial English tendency to claim the positive attributes of Britain as a whole when it suited them, and forget that Scotland and Wales existed the rest of the time.[61] But they also, crucially, widened out the bounds of nationalism to a nostalgia that was epic in scope, imagining an 'England' – or Britain – that reached back into the mists of time immemorial.

Most importantly, 'this other Eden' was long since lost. Gaunt's speech is often remembered out of context as a misty-eyed celebration of English/British landscape and ancestry, and yet it is a bitter deathbed soliloquy of grief and loss, as Gaunt seethes that 'England, that was wont to conquer others, hath made a shameful conquest of itself' under Richard II's misrule. Yet what is it that has supposedly vanished from the land – what is Gaunt nostalgic *for*? He does not seem to describe it specifically, repeating 'this' again and again. What seems most important of all is the *idea* of the nation he is conjuring, the atmosphere it evokes, as if the very essence of national pride is to long for and desire something that can never quite be seen or held completely, never truly inhabited. Paradise is always lost, and to be a nationalist is to be always nostalgic, to dream of the idea that it could one day be recovered.[62]

It was a mood that pervaded so many developments in the Tudor era. The Reformation was pictured as a nostalgic quest to restore England's ancient status as an empire, after a thousand years of colonisation by Rome. The Tudors themselves, hailing from Wales, presented their lineage as descending from the ancient kings of the Britons. The Welsh soldiers who had fought with Henry VII against Richard III at the Battle of Bosworth in 1485 had seen him as their prophesied redeemer, who had returned to claim his birth right and who would liberate them from centuries of English domination. Naming his firstborn son Arthur in 1486, Henry unmistakeably evoked for people the famous legend that King Arthur would one day return and lead the Britons to victory over their Saxon oppressors, uniting the island once more. At his birth, both Welsh and Scottish poets hailed Prince Arthur as the resurrection of the ancient British king. Under Henry VIII and Edward VI's rule in the 1540s, England attempted to impose a union between the English and Scottish crowns, in what is known as the 'Rough

Wooing' (read: warfare), spinning it as a restoration of ancient history. English politicians and propagandists in favour of the union urged the Scots to recover their true identity, and take up the 'old name of Britons' again. Protector Somerset, appointed as regent to the young Edward VI, was acclaimed as the descendant of an ancient British earl who had slain Saxon invaders, and who would emulate his ancestor's courage by restoring 'the whole Empire & name of great Britain.'[63]

Even before this Britain would be created by the union of the Scottish and English crowns under James VI and I in 1603, the British Empire itself was being promoted as a nostalgia-soaked quest to regain lost glory by claiming new territories abroad. Elizabeth I's advisor, the mathematician and occultist John Dee – known in his time as 'the conjurer' – offered a seductive justification for expanding England's territories in the New World. It would be a *restoration*, Dee argued in 1576, of Britain's ancient imperial status; a tantalising promise of resurrection that must be seized before the opportunity passed forever out of reach. 'There is a little lock of Lady Occasion, flickering in the air,' he proclaimed, and if people could just 'catch hold' of these golden strands of opportunity,

> we may yet once more (before all be utterly past, and for ever) ... valiantly recover and enjoy, if not all our ancient and due appurtenances to this Imperial British monarchy, yet at least some such notable portion thereof ... [and] this may become the most peaceable, most rich, most puissant, & most flourishing monarchy of all else (this day) in Christendom.

It was a mood of fleeting chance not far from Margaret Thatcher's conjuring of Arthurian legend on the eve of the general election in 1979: that if Britain didn't seize this opportunity for change, then all would be lost completely, as the nation drifted into 'a distant memory of an offshore island, lost in the mists of time, like Camelot, remembered kindly, for its noble past.' Thatcher's feeling for Britain in the wake of decolonisation was the same feeling that, 400 years before, was motivating imperialism at the very start – before England would establish its first colony in America, before Britain really even existed in a political or military sense. If they didn't act now to take back the glory they had lost, Dee urged, the chance would 'be utterly past, and for ever.'[64] To restore the past, they had to start something new. Imperial nostalgia was being written into the British Empire from the very beginning.

As the Britain that had long been dreamed of started to become a reality – as the crowns were joined in 1603, and as England and Scotland established colonies in the Americas over the course of the seventeenth century, an empire that would become an officially British project with political union in 1707 – people stopped conceiving of Britishness in quite such mythic and poetic language.[65] It is hard to keep dreaming of a long-lost object of desire when the thing you longed for actually happens. But there was one lost empire that England could always yearn for, forever out of reach of recovery. The quest to regain England's medieval empire in France had long been dreamed of by Tudor monarchs – when England was stripped of its last possession with the fall of Calais in 1558, Mary I was famously said to have declared that when she died, they would find the word Calais inscribed on her heart. By the end of the Elizabethan era, tales of English glory in France were becoming hopelessly nostalgic reveries – though it would not be until the 1800s that British monarchs formally gave up their claim to the French throne.

Shakespeare's *Henry V* (1599) piled nostalgia upon nostalgia in its celebration of England's unexpected victory at Agincourt in 1415. It had been a brief window of time in which plucky English soldiers, heavily outnumbered, had momentarily recaptured the glory of an earlier era – the dream of living up to England's famed victory at Crécy in 1346, and still further to when the Angevin kings of England had ruled over swathes of France in the twelfth and thirteenth centuries. Vowing to redeem his nation, Henry V is called upon to 'rouse' the 'lions' of his ancestral blood, to 'awake remembrance of the valiant dead' and 'renew their feats' – a dream that seemed almost impossible in the face of overwhelming odds. It seems such a valiantly doomed endeavour that when Henry makes his speech on the morning of battle, in what has come to be seen as one of the most enduring literary expressions of Englishness, he tells anyone that doesn't want the honour of dying in the company of this 'happy few', this 'band of brothers', to leave. And yet audiences watching the play know, of course, that Henry will actually win at Agincourt. They know, too, that it will be a short-lived moment of victory; that England will come to lose in France again, and they will be forever dreaming of this one moment of glory. So even before the battle has played out on stage, Shakespeare projects nostalgia far into the future: past Henry's ancestors, past Crécy, past the battle that is about to take place. Henry invites his soldiers to imagine themselves as old men, sitting down to enjoy a feast with their family and neighbours, where one day they will strip their sleeves, show their scars, and tell tales of the day they fought at Agincourt.[66]

In time, future generations would watch *Henry V* through the lens of their own nostalgic hopes and retrospects. When Laurence Olivier released his version in cinemas in 1944, funded as a wartime morale booster by the British government, audiences were filtering these scenes through their own generation's experiences in France. Henry's centuries-old victory against the odds, his struggle to redeem what had been lost, seemed especially poignant in the months after D-Day, when Britain had again returned to the continent after evacuating at Dunkirk in 1940. And in turn, generations since 1945 would look back to the Second World War as their 'finest hour' of courage and unity, in memory and on film – a golden age of heroism that Britain would never again be able to recover. It is the same nostalgia people were feeling in the sixteenth century, and before. Trace it back to its source, and you simply find more nostalgia.

Conclusion

In the Past, Even the Future Was Better

To be nostalgic for a nation – to be nostalgic for anything – is always to dream of what is lost; to long for something beyond the realm of the possible. Because if we could really reach it again, and keep it safe from time, really inhabit the time we long for or restore the thing we miss, then we would no longer feel nostalgia for it. It is a desire that exists only in its denial, forever yearning for impossible satisfaction. Is this why it some-times feels like a guilty pleasure, something slightly unseemly in excess – a pleasurable pain that generates its own perpetual frustration?

The Swiss soldiers to whom Johannes Hofer first gave the diagnosis of nostalgia in 1688 longed to return home with such force that they were losing touch with reality, confusing real and imaginary events as they dwelt on their faraway object of desire with single-minded fixation, yearning to feel whole again and become part of their home once more. Like the soldiers who wrote letters to their families back home in Britain during the First World War, we can imagine that they told themselves they would never again complain about the goodness of their civilian lives, if only they could return home safely – only now with a renewed appreciation for just how good they had had it. We imagine, too, that those who returned to their heart's desire did not experience their lives back home as a dream of unend-ing bliss. We are always primed to forget the daily frustrations, the squabbles, the minor aches and pains, and remember the good times, even if sometimes we don't truly appreciate them until it's too late. 'Just wait until now becomes then,' reflects the protagonist of Susan Sontag's short story 'Unguided Tour' (1977) – on holiday, in love, a bundle of complicated thoughts and wants and memories, carrying a heavy suitcase – 'you'll see how happy we were.'[1] But that's life – we all spend our time veering between expectations and retrospections, dreams and reality, illusions and disillusionment, and discovering how it feels to end up somewhere in the middle.

But what happens when we can never go back? The Swiss soldiers weren't able to return to an earlier time in their lives, of course, but they *could* return to a place: a place where they would have found that some things had changed while they were away, while others remained just as they had left them. Except what if the 'home' you yearn for was one you had never lived in; a time long ago that you had never experienced directly? What if it was an idea: an imaginary time and place inhabited by people who never knew each other, where medieval Anglo-Saxons grew up into Elizabethan explorers, who gave birth to Victorian industrialists and imperial conquerors; people untroubled by complex motivations and nostalgias of their own, who are there only to reassure you that you are at home, here, among the great and the good; where everything can be found in its right and proper order, in a story with its heroes and villains, its beginning, middle, and happy end? If you denied that these people were real – that they really existed in the way that you imagined them, as heroes in a courageous story – would it feel like betrayal? Maybe, like the Edwardian audiences who first watched *Peter Pan*, you could will this world of the imagination into existence, to keep its power going, if people could just wish for it hard enough. Who on earth wants to bring the play to a halt by admitting that they don't believe in fairy tales? But sometimes, like the readers of *The Wind in the Willows*, it is time to leave these worlds of the imagination behind us, these stories we have learnt since child-hood, and view them from the 'wide world' outside.

The historian Herbert Butterfield, who was born at the twi-light of the Victorian era in 1900, began his career critiquing the errors that nineteenth-century historians had made in read-ing Britain's past as the upwards march of a glorious history of progress. The Whig historians who had been writing a story of unfolding liberty and improvement had actually, Butterfield argued, warped the past in order to depict it as something run-ning smoothly into the present. What his predecessors had *really* been doing with this, he suspected, was looking back to history in a way that reflected well on *them*: reaching back through the generations and looking for people who reminded them comfortingly of themselves. With the benefit of hindsight, they had been peeling away anything they thought was a false start or a dead end, and downplaying all the contending and complicated forces of the past, in trying to trace a single thread of unbroken continuity through the ages. It was a thread which confirmed that England and Britain had always contained the essence of greatness, and that even as time changed some things beyond recognition, its essence remained the same: a glorious inheritance that people could only improve on in the present, and bequeath to future generations in their turn, as Britain became greater and greater still. But for Butterfield, even as this story flattered people in the present, it did a real disservice to the past as it actually existed. What historians needed to do, he argued, was to try to see things as they had looked to the people who lived through them at the time.

Perhaps this is the kind of thing that young historians write, as they slay the idols of older generations, impatient with the way that people around them try to make a familiar place out of the past, a story they feel uncomplicatedly connected to. But-terfield was 30 when he published his critique of *The Whig Interpretation of History* in 1931, writing that 'if history can do anything it is to remind us of those complications that undermine our certainties.'[2] He was, as today's cabinet ministers and culture-war columnists would put it, 'rewriting history', precisely because he felt that people had got their history so very wrong, in ways that were making them all too certain of the rightness of their own assumptions.

This strikes me as a good thing to do, at the start of my thirties, but I hope I don't become like Herbert Butterfield. Thirteen years of time, and history, separate *The Whig Interpretation of History* from *The Englishman and his History* of 1944, in which Butterfield had come to the conclusion that

> We are all of us exultant and unrepentant whigs. Those who, perhaps in the misguided austerity of youth, wish to drive out that whig interpretation . . . are sweeping a room which humanly speaking cannot long remain empty. They are opening the door for seven devils which, precisely because they are newcomers, are bound to be worse than the first.
>
> We, on the other hand, will not dream of wishing it away, but will rejoice in an interpretation of the past which has grown up with us, has grown up with the history itself, and has helped to make the history.

Getting history wrong was, Butterfield now argued, the way people found their way forward to a better future. 'We must congratulate ourselves,' he felt, that our

> Forefathers . . . did not resurrect and fasten upon us the authentic middle ages . . . in England we made peace with our middle ages by misconstruing them; and, therefore, we may say that 'wrong' history was one of our assets. The whig interpretation came at exactly the crucial moment and, whatever it may have done to our history, it had a wonderful effect on English politics.[3]

Perhaps this is the kind of thing that a historian in his forties writes, five years into the colossal, preventable tragedy of a war against fascism – the culmination of an age of totalitarianism, people have begun to feel, that had rushed in to fill the space that had been left when people gave up on their faith in the steady unfolding of liberty and progress. (Certainly, some reinterpretation was needed. Butterfield had in the 1930s found much in Hitler's Germany to admire – though much, too, to be distressed by – and indeed had accepted an invitation there to give a series of lectures on the Whig interpretation in 1938.[4]) *The Englishman and his History* was part of a turn towards nationalist history by historians across the political spectrum in wartime, as people looked for reassurance at a time of crisis in the enduring characteristics and traditions of 'Englishness'; the values that people were fighting to preserve. For many of their readers, it was a tempting explanation for why England and Britain had not ended up like Nazi Germany – a story that flattered people in the present, casting Britons as the creators and inheritors of a 'past which has grown up with us' with which they would fight to keep the world on the 'right' side of history. It was just the kind of interpretation that Butterfield had argued as a younger man was 'the source of all sins and sophistries in history . . . the essence of what we mean by the word "unhistorical".'[5]

Unfortunately, Nazi Germany had also been rooting itself in 'wrong' history. Fascist propagandists in Europe throughout the 1930s had themselves felt that promises to reconnect people with the mythic racial purity of their ancestral homelands were having a 'wonderful effect' on their own nations' politics. And it was hardly something that the 'Whig tradition' had rendered England immune from: as we know, the drive to trace a line of continuity between the present and a putative 'Anglo-Saxon' inheritance compelled many English fascists to sympathise with Nazism. It continues to motivate them today, in frightening numbers. And I am not sure what is more frightening: that fact in itself, or the enthusiasm with which politicians and right-wing newspapers warn that historians who seek to debunk these foundation myths and dispassionately examine the past are sinister Marxist ideologues seeking to undermine the freedom of 'Western civilisation' as we know it. It sounds a bit fashy to me.

What can historians do, when newspapers and politicians tell people we cannot be trusted with history? As Peter Mitchell writes in his history of imperial nostalgia, 'the best suggestion I can offer is to historicise: not only to historicise the nostalgic imagination itself . . . but to historicise the experience of living in the present, the fantasies with which we structure our politics, our culture and the textures of our everyday lives.'[6] I think it is reassuring, in a way, to remind ourselves that people have always been nostalgic for what has gone before; always inter-preting their own experiences by looking back to the past, and rewriting that past, in turn, in the light of the present. There is an irony to our perpetual nostalgia: that we look back to people who themselves were looking backwards, and that even as we remember them, we can forget how powerfully they felt their *own* nostalgia. No one has ever lived entirely in the present, feeling that their nation or their community was a perfect whole, untouched by grief or loss or regret. Everything changes, nothing stands still, and nostalgia is sometimes the feeling we sit with, as we recognise what it means to move forward in time, perpetually seeing presents turn into pasts that become both strange and familiar.

And I think this is where historians have an important role to play. Nostalgia is not history – in the sense that we mean history as an intellectual discipline, with its own methods and standards for interpreting the past from the evidence available to us. But historians, too, are dealers in the strange and the familiar. For the historian Peter Mandler, our job is to 'be the past's advocate, constantly jabbing the modern observer in the side with the strangeness and difference of the past, to offset the effects of phony familiarisation.' And yet I think at the same time we also need to offset phony estrangement. When it comes to twenty-first-century nostalgia for the empire-builders of the past, for instance, we need both to recognise that people's values in the past were often very different to our own – but not so very dif-ferent that many people in the eighteenth and nineteenth centuries were unable to recognise the atrocity of slavery. In discovering how very different the world has been in the past, and how deeply strange people's ways of thinking and feeling can seem to us across time, we realise that things need not always be the way we have been told they are. And yet, at the same time, we can be shocked by how familiar the past can seem to us, how moved we are by stories that resonate across time, and how intimately we recognise the anxieties and grief as well as the joys of people living hundreds of years ago. As Mandler argues, history at its best has 'imaginative' as well as 'intellectual' capabilities: 'simply put, history broadens the mind,' exposing us to

> the full range of human possibilities, only a small sampling of which is available in the present . . . One of the purposes of historical time travel is to transport our modern selves into alien situations which allow us to highlight by contrast our own values and assumptions . . . In this aspect history asks us not to lose ourselves in the past but to view the past from our own standpoint; in fact, one of its functions is to help us define our standpoint more clearly.[7]

The ways in which history is viewed today by politicians and the media – just like the ways it has been used for centuries – is so often to set out in search of confirmation for what we think we already know. It turns the past into a familiar place, a terrain where we feel comfortable – somewhere we can return to again and again, secure in the certainty that it will always be waiting there for us just as we had left it. It gives British history all the emotional value of a home, a stable base from which to set out and explore the future. People often talk about the value of history in terms of the 'lessons' it can impart to us, arguing that 'if you don't know where you came from, you can't know where you are going', or 'those who do not learn from history are doomed to repeat it'. Well, yes and no. We can always pick and choose the 'lessons' we take from history, especially if we turn to the past to confirm our preconceptions, or bolster our worldview or identity. Sometimes, it should be a place we go to sit with our uncertainty, until what we thought was familiar becomes strange to us, and the strange begins to feel a little more familiar – because, empathising at a distance with people who both are and are not like us, we start to understand things better.

I have ended this book in the sixteenth century, because it is here that so many of our national myths, and ideas about English and British identity, first began to take shape: the image of a proudly independent island nation, setting its eyes on expansion around the globe, and articulating this vision of greatness through appeals both to England's Anglo-Saxon inheritance, and the ancient Britons who resisted it. It is an image that people ever since have looked back to both with pride and nostalgia, yearning to infuse that 'essence' or 'spirit' back into the nation once more. We could go back still further, and explore how medieval chroniclers, kings, poets and political figures were framing English, Welsh and Scottish identities even earlier; and we would find people, too, experiencing nostalgias of their own amid the changes they were living through. As long as people have been writing, they have been writing about nostalgia. We could work our way back step by step to Greek and Roman philosophers and classical myths that told of a Golden Age of primordial peace and harmony, degenerated into Silver, then Bronze, and then the Iron Age of their present, where men had become warlike and greedy, and loyalty and truth were apparently nowhere to be found; or to Odysseus's decade-long quest for *nostos* – homecoming. Archaeologists could take you back further still, as they explore why people might have taken such care to fix moments and memories in wood and stone, carving what was important to them into objects they could keep hold of or carry far from home.

Nostalgia is a universal human impulse, and not something that would be realistic, or even desirable, to think we can do away with. I am not suggesting that we should never look to the past for comfort, or live our lives resolutely faced away from it unless to criticise it by our own standards. But our innate and very human tendency to rose-tint the past is something that we need to handle extremely carefully: something we need to balance against reminding ourselves of the messiness of reality; that the stories we tell about the past are not the same thing as the past as it was lived at the time.

We need to tell ourselves stories about the past, to simplify and make sense of the complexity of human experience. But we also need to debunk dangerous myths about the past, especially when those myths are mistaken for reality and used as a blueprint for the future. Never more so than now, as politicians draw on mistaken ideas about history to shape the future of Britain's place in the world, while newspapers launch attacks on historians and heritage workers whose scholarship challenges this 'official' narrative. We are in dangerous territory when we are told that to undermine an image of British history as a single, overarching tale of unerring triumph and pride, 'our island story', is to attack the foundations of people's identities in the present. It should not feel like an existential threat to explore the complexities of the past, or to find out that things were rarely as straightforward as we had first been told. I am not telling you how you should feel about British history on the whole, or how to relate to it on a personal level, but it does not need to be defended from itself.

Historians are probably not the best experts at predicting the future, but if one thing is certain, it is that both within and beyond the borders of our nations, and the histories they connect us to, is a future of environmental crisis. Just as our nostalgia extends to embrace times in the past we have never known ourselves, it reaches to places we have never been to. Sometimes, it extends to anticipation: a nostalgia for things we have not yet lost, or that we are on the point of losing. Watching nature documentaries, for instance, the scope of our nostalgia extends far beyond the horizons of our personal experience, taking in once-pristine oceans, melting ice caps and disappearing rainforests. We anticipate the grief we will feel at the loss of more and more habitats; the ways it will change the lives of people we do not know as well as our own. When we look back upon what has been lost, the nostalgia we can feel is not always just for the vanished past: it can also embrace our grief for lost futures. 'In the past,' quipped the German comedian and philosopher of the absurd Karl Valentin in the 1920s, 'even the future was better' – gently skewering the paradoxes of people's nostalgia for the 'good old days'. Only the irony hits us differently, as a joke from a time in which the future still held, as we know today, some of the most catastrophic events of the twentieth century.[8] The future almost always isn't what it used to be. Will the irony hit us differently again, as the world becomes a hotter and less habitable place, that opportunities for a different and better future are constantly falling behind our reach? It is hard to escape the feeling shared by the participants of the *Recording Britain* project, as they began to document Britain's dwindling countryside in 1939 – that, 'like a spendthrift heir', we have begun, 'too late, to keep accounts.'[9] But perhaps, like the generations of observers before us, our best hope is that an awareness of what is being lost can be harnessed in the drive to preserve, create and restore.

'There is only the fight to recover what has been lost / And found and lost again and again: and now, under conditions that seem unpropitious', wrote T.S. Eliot in *East Coker*, at the outset of the Second World War. 'But perhaps neither gain nor loss. / For us, there is only the trying. The rest is not our business.'[10] I am very moved by *East Coker* – a poem of almost unbearably poignant nostalgia, made all the more poignant in its hope for the future. Eliot is also a poet whose views and values I find in many respects repellent, not least his anti-Semitism – a perverse intolerance made all the more perverse by the humanity with which he wrote of the unbearable sense of grief and loss in 1940. It is OK to sit with both of those feelings. That's life; that's history.

Acknowledgements

To change direction, and begin at the beginning: thank you to John Chartres, Malcolm Chase and Peter Mandler, for being the best mentors in history I could have asked for, and to whose expertise and encouragement this book owes so very much.

My thanks to my agent, Charlotte Merritt, and to my editor, Suzanne Connelly, for their faith in me, and for their many incisive comments and suggestions – it has been such a pleasure to develop this book with their expert guidance and support. And to my copyeditor, Fraser Crichton, both for his eye for detail and for enlightening me on some of the finer points of Scottish history. I would also like to thank the teams at Andrew Nurnberg Associates and Ebury.

I would like to thank all those who gave their time to read drafts of the chapters: Agnes Arnold-Forster, Laura Carter, Jonathan Healey, Simon John James, Andrew Seaton and James Stafford. Thank you very much for your thoughts and advice.

I am indebted to the Arts and Humanities Research Council for funding research during my PhD that I have drawn on throughout the book, and to Peterhouse, Cambridge for funding research undertaken in the Burnett Archive of Working Class Autobiographies at Brunel University. I am enormously grateful to everyone who organised and participated in the New York–Cambridge Training Collaboration at NYU, Columbia and Cambridge Universities, for teaching me so much about twentieth-century British history, and for doing it so enjoyably on both sides of the Atlantic. My thanks also go to Margit Franz-Riethdorf, who generously gave me the use of her studio, and in whose beautiful garden I wrote much of the proposal.

I am grateful beyond words to Daisy Dixon, Matthew Green, Emma Greensmith, Emma Neville, Cornelius Riethdorf, Anna Savoie and Mat Simpson – for our many late-night discussions, and the *nostos* without the *algia*. My final thanks, as ever, go to my parents, Deborah and Duncan, and my sister, Jessica Woods – for their love, support and encouragement.

Picture credits

p 15:   PA Images / Alamy Stock Photo

p 67:   Pictorial Press Ltd / Alamy Stock Photo

p 98:   Punch Cartoon Library / TopFoto

p 129:   Courtesy Shell Heritage Art Collection.
                 Copyright Shell Brands International AG

p 132:   Library of Congress, Prints & Photographs
                 Division, LC-USZC4-11202

p 139 (top):   Pictorial Press Ltd / Alamy Stock Photo

p 139 (bottom): De Luan / Alamy Stock Photo

p 154:   Illustrated London News / Mary Evans Pic-
                 ture Library

p 155:   Illustrated London News/Mary Evans Picture
                 Library

p 180:   Wikimedia Commons / Internet Archive

p 207:   Wellcome Collection

p 227:   Chronicle / Alamy Stock Photo

p 243:   Wikimedia Commons / Biodiversity Heritage
                Library

p 247:   Wikimedia Commons / The Yorck Project

Notes

INTRODUCTION: NOSTALGIA TELLS IT LIKE IT WASN'T

1. 'Boris Johnson "cannot believe" BBC Proms decision', BBC News, 25 August 2020 [https://www.bbc.co.uk/news/entertainment-arts-53902065]; Matthew Moore, 'Don't airbrush British history, government tells heritage groups', *The Times*, 15 February 2021

2. Boris Johnson, 'The rest of the world believes in Britain. It's time that we did too', *Telegraph*, 15 July 2018; Robert Saunders, 'Brexit and Empire: "Global Britain" and the Myth of Imperial Nostalgia', *The Journal of Imperial and Commonwealth History*, 48, 6 (2020), p.1164

3. Johannes Hofer, *Dissertatio Medica de nostalgia* (Basel, 1688), quoted in Svetlana Boym, *The Future of Nostalgia* (New York: Basic Books, 2002), p.3; Peter Mitchell, *Imperial Nostalgia: How the British Conquered Themselves* (Manchester: Manchester University Press, 2021), pp.18–19. See also Thomas Dodman, *What Nostalgia Was: War, Empire, and the Time of a Deadly Emotion* (Chicago: University of Chicago Press, 2018); Susan J. Matt, *Homesickness: An American History* (Oxford: Oxford University Press, 2014), esp. p.5

4. For surveys of the literature on nostalgia, change and modernity, see Malcolm Chase and Christopher Shaw, 'The Dimensions of Nostalgia', in Christopher Shaw and Malcolm Chase (eds), *The Imagined Past: History and Nostalgia* (Manchester: Manchester University Press, 1989), pp.6–8; Brecht Deseure and Judith Pollmann, 'The experience of rupture and the history of memory', in

Erika Kuijpers, Judith Pollmann, Johannes Muller and Jasper van der Steen (eds), *Memory Before Modernity: Practices of Memory in Early Modern Europe* (Leiden: Brill, 2013), pp.315–29

5. Jonathan Coe, *Middle England* (London: Penguin, 2019), p.391
6. Mitchell, p.16
7. Peter Mandler, *History and National Life* (London: Profile, 2002), pp.20 and 22
8. Raphael Samuel, *Island Stories* (London: Verso, 1998), pp.4, 81–2 and 210–11
9. Harriet Phillips, *Nostalgia in Print and Performance, 1510–1613: Merry Worlds* (Cambridge: Cambridge University Press, 2019), pp.131–2
10. David Lowenthal, 'Nostalgia tells it like it wasn't', in Chase and Shaw, p.29

CHAPTER 1: KEEP CALM AND TAKE BACK CONTROL

1. For the history of nostalgia on the political left since 1950, see for example Richard Jobson, *Nostalgia and the Postwar Labour Party: Prisoners of the Past* (Manchester: Manchester University Press, 2018)
2. Roya Nikkhah, 'Labour's Ashes to Ashes Gene Hunt poster attack on Tories backfires', *Telegraph*, 3 April 2010
3. See, for example, Robert Jenrick, 'We will save Britain's statues from the woke militants who want to censor our past', *Telegraph*, 16 January 2021; Matthew Moore, 'Don't airbrush British history, government tells heritage groups', *The Times*, 15 February 2021; Richard Evans, 'The Wonderfulness of Us (the Tory Interpretation of History)', *London Review of Books*, 33, 6 (17 March 2011)
4. Alexandra Haddow, 'From music streaming to TV shows, nostalgia's on the rise – and where's the harm in that?', *NME*, 1 May 2020
5. Hunter Davies, 'I'm 84. I survived rationing. I'm not scared of coronavirus', *Sunday Times*, 15 March 2020
6. 'Maureen from Barnsley awaits her freedom', MailOnline, 15 January 2021 [https://www.dailymail.co.uk/news/article-9152133/

Maureen-Barnsley-said-didnt-sod-Covid-restrictions-set-vaccine.
html]

7. Matt Hancock, 'We must all do everything in our power to protect lives', *Telegraph*, 14 March 2020; 'The Queen's Coronavirus
   Address', BBC News, 5 April 2020 [https://www.bbc.co.uk/news/
   av/uk-52174772]; Henry Mance, 'Captain Tom and why we need
   heroes', *Financial Times*, 24 April 2020

8. Sophie Gaston and Sacha Hilhorst, *At Home in One's Past: Nostalgia as a Cultural and Political Force in Britain, France and
   Germany*, Demos (2018), pp.74 and 85

9. Harriet Sherwood, 'Volunteer lockdown army helps to make Britain brighter', *Observer*, 28 February 2021; Patrick Butler, 'A
   million volunteer to help NHS and others during Covid-19 outbreak', *Guardian*, 13 April 2020

10. Marina Hyde, 'The horror of coronavirus is all too real. Don't
    turn it into an imaginary war', *Guardian*, 7 April 2020

11. Owen Hatherley, *The Ministry of Nostalgia* (London: Verso,
    2016), pp.16 and 18–19

12. Boris Johnson, *Hansard's Parliamentary Debates*, 22 September
    2020, vol. 680, column 815

13. Dan Bloom, 'Boris Johnson accused of calling ventilator crisis
    drive "Operation Last Gasp"', *Metro*, 17 March 2020

14. Boris Johnson, 'We are so nearly out of our captivity, we can see
    the sunlit upland pastures ahead', *Daily Mail*, 28 November 2020

15. Jonathan Chadwick, 'War on coronavirus', *Daily Mail*, 20 April
    2020

16. Daniel Hannan (@DanielJHannan), 'During WW2, boys from @
    CityofLdnSchool (including a young Kingsley Amis) were evacu-
    ated to @MarlboroughCol. The two schools shared premises, one
    set of boys doing games while the other was in class. Even at the
    height of the Blitz, no one missed a day of schooling', 25 January
    2021. Tweet; Daniel Hannan, 'If coronavirus has a silver lining, it
    should be the return of the bow and the curtsy', *Telegraph*, 15
    March 2020

17. Michael Ashcroft (@LordAshcroft), 'Perhaps if World War 2 hap-
    pened today the questions would include:–', 17 May 2020. Tweet

18. Peter Mitchell, *Imperial Nostalgia: How the British Conquered
    Themselves* (Manchester: Manchester University Press, 2021), p.26

19. Olivia Petter, 'Prince William says Britain is at its best when we're in a crisis', *Independent*, 13 April 2020; Rod Liddle, 'A peaceful, easy life hasn't made us happy. Perhaps it's time to give war a chance', *The Times*, 11 August 2019

20. Sebastian Payne and Robert Wright, 'Labour accuses Johnson of stoking "culture war" to distract from failings', *Financial Times*, 15 June 2020; Laura Webster, 'Downing Street stoking "war on woke" to shore up Tory support', *National*, 16 June 2020

21. Anna Mikhailova, 'Boris Johnson attacks "dubious" campaign to "photoshop" Britain's history', *Telegraph*, 14 June 2020; Boris Johnson, 'Rather than tear some people down we should build others up', *Telegraph*, 14 June 2020

22. Robert Jenrick, 'We will save Britian's statues from the woke militants who want to censor our past', *Telegraph*, 16 January 2021; Moore; Geraldine Kendall Adams, 'Fears over editorial freedom as heritage bodies summoned to discuss contested history', News, Museums Association, 16 February 2021 [https://www.museumsassociation.org/museums-journal/news/2021/02/fears-over-editorial-freedom-as-heritage-bodies-summoned-to-discuss-contested-history/]

23. Press Release, 'Charity Commission finds National Trust did not breach charity law', The Charity Commission, 11 March 2021 [https://www.gov.uk/government/news/charity-commission-finds-national-trust-did-not-breach-charity-law]

24. 'Boris Johnson "cannot believe" BBC Proms decision', BBC News, 25 August 2020

25. David Olusoga, 'Britain cannot be reborn while we're still lost in fantasies about the past', *Guardian*, 2 June 2019

26. Craig Simpson, 'Heroes of Rorke's Drift branded "imperialist" over links to empire', *Telegraph*, 17 December 2020

27. Sathnam Sanghera, *Empireland: How Imperialism Has Shaped Modern Britain* (London: Viking, 2021), pp.16–17

28. Afua Hirsch, *Brit(ish): On Race, Identity and Belonging* (London: Vintage, 2018), p.271

29. Akala, *Natives: Race and Class in the Ruins of Empire* (London: Two Roads, 2018), p.7

30. For example, Danny Dorling and Sally Tomlinson, *Rule Britannia: Brexit and the End of Empire* (London: Biteback, 2019), pp.55–6

31. Adam Ramsay, 'For Britain to solve its economic problems, it needs to stop lying to itself about its past', Open Democracy, 9 March 2017 [https://neweconomics.opendemocracy.net/trade-empire-2-0-and-the-lies-we-tell-ourselves/]

32. Liam Fox (@LiamFox), 'The United Kingdom, is one of the few countries in the European Union that does not need to bury its 20th century history', 4 March 2016. Tweet

33. Ramsay

34. Reni Eddo-Lodge, *Why I'm No Longer Talking to White People About Race* (London: Bloomsbury, 2018), p.9; Sanghera, pp.73–4 and 76

35. 'Laurence Fox apologises to Sikhs for "clumsy" 1917 comments', BBC News, 24 January 2020 [https://www.bbc.co.uk/news/entertainment-arts-51233734]

36. Sanghera, pp.77–80

37. Sarah Bodesley, 'Mary Beard abused on Twitter over Roman Britain's ethnic diversity', *Guardian*, 6 August 2017

38. Richard Evans, '"One man who made history" by another who seems to make it up: Boris on Churchill', *New Statesman*, 13 November 2014

39. See, for example, Priyamvada Gopal, 'Why can't Britain handle the truth about Winston Churchill?', *Guardian*, 17 March 2021

40. Leah Sinclair, 'Police guard statue of Winston Churchill as protesters gather around monument chanting "protect women, not statues"', *Evening Standard*, 14 March 2021; Alain Tolhurst, 'Policing Minister Says 10-Year Jail Term for Defacing Statues Reflects their "Emotional Value"', Politics Home, 15 March 2021 [https://www.politicshome.com/news/article/kit-malthouse-sarah-everard-clapham-vigil-policing-bill-defending-statues]

41. David Reynolds, *Island Stories: Britain and its History in the Age of Brexit* (London: William Collins, 2019), pp.3, 104 and 240; Fintan O'Toole, *Heroic Failure: Brexit and the Politics of Pain* (London: Head of Zeus, 2019), p.172

42. James Cooray Smith, 'Nigel Farage's love of Dunkirk shows how Brexiteers learned the wrong lessons from World War II', *New Statesman*, 26 July 2017

43. O'Toole, p.68

44. Mark Mazower, 'Wartime nostalgia blinds us to Britain's changed realities', *Guardian*, 2 September 2009; Cooray Smith

45. Amy Walker, 'Do mention the war', *Guardian*, 4 Febuary 2019; Jacob Rees-Mogg, 'The Brexit white paper is a bad deal for Britain', *Spectator*, 12 July 2018

46. Boris Johnson, 'We are heading for a car crash Brexit under Theresa May's Chequers plan', *Telegraph*, 16 September 2018

47. Anoosh Chakelian, '1066, Hitler, the Corn Laws ... Why are Brexiteers the basic bitches of history?', *New Statesman*, 17 September 2018

48. Tim Shipman, *All Out War: the full story of Brexit* (London: William Collins, 2017), pp.54–5; Pat Kane, 'Dominic Cummings tries to "take back control". Here's the alternative', The Alternative, 28 July 2019 [https://www.thealternative.org.uk/dailyalternative/2019/7/28/editorial-cummings-power]

49. 'Brexit: Too many older Leave voters nostalgic for "white" Britain, says Cable', BBC News, 11 March 2018 [https://www.bbc.co.uk/news/uk-politics-43364331]

50. For example, Ishaan Tharoor, 'Brexit and Britain's delusions of empire', *Washington Post*, 31 March 2017; Tharoor, 'Britain clings to imperial nostalgia as Brexit looms', *Washington Post*, 4 January 2019; Ben Judah 'England's Last Gasp of Empire', *New York Times*, 12 July 2016

51. Gary Younge, 'Britain's imperial fantasies have given us Brexit', *Guardian*, 3 February 2018; Hirsch, p.270; David Olusoga, 'Empire 2.0 is dangerous nostalgia for something that never existed', *Guardian*, 8 March 2017

52. Robert Saunders, 'The myth of Brexit as imperial nostalgia', *Prospect*, 7 January 2019; Saunders, 'Brexit and Empire: "Global Britain" and the Myth of Imperial Nostalgia', *The Journal of Imperial and Commonwealth History*, 48, 6 (2020), p.1142. For distinctions between nostalgia and amnesia, remembering and forgetting, see, for example: Paul Gilroy, *Postcolonial Melancholia* (New York: Columbia University Press, 2008); Gilroy, *After Empire: Melancholia or Convivial Culture* (London: Routledge, 2008); Mitchell; Shashi Tharoor, *Inglorious Empire: What the British Did to India* (London: C. Hurst & Co., 2017), esp. ch.8; Patricia M.E. Lorcin, 'Imperial Nostalgia; Colonial Nostalgia;

Differences of Theory, Similarities of Practice?', *Historical Reflections*, 39, 3 (2013), pp.97–111

53. Boris Johnson, 'The rest of the world believes in Britain. It's time that we did too', *Telegraph*, 15 July 2018

54. Ash Sarkar, 'The colonial past is another country. Let's leave Boris Johnson there', *Guardian*, 10 July 2018

55. 'Full text: Boris Johnson's conference speech', *Spectator*, 2 October 2016

56. Quoted in Saunders, 'Brexit and Empire', p.1164

57. O'Toole, esp. p.3

58. Saunders, 'Brexit and Empire', pp.1147–8

59. Saunders, 'Brexit and Empire', p.1142

60. See, for example, John Denham, 'Cable's Confusion', *Open Democracy*, 15 March 2018

61. Rowena Mason, 'Jamaica should "move on from the painful legacy of slavery", says Cameron', *Guardian*, 30 September 2015

62. Quoted in Saunders, 'Brexit and Empire', p.1166

63. John Kampfner, *Blair's Wars* (London: Simon & Schuster, 2004), p.4; Robert Cooper, 'Why we still need empires', *Observer*, 7 April 2002

64. 'The British Empire is "something to be proud of"', YouGov, 26 July 2014 [https://yougov.co.uk/topics/politics/articles-reports/2014/07/26/Britain-proud-its-empire]; 'Attitudes to Racism in Britain, research for the Economist', Ipsos MORI, September 2020 [https://www.ipsos.com/sites/default/files/ct/news/documents/2020-10/economist-survey-on-racism-2020-slides.pdf]

65. Quoted in Gaston and Hilhorst, pp.63 and 66

66. '45 of the funniest signs from the anti-Brexit march', Bored Panda, 2019 [https://www.boredpanda.com/funny-anti-brexit-protest-signs-london/]; Tom Nicholson, 'There is a crisis in British swearing', *Esquire*, 30 August 2018

67. 'A Five-Ring Opening Circus, Weirdly and Unabashedly British', *New York Times*, 27 July 2012

68. Yasmin Alibhai-Brown, 'Mo's joyful embrace of Britishness', *Daily Mail*, 12 August 2012; Nasar Meer and Tariq Modood, 'Accentuating Multicultural Britishness: An Open or Closed Activity?', in Richard T. Ashcroft and Mark Bevir (eds), *Multiculturalism in the British Commonwealth: Comparative Perspectives*

on Theory and Practice (Berkeley, CA: University of California Press, 2019), p.47

69. See, for example, Stuart Heritage's satirical piece, 'The London Olympics opening ceremony: a moment of optimism that destroyed the decade', *Guardian*, 26 December 2019

70. 'Media reaction to the London 2012 Olympic opening ceremony', BBC News, 28 July 2012 [https://www.bbc.co.uk/news/uk-19025686]; Ian Birrell, 'The London 2012 opening ceremony, and a night that set NHS reform back years', *Mail on Sunday*, 6 August 2012

71. Nicholas Watt, 'Olympics opening ceremony was "multicultural crap", Tory MP tweets', *Guardian*, 28 July 2012

72. 'London 2012: Opening ceremony – reviews', *Observer*, 29 July 2012

73. David Lowenthal, *The Past is a Foreign Country Revisited* (Cambridge: Cambridge University Press, 2015), p.39

74. Hatherley, p.23

75. They are probably not. Grace Cook, 'The Cotton Tote Crisis', *New York Times*, 24 August 2021

76. Hatherley, p.4. See also Elizabeth Wilson, 'Austerity in Retrospect: The Glamour of Masochism', *AA Files*, 57 (2008), pp.46–50

77. Hatherley, pp.115–9; Tom Harrisson, *Living Through the Blitz* (1976; London: Penguin, 1990)

78. Hatherley, pp.21 and 41

79. See, for example, Patrick Wright, *On Living in an Old Country* (1985; Oxford: Oxford University Press, 2009); Robert Hewison, *The Heritage Industry: Britain in a Climate of Decline* (London: Meuthen, 1987); David Cannadine, 'Brideshead Revered', *London Review of Books*, 5, 5 (17 March 1983). For critical surveys of the 'heritage debates' of the 1980s, see Peter Mandler, *History and National Life* (London: Profile, 2002), pp.124–9; George K. Behlmer, 'Introduction', in George K. Behlmer and Fred M. Leventhal (eds), *Singular Continuities: Tradition, Nostalgia and Identity in Modern British Culture* (Stanford: Stanford University Press, 2000), pp.4–7

80. For example, Martin J. Wiener, *English Culture and the Decline of the Industrial Spirit 1850–1980* (1981; London: Penguin, 1992)

NOTES

81. Tom Paulin, quoted in Raphael Samuel, *Theatres of Memory* (London: Verso, 1994), p.260; Stephen Pile, quoted in Lowenthal, p.107

82. John Major, Speech to Conservative Group for Europe, 22 April 1993

83. Lowenthal, pp.587–8

84. Samuel, *Theatres of Memory*, esp. p.262; Keith Thomas, 'Retrochic', *London Review of Books*, 17, 8 (20 April 1995); Lara Rutherford-Morrison, 'Playing Victorian: Heritage, Authenticity, and Make-Believe in Blists Hill Victorian Town, the Ironbridge Gorge', *The Public Historian*, 37, 3 (2015), esp. pp.78–9 and 82–3

85. Margaret Thatcher, *The Downing Street Years* (1993; London: Harper Press, 2011), p.758; Jonathon Porritt, 'Environmental Politics: The Old and the New', *The Political Quarterly*, 68, B (1997), p.62; John McCormick, *British Politics and the Environment* (London: Routledge, 1991), p.57

86. Nicholas Ridley, speech to National Association of Conservation Graduates, January 1988; Ryan Trimm, *Heritage and the Legacy of the Past in Contemporary Britain* (London: Routledge, 2017), p.237; 'Would YOU live next to a Nimby?', BBC News, 21 May 2002 [http://news.bbc.co.uk/1/hi/uk/2000000.stm]

87. Thomas; see also Samuel, *Theatres of Memory*, p.291

88. Margaret Thatcher, speech to the Conservative Party rally at Cheltenham Racecourse, 3 July 1982

89. Margaret Thatcher, speech to Conservative Rally in Bolton, 1 May 1979

90. Raphael Samuel, *Island Stories* (London: Verso, 1998), pp.330–2

91. Mandler, p.125

92. Samuel, *Island Stories*, pp.346, 335, 337 and 329

93. Samuel, *Island Stories*, pp.334 and 338

94. Margaret Thatcher, Interview for *Woman's Own*, 23 September 1987 [https://www.margaretthatcher.org/document/106689]

95. Samuel, *Island Stories*, p.338

CHAPTER 2: I WAS LORD
KITCHENER'S VALET

1. Andy Beckett, *When the Lights Went Out: What Really Happened to Britain in the Seventies* (London: Faber & Faber, 2009), pp.177–8; Tom Nairn, *The Break-Up of Britain: Crisis and Neo-nationalism* (1977; London: Verso, 1981), p.13

2. Michael Shanks, *The Stagnant Society* (London: Penguin, 1961), p.29; Arthur Koestler, *Suicide of a Nation* (London: Macmillan, 1964)

3. Harold Macmillan, speech at Bedford, 20 July 1957

4. Beckett, p.416

5. Beckett, p.417

6. Raphael Samuel, *Theatres of Memory* (London: Verso, 1994), pp. 56–7; David Lowenthal, *The Past is a Foreign Country Revisited* (Cambridge: Cambridge University Press, 2015), p.25

7. David Kynaston, *Austerity Britain:1945–51* (London: Bloomsbury, 2007), p.249; Brian Mitchell, *International History Statistics: Europe, 1750–1988* (Basingstoke: Palgrave Macmillan, 1992), p.132; Clair Wills, *Lovers and Strangers: An Immigrant History of Post-War Britain* (London: Penguin, 2018), p.xiv

8. David Kynaston, *Modernity Britain:1957–62* (London: Bloomsbury, 2015), pp.428–9

9. Kynaston, *Austerity Britain*, pp.161–2

10. Quoted in David Kynaston, *Family Britain: 1951–57* (London: Bloomsbury, 2009), pp.5–7 and 60–1

11. Samuel, pp.92–3

12. Kynaston, *Austerity Britain*, p.31; Jonathan Rose, *The Literary Churchill: Author, Reader, Actor* (New Haven, Conn.: Yale University Press, 2014), p.370

13. Quoted in Kynaston, *Family Britain*, pp.667–8; Samuel, pp.51 and 54

14. 'Interview with Robert Orbach', Victoria and Albert Museum, [http://www.vam.ac.uk/content/articles/i/robert-orbach/]

15. Samuel, pp.96–8; Peter Mandler, *History and National Life* (London: Profile, 2002), pp.93–4

16. Mandler, pp.94 and 103–4

17. Samuel, pp.60–2

18. Mandler, pp.94–5

19. Mandler, p.95; Kynaston, *Austerity Britain*, p.20; and Jon Lawrence, *Me, Me, Me?: The Search for Community in Post-war England* (Oxford: Oxford University Press, 2019), p.44

20. Kynaston, *Modernity Britain*, p.84; and *Austerity Britain*, pp. 594–5. For the history of slum clearance, see Ben Jones, 'Slum Clearance, Privatization and Residualization: the practices and politics of council housing in mid-twentieth-century England', *Twentieth Century British History*, 21, 4 (2010), esp. pp.512–5; and Jim Yelling, 'The incidence of slum clearance in England and Wales, 1955–85, *Urban History*, 27 (2000), pp.234–54

21. Quoted in Kynaston, *Austerity Britain*, pp.161–2

22. Wills, p.250; Kynaston, *Modernity Britain*, p.650. See also Lawrence, esp. p.91

23. Reginald Turnor, *Nineteenth Century Architecture in Britain* (London: Batsford, 1950), p.111; Kenneth Clark, *The Gothic Revival: An Essay in the History of Taste* (1928; London: John Murray, 1983), p.191; Kynaston, *Modernity Britain*, pp.290, 280 and 651

24. For people's housing aspirations, see Mark Clapson, 'The suburban aspiration in England since 1919', *Contemporary British History*, 14 (2000), pp.151–74; and Claire Langhamer, 'The Meanings of Home in Postwar Britain', *Journal of Contemporary History*, 40, 2 (2005), esp. p.346

25. Quoted in Kynaston, *Family Britain*, pp.418–20; Ian Nairn, 'Outrage', *Architectural Review*, June 1955, republished August 2015 [https://www.architectural-review.com/essays/outrage/outrage-the-birth-of-subtopia-will-be-the-death-of-us]

26. Letter from John Summerson to John Betjeman, 15 June 1966, in Candida Lycett Green (ed), *John Betjeman, Letters: 1951–84* (London: Methuen, 1995), pp.319–20; 'Euston portico fate inevitable says Mr Macmillan', *The Times*, 4 November 1961; Kynaston, *Modernity Britain,* p.647

27. Quoted in Kynaston, *Modernity Britain*, pp.289 and 291

28. Kynaston, *Modernity Britain*, pp.444–5, 636–7 and 675

29. Philip Larkin, 'Here', *New Statesman*, 24 November 1961

30. Kynaston, *Modernity Britain,* pp.637, 79–80, 669 and 443; Samuel, p.153

31. Quoted in Kynaston, *Modernity Britain*, pp.84, 664–5, 669 and 281

32. Kynaston, *Modernity Britain*, pp.637 and 668

33. Quoted in Kynaston, *Family Britain*, p.59; Lawrence, esp. pp.80 and 91; Langhamer, p.349

34. Beckett, p.423; see also Guy Ortolano, *Thatcher's Progress: Democracy to Market Liberalism through an English New Town* (Cambridge: Cambridge University Press, 2019)

35. Lawrence, esp. pp.2, 75, 86, 89 and 94–5

36. Quoted in Kynaston, *Modernity Britain*, p.191; and *Family Britain*, p.635

37. Lawrence, p.51; Langhamer, pp.351–2

38. V.W. Garratt, *A Man in the Street* (London: J.M. Dent & Sons Ltd, 1939), p.64

39. Grace Foakes, *My Part of the River* (London: Shepheard–Walwyn, 1974), p.56; and *My Part of the River: Memories of people and places in the East End of Edwardian London* (London: Futura, 1988), p.192

40. Walter Southgate, *That's the Way it Was: A Working Class Autobiography, 1890–1950* (Oxted, Surrey: New Clarion Press, 1982), pp.21–2 and 100–1. For nostalgia, myths and realities of 'traditional' working-class communities, see also Joanna Bourke, *Working-Class Cultures in Britain, 1890–1960* (London: Routledge, 1994), esp. pp.137–8; Robert Colls, 'When we lived in communities: working-class culture and its critics', in Robert Colls and Richard Rogers (eds), *Cities of Ideas* (Aldershot: Ashgate, 2004), pp.283–307; Ben Jones, 'The Uses of Nostalgia: autobiography, community publishing and working-class neighbourhoods in post-war England', *Cultural and Social History*, 7, 3 (2010), pp.355–74; Lawrence, esp. pp.1–15; Ortolano, pp.143–6

41. Arthur T. Collinson, 'One way only: an autobiography of an old-time trade unionist', 3:30, Burnett Archive of Working Class Autobiographies, Brunel University, p.5

42. John Bull, 'Letter to Olive', 10 April 1970, in 'Early Childhood', 2:114, Burnett Archive

43. Winifred Till, 'The Early Years of a Victorian Grandmother', 2:763, Burnett Archive, p.38

44. Jack William Jones, Untitled, 2:443, Burnett Archive, p.48

45. Jack Jones, p.49
46. For a summary of historical recorded crime, 1898–2001, see Home Office crime data [https://www.gov.uk/government/statistics/historical–crime–data]
47. Edie Rutherford, and B. Charles, quoted in Simon Garfield, *Our Hidden Lives: the remarkable diaries of post-war Britain* (London: Ebury Press, 2005), pp.144 and 150
48. Charles, Rutherford, and Herbert Brush, quoted in Garfield, pp.261, 148 and 508
49. Brush, quoted in Garfield, p.508
50. John Bull, pp.9 and 36
51. Jack Lanigan, 'The Kingdom Did Come', 1:421, Burnett Archive, pp.2 and 5
52. Linda McDowell, 'Workers, migrants, aliens or citizens? State constructions and discourses of identity among post-war European labour migrants in Britain', *Political Georgraphy*, 22, 8 (2003), p.865; Wills, pp.24–5
53. *Evening Standard*, 22 June 1948
54. George Lamming, quoted in Wills, p.7
55. Interview with Ivan Weekes, in Mike Phillips and Trevor Phillips, *Windrush: The Irresistible Rise of Multi-Racial Britain* (London: Harper Collins, 1999), p.128; Tony Moore, *Policing Notting Hill: Fifty Years of Turbulence* (Hook, Hampshire: Waterside Press, 2013), pp.80–1
56. Interviews with Cecil Holness and Cy Grant, in Phillips, pp.38 and 50. See also 'Cy Grant: Into the Wind', in Stephen Bourne, *The Motherland Calls: Britain's Black Servicemen and Women 1939–45* (Cheltenham: The History Press, 2012), ch.6
57. Interview with Tryphena Anderson, in Phillips, pp.97 and 119
58. Wills, pp.45 and 62
59. Interview with Diane Abbott, in Phillips, p.211
60. Interview with Rudy Braithwaite, in Phillips, pp.397–8; Phillips, p.395. See also, Colin Grant, *Homecoming: Voices of the Windrush Generation* (London: Jonathan Cape, 2019)
61. Wills, pp.358–60
62. Wills, pp.352–3
63. Brigid Keenan, 'Passage from India', *Spectator*, 26 August 2017; Keenan, 'The lifelong effects of being a child in the British Raj',

Spectator, 27 March 2021; Keenan, *Full Marks for Trying: An unlikely journey from the Raj to the rag trade* (London: Bloomsbury, 2016), ch.1. For nostalgia for the British Raj in England, see also Sathnam Sanghera, *Empireland: How Imperialism Has Shaped Modern Britain* (London: Viking, 2021), pp.95–6

64. Quoted in Ian Patel, 'Enoch Powell's Altered World', blog, *London Review of Books*, 20 April 2018. See also Peter Brooke, 'India, Imperialism and the origins of Enoch Powell's "Rivers of Blood" speech', *The Historical Journal*, 50, 3 (2007), pp.669–87

65. Enoch Powell, 'Imperial Sickness', *Spectator*, 12 September 1968, pp.13–14; Speech to the St George's Day Banquet, 23 April 1961; Phillips, p.76; David Reynolds, *Island Stories: Britain and its History in the Age of Brexit* (London: William Collins, 2019), pp.169–70; Robert Saunders, 'Brexit and Empire: "Global Britain" and the Myth of Imperial Nostalgia', *The Journal of Imperial and Commonwealth History*, 48, 6 (2020), p.1148; Camilla Schofield, 'A nation or no nation? Enoch Powell and Thatcherism', in Ben Jackson and Robert Saunders (eds), *Making Thatcher's Britain* (Cambridge: Cambridge University Press, 2012), p.95; and Stephen Howe, 'Decolonisation and its imperial aftershocks', in *Making Thatcher's Britain*, pp.238–9

66. Quoted in Kynaston, *Austerity Britain*, p.16. For the longing for home in wartime, see Langhamer, p.343

67. *Punch*, 4 October 1944

68. Quoted in Kynaston, p.109

69. Kynaston, *Austerity Britain*, p.97; For divorce figures in the 1970s, see statistical bulletin, 'Divorces in England and Wales', Office for National Statistics [https://www.ons.gov.uk/peoplepopulation-andcommunity/birthsdeathsandmarriages/divorce/bulletins/divorcesinenglandandwales/latest#divorces-in-england-and-wales-data]

70. Rutherford and Charles, quoted in Garfield, pp.226 and 177

71. Quoted in Kynaston, *Austerity Britain*, p.191

72. Maggie Joy Blunt [pseud] in May 1948, quoted in Garfield, pp.394–5

73. Elizabeth David, 'John Wesley's Eye', *Spectator*, 1 February 1963, collected in Elizabeth David, *An Omelette and a Glass of Wine* (London: Grub Street, 2009), pp.19–21

74. Evelyn Waugh, preface to revised edition of *Brideshead Revisited* (London: Penguin, 1959)

75. George Taylor, quoted in Garfield, p.352

76. Quentin Crisp, *The Naked Civil Servant* (1968; London: Penguin, 1997), p.168

77. Tom Harrisson, *Living Through the Blitz* (1976; London: Penguin, 1990), pp.85, 80–1 and 322

78. Harrisson, pp.80–1 and 126–7

79. David Reynolds, *Island Stories: Britain and its History in the Age of Brexit* (London: William Collins, 2019), pp.85–6

80. Harrisson, pp.134–7 and 274

81. Crisp, p.168

82. Quoted in Leo Robson, 'The Novelist of Human Unknowability', *New Yorker*, 10 October 2016

83. Lara Feigel, *The Love Charm of Bombs: Restless Lives in the Second World War* (London: Bloomsbury, 2013), esp. pp.2–4

84. Quoted in Feigel, p.465; and Victoria Glendinning, 'I am in your keeping', *Guardian*, 7 February 2009

85. Stephen Spender, quoted in John Sutherland, 'The Blitz in London: a metropolis's orgasm', *New Statesman*, 10 January 2013; Graham Greene, quoted in Feigel, p.129

86. For the reception of *Brief Encounter* in post-war Britain, see Thomas Dixon, *Weeping Britannia: Portrait of a Nation in Tears* (Oxford: Oxford University Press, 2015), pp.230–1 and 240–4

CHAPTER 3: THE END OF THE
GARDEN PARTY

1. Stanley Baldwin, 'What England means to me', speech to the Royal Society of St George, 6 May 1924; David Cannadine, 'Emollience: Stanley Baldwin and Francis Brett Young', in David Cannadine, *In Churchill's Shadow: Confronting the Past in Modern Britain* (Oxford: Oxford University Press, 2003), pp.160–8; Martin Wiener, *English Culture and the Decline of the Industrial Spirit* (London: Penguin, 1992), p.100

2. Charles Ferrall and Dougal McNeill, 'Introduction', in *British Literature in Transition, 1920–1940: Futility and Anarchy* (Cambridge:

Cambridge University Press, 2018), pp.3–14; Gabrielle McIntire, 'History: The Past in Transition', in Ferrall and McNeill, pp.149–50; Cannadine, p.180

3. Baldwin, 'What England means to me', Cannadine, pp.161 and 180–1

4. Ferrall and McNeill, pp.23–4; Peter Mandler and Susan Pedersen, 'Introduction: The British intelligentsia after the Victorians', in Susan Pedersen and Peter Mandler (eds), *After the Victorians: Private conscience and public duty in modern Britain* (London: Routledge, 1994), p.18; John Carey, *The Intellectuals and the Masses: Pride and Prejudice among the Literary Intelligentsia, 1880–1939* (London: Faber & Faber, 1992)

5. J.B. Priestley, *English Journey* (London: William Heinemann, 1934), pp.4–5; Chris Waters, 'J.B. Priestley: Englishness and the politics of nostalgia', in Pedersen and Mandler, pp.210–11; Owen Hatherley, *The Ministry of Nostalgia* (London: Verso, 2015), pp.77–8; Stefan Collini, 'From the Motorcoach', *London Review of Books*, 31, 22 (2009)

6. Wiener, pp.74–5

7. Evelyn Waugh, *Labels* (1930; London: Penguin, 1985), p.46; Peter Mandler, 'Politics and the English Landscape since the First World War', *Huntingdon Library Quarterly*, 55, 3 (1992), pp.455–6; Alexandra Harris, *Romantic Moderns: English Writers, Artists and the Imagination from Virginia Woolf to John Piper* (London: Thames & Hudson, 2015), p.80

8. Robert Graves, *Goodbye to All That* (1929; London: Penguin, 2000), pp.7 and 157; Robert McCrum, 'Goodbye to All That by Robert Graves', *Guardian*, 28 November 2016

9. Peter Mandler, *History and National Life* (London: Profile, 2002), pp.60–1 and 78; Raphael Samuel, *Island Stories: Unravelling Britain* (London: Verso, 1998), pp.82 and 210; W.C. Sellar and R.J. Yeatman, *1066 and All That* (1930; London: Methuen, 2009), pp.v, 3, 32, 42 and 56

10. Roger Fry, quoted in Christoper Reed, *A Roger Fry Reader* (Chicago: University of Chicago Press, 1996), p.57; Christine Froula, 'War, Peace and Internationalism', in Victoria Rosner (ed), *The Cambridge Companion to the Bloomsbury Group* (Cambridge: Cambridge University Press, 2014), p.97; Paul Levy,

'Rereadings: Eminent Victorians by Lytton Strachey', *Guardian*, 20 July 2002

11. W.S.F.B, 'Introduction', in Lytton Strachey, *Eminent Victorians* (1918; London: Folio Society, 1967), pp.12–14; Lytton Strachey, *Eminent Victorians* (1918; Oxford: Oxford University Press, 2009), pp.145 and 243; Edmund Wilson, 'Lytton Strachey', *New Republic*, 72 (21 September 1932), pp.146–8

12. Laura Carter, 'The Quennells and the "History of Everyday Life" in England, c. 1918–1969', *History Workshop Journal*, 81, 1 (2016), pp.106–34; Frank Roscoe, 'A note on the methods and influence of C.H.B. and Marjorie Quennell on History Teaching in Schools', in C.H.B. and Marjorie Quennell, *A History of Everyday Things in England*, vol. 2, *1500–1799* (London: B.T. Batsford, 1937), p.vi; Marjorie and C.H.B. Quennell, 'Preface' (1919) in *A History of Everyday Things*, pp.x–xi

13. Laura Carter, *Histories of Everyday Life: The Making of Popular Social History in Britain, 1918–1979* (Oxford: Oxford University Press, 2021), esp. ch.2; Michael Gove, 'All pupils will learn our island story', speech at the Conservative Party Conference, 5 October 2010

14. Laura Carter, 'Rethinking Folk Culture in Twentieth-Century Britain', *Twentieth Century British History*, 28, 4 (2017), pp.555 and 558; Samuel, p.81; Isabel Frances Grant and Alexander Fenton, *The Making of Am Fasgadh: An Account of the Origins of the Highland Folk Museum, by its Founder* (Edinburgh: National Museums Scotland, 2007); Bob Powell, 'Scotland's Open Air Museums', in Alexander Fenton and Margaret A. Mackay (eds), *An Introduction to Scottish Enthnology* (Edinburgh: Birlinn, 2013)

15. D.N. Jeans, 'Planning and the Myth of the English Countryside, in the Interwar Period', *Rural History*, 1, 2 (1990), p.252; Sean O'Connell, 'Motoring and Modernity, 1900–50', in Francesca Carnevali and Julie-Marie Strange (eds), *20th Century Britain: Economic, Cultural and Social Change* (London: Routledge, 2007), p.113

16. Harris, p.10; Jed Esty, *A Shrinking Island: Modernist Culture in England* (Princeton, NJ: Princeton University Press, 2003), pp.7–17; Mandler, *History and National Life*, p.57; Malcolm Chase, 'This is no claptrap: this is our heritage', in Malcolm Chase and

Christopher Shaw (eds), *The Imagined Past: History and Nostalgia* (Manchester: Manchester University Press, 1989), pp.128–33

17. Peter Mandler, 'Against Englishness: English Culture and the Limits to Rural Nostalgia, 1850–1940', *Transactions of the Royal Historical Society*, 7 (1997), pp.171–2

18. C.E.M. Joad, 'The people's claim', in Clough Williams-Ellis (ed), *Britain and the Beast* (London: Readers Union, 1938), pp.72–3; Peter Mandler, 'Politics and the English Landscape since the First World War', *Huntington Library Quarterly*, 55, 3 (1992), p.465; Alun Howkins, *The Death of Rural England: A Social History of the Countryside Since 1900* (London: Routledge, 2003), esp. pp. 95–112; Allan R. Ruff, *Arcadian Visions: Pastoral Influences on Poetry, Painting and the Design of Landscape* (Macclesfield: Windgather Press, 2015), p.226

19. Jeans, pp.259–60; Mandler, 'Against Englishness', p.172

20. Jeans, p.252

21. Jeans, p.260

22. Jeans, pp.257–8; Todd Kutcha, *Semi-detached Empire: Suburbia and the Colonization of Britain, 1880 to the present* (Charlottesville, VA: University of Virginia Press, 2010), p.14; Ian Nairn, 'Outrage', *Architectural Review*, June 1955, republished August 2015 [https://www.architectural-review.com/essays/outrage/outrage-the-birth-of-subtopia-will-be-the-death-of-us]; Howard Marshall, 'The rake's progress', in *Britain and the Beast*, p.164; Thomas Sharp, 'The North East', in *Britain and the Beast*, pp. 144–5

23. Mandler, 'Against Englishness', p.172

24. Jeans, p.259; Chase, esp. pp.134–8; Robert Hemmings, *Modern Nostalgia: Siegfried Sassoon, Trauma and the Second World War* (Edinburgh: Edinburgh University Press, 2008), p.21; David Cannadine, 'The National Trust and the National Heritage', in *In Churchill's Shadow*, p.229; David Cannadine, *The Decline and Fall of the British Aristocracy* (London: Penguin, 2005), esp. p.89

25. E.M. Forster, 'The point of view of the creative artist', in Arthur Koestler (ed), *The Challenge of Our Time* (London: P. Marshall, 1948), p.34; Carey, p.49

26. George Orwell, *Coming Up for Air* (1939; Oxford: Oxford University Press, 2021), pp.179 and 151; D.H. Lawrence, *Lady Chatterley's*

Lover (1928; London: Penguin, 1960), pp.162–3; David Gervais, *Literary Englands: Versions of "Englishness" in Modern Writing* (Cambridge: Cambridge University Press, 1993), pp.86–7

27. Evelyn Waugh, *Decline and Fall* (1928; London: Penguin, 2001), p.109; Gervais, esp. pp.86–94 and 157–75
28. Mandler, 'Against Englishness', p.174
29. Jeans, p.260
30. Jeans, p.255
31. Harris, pp.214–21; Samuel 217–8
32. Wiener, p.76
33. Ernest Rhys, *The Old Country: a book of love and praise of England* (1917: London: J.M. Dent & Sons, 1922), p.v
34. James Fox, *British Art and the First World War, 1914–1924* (Cambridge: Cambridge University Press, 2015), pp.114–5; Wiener, p.63; Harry Smith and Robert J. Bennett, 'Urban–Rural Classification using Census data, 1851–1911', Working Paper 6: ESRC project ES/M0010953: 'Drivers of Entrepreneurship and Small Businesses', University of Cambridge, Department of Geography and Cambridge Group for the History of Population and Social Structure (2017), p.8; Hemmings, p.20
35. Fox, pp.2, 9, 38 and 111
36. Fox, pp.114–6
37. Fox, p.111
38. Michael Roper, 'Trauma as an emotional experience in the Great War', *The Historical Journal*, 52, 2 (2011), pp.427–8 and 436–7; Joanna Bourke, *Dismembering the Male: Men's Bodies, Britain and the Great War* (London: Reaktion, 1996), esp. p.22
39. Roper, p.438
40. Roper, pp.436, 439, 441 and 449
41. Fox, p.127
42. Harry Ricketts, 'Out of Mrs Colefax's Drawing Room: Poets and Poetry Between the Wars', in Ferrall and McNeill, p.36; Hemmings, p.63; Blunden in Ricketts, pp.36–7; Sassoon in Hemmings
43. Roper, p.429; E. Leed, *No Man's Land: Combat and Identity in World War I* (Cambridge: Cambridge University Press, 1979), p.189; Jon Lawrence, 'Forging a peaceable kingdom: war, violence, and fear of brutalization in post-First World War Britain', *Journal of Modern History*, 75 (2003), pp.3–4

44. Hemmings, pp.82, 91, 14 and 74

45. Hemmings, pp.85 and 88–90; Jean Moorcroft Wilson, 'The Hermit of Heytesbury', *Guardian*, 29 March 2003; Winston Churchill, *The Second World War: The Gathering Storm* (London: Cassell, 1948), p.320

46. Samuel, p.48

47. Samuel, pp.82–3 and 218–9; George Orwell, *The Lion and the Unicorn: Socialism and the English Genius* (1941; London: Penguin, 2018), p.7; Churchill, p.320

48. Samuel, p.208

49. Waters, pp.218–9

50. Harris, pp.206–7; Samuel, p.30; Gill Sanders, *Recording Britain* (London: V&A, 2011)

51. Phillip Kennedy, 'Illustrating the Lost Landscapes of Pre-war Britain', Illustration Chronicles (blog) [https://illustrationchronicles.com/illustrating-the-lost-landscapes-of-pre-war-britain]; Harris, p.207

CHAPTER 4: NEVER NEVER LAND

1. James Vernon, *Distant Strangers: How Britain Became Modern* (Berkeley and Los Angeles: University of California Press, 2014), pp.9 and 24

2. David Edgerton, *The Shock of the Old: Technology and Global History Since 1900* (London: Profile Books, 2008), pp.xxi and 33

3. Alfred Austin, *Haunts of Ancient Peace* (London: Macmillan, 1902), pp.18–19; Virginia Woolf, *Mr. Bennett and Mrs. Brown* (London: Hogarth Press, 1924)

4. Stephen Kern, *The Culture of Time and Space, 1880–1918* (Cambridge, Mass.: Harvard University Press, 2003); Lynda Nead, *Victorian Babylon: People, Streets and Images in Nineteenth-Century London* (New Haven, Conn.: Yale University Press, 2000), pp.3–10

5. Peter Mandler, *History and National Life* (London: Profile, 2002), p.54

6. H.G. Wells, *Anticipations of the Reaction of Mechanical and Scientific Progress upon Human Life and Thought* (1901; New York: Dover Publications, 1999), p.40

NOTES

7. Arnold Toynbee, *Lectures on the Industrial Revolution* (London, 1884), pp.85 and 5; Daniel Wilson, 'Arnold Toynbee and the Industrial Revolution: The Science of History, Political Economy and the Machine Past', *History & Memory*, 26, 2 (2014), pp.133–61

8. C.F.G. Masterman, *In Peril of Change: Essays Written in Time of Tranquility* (New York: B.W. Huebsch, 1905), p.xii

9. Andrew Mearns, *The Bitter Cry of Outcast London. An Inquiry into the Condition of the Abject Poor* (London: James Clarke & Co., 1883); William Booth, *In Darkest England and the Way Out* (London; New York: Funk & Wagnalls, 1890). For surveys of Victorian and Edwardian enquiries into urban problems, see Andrew Lees, *Cities Perceived: Urban Society in European and American Thought, 1820–1940* (New York: Columbia University Press, 1985); Bruce Coleman, *The Idea of the City in Nineteenth-Century Britain* (Sydney: Law Book Co. of Australasia, 1973); Hannah Rose Woods, 'Anxiety and Urban Life in Late Victorian and Edwardian Culture, 1880–1914', PhD thesis, University of Cambridge (2018)

10. C.F.G. Masterman, *The Condition of England* (London: Meuthen & Co., 1909), p.163

11. Jonathan Rose, *The Edwardian Temperament, 1895–1919* (Athens, Ohio: Ohio University Press, 1986), pp.1–2. For a range of estimates for 1851 attendance figures, see Steve Bruce, 'Christianity in Britain, R.I.P', *Sociology of Religion*, 62, 2 (2001), p.194

12. Vanessa Heggie, 'Lies, Damn Lies and Manchester's Recruiting Statistics: Degeneration as an "Urban Legend" in Victorian and Edwardian Britain', *Journal of the History of Medicine and Allied Sciences*, 63, 2 (2008), p.178

13. See, for example, Max Nordau, Extract from *Degeneration* (1895), in Sally Ledger and Roger Luckhurst, *The Fin de Siècle, A Reader in Cultural History c.1880–1900* (Oxford: Oxford University Press, 2000), p.15; Daniel Pick, *Faces of Degeneration: A European Disorder, c.1848–1918* (Cambridge: Cambridge University Press, 1993)

14. Raphael Samuel, *Island Stories: Unravelling Britain* (London: Verso, 1998), p.81; Mandler, pp.44–5

15. Quoted in Stewart J. Brown, *Providence and Empire: Religion, Politics and Society 1815–1914* (Harlow: Pearson Longman, 2008), p.424

16. Peter Gay, *The Bourgeois Experience, Victoria to Freud*, vol. 5, *Pleasure Wars* (London: Fontana Press, 1998), p.12; Gay, *The Bourgeois Experience*, vol. 3, *The Cultivation of Hatred* (London: Fontana Press, 1995), p.506–7. See also Howard I. Kushner, 'Suicide, gender and the fear of modernity in nineteenth-century medical and social thought', *Journal of Social History*, 26 (1993), pp.461–90; Mark Jackson, *The Age of Stress: Science and the Search for Stability* (Oxford: Oxford University Press, 2013), pp. 21–55; Janet Oppenheim, *'Shattered Nerves': Doctors, Patients and Depression in Victorian England* (New York: Oxford University Press USA, 1991). For anxieties about technology, see Bernhard Rieger, *Technology and the Culture of Modernity in Britain and Germany, 1890–1945* (Cambridge: Cambridge University Press, 2009), pp.2–19; Wolfgang Schivelbusch, *The railway journey: the industrialisation of time and space in the nineteenth century* (Leamington Spa: Berg, 1986)

17. 'Phospherine', 1901–2, History of Advertising Trust, Norfolk

18. 'Eno's Fruit Salt', *Penny Illustrated Paper*, 3 August 1889. See also Takahiro Ueyama, *Health in the Marketplace: Professionalism, Therapeutic Desires, and Medical Commodification in Late Victorian London* (Palo Alto, CA: The Society for the Promotion of Science and Scholarship, 2010)

19. 'Sanatogen', *Graphic*, 7 November 1908

20. 'Sunlight Soap', *Illustrated London News*, 3 May 1901; Karen Sayer, *Country Cottages: A Cultural History* (Manchester: Manchester University Press, 2000), p.34. See also Lori Anne Loeb, *Consuming Angels: Advertising and Victorian Women* (Oxford: Oxford University Press, 1994)

21. Patrick Geddes, *Cities in Evolution: An Introduction to the Town Planning Movement and to the Study of Civics* (London: Williams & Norgate, 1915), p.74; Geddes, *City Development: A Study of Parks, Gardens and Culture-Institutes* (Birmingham: The Saint George Press, 1904), p.212; Geddes, *Cities in Evolution*, p.66

22. Masterman, *In Peril of Change*, pp.xii, 13 and 71

23. C.F.G. Masterman, 'Realities at Home', in *The Heart of the Empire: Discussions of Problems of Modern City Life in England* (London: T. Fisher Unwin, 1907), pp.8–9; G.M. Trevelyan, 'Past and Future', in *The Heart of the Empire*, p.407

24. Eric Hobsbawm and Terence Ranger (eds), *The Invention of Tradition* (1983; Cambridge: Cambridge University Press, 2012)
25. Mandler, pp.56 and 58
26. Reginald Bray, 'The Children of the Town', in *The Heart of the Empire*, pp.127 and 131–4
27. Winifred Till, 'The Early Years of a Victorian Grandmother', 2:763, pp.27–8, Burnett Archive of Working Class Autobiographies, Brunel University
28. James Whittaker, *I, James Whittaker*, foreword by Gilbert Frankau (London: Rich & Cowan Ltd, 1934), pp.44–6
29. George Acorn [pseud], *One of the Multitude* (London: William Heinemann, 1911), p.10
30. Lynne Hapgood, *Margins of Desire: The Suburbs in Fiction and Culture 1880–1925* (Manchester: Manchester University Press, 2005), p.69
31. Richard Jefferies, *Nature Near London* (London: Chatto and Windus, 1892)
32. Hapgood, p.69
33. Thomas Hardy, 'The Dorsetshire Labourer', *Longman's Magazine*, 2, 9 (July 1883), pp.252–69; Jan Marsh, *Back to the Land: The Pastoral Impulse in England, from 1880–1914* (London: Quartet Books, 1982), pp.29–30
34. Henry Snell, *Men, Movements and Myself* (London: J.M. Dent and Sons Ltd, 1936), pp.8 and 1
35. Edward Thomas, 'Adlestrop' (1917); Edward Thomas, *The Woodland Life* (Edinburgh and London: W. Blackwood and Sons, 1897); Hapgood, p.61
36. Trevelyan, pp.410 and 415
37. Marsh, p.3
38. Raphael Samuel, *Theatres of Memory* (London: Verso, 1994), pp.294–6
39. William Morris, 'The Beauty of Life' (1880); and 'Art and the Beauty of the Earth' (1884)
40. William Morris, *News from Nowhere, or, An Epoch of Rest* (1890), in *News from Nowhere and Other Writings* (London: Penguin, 2004), p.201
41. C.R. Ashbee, *Where the Great City Stands: A Study in the New Civics* (London: B.T. Batsford, 1917), p.21

42. Quoted in Joseph Bizup, *Manufacturing Culture: Vindications of Early Industry* (Charlottesville, VA: University of Virginia Press, 2003), p.187

43. William Morris, 'The Lesser Arts' (1882), in *News from Nowhere and Other Writings*, p.250; Morris, *News from Nowhere*, p.122. See also discussion of Ruskin's and Morris's philosophies of labour in John Hughes, *The End of Work: Theological Critiques of Capitalism* (Oxford: Blackwell, 2007), pp.116–8

44. H.G. Wells, *A Modern Utopia* (1905; London: Penguin, 2005), p.72

45. Wells, *A Modern Utopia*, pp.73 and 78–9

46. Marsh, p.196

47. Talia Schaffer, *The Forgotten Female Aesthetes: Literary Culture in Late Victorian England* (Charlottesville, VA: University of Virginia Press, 2000), pp.102–9

48. Edward Carpenter, *Civilisation: Its Cause and Cure, and Other Essays* (1889; London: George Allen & Unwin Ltd, 1921), pp.47 and 58; and 'Simplification of Life', in *England's Ideal, And other Papers on Social Subjects* (London: Swan Sonnenschein, Lowrey & Co., 1887), p.94

49. Edward Carpenter, *The Intermediate Sex* (London: George Allen & Co., 1912), pp.166–7, 40 and 24

50. Quoted in Marsh, pp.18–9; Carpenter, *England's Ideal*, p.84

51. Marsh, pp.18–22

52. Edward Carpenter, *Love's Coming of Age: A Series of Papers on the Relations of the Sexes* (1896; New York and London: Mitchell Kennerley, 1911), p.22

53. H.G. Wells, *Tono-Bungay* (1908; London: Penguin, 2005), pp.372–3

54. Wilfrid Scawen Blunt, *My Diaries*, Part Two (New York: Knopf, 1921), pp.329–30

55. Samuel Hynes, *The Edwardian Turn of Mind* (London: Pimlico, 1991), p.328

56. See, for example, Micheal Sturma, *South Sea Maidens: Western Fantasy and Sexual Politics in the South Pacific* (Westport, Conn.: Greenwood Press, 2002), pp.87–9

57. Quoted in Hynes, p.328

58. *The Times*, 7 November 1910, p.12

59. Rose, p.186

60. Edith Nesbit, *Wings and the Child: Or, the Building of Magic Cities* (London: Hodder and Stoughton, 1913), p.52

61. See for example, Alex Owen, 'Occultism and the "Modern" Self in Fin-de-Siècle Britain', in Martin Daunton and Bernhard Rieger (eds), *Meanings of Modernity: Britain from the Late-Victorian Era to World War II* (Oxford; New York: Berg, 2001)

62. Kenneth Grahame, *The Wind in the Willows* (1908), in *The Penguin Kenneth Grahame* (London: Penguin, 1983), pp.245–7; Rosemary Hill, 'Wild Waters are upon us', *Guardian*, 13 June 2009

63. Rose, p.186

64. H.G. Wells, *The New Machiavelli* (1911; Harmondsworth: Penguin, 1978), p.37

65. See also Simon J. James, *Maps of Utopia: H.G. Wells, Modernity and the End of Culture* (Oxford: Oxford University Press, 2012), esp. p.15

66. George Gissing, *The Whirlpool* (1897; Hemel Hempstead: Harvester, 1977), p.342; Rudyard Kipling, 'If', *Rewards and Fairies* (London: Macmillan, 1910).

67. Thomas Dixon, *Weeping Britannia: Portrait of a Nation in Tears* (Oxford: Oxford University Press, 2015), pp.211–3. For the history of the stiff upper lip, see also Stephen Heathorn, 'How Stiff Were their Upper Lips? Research on Late-Victorian and Edwardian Masculinity', *History Compass*, 2 (2004), pp.1–7; and John Tosh, *Manliness and masculinities in nineteenth-century Britain: essays on gender, family and empire* (Harlow: Pearson Longman, 2005)

68. W. Graham Robertson, *Pinkie and the Fairies* (London: Heinemann, 1909); Dixon, p.209

69. G.K. Chesterton, *Autobiography* (1936; London: Hutchinson, 1969), pp.234–5

CHAPTER 5: THOSE INFERNAL AND DAMNABLY GOOD OLD TIMES

1. David Lowenthal, *The Past is a Foreign Country Revisited* (Cambridge: Cambridge University Press, 2015), p.173

2. *Hansard's Parliamentary Debates*, 15 March 1838, vol. 41, column 941

3. *London Chronicle*, 5114 (14–16 July 1789); William Wordsworth, *Prelude* (1805), bk. 10, l. 696; Ruth Mather, 'The impact of the French Revolution in Britain', British Library online resource [https://www.bl.uk/romantics-and-victorians/articles/the-impact-of-the-french-revolution-in-britain]

4. Robert Poole, *Peterloo: the English Uprising* (Oxford: Oxford University Press, 2019), p.1

5. 'Destruction by fire of the Houses of Parliament', *Manchester Guardian*, 18 October 1834

6. Caroline Shenton, 'The Fire of 1834', The History of Parliament online [https://www.historyofparliamentonline.org/periods/modern/fire-1834]; Rosemary Hill, '*The Day Parliament Burned Down* by Caroline Shenton – review', *Guardian*, 5 October 2012

7. Michael Levin, *The Condition of England Question: Carlyle, Mill, Engels* (Basingstoke: Macmillan Press, 1998), p.34; extract from the *Standard*, reprinted in *Cobbett's Weekly Political Register*, 86, 4 (25 October 1834), p.202; Caroline Shenton, *The Day Parliament Burned Down* (Oxford: Oxford University Press, 2012), pp.132–3

8. Tanya Gold, 'The Houses of Parliament are falling down', *New Statesman*, 5 February 2018; Caroline Shenton, *Mr Barry's War: Rebuilding the Houses of Parliament after the Great Fire of 1834*, (Oxford: Oxford University Press, 2016), p.5

9. Rosemary Hill, *God's Architect: Pugin and the Building of Romantic Britain* (New Haven, Conn.: Yale University Press, 2009), esp. pp.304–5; Stephen Farrell, 'The New Palace of Westminster', History of Parliament online [https://www.historyofparliamentonline.org/periods/modern/new-palace-westminster]

10. Shenton, *Mr Barry's War*, p.5; Edward J. Gillin, *The Victorian Palace of Science: Scientific Knowledge and the Building of the Houses of Parliament* (Cambridge: Cambridge University Press, 2017), pp.19–29

11. James A. Secord, *Visions of Science: Books and readers at the dawn of the Victorian age* (Oxford: Oxford University Press, 2014), p.4

12. Edmund Burke, *Reflections on the Revolution in France* (1790), in Duncan Wu (ed), *Romanticism: An Anthology* (Oxford: Wiley-Blackwell, 2012), pp.12–13

13. Robert Miles, 'The 1790s: the effulgence of Gothic', in Jerrold E. Hogle (ed), *The Cambridge Companion to Gothic Fiction* (Cambridge: Cambridge University Press, 2002), p.47; William Blackstone, *Commentary on the Laws of England*, 4 vols, 15th edn (London, 1809), vol. 3, p.268

14. Secord, p.2; Antonia Fraser, *The King and the Catholics: The Fight for Rights, 1829* (London: Weidenfeld & Nicolson, 2019)

15. John Coffey, '"Tremble, Britannia!" Fear, Providence and the Abolition of the Slave Trade, 1758–1807', *The English Historical Review*, 127, 527 (2012), pp.844–6; Linda Colley, *Britons: Forging the Nation, 1707–1837* (New Haven, Conn.: Yale University Press, 1992), p.4

16. Colley, pp.354–9

17. Colley, pp.354–9 and 373

18. Hannah More, *Slavery: A Poem* (London: T. Caddell, 1788)

19. Coffey, p.860; Lois G. Schwoerer, 'Celebrating the Glorious Revolution', *Albion: A Quarterly Journal Concerned with British Studies*, 22, 1 (1990), pp.2–8

20. Colley, p.354

21. See, for example, Marika Sherwood, *After Abolition: Britain and the Slave Trade since 1807* (London: Bloomsbury Academic, 2009)

22. Peter Mandler, *History and National Life* (London: Profile, 2002), p.20

23. David Reynolds, *Island Stories: Britain and its History in the Age of Brexit* (London: William Collins, 2019), p.29

24. Michael Angelo Garvey, *The Silent Revolution: Or the Future Effects of Steam and Electricity upon the Condition of Mankind* (London: William and Frederik G. Cash, 1852), pp.1–2

25. Mandler, p.20

26. Mandler, pp.25–7. See also Andrew Sanders, *In the Olden Time: Victorians and the British Past* (New Haven, Conn.: Yale University Press, 2013)

27. Thomas Carlyle, 'Signs of the Times' (1829) in *The Works of Thomas Carlyle*, vol. 27 (Cambridge: Cambridge University Press, 2012), pp.62 and 60

28. Peter Gaskell, *The Manufacturing Population of England* (London: Baldwin and Craddock, 1833), pp.14, 19, 23 and 10

29. Carlyle, 'Signs of the Times', p.58

30. Thomas Carlyle, *Past and Present* (1843), book IV, in *The Works of Thomas Carlyle*, vol. 10 (Cambridge: Cambridge University Press, 2011), p.274

31. William Cobbett, quoted in Raymond Chapman, *The Sense of the Past in Victorian Literature* (Beckenham: Croom Helm, 1986), p.35

32. Quoted in Mike Sanders, *The Poetry of Chartism* (Cambridge: Cambridge University Press, 2009), p.162

33. Colley, pp.336–7

34. Henry James, 'In Warwickshire' (1877), in *Portraits of Places* (1883; Cambridge: Cambridge University Press, 2010), pp.249–50 and 257–8; Whitman paraphrased by Stephen Spender, quoted in Lowenthal, p.129

35. John Stuart Mill, 'The Spirit of the Age' (1831), in Gertrude Himmelfarb (ed), *The Spirit of the Age: Victorian Essays* (New Haven, Conn.: Yale University Press, 2007), p.52; John Constable, 'Lecture on Landscape' (1834–5), in R.B. Beckett (ed), *John Constable's Discourses* (Ipswich: Suffolk Records Society, vol. 14, 1970), p.70; George Gilbert Scott, *Remarks on Secular & Domestic Architecture* (London: John Murray, 1857), p.258

36. Thomas Babington Macaulay, 'Review of Sir James Mackintosh, *History of the Revolution*', in *Edinburgh Review*, 61, 121 (July 1835), pp.287–8; *Hansard's Parliamentary Debates*, 10 July 1833, vol. 19, column 535; Reynolds, p.186

37. Boris Johnson, *Hansard's Parliamentary Debates*, 22 September 2020, vol. 680, column 815

38. Edward A. Freeman, *The Growth of the English Constitution from the Earliest Times* (London: Macmillan and Co., 1872), p.vii; Mandler, p.36

39. G.A. Bremner and Jonathan Conlin, '1066 and All That: E.A. Freeman and the Importance of Being Memorable', in Bremner and Conlin (eds), *Making History: Edward Augustus Freeman and Victorian Cultural Politics* (Oxford: Oxford University Press, 2015), pp.7–9

40. Mandler, p.34

41. Quoted in Jonathan Rose, *The Intellectual Life of the British Working Classes* (New Haven, Conn.: Yale University Press, 2002), p.130

42. 'Coming of Age', *The Art Journal*, New series vol. 1 (1855), p.67

43. Mandler, pp.22, 31 and 45

44. Prys Morgan, 'From a Death to a View: The Hunt for a Welsh Past in the Romantic Period', in Eric Hobsbawm and Terence Ranger (eds), *The Invention of Tradition* (Cambridge: Cambridge University Press, 2012), esp. pp.43–4 and 58–62

45. Hugh Trevor-Roper, 'The Invention of Tradition: The Highland Tradition of Scotland', in Hobsbawm and Ranger, pp.29–30

46. J.G. Lockhart, *Memoirs of the Life of Sir Walter Scott*, vol. 3 (Paris: Baudry's European Library, 1837), p.115

47. For Romantic nostalgia for Highland culture, see Julie Shields, 'Highland Emigration and the Transformation of Nostalgia in Romantic Poetry', *European Romantic Review*, 23, 6 (2012), pp. 765–84

48. Chapman, p.34; Andrew Lincoln, *Walter Scott and Modernity* (Edinburgh: Edinburgh University Press, 2007), pp.1–2

49. Lowenthal, p.177

50. Elizabeth Barrett Browning, *Aurora Leigh* (1856; Oxford: Oxford University Press, 2008), pp.151–2; George Eliot, *Essays and Leaves from a Notebook* (Edinburgh and London, 1884), p.37

51. Charles Dickens, Letter to Douglas Jerrold, 3 May 1843, in *The Letters of Charles Dickens, 1820–1870* (Oxford: Clarendon Press, 1965–2002), vol. 3, p.481

52. Charles Dickens, *A Child's History of England* (1851–3; Cambridge: Cambridge University Press, 2015), vol. 1, p.137, vol. 3, p. 65, and vol. 2, p.96

53. Dickens, *A Child's History*, vol. 3, pp.52, 84, 53 and 248–9

54. Dickens, *A Child's History*, vol. 3, pp.139–40

55. Dickens, *A Child's History*, vol. 3, p.320

56. Charles Dickens, *A Tale of Two Cities* (1859; London: Penguin, 2003), p.5

57. *Saturday Review*, 8 (17 December 1859), pp.741–3

58. George Eliot, *Adam Bede* (1859; London: Penguin, 2008), p. 559–60

59. Emily Brontë, *Wuthering Heights* (1847; London: Penguin, 2003), p.25

60. Jane Austen, *Sense and Sensibility* (1811; London: Penguin, 2004), p.29; Tamara S. Wagner, *Longing: Narratives of Nostalgia in the British Novel, 1740–1890* (Lewisburg: Bucknell University Press, 2004), pp.95–6; Nicholas Dames, 'Austen's nostalgics',

Representations, 73, 1 (2001), pp.119–20; Jane Austen, *Pride and Prejudice* (1813; London: Penguin, 2003), p.348

61. Elizabeth Gaskell, *North and South* (1855; London: Penguin, 1996), pp.169, 14 and 299; Jane Mansfield, 'Nostalgia for Places: The Brontës and Elizabeth Gaskell', *Peer English*, 4 (2009), esp. p.64

62. Susan Zlotnick, *Women, Writing and the Industrial Revolution* (Baltimore, MD: Johns Hopkins University Press, 1998), pp.1–9, 63 and 96

63. Ellen Johnston, 'An Address to Napiers Dockyard', in *Autobiography, Poems and Songs* (Glasgow: William Love, 1867), pp. 19–21; Susan Zlotnick, '"A Thousand Times I'd Be a Factory Girl": Dialect, Domesticity, and Working-Class Women's Poetry in Victorian Britain', *Victorian Studies*, 35, 1 (1991), pp.20–3

64. Emma Griffin, *Liberty's Dawn: A People's History of the Industrial Revolution* (New Haven, Conn.: Yale University Press, 2013), pp.1–19

65. Griffin, pp.24 and 168–85

66. Thomas Wood, 'Autobiography by Thomas Wood, 1822–1880', collected in John Burnett, *Useful Toil: Autobiographies of Working People from the 1820s to the 1920s* (London: Routledge, 1974), pp.311–20

67. Wood, p.314

68. Griffin, pp.241–7; Isaac Anderson, *The Life History of Isaac Anderson. A Member of the Peculiar People* (1896), p.7; Benjamin North, *Autobiography of Benjamin North* (Aylesbury, 1882), p.95

69. George Mitchell, 'Autobiography and reminiscences of George Mitchell, "One from the Plough"', in Stephen Price (ed), *The Skeleton at the Plough, or the Poor Farm Labourers of the West: with the Autobiography and Reminiscences of George Mitchell* (London, 1875[?]), p.100

70. Noah Cooke, 'Autobiography' in his *Wild Warblings* (Kidderminster, 1876), p.34

71. Griffin, p.243; and Jane Humphries, *Childhood and Child Labour in the British Industrial Revolution*, (Cambridge: Cambridge, University Press, 2010), pp.220 and 249

72. James Hawker, 'The life of a poacher', in Garth Christian (ed), *A Victorian Poacher. James Hawker's Journal* (Oxford: Oxford University Press, 1978), p.76

73. James Dawson Burn, *The Autobiography of a Beggar Boy* (London: William Tweedie, 1855), pp.116–17

74. Deirdre Shauna Lynch, 'Gothic Fiction', in Richard Maxwell and Katie Trumpener (eds), *The Cambridge Companion to Fiction of the Romantic Period* (Cambridge: Cambridge University Press, 2008), pp.47–8 and 53; Carol Margaret Davidson, ' "There's No Place Like Home?" Nostalgia, Perversion, and Trauma in the Female Gothic', in Isabella van Elferen (ed), *Nostalgia or Perversion? Gothic Rewriting from the Eighteenth Century until the Present* (Newcastle: Cambridge Scholars Publishing, 2007), p.30

75. William Stafford, ' "This once happy country": nostalgia for pre-modern society', in Christopher Shaw and Malcolm Chase (eds), *The Imagined Past: History and Nostalgia* (Manchester: Manchester University Press, 1989), p.40; Lynch, p.47

76. Lynch, p.53; Adam Roberts, 'Gothic and Horror Fiction', in Edward James and Farah Mendlesohn (eds), *The Cambridge Companion to Fantasy Literature* (Cambridge: Cambridge University Press, 2012), p.29

77. Raphael Samuel, *Theatres of Memory* (London: Verso, 1994), p.16; Samuel, *Island Stories: Unravelling Britain* (London: Verso, 1998), pp.86 and 101–24

78. Dickens, *A Child's History*, vol. 2, p.197

79. Mandler, pp.27–9; Samuel, *Island Stories*, p.113

80. Samuel, *Island Stories*, pp.102–7

81. Andrew Sanders, 'A Gothic Revival: William Harrison Ainsworth's The Tower of London', in *The Victorian Historical Novel, 1840–1880* (Basingstoke: Palgrave Macmillan, 1979), pp.32–3; Samuel, *Island Stories*, p.116

82. William Hazlitt, 'On the Pleasure of Hating' (1826), in *The Spirit of Controversy and Other Essays* (Oxford: Oxford University Press, 2021) pp.299–300

CHAPTER 6: DECLINE AND FALL

1. Linda Colley, *Britons: Forging the Nation* (New Haven, Conn.: Yale University Press, 1992), pp.12–13

2. James Hodges, *The Rights and Interests of the Two British Monarchies* (London, 1703), p.20

3. Quoted in Matthew Adams, 'Imagining Britain: The Formation of British National Identity during the Eighteenth Century', PhD thesis, University of Warwick (2002), p.110

4. Daniel Defoe, *An Essay at Removing National Prejudices Against a Union With Scotland* (Edinburgh, 1706), p.11; Defoe, *The History of the Union of Great Britain* (Edinburgh, 1709)

5. Daniel Defoe, *The True-Born Englishman* (1701), in William Hazlitt (ed), *The Works of Daniel Defoe*, vol. III (London, 1843), p.9

6. William Robertson, quoted in Tim Stuart-Buttle, 'Gibbon and Enlightenment History in Eighteenth-Century Britain', in Karen O'Brien and Brian Young (eds), *The Cambridge Companion to Edward Gibbon* (Cambridge: Cambridge University Press, 2018), p.111

7. David Hume, 'Of Commerce' (1752), in *Selected Essays* (Oxford: Oxford University Press, 1998), p.169; Stuart-Buttle, p.115; and J.G.A. Pocock, 'Gibbon's Decline and Fall and the World View of the Late Enlightenment', *Eighteenth-Century Studies*, 10, 3 (1977), p.292

8. Richard Price, *Observations on the Importance of the American Revolution* (1785; Cambridge: Cambridge University Press, 2013), p.5

9. Stuart-Buttle, p.111; Karen O'Brien, *Narratives of Enlightenment: Cosmopolitan History from Voltaire to Gibbon* (Cambridge: Cambridge University Press, 1997), pp.3–5

10. Edward Gibbon, *The History of the Decline and Fall of the Roman Empire*, ch. xxxviii (1776–89; London: Penguin, 2000), p.435

11. Karen O'Brien, 'Introduction', in *The Cambridge Companion to Edward Gibbon*, p.17; J.G.A Pocock, 'An Overview of *The Decline and Fall of the Roman Empire*', in *The Cambridge Companion to Gibbon,* pp.21–2; Pocock, 'Gibbon's Decline and Fall and the World View of the Late Enlightenment', pp.290–3; and Piers Brendon, 'The Decline and Fall of the British Empire', *History Extra*, January 2008

12. Quoted in John Carswell, *The South Sea Bubble* (Stroud: Alan Sutton, 1960), p.133. See also Malcolm Balen, *A Very English Deceit: The Secret History of the South Sea Bubble and the First*

Great Financial Scandal (London: Fourth Estate, 2009); Virginia Cowles, *The Great Swindle: A History of the South Sea Bubble* (London: Sharpe Books, 2018)

13. Christopher Christie, *The British Country House in the Eighteenth Century* (Manchester: Manchester University Press, 2000), p.9; Gregory Clark, 'Debts, deficits, and crowding out: England, 1727–1840', *European Review of Economic History*, 5, 3 (2001), p.403

14. Colley, pp.101–2

15. Ottobah Cugoano, *Thoughts and Sentiments on the Evil of Slavery* (1787), quoted in John Coffey, '"Tremble, Britannia!" Fear, Providence and the Abolition of the Slave Trade, 1758–1807', *The English Historical Review*, 127, 527 (2012), p.860; Nicholas Hudson, '"Britons Never Will Be Slaves": National Myth, Conservatism, and the Beginnings of British Antislavery', *Eighteenth-Century Studies*, 34, 4 (2001), esp. p.570; Colley, p.141

16. Horace Walpole, Letter to Sir Horace Mann, 24 November 1774, in Wilmarth Sheldon Lewis (ed), *The Yale Edition of Horace Walpole's Correspondence*, vol. 24 (New Haven, Conn.: Yale University Press, 1937), p.62

17. John Brown, *An estimate of the manners and principles of the times* (Belfast, 1758), pp.12, 16 and 23–4

18. R. Campbell, *The London Tradesman* (1742; London, 1758)

19. *London Magazine*, 25 (1756), pp.15–16

20. Christopher Christie, *The British Country House in the Eighteenth Century* (Manchester: Manchester University Press, 2000), p.4; and Jonathan Finch and Jan Woudstra, '"Capability" Brown: An Eighteenth-Century Life', in Finch and Woudstra (eds), *Capability Brown, Royal Gardener: The Business of Place-Making in Northern Europe* (York: White Rose University Press, 2020), p.5

21. Christie, pp.4, 9 and 38

22. William Shenstone, 'Unconnected Thoughts on Gardening', in *The Works in Verse and Prose of William Shenstone*, vol. II (London, 1765), p.112; see also Joan Bassin, 'The English Landscape Garden in the Eighteenth Century: The Cultural Importance of an English Institution', *Albion: A Quarterly Journal Concerned with British Studies*, 11, 1 (1979), p.18

23. Christie, p.37

24. Horace Walpole, Letter to Sir Horace Mann, 27 April 1753, in *The Yale Edition of Horace Walpole's Correspondence*, vol. 20, p.372

25. Horace Walpole, Letter to Sir Horace Mann, 28 October 1752, in *The Yale Edition of Horace Walpole's Correspondence*, vol. 20, p.341; Christie, p.37

26. Christie, pp.69 and 82

27. Isaac Kramnick, *Bolingbroke and His Circle: The Politics of Nostalgia in the Age of Walpole* (Ithaca, NY: Cornell University Press, 1992), p.4

28. Colley, p.59; Bassin, pp.26–7

29. Christie, p.19

30. Stephen Bending, 'Re-Reading the Eighteenth-Century English Landscape Garden', *Huntingdon Library Quarterly*, 55, 3 (1992), p.382; Finch and Woudstra, p.3; Jonathan Lamb, 'The Medium of Publicity at the Garden at Stowe', *Huntingdon Library Quarterly*, 59, 1 (1996), p.62

31. Bassin, p.27; E.P. Thompson, 'Patrician Society, Plebian Culture', *Journal of Social History*, 7, 4 (1974), pp.382–405

32. First published in *Common Sense*, quoted in *The Gentleman's Magazine*, 9 (1739), p.640

33. Bassin, pp.18 and 32; Finch and Woudstra, p.6; and Michael Symes, 'Enlightenment, the "Natural Garden" and Brown', *Garden History*, 44, supplement 1 (2016), p.11

34. Bassin, p.28; Mark Girouard, *Life in the English Country House: a Social and Architectural History* (New Haven, Conn.: Yale University Press, 1993), pp.214–8

35. Quoted in Christie, p.32

36. Girouard, pp.10, 142–3 and 189; Raymond Williams, *The Country and the City* (London: Hogarth Press, 1985), esp. pp.55–9

37. Quoted in Finch and Woudstra, p.9

38. Brown, p.63

39. Christie, p.19

40. Quoted in Beverly Lemire, 'Developing Consumerism and the Ready-Made Clothing trade in Britain 1750–1800', *Textile History*, 15, 1 (1984), p.41

41. Bethan Bell, 'The Rise, Fall and Rise of the Status Pineapple', BBC News, 2 August 2020 [https://www.bbc.co.uk/news/uk-england-53432877]; 'How pineapples became a status symbol', *Week*, 22

July 2018; Michael Olmert, 'The Hospitable Pineapple', *Colonial Williamsburg Journal*, 20, 2 (1998), pp.56–7; Fran Beauman, *The Pineapple: King of Fruits* (London: Vintage, 2006), esp. p.111

42. Henry Fielding, *An enquiry into the causes of the late increase of robbers* (London, 1751), p.6; Michael McKeon, 'Aestheticising the critique of luxury: Smollett's Humphry Clinker', in Maxine Berg and Elizabeth Eger (eds), *Luxury in the Eighteenth Century: Debates, Desires and Delectable Goods* (Basingstoke: Palgrave Macmillan, 2003), p.58

43. John Dennis, *An essay upon publick spirit* (London, 1711), p.vi

44. *London Chronicle*, 9 (3–6 January 1761), p.20

45. Bernard de Mandeville, *The Fable of the Bees: or, Private Vices, Publick Benefits* (London, 1714)

46. Maxine Berg and Elizabeth Eger, 'The Rise and Fall of the Luxury Debates', in Berg and Eger, *Luxury in the Eighteenth Century*, esp. p.7; John Sekora, *Luxury: the Concept in Western Thought, Eden to Smollet* (Baltimore, MD: The Johns Hopkins University Press, 1977); C.J. Berry, *The Idea of Luxury: a conceptual and historical investigation* (Cambridge: Cambridge University Press, 1994), pp.101–76

47. [anon], *The Tryal of the Lady Allurea Luxury, before the Lord Chief-Justice Upright, On an Information for a Conspiracy* (1757; London, 1763), pp.8 and 21

48. Jonas Hanway, *A journal of eight days journey. To which is added, an essay in tea* (London, 1756), p.245

49. Tobias Smollett, *The Life and Adventures of Sir Launcelot Greaves* (1760; Oxford: Oxford University Press, 1973), p.23

50. Arthur Young, *The Farmer's letters to the people of England: Containing the sentiments of a practical husbandman, on various subjects of great importance* (London, 1768), p.282

51. John Burnett, *Liquid Pleasures: A Social History of Drinks in Modern Britain* (London: Routledge, 1999), pp.51–57. For tea import estimates, see David Richardson, 'The Slave Trade, Sugar and British Economic Growth', in Barbara L. Solow and Stanley L. Engerman (eds), *British Capitalism and Caribbean Slavery* (Cambridge: Cambridge University Press, 2004), p.117

52. Sir Frederick Morton Eden, *The State of the Poor*, vol. I (London, 1797), p.555

53. Horace Walpole, Letter to Sir Horace Mann, 15 November 1779, in *The Yale Edition of Horace Walpole's Correspondence*, vol. 33, p.138

54. Quoted in Srinivas Aravamundam, 'Defoe, Commerce and Empire', in John Richetti (ed), *The Cambridge Companion to Daniel Defoe* (Cambridge: Cambridge University Press, 2009), p.48

55. Adam Smith, *The Wealth of Nations,* books I–III (1776; London: Penguin, 1982), bk II, ch. 3, p.443

56. David Hume, 'Of Refinement in the Arts' [originally titled 'Of Luxury'] (1742), in *Selected Essays*, pp.167–9; Sekora, p.119

57. Maxine Berg, *Luxury and Pleasure in Eighteenth Century Britain* (Oxford: Oxford University Press, 2005), p.7

58. Hume, 'Of Refinement in the Arts', pp.169 and 171

59. Lawrence Klein, 'Politeness and the Interpretation of the British Eighteenth Century', *The Historical Journal*, 45, 4 (2002), pp. 869–98

60. Felix Waldmann, 'David Hume was a brilliant philosopher but also a racist involved in slavery', *Scotsman*, 17 July 2020; Robin Mills, 'David Hume's racism was attacked by an 18th century Scottish philosopher, as well as modern Black Lives Matter protesters', *Scotsman*, 18 September 2020; Andrew Valls, '"A Lousy Empirical Scientist": Reconsidering Hume's Racism', in Andrew Valls (ed), *Race and Racism in Modern Philosophy* (Ithaca, NY: Cornell University Press, 2005), pp.127–49

61. Daniel Defoe, *Everybody's Business is No-body's Business* (London, 1725), pp.15–16

62. Daniel Defoe, *An humble proposal to the people of England, for the encrease of their trade, and encouragement of their manufactures* (London, 1729), pp.56–7; Defoe, *A brief deduction of the original, progress, and immense greatness of the British woollen manufacture* (London, 1727), pp.39–40. See also Peter Earle, *The World of Defoe* (London: Weidenfeld & Nicolson, 1976), esp. pp.107–8 and 143. For the trade in foreign textiles, see Beverly Lemire, *Fashion's Favourite: The Cotton Trade and the Consumer in Britain, 1660–1800* (Oxford: Oxford University Press, 2001), esp. pp.16–38

63. Malachy Postlethwayt, *Britain's Commercial Interest Explained and Improved* (London, 1757), vol. II, p.307

64. Joyce Appleby, 'Consumption in early modern social thought', in John Brewer and Roy Porter (eds), *Consumption and the World of Goods* (London: Routledge, 1993), pp.506–11

65. S.J. Thompson, 'Parliamentary Enclosure, Property, Population, and the Decline of Classical Republicanism in Eighteenth-Century Britain', *The Historical Journal*, 51, 3 (2008), p.628; Ellen Rosenman, 'On Enclosure Acts and the Commons', in Dino Franco Felluga (ed), *BRANCH: Britain, Representation and Nineteenth-Century History*. Extension of *Romanticism and Victorianism on the Net*. [http://www.branchcollective.org/?ps_articles=ellen-rosenman-on-enclosure-acts-and-the-commons]. For rent increases following enclosure, see D. McCloskey, 'The open fields of England: rent, risk and the rate of interest, 1300–1815', in David W. Galenson (ed), *Markets in History: Economic Studies of the Past* (Cambridge: Cambridge University Press, 1989), p.17

66. Joyce Burnett, 'Agriculture, 1700–1870', in Roderick Floud, Jane Humphries and Paul Johnson (eds), *The Cambridge Economic History of Modern Britain*, vol. 1 (Cambridge: Cambridge University Press, 2014), p.104; Robert C. Allan, *The British Industrial Revolution in Global Perspective* (Cambridge: Cambridge University Press, 2009), p.17; James Simpson, 'European Farmers and the British "agricultural revolution"', in Leandro Prados de la Escosura (ed), *Exceptionalism and Industrialisation: Britain and its European Rivals, 1688–1815* (Cambridge: Cambridge University Press, 2004), p.70

67. Caryn Chaden, 'Oliver Goldsmith, *The Deserted Village*, and George Crabbe, *The Village*', in Christine Gerrard (eds), *A Companion to Eighteenth-Century Poetry* (Oxford: Blackwell, 2006), p.303

68. Oliver Goldsmith, *The Deserted Village* (London, 1770), p.7

69. Goldsmith, pp.8 and 18–19

70. Chaden, pp.303–4

71. Alastair Bonnett, 'Nostalgia and Anti-nostalgia in English Radical History: The Case of Thomas Spence (1750–1814)', *Groniek: Historisch Tijdschrift*, 214 (2017), pp.45–7

72. Quoted in Andy Wood, *The Memory of the People: Custom and Popular Senses of the Past in Early Modern England* (Cambridge: Cambridge University Press, 2013), p.344

73. John Payne Collier, *A Book of Roxburghe Ballads* (London, 1847), p.99

74. Rosenman

75. S.J. Thompson, pp.621–2 and 630; Pocock, 'Gibbon's Decline and Fall and the World View of the Late Enlightenment', p.292

76. Quoted in S.J. Thompson, p.630

77. Colley, pp.87–8 and 289–300

78. Sir James Steuart, paraphrased by John Arbuthnot, in *An Inquiry into the Connection between the present price of provisions, and the size of farms* (London, 1773), p.140; S.J. Thompson, p.639

79. Pocock, 'Gibbon's Decline and Fall and the World View of the Late Enlightenment', p.292

80. David Hume, *An Enquiry concerning the Principles of Morals* (1751; Oxford: Oxford University Press, 1998), p.63

81. Gibbon, ch. II, p.62

82. Adam Ferguson, *An Essay on the History of Civil Society* (1767; Cambridge: Cambridge University Press, 1995), esp. pp.32–4, 38–9 fn and 42–4; Stuart-Buttle, pp.117–8

83. Adam Smith, *The theory of moral sentiments*, second edition (Edinburgh, 1761), p.271

84. George Cheyne, *The English Malady* (London, 1733), p.174; see also Roy Porter, 'Consumption: disease of the consumer society?' in Brewer and Porter, esp. p.63

85. Roy Porter, 'Introduction', in George Cheyne, *The English Malady*, ed. Roy Porter (1733; London: Routledge, 1991), pp.xxvii–xxxii; Johan A. Aarli, 'Why was the English Malady "English"?' *Brain*, 134, 2 (2011), pp.627–30

CHAPTER 7: THE COMMITTEE FOR THE DEMOLITION OF MONUMENTS

1. Philip Schwyzer, *Literature, Nationalism and Modern Memory in Early Modern England and Wales* (Cambridge: Cambridge University Press, 2004), pp.13–32; J.H.M. Salmon, 'Precept, example, and truth: Degory Wheare and the *ars historica*', in Donald R. Kelley and David Harris Sacks (eds), *The Historical Imagination in Early Modern Britain: history, rhetoric and fiction*

1500–1800 (Cambridge: Woodrow Wilson Center and Cambridge University Press, 1997), pp.16 and 28–9; Patrick Collinson, 'Truth, lies and fiction in sixteenth-century Protestant historiography', in Kelley and Sacks, pp.43–5

2. Schwyzer, pp.32–3; Alexandra Walsham, 'History, Memory and the English Reformation', *The Historical Journal*, 55, 4 (2012), p.904

3. Jamie A. Gianoutsos, *The Rule of Manhood: Tyranny, Gender and Classical Republicanism in England, 1603–1660* (Cambridge: Cambridge University Press, 2021), p.25. NB spelling of primary sources modernised throughout the chapter

4. Andy Wood, *The Memory of the People: Custom and Popular Senses of the Past in Early Modern England* (Cambridge: Cambridge University Press, 2013), pp.74 and 77–8; Brecht Deseure and Judith Pollmann, 'The experience of rupture and the history of memory', in Erika Kuijpers, Judith Pollmann, Johannes Muller and Jasper van der Steen (eds), *Memory Before Modernity: Practices of Memory in Early Modern Europe* (Leiden: Brill, 2013), pp.318 and 324–5; Keith Thomas, 'The Perception of the Past in Early Modern England', Creighton Trust Lecture, 1983; Adam Morton, 'Remembering the Past at the End of Time', in Alexandra Walsham, Bronwyn Wallace, Ceri Law and Brian Cummings (eds), *Memory and the English Reformation* (Cambridge: Cambridge University Press, 2020), p.80; Daniel Woolf, *The Social Circulation of the Past: English Historical Culture, 1500–1730* (Oxford: Oxford University Press, 2003), pp.1–16

5. David Lowenthal, *The Past is a Foreign Country Revisited* (Cambridge: Cambridge University Press, 2015), p.361; Francis Young, 'Not what it used to be? Nostalgia in Early Modern England', blog post, Februrary 2020 [https://manyheadedmonster.com/2020/02/11/not-what-it-used-to-be-nostalgia-in-early-modern-england/]

6. Carlos M.N. Eire, *Reformations: The Early Modern World, 1450–1650* (New Haven, Conn.: Yale University Press, 2016), pp.318–9

7. Young

8. Alexandra Walsham, 'The Reformation of the Generations: youth, age and religious change in England, c. 1500–1700', *Transactions of the Royal Historical Society*, 21 (2001), p.99; Walsham,

'History, Memory and the English Reformation', p.202; Keith Thomas, 'Art and Iconoclasm in Early Modern England', in Kenneth Fincham and Peter Lake (eds), *Religious Politics in Post-Reformation England* (Woodbridge: Boydell Press, 2006), p.18

9. Alexandra Walsham, Brian Cummings and Ceri Law, 'Introduction: Memory and the English Reformation', in Walsham et al, *Memory and the English Reformation*, pp.37–8; Walsham, 'History, Memory and the English Reformation', pp.903 and 911; Collinson, p.37

10. Walsham, 'History, Memory and the English Reformation', pp. 911–5

11. Gianoutsos, p.21. For Jacobean nostalgia for Elizabeth I, see Yuichi Tsukada, *Shakespeare and the Politics of Nostalgia: Negotiating the Memory of Elizabeth I on the Jacobean Stage* (London: The Arden Shakespeare, 2019), esp. pp.4–9

12. Alexandra Walsham, 'Impolitic Pictures: Providence, History, and the Iconography of Protestant Nationhood in Early Stuart England', in R.N. Swanson (ed), *The Church Retrospective: Depictions and Representations* (The Ecclesiastical History Society, 1997), pp.307 and 310–1; Julie Spraggon, *Puritan Iconoclasm during the English Civil War* (Woodbridge: Boydell Press, 2003), p.28

13. David Cressy, *Bonfires and Bells: National Memory and the Protestant Calendar in Elizabethan and Stuart England* (London: Weidenfeld & Nicolson, 1989); Cressy, 'The Fifth of November Remembered', in Roy Porter (ed), *Myths of the English* (Cambridge: Polity Press, 1992), pp.68–90; Spraggon, p.129

14. Walsham, 'Impolitic Pictures', pp.321–5

15. David Cressy, 'Remembrancers of the Revolution: Histories and Historiographies of the 1640s', *Huntingdon Library Quarterly*, 68, 1–2 (2005), p.258

16. Christopher Hill, *Puritanism and Revolution: Studies in Interpretation of the English Revolution of the 17th Century* (Basingstoke: Palgrave Macmillan, 1997), ch. 3, 'The Norman Yoke', esp. pp.59 and 62

17. Wood, *Memory of the People*, p.96

18. Cressy, 'Remembrancers of the Revolution', pp.259 and 262–3

19. Christopher Highley, 'Henry VIII's Ghost in Cromwellian England', in Walsham et al, *Memory and the English Reformation*,

p.106; Susan A. Clarke 'Royalists Write the Death of Lord Hastings: Post-Regicide Funerary Propaganda', *Parergon*, 22, 5 (2005), pp.113–30; John McWilliams, '"A Storm of Lamentations Writ": "Lachrymae Musarum" and Royalist Culture after the Civil War', *The Yearbook of English Studies*, 33 (2003), pp.273–89

20. Ingo Berensmeyer, 'The art of oblivion: Politics of remembering and forgetting in Restoration England', *European Journal of English Studies*, 10, 1 (2006), pp.81–96; Victoria Moul, 'Abraham Cowley's *1756 Poems*: Form and Contexts', in Philip Major (ed), *Royalists and Royalism in 17th-Century Literature: Exploring Abraham Cowley* (London: Routledge, 2013), pp.150–2

21. Berensmeyer, pp.81–96

22. Thomas Hobbes, quoted in Lowenthal, p.139; Matthew Neufeld, 'Putting the Past to Work, Working through the Past', *Huntingdon Library Quarterly*, 76, 4 (2013), p.484; Neufeld, *The Civil Wars after 1660: Public Remembering in Late Stuart England* (Woodbridge: Boydell Press, 2013), esp. pp.4–5, 17–8 and 20

23. Neufeld, *The Civil Wars*, pp.20–7, 33, 35 and 42–6

24. Neufeld, *The Civil Wars*, esp. p.22; Warren Chernaik, 'Harsh Remedies: Satire and Politics in "Last Instructions to a Painter"', in Martin Dzelzainis and Edward Holberton (eds), *The Oxford Handbook of Andrew Marvell* (Oxford: Oxford University Press, 2019), pp.444–62

25. Andy Wood, 'Coda: history, time and social memory', in Keith Wrightson (eds), *A Social History of England, 1500–1750* (Cambridge: Cambridge University Press, 2017), pp.385–6

26. Thomas, 'Art and Iconoclasm', pp.16–17; Alexandra Walsham, 'Recycling the Sacred: Material Culture and Cultural Memory after the English Reformation', *Church History*, 86, 4 (2017), pp.1127 and 1135

27. Harriet Lyon, 'Remembering the Dissolution of the Monasteries', in Walsham et al, *Memory and the English Reformation*, pp. 69–70

28. Walsham, 'Reformation of the Generations', pp.101–2; and 'Recycling the Sacred', p.1143

29. Alexandra Walsham, 'The Reformation and "the disenchantment of the world" reassessed', *The Historical Journal*, 51, 2 (2008), p.507

30. Steward Mottram, 'Rereading Ruins: Edmund Spenser and Scottish Presbyterianism', in Walsham et al, *Memory and the English Reformation*, p.228; Walsham, 'Recycling the Sacred', pp.1126 and 1129

31. Alexandra Walsham, 'Converting the Cross: Monuments, Memory and Time in Post-Reformation England', in Walsham et al, *Memory and the English Reformation*, p.139; Walsham, 'Disenchantment of the world', p.512; Walsham, 'Recycling the Sacred', p.1130; Margaret Aston, *Broken Idols of the English Reformation* (Cambridge: Cambridge University Press, 2016), p.14

32. Matthew Moore, 'Don't airbrush British history, government tells heritage groups', *The Times*, 15 February 2021; Sophie Sleigh and Alexandra Rogers, 'Boris Johnson says he will "defend British history" from "cancel culture"', Huffington Post, 6 October 2021 [https://www.huffingtonpost.co.uk/entry/boris-johnson-british-history-cancel-culture_uk_615d7497e4b08d08062c45c4]

33. Quoted in Wood, *Memory of the People*, p.68; Margaret Aston, 'English Ruins and English History: The Dissolution and the Sense of the Past', *Journal of the Warburg and Courtauld Institutes*, 36 (1973), esp. p.232

34. Wood, *Memory of the People*, pp.89 and 91–2. See also Eamon Duffy, *The Voices of Morebath: Reformation and Rebellion in an English Village* (New Haven, Conn.: Yale University Press, 2003)

35. Alexandra Walsham, 'Relics, writing and memory in the English Counter Reformation: Thomas Maxfield and his afterlives', *British Catholic History*, 34, 1 (2018), pp.90–1; Walsham, 'Recycling the Sacred', p.1145; Walsham, 'Converting the Cross', pp.137–8; Emilie Murphy, 'Making Memories in Post-Reformation English Catholic Musical Miscellanies,' in Walsham et al, *Memory and the English Reformation*, esp. pp.408 and 411

36. Thomas, 'Art and Iconoclasm', p.21; Aston, 'English Ruins', pp. 243–4

37. Lyon, p.76; Aston, 'English Ruins', pp.236–8 and 252

38. Aston, 'English Ruins', p.248; Walsham, 'History, Memory and the English Reformation', pp.919; Raphael Samuel, *Theatres of Memory* (London: Verso, 1994), p.30

39. Walsham, 'History, Memory and the English Reformation', p.908

40. Aston, 'English Ruins', pp.244–6; Schwyzer, pp.62–4

41. Spraggon, esp. pp.177–8
42. Spraggon, esp. pp.73–85
43. Spraggon, pp.187, 197 and 204–14
44. Spraggon, pp.189 and 198–9
45. Alexandra Walsham, *The Reformation of the Landscape: Religion, Identity, and Memory in Early Modern Britain* (Oxford: Oxford University Press, 2012); Keith Thomas, 'Killing Stones: Holy Places', *London Review of Books*, 33, 10 (19 May 2011); Spraggon, p.82; Thomas, 'Art and Iconoclasm', p.40
46. Aston, 'English Ruins', pp.250 and 254–5; Walsham, 'Converting the Cross', p.146
47. Schwyzer, pp.54 and 60; Walsham, *Reformation of the Landscape*, p.296; Aston, 'English Ruins', p.234
48. Harriet Phillips, *Nostalgia in Print and Performance, 1510–1613: Merry Worlds* (Cambridge: Cambridge University Press, 2019), pp.1–2. See also Ronald Hutton, *The Rise and Fall of Merry England: The Ritual Year 1400–1700* (Oxford: Oxford University Press, 1994)
49. See, for example, Wood, *Memory of the People*, pp.74–5; Deseure and Pollmann, pp.318 and 324–5; Thomas, 'The Perception of the Past'; Morton, p.80
50. Wood, *Memory of the People*, esp. pp.69–71 and 242
51. Adam Fox, 'Remembering the Past in Early Modern England: Oral and Written Tradition', *Transactions of the Royal Historical Society*, 6th series (1999), p.239; Wood, *Memory of the People*, pp.67–8. See also Walsham, 'Reformation of the Generations', esp. p.100
52. Phillips, pp.31, 37 and 44
53. Phillips, pp.35–8
54. Phillips, pp.1–3, 164 and 167–8; Fox, p.240
55. Phillips, pp.57, 68 and 12–13
56. Phillips, pp.2, 46–7 and 98; Spraggon, p.xiv and 255
57. Phillips, pp.131–2
58. Berensmeyer, fn. 4; Phillips, p.61
59. See, for example, Benedict Anderson, *Imagined Communities: Reflections on the Origin and Spread of Nationalism* (London: Verso, 1991), pp.11–12
60. Schwyzer, pp.2–4

61. Schwyzer, pp.4–6, 33 and 39–40. For sixteenth-century perspectives on the Anglo-Saxons, see also Rebecca Brackmann, *The Elizabethan Invention of Anglo–Saxon England* (Cambridge: D.S. Brewer, 2012); John D. Niles, 'The Discovery of Anglo-Saxon England in Tudor Times', in *The Idea of Anglo-Saxon England: Remembering, Forgetting, Deciphering and Renewing the Past* (Oxford: Wiley-Blackwell, 2015), pp.49–76

62. Schwyzer, pp.9–10; Hester Lees-Jefferies, 'Nostalgia: Richard II, Henry V, Henry VI', in Katherine A. Craik (ed), *Shakespeare and Emotion* (Cambridge: Cambridge University Press, 2020), pp. 304–8; Katherine A. Craik, 'Introduction', in *Shakespeare and Emotion*, p.15

63. Schwyzer, pp.13, 21–3 and 34–5

64. Schwyzer, p.11; Raphael Samuel, *Island Stories: Unravelling Britain* (London: Verso, 1998), p.46; Margaret Thatcher, speech to Conservative rally in Bolton, 1 May 1979

65. Schwyzer, pp.173–4

66. Schwyzer, pp.128–131; Lees-Jefferies, pp.314–5

CONCLUSION: IN THE PAST, EVEN THE FUTURE WAS BETTER

1. Quoted in David Lowenthal, *The Past is a Foreign Country Revisited* (Cambridge: Cambridge University Press, 2015), p.110

2. Herbert Butterfield, *The Whig Interpretation of History* (1931; London: G. Bell and Sons, 1968), p.75

3. Herbert Butterfield, *The Englishman and his History* (Cambridge: Cambridge University Press, 1944), pp.3–4 and 6–7

4. For Butterfield's ambivalent relationship to Nazism, see Michael Bentley, *Herbert Butterfield: History, Science and God* (Cambridge: Cambridge University Press, 2011), pp.119–45

5. Butterfield, *Whig Interpretation*, pp.31–2. See also Keith C. Sewell, 'The "Herbert Butterfield Problem" and its Resolution', *Journal of the History of Ideas*, 64, 4 (2003), pp.599–618

6. Peter Mitchell, *Imperial Nostalgia: How the British Conquered Themselves* (Manchester: Manchester University Press, 2021), p.184

7. Peter Mandler, *History and National Life* (London: Profile, 2002), pp.146–9

8. Quoted in Heike Paul, 'Introduction', in Heike Paul (ed), *Critical Terms in Futures Studies* (Basingstoke: Palgrave Macmillan, 2019), p.1

9. Quoted in Alexandra Harris, *Romantic Moderns: English Writers, Artists and the Imagination from Virginia Woolf to John Piper* (London: Thames & Hudson, 2010), p.207

10. T.S. Eliot, *East Coker* (1940), in *Four Quartets* (London: Faber & Faber, 1943)

Index

Page references in *italics* indicate images.

agricultural labourers transition to
industrial work 10, 162–3, 164,
165, 166, 202, 216, 218, 221,
222–3, 250
consumerism and
see consumerism
countryside/rural nostalgia and
see countryside/rural nostalgia
factory labour and see factories
'Industrial Revolution', invention
of term
147–8, 187
inequality and 3, 148, 215, 263
landscape, industrial 147
medievalism as reaction against
see medievalism
nervous disorders and 3, 152–6,
154, 156, 198, 201, 269–70
overwork, ushers in culture of 3,
198, 201
pride in 148, 168, 187, 191–2,
198–9
social problems created by 147–9,
150–5, 168–9, 187, 198, 200–1,
203
technological change and
see technological change
'Workshop of the World', Britain
as 3, 43, 148, 187
inequality 3, 52, 136, 215, 263, 264
Interregnum (1649–60) 272, 283,
286, 288, 299, 307
interwar period (1918–40) 108–43
Iraq War (2003–11) 40, 43
Ireland 7, 90, 92, 94,
195, 230
Isherwood, Christopher 100
Islington 80
I Was Lord Kitchener's Valet
66, 67, 67

Jamaica 39, 91, 92, 93, 241
James I of England, VI of Scotland,
King 273, 279, 280, 297, 310

James II of England, VII of Scotland,
King 196, 230, 275, 286
James, Henry 203–4
Jefferies, Richard 164–5
Nature Near London 163
The Woodland Life 165
Jenrick, Robert 22
jingoism 30, 31, 35, 114
Joad, Cyril 121
Johnson, Boris 1, 19–20, 22, 23,
25–6, 29, 30–1, 32, 35–6, 205,
291
Johnston, Ellen 219
Jones, Jack 85, 86
Jonson, Ben 279
Joseph of Arimathea 274

Kampfner, John 40
Keenan, Brigid 95–6
'Keep Calm and Carry On' 11, 14,
18, 46–50
Kinks, The 67
Kipling, Rudyard 35, 36
'If' 183
'The Road to Mandalay' 35
Kitchener, Lord 129, 183
Knight, Laura: Spring 135–6

Labour Party 11–12, 43, 51, 52, 54,
63, 100, 164
laissez-faire economics
54–5, 202
Lamming, George 90–1
land ownership 124, 240–1, 244–5,
261–9, 301–2
Langley, Lee 96
Lanigan, Jack 88
Larkin, Philip
'Here' 76
'MCMXIV' (1964) 133
Lascelles family 241
Latimer, Bishop Hugh 305
Laud, Archbishop William 280, 281,
282, 296, 297

Henry V and 312
immigration and 89–90, 91
'Keep Calm and Carry On' slogan
    and 11, 14, 18, 46–50
'muddling through' concept and
    49, 140
nostalgia for 1, 2, 11, 14, 15, 16,
    18, 20, 30–1, 32, 38, 40–1,
    98–104, 98, 141–2, 312
'our finest hour', as 11, 16, 312
patriotic self-image during 139–40
post-war decline, narrative of
    58–107
rationing 14, 15, 16, 47, 48, 63,
    64, 96, 98, 99, 100
Recording Britain project 141–2,
    322
recruitment posters 138, 139, *139*
return 'home' to 'normal' after
    97–105, *98*
seventieth anniversary of outbreak
    (2009) 32
underdog, image of Britain as
    plucky and 38
VE Day (1945) 15, *15*
Seeley, J.R.: *The Expansion of
    England* 152
Sellar, W.C.: *1066 and All That* 9,
    114–15, 206
Seurat, Georges 175
Seven Years War (1756–63)
    238, 239
sex
    homosexuality 60, 68, 151, 172–4
    'permissive society' and
        60, 62
    rural nostalgia/late Victorian and
        Edwardian cultural dissidents
        and 172–4
    Second World War and 104
Shakespeare, William 9, 245, 280,
    305, 307, 308
    As You Like It 304
    Henry V 311–12

Richard II 308–9
Shanks, Michael: *The Stagnant
    Society* 59, 106
Shapps, Grant 36–7
Sharp, Thomas 123, 124
Shaw, George Bernard 171
Shell 128
Shell Guides 119, 128
Shelley, Mary: *Frankenstein* 148,
    225
Shenstone, William 242
Silkin, Lewis 71
Simpsons, The 31
Skyfall (film) 1
slave trade 2, 12, 22, 23, 39, 220,
    237, 259, 271, 291, 319
    abolition of 195–7, 239
slum clearances 70, 77–8, 80
Smith, Adam 269
    The Wealth of Nations 257, 261
Smith, James Cooray 31, 32
Smollett, Tobias 254–5
Snell, Henry 164
social hierarchies 192, 193, 194,
    202, 231–2, 238, 244–5, 246,
    248, 250, 252–3
socialism 45, 83, 167, 170, 177–8,
    264
Somme, battle of the (1916)
    38, 134
Sontag, Susan: 'Unguided Tour' 314
Southgate, Walter 83–4
South Sea Bubble (1720) 237
South Sea Company 237, 241
Space Age 61
Spanish Armada (1588) 188, 278,
    280
Spectator 38–9, 137
speed of change 144, 146–7, 153,
    251
Spence, Basil 75
Spence, Thomas 264–5
Spender, Stephen 104
standards of living 3, 58, 60, 153